Contents

ASIAN MEDIA INFORMATION AND COMMUNICATION CENTRE
(AMIC)

PUBLIC SERVICE
BROADCASTING

IN THE

AGE OF GLOBALIZATION

EDITED BY
Indrajit Banerjee
Kalinga Seneviratne

Published by
Asian Media Information and Communication Centre (AMIC)
and
The School of Communication and Information (SCI)
Nanyang Technological University, Singapore

Correspondence address:
AMIC
Jurong Point PO Box 360
Singapore 916412
Tel: (65) 67927570
Fax: (65) 67927129
Website: http://www.amic.org.sg

First published 2006

Body text set in Dutch 801 11/14 pt

Produced by BOOKSMITH (E-mail: chrys2@singnet.com.sg)

ISBN 981-4136-01-8

Foreword

This book on *Public Service Broadcasting in the Age of Globalization* could not have appeared at a more relevant time. It is clear now that in the information age, public service broadcasting can play a critical role in informing and educating citizens in an accurate and unbiased manner, keeping in mind the public interest and the citizens' right to know.

For the past two decades or more, public service broadcasting has been facing stiff competition from its commercial counterparts. Cable, satellite and terrestrial commercial broadcasters have unleashed a competitive assault for the advertising dollar and, in the process, broadcasting content has witnessed a significant decline in terms of quality. Commercial logic dominates the global broadcasting landscape today, with little concern for public interest and for the need to inform and educate citizens to understand the complex challenges of the world they live in.

Public service broadcasting is therefore all the more necessary; indeed, it is more relevant than ever. This book eloquently points to the imperative need for public service broadcasters to refuse to follow their commercial counterparts and succumb to the commercial bottom line, as they will then lose their legitimacy. Public service broadcasting has a clear mission and mandate of its own. It must stick to its own *raison d'etre* if it is to continue to grow and thrive.

This publication contains a compendium of critical essays that outline the issues and challenges faced by public service broadcasters around the world. It provides valuable insights into specific national public service broadcasting experiences, while highlighting a range of common issues faced by public service broadcasters in different national contexts.

A clear theme that emerges from the book is the critical need to strengthen public service broadcasting institutions around the globe to enhance democracy, good governance and informed public debate. I am sure that this volume will contribute immeasurably to the contemporary debate on the key issues facing all who are concerned with the future of public service broadcasting across the world.

Dr Shashi Tharoor
Under Secretary-General
Department of Public Information
United Nations

Public Service Broadcasting in the Age of Globalization—An Introduction

Neither commercial nor state-controlled, public broadcasting's only raison d'etre is public service. It is the public's broadcasting organization; it speaks to everyone as a citizen. Public broadcasters encourage access to and participate in public life. They develop knowledge, broaden horizons and enable people to better understand themselves by better understanding the world and others.
  – *Public Broadcasting: Why? How?* (UNESCO/WRTVC, 2001)

For the past two decades, public service broadcasting around the world has witnessed intense competition and pressures from commercial broadcasters as well as a whole range of new media channels. One can say that public service broadcasting has been under siege from a new breed of commercially oriented and profit-seeking broadcasters. Ironically though, it is when it seems most vulnerable that public service broadcasting is proving to be the most relevant. Today, more than ever before, the need for public service broadcasting is becoming evident.

Since the 1980s, when most countries in the world had either public service broadcasting or state broadcasting monopolies, the broadcasting landscape has witnessed profound and fundamental transformations. The advent of terrestrial commercial broadcasting, followed by a plethora of commercial cable and satellite channels, has invaded the broadcasting landscape and pushed public service broadcasting to the wall. Faced by intense competition from their commercial rivals, public service broadcasters have had to struggle for their survival and have adopted a variety of strategies and responses to commercial broadcasting.

In some countries, public service broadcasters have succumbed to competitive pressures and have taken up an increasingly commercial stance. While this strategy has enhanced the "profitability" of public service broadcasting, it has hurt its credibility as a public service institution. In other countries, public service broadcasters have moved "upstream" in order to provide quality broadcasting services and to distinguish themselves from their purely commercially oriented rivals. This is undoubtedly the best possible strategy for public service broadcasters—sticking to their main role and mission, and challenge commercial broadcasters by providing quality broadcasting services by promoting and protecting the public interest.

One of the key challenges for public service broadcasting around the world has been to find a balance between commercial viability and the public interest. Whenever commercial bottom lines and profit considerations guide the public service broadcasting agenda, it leads to the dilution of the main functions of public service broadcasting. A genuine public service broadcaster cannot be expected to serve the public interest while at the same time compete with commercial broadcasters for advertising revenue and profitability. Financial independence has therefore always been one of the best ways of ensuring the success and stability of public service broadcasting institutions. This is why many of the most successful and distinguished public service broadcasters are supported by public funding, either in the form of parliamentary allocations or license fees, as is the case with the BBC in the UK, the NHK in Japan and the ARD and ZDF in Germany (Banerjee & Seneviratne, 2005).

In the current global broadcasting landscape, however, many public service broadcasting institutions rely on commercial and advertising revenue and this distracts them from their main mission and purpose. This has been one of the core problems with public service broadcasting institutions and will continue to constitute one of the single most important challenges for public service broadcasters in the 21st century.

While public service broadcasting is facing many daunting challenges, it is unquestionable that at a time when commercial broadcasters ignore public service issues and devote all their resources to producing and broadcasting entertainment and commercially popular content, the need for public service broadcasting is greater than ever before. In an increasingly globalized world, it is essential to have broadcast institutions that address viewers and listeners as social beings and citizens rather than as mere consumers. In a world wrought with wars, conflicts, disasters and ethnic and religious strife, it is critical to have committed public service broadcasting institutions which enlighten citizens with accurate and unbiased news and information, educate citizens and help overcome the numerous divides that characterize the world today.

As the noted American scholar Neil Postman (1985) had observed, the media seem to have lost all sense of purpose and essentially content themselves by "amusing ourselves to death". Entertainment has emerged as the staple diet for commercial broadcasters all over the world, and information and education has ceased to be a matter of any concern for these broadcasters. In this context, an independent public service broadcasting institution can play a vital role in bringing public interest issues back in the foreground and provide a more wholesome broadcasting environment.

It is important for public service broadcasters to take up the challenge instead of either moving to more commercially oriented programming or abandoning their mission. It has been proved time and again that when public service broadcasters dedicate themselves to good quality programming, they perform better than even their strongest commercial rivals. In fact, it is interesting to note that many of the programme genres that were first developed by public service broadcasters, such as the TV documentary, have been taken up successfully by commercial broadcasters and turned into one of the most popular and successful genres. Even news has become a popular genre and there are numerous commercial broadcasters that have concentrated on the news genre alone and made it a successful commodity. It is niche educational and informational programming of this kind which had established quality public service broadcasters and can continue to give them the edge while their commercial counterparts devote themselves to pure entertainment-oriented content.

A supportive policy environment encouraging the development of public service broadcasting as well as viable funding models are key factors to ensure the survival and development of public service broadcasting. Public commitment to public service broadcasting thus becomes essential and citizens must rally around the cause of public service broadcasting to ensure that it gets the proper acknowledgement and support from government and public institutions. Citizens themselves should take part of the blame when public service broadcasting is in decline as they are, even if only in part, responsible for protecting and promoting public service broadcasting.

Another important development for public service broadcasting in the long term is the ability and commitment of governments to transform state broadcasting institutions into genuine public service broadcasting organizations. This transition is critical as it will ensure that every country has at least one well-established public service broadcaster. In addition, such a move to increase the credibility of governments as state broadcasters are generally looked at with suspicion, given their clear pro-establishment bias. If all state broadcasters are transformed into public service broadcasting institutions, it will usher in a new age of public service broadcasting around the world. Given their long history and experience in the broadcasting sector, their territorial reach as well as committed public funding, state broadcasters could be turned into effective public service broadcasting institutions. This will, however, require strong political will and commitment as governments are always reluctant to give up their control over the airwaves and media channels.

In some ways then, public service broadcasting can be said to be poised at a historical crossroad. Digital technologies and platforms offer new and powerful tools to public service broadcasters to develop themselves. Commercial broadcasting has plunged to the depths of mass and popular entertainment, providing public service broadcasting with an unprecedented opportunity to capture viewers and listeners who are interested in quality educational and informational content.

This publication is a modest attempt to identify some of the principal issues and challenges faced by public service broadcasting in various parts of the world. This compendium of essays aims to focus on various key aspects of public service broadcasting as well as to highlight best practices and critical issues relating to public service broadcasting. These essays look at various aspects of public service broadcasting ranging from definitions of public service broadcasting to challenges faced by established public service broadcasters such as the BBC in the UK and ABC in Australia. Several of the essays also highlight specific experiences of public service broadcasting in countries as varied as Malta, India, Papua New Guinea, Japan, Germany and many others.

It is with the intention of highlighting the opportunities and challenges faced by public service broadcasting in the 21st century that we embarked on this project to produce a book which will help to enhance our understanding of public service broadcasting and contribute to the debate and, most importantly, take action to make the above a possibility and not a utopian dream—as some like to argue—in today's excessively commercialized and globalized world of broadcasting.

In Chapter 2, Kalinga Seneviratne looks at the various definitions and models of PSBs, as well as the historic background to the development of public service broadcasting in various countries and regions of the world.

In the third chapter, Andrew Taussig takes us through the trials and tribulations of the BBC in the UK, and he suggests that the drama is not yet over. He also looks at the experience of other parts of Europe in recent years, especially the former communist countries, as they try to turn the old state broadcasting services into PSBs.

"Keep the essence, change (almost) everything else" is the theme of Chapter 4, where Karol Jakubowicz tries to redefine PSBs for the 21st century, taking into account the recent experiences of PSBs in Europe and the ongoing battle to make them relevant and economically viable. In the fifth chapter, Sundeep Mupiddi explores a conceptual model for public service television programming with examples from India, New Zealand and the US.

In Chapter 6, Venkat Iyer looks at the legal and regulatory aspects of PSBs in the current commercial environment, taking examples from Europe, Africa and Asia. He also discusses regulatory challenges faced by PSBs in the current climate and how one may respond to them. In Chapter 7, Binod Agrawal and Shalini Raghaviah discuss the historic development of PSB in India, and how it has transformed from a public service to a commercial entertainment medium.

How a model public service broadcaster could survive in the age of competition is the theme of Chapter 8 by Elizabeth Jacka, who discusses the situation in Australia, and the ABC in particular. There are important lessons to be learnt from ABC's continuing battle to protect itself and survive as a model PSB in the world. In Chapter 9, Umi Khattab examines the role of public culture, ethnicity and identity in the context of public service broadcasting in Malaysia. She also explores the role of the government in directing the PSB's role in the country.

The interesting story of broadcast development in post-apartheid South Africa is addressed by Ruth Elizabeth Teer-Tomaselli in Chapter 10, where she discusses the trials and tribulations of turning a state service broadcaster into a PSB. The impact of media liberalization on a German PSB is the focus of Chapter 11 by Sigrid Baringhorst, where she looks at the struggle of German PSBs to improve their ratings in a commercially driven entertainment media climate, while still leading the field in the provision of educational and information programmes.

Malta provides an interesting example of—perhaps a successful—battle between David and Goliath, to make a PSB relevant in a small island nation at the crossroads of Europe, with much global and cross-border infiltration of broadcast media. This topic is addressed by Joseph Borg in Chapter 12.

Another island nation, Sri Lanka, is the focus of Chapter 13 by Ariayaratne Athugala, where he looks at how a PSB has become increasingly commercialized to compete with the rapidly expanding private broadcasters while, on the other hand, some commercial radio has been taking a leaf out of PSBs in news and information programming.

In Chapter 14, Thomas Yesudhasan takes an interesting trip into the hill tribes of South India to discover that the tribal people are gradually getting hooked onto television, especially cable TV as an entertainment medium, but at the same time prefer PSB radio as an information source. With NHK in Japan, another model PSB, in the midst of a battle to regain the confidence of the people, Kuniko Sakata Watanabe argues in Chapter 15 that NHK could make themselves more relevant to the needs of the people by introducing more community access style of programming by adopting some of the production models being tried out by small community television channels in Japan.

In Chapter 16, Marie Mater, taking the example of Pacifica Radio, discusses how the state of public broadcasting in the United States could be improved by promoting more democratic access to the airwaves. And in the final chapter, Dick Rooney looks at the development of PSB in the Pacific island nation of Papua New Guinea and argues that public service radio could be revitalized in the country as an effective communication tool in a culturally diverse country by a greater emphasis on community-based broadcasting by the state radio sector.

Thus, in this book, we have not tried to separate community broadcasting from public service broadcasting but presented the idea that both sectors of broadcasting may be able to come together in some countries and communities for the benefit of citizens.

This book was inspired by a project that we had undertaken for UNESCO and which resulted in the publication of *Public Service Broadcasting—A Best Practices Sourcebook*. We would like to acknowledge UNESCO's support for our work on public service broadcasting as well as its long history and commitment in the promotion and support of public service broadcasting.

We hope this book will be a useful resource for public service broadcasters, policymakers and tertiary educational institutions as well as for students and the general public around the world. The broad range of case studies and analysis that this book provides will hopefully help to stimulate the debate and eventually to rekindle the commitment of experts and citizens to public service broadcasting.

References

Banerjee, I., & Seneviratne, K. (2005). *Public Service Broadcasting—A Best Practices Sourcebook*. Paris: UNESCO.

Postman, N. (1985). *Amusing Ourselves to Death—Public Discourse in the Age of Show Business*. New York: Penguin.

Definition and History of Public Service Broadcasting

The importance of public broadcasting is far from self-evident. It took several decades to find its place alongside entirely commercial media and media controlled by the state. Today, the unique contribution of public broadcasting is no longer in doubt and well-known examples, such as the BBC, are universally acclaimed. Public service plays an irreplaceable role in providing citizens with information, education and entertainment free of commercial, state or political influences ... Public service must enable each citizen to become a stakeholder in society, participating fully in the life of the community to which they belong and actively involved in its organization. Public service must be free from partisan or state pressure. It aims to serve all in the quest for the common good. It must preserve its independence while at the same time having its long-term financial resources guaranteed.

> – Claude Ondobo, Deputy Assistant Director General and Director of Communication Development Division, UNESCO, 2001

Today, all forms of public broadcasting—and the democratic promise that is always implicit in public broadcasting systems—are in rapid retreat. To some extent, this decline is the result of the rise of the cable and satellite broadcasting technologies that have dramatically increased the number of television channels. When public broadcasting accounts for an ever smaller portion of the audience, it is ever more difficult to earn or maintain a public subsidy. To an even greater extent, however, the decline of public service broadcasting is the logical consequence of the worldwide neo-liberal adoption of the market and commercial values as the superior regulator of the media.

> – Prof Robert MacChesney, University of Wisconsin, USA, 1997

Now is the time to move towards a market in broadcasting where viewers pay for what they choose to watch and not for much else.

> – Tim Yeo, Conservative Party Media Spokesperson, UK, 2002

A division is clearly growing between channels whose primary purpose is public service, and those which are obviously businesses seeking to maximize profits. For the former the ambition is to succeed in innovation, in refreshing the pool of home grown programmes, in accurately reflecting and stimulating the public mood and taste ... Perhaps the best medicine is to make sure that the public service broadcasters, those who put the public interest first, those who are committed to sustaining a creative, non-derivative production base, are properly supported, properly sustained and properly funded.

– Michael Grade, CEO, Channel 4 Television, UK, 1996

With the rapid spread of digital communication technologies in the 1990s, broadcasting, telecommunications and the computer have blended together to revolutionize the way we receive and consume broadcasting services today. It has dramatically increased the speed at which we can receive these services and also in many cases made it a lot cheaper to receive an ever more increasing number of channels. Thus, in this multi-channel environment the very notion or definition of Public Service Broadcasting (PSB) has become a topic of debate all over the world.

In this new information age, there are many questions being asked about the new role for PBS. What role should it be given to play? Are there social and cultural goals attributed to broadcasting which requires a specially mandated non-commercially driven organization, publicly funded if necessary and publicly owned so as to be publicly accountable? If so, how would you fund such a service?

The evolution of the new broadcasting environment has been marked by three sets of parallel developments (Raboy, 1999) namely:

- The explosion in channel capacity and disappearance of audiovisual borders made possible by new technology.
- The disintegration of the state broadcasting model with the collapse of the socialist bloc and the move towards democratization in various parts of the world.
- The upsurge in market broadcasting and the introduction of mixed broadcasting systems in the countries with former public service monopolies.

The last two developments may in fact help to device a more universally applicable model of PSB because for long Public Service Broadcasting (PSB) has been misunderstood as Government Service Broadcasting (GSB) in some parts of the world, especially in the former Communist bloc and in many developing countries.

While PSB has been widely accepted as the style of broadcasting established by the first Director-General of the BBC, John Reith with its mission to "inform, educate and entertain", yet, there has been no standard definition of what PSB is exactly about. Because in some countries PSB was referred to in terms of a particular organization or system of broadcasting, usually the national government owned broadcasting monopoly, which was part of the public service. Its role was also seen as developmental in nature rather than entertaining or even informing (independent of government policy).

Main principles of PSB

Neither commercial nor state-controlled, public broadcasting's only *raison d'etre* is public service. It is the public's broadcasting organization; it speaks to everyone as a citizen. Public broadcasters encourage access to and participation in public life. They develop knowledge, broaden horizons and enable people to better understand themselves by better understanding the world and others.

– World Radio And Television Council, 2002

The BBC or the British model has been widely accepted as a universal definition of PSB and UK's now defunct Broadcasting Research Unit has summarized its main principles as the following:

- Universal accessibility (geographically)
- Universal appeal (general tastes and interests)
- Paying particular attention to minorities
- Contributing to a sense of national identity and community
- Keeping a distance from vested interests
- Direct funding and universality of payment
- Competition in good programming rather than for numbers
- Guidelines that liberate rather than restrict programme makers

(Raboy, 1999: 8)

New definitions of "public service", which are in circulation, have moved decisively away from any such priority for universality, independence and diversity argue Holland (2003).

She lists three prevalent viewpoints on this:

- *Extreme market view*
  A television service, which has a guaranteed income from taxation or a license fee simply creates "a distortion in the market" and thus is illegitimate.

- *Compensates for market failure*
  Beyond simply using the catch phrase that public service broadcasting must "inform, educate and entertain", one may add "inform, educate and entertain in a way in which the private sector, left unregulated, would not do so".

- *Present specific, worthy programming*
  This sees some programmes and channels as public service and some not. This is a compromise view to the other two.

Raboy (1999) identifies three principle types of broadcasting systems as:

- *Public service core system*
  Dominant among these are the public service monopolies which existed in most Western European countries until the 1980s, where there was a very strong public service remit, lack of direct competition and a relative degree of autonomy from the state depending on the country's political culture.

- *Private enterprise core system*
  These are national systems built around commercial broadcasting practices, where the role of the state has been limited to frequency allocation and regulating of privately-owned broadcasting undertakings. This is the system prevalent in the US, many parts of Latin America and Asia.

- *State broadcasting core system*
  These systems exist today in countries which have not yet broken away from the tradition of a single, monolithic state-owned broadcaster or emerging systems, which although having been built on the state-owned and controlled system is now slowly opening out to commercial and community broadcasting. These systems are today found in parts of Africa and Asia, where democratization is gathering momentum, with South Africa providing a very stunning example of this.

Tongue (1996) argues that democratic societies require shared information or "common knowledge" in order to function effectively and democratically and warns that when differentiation and fragmentation arise within society, common knowledge is lost. This is a fact which should strengthen the case for public information and for public service broadcasting, she says, because diversity and access are the key principles of PSB.

"PSB has been built on the principle that public service television is free at the point of use. There is no reason why this principle should be aban-

PSB is a means for the community to express, discuss and shift through the issues and matters that are important and meaningful for it. To perform this function, it must achieve and retain a significant share of voice and meaningful presence in the social, public and cultural debate and communication. PSB is also a means for the community to invest in the production and mediation of pluralistic programming, without regard to its market value.

PSB must be a force to enable the effective working of a pluralist democracy and serve as a watchdog of the authorities. It must also include media content, which preserves and develops cultural diversity, identity and culture—not just "high culture", but culture generally. It has an important educational role to play.

– Report on PSB by the Committee on Culture, Science and Education of the – Parliamentary Assembly of the Council of Europe, January 2004.

doned. The new world of TV with multiple channels and as a consequence the fragmentation of audiences, increases the case for PSB being available to all and by all means via all technologies," Tongue argued in the report to the EU's Committee on Culture, Youth, Education and the Media.

PUBLIC SERVICE BROADCASTING AND THE DIGITAL CHALLENGE

Today, the commercial mass media looks very different from what existed until about the 1980s. During their heyday, mass media sources were a few large corporate entities that hired professionals who served as gatekeepers of what the national audiences would receive, hear or see. Since the popularity of cable television that started in the early 1980s, the media scene has been one of audience fragmentation. Today, with advances in information technology, we have desktop computers, the Internet, portable digital cameras and recorders that make it possible for multiple sources to cater to distinct types of listeners, viewers and readers. Thus, what we are seeing today is the erosion of the authority of centralized media sources in defining culture and popular opinion and, concomitantly, more access to the media of communication and information by laypeople.

In terms of media messages, earlier they tended to be homogenized, undifferentiated, one-way, and addressed primarily to national audiences. Today, there is a clear move towards narrowcasting and market segmentation into niche audience groups. Newer concepts such as "one to one communication" are moving towards an audience of one person. Therefore, a significant change in the nature of mass mediated messages is a move from homogenization of tastes and cultures to targeting of niche groups and individuals with customized products that cater to specific tastes and values.

The interactive media technologies provide rapid feedback thus fundamentally altering the nature of the mass communication process from the patterns of the past. Media and information signals today are increasingly digitized and integrated into a single network. The hybrid media of today that combine sound, voice, text, graphics, video, etc. are erasing the earlier distinctions between radio, television, print or telephone.

Probably, the most significant change in the nature of media messages is the conversion of signals from analogue to digital and the convergence of different media into one all-purpose data network. The Internet, for example, is a combination of all the media we have known until now. Technical advances such as the increase in bandwidth, digital compression, high speed lines and modems, and fibre optic networks have greatly increased the number of channels, the speed of transmission and the level of interactivity. On-demand entertainment, information and educational services will give the users a new measure of control. Also, the new technologies make it possible for individuals and groups to produce and distribute professional multimedia presentations and products from their desktop computers and workstations giving rise to personal electronic media as a new form of mass communications. These decentralized and interactive information sources are proving to be popular and increasingly taking the place of traditional mass media.

What are the roles of the mass media in this climate of constant change?

The term "public service broadcasting" (PSB) describes very aptly its role and function. I see PSB as a forum for and an advocate of public service. Therefore, PSB has a primary stake in social responsibility and should be held accountable to it unlike the commercial media. PSB, public journalism and other public service media outlets should be committed to facilitating and invigorating public discourse. It facilitates public discourse and service by giving a voice to the genuine public. Scholars in public journalism have posited that media outlets such as PSB's tasks must include a proactive role in identifying and honing matters of public interest and concern and facilitate interaction with and between members of the public on such issues. The outcomes expected of PSB include serving as an effective and free marketplace of ideas and information on matters of public interest and thus empower members of the public to connect with important issues concerning public life in their societies.

The new media technologies are opening up a diverse range of options for consumers and producers of informational materials and services. This is a positive trend for a democratic society that values choices. However, what are the cultural, social and political implications of the changes wrought by the newer media and the commercial broadcasting industries around the world? What are the risks to a modern and democratic society?

PSB and other public service media have to be at the centre of the debate, asking questions, providing an informed critique of the dangers or risks involved and educating citizens on the social, political, economic, cultural and moral implications of the changes taking place. PSB must be a leader in facilitating public policy decisions towards the strengthening of the benefits offered by the new media and commercial media systems and reducing or eliminating the negative consequences.

There are four areas of concern that I would like to identify that PSB should address in a meaningful way:

- Social equality or ensure full citizen access to the new media/information technologies
- Issues relating to freedom to produce, transmit and receive information
- Invasion of privacy issues
- Certain cultural effects

Social equality

Equitable access to information and media channels is of paramount importance to a democratic polity. Today, the distribution of the new media is unequal in most regions of the world including the United States. Factors that inhibit access to the new media include functional illiteracy, computer illiteracy, economic disadvantage and unequal infrastructural facilities and development. Research has shown that certain sections of the population such as women, minorities and the economically poor are worse off in their lack of access to the new hardware and software. Meanwhile, other research results indicate that the information rich are getting richer and that the information gap is increasing between the information rich and the information poor due to disparities in education, income and access.

Freedom-related issues

The debate on media freedom is both lively and important. In democratic societies, the overriding interest has been to protect media freedom under the assumption that the media will function as a free marketplace of ideas and opinions. For example, in the United States though the mass media has been criticized for allowing the economic and commercial interests to dominate at the cost of other interests vital to the community, on the whole, the scene is one of unfettered media catering to the information and entertainment needs of that country. However, there have been attempts by the government and other groups to impose censorship on certain types of content especially the Internet. Is the Internet a vehicle for personal conversations or is it an electronic newspaper? Should the content of the Internet be completely free or should it be liable to laws that newspapers and the electronic media are required to subscribe to? How do we deal with the increased number of individuals who are serving as media sources (in the newer media) and some of whom are spewing hatred about others or expressing very controversial and unsubstantiated opinions? How does one deal with deception in the digitized representations of events, people or places on the Internet and other newer graphics technologies? In the realm of the newer information and media technologies, how do we balance individual freedoms with community interest? PSB must take a leadership role in debating these issues.

Privacy issues

How do we protect the electronic privacy of individuals in this age of globalization? Individuals, who are active online or regularly use credit cards or cheques to purchase products, pay membership dues to professional associations, etc. leave an indelible electronic fingerprint with every transaction. Those who use the Internet may be susceptible to monitoring by someone. Many users are unaware of "listening" devices such as cookies that are imbedded in the computer code of their machines or Internet accounts. Thus, the threat to personal liberties is a real one in this age of interactive media due to the lack of privacy or anonymity. This represents another set of concerns wherein PSB can play a leadership role by disseminating facts, views and opinions of a wide swath of constituencies in a society and thus facilitate a "grassroots" dialogue and discussion.

Cultural effects

In the rush to reap the advantages offered by the new communication and media technologies, we may be reifying technology. Some scholars such as Neil Postman have discussed the dangers of a technology in which technology is deified and extends an authoritarian control over all aspects of civil society. At the crux of this debate is the scientific method that exhibits an anthropomorphic view of reality, uses technology to extend greater control at the expense of other issues and interests. Should civil society institutions be the cheerleaders for the new technologies and, inadvertently, help establish a technological elite that comprises engineers, managers, scientists, etc. who bring with them a very technology-oriented world view? Or, should civil society institutions also pay sufficient attention to the social, cultural, ethical, and moral implications of the newer technologies? Again, in my view, PSB is an ideal conduit to provide an informed and critical view of the profound changes affecting all of us in the age of globalization.

Another important issue is the role of the traditional mass media in uniting a society. With the proliferation of media sources, will there be a serious fragmentation of the national society where we have numerous information islands unconnected by a national medium? What then would the consequences be to national identity and national unity? Or is "nation" an obsolescent concept in this age of the global village that the new media are ushering in?

PSB has an important role to play here by initiating a dialogue with civil society on the implications of these developments to the future of that society and the national culture.

– Prof Srinivas R. Melkote, School of Communication Studies –
Bowling Green State University[1]

---

[1] This article was specially contributed for this publication in September 2005.

Main categories of PSB

PSB models have been developed due to the mistrust of two systems—the profit motivated commercial model and the state-controlled motivated state broadcasting model.

In the United States, after many debates, it was deemed that the public good would be better served if broadcasting was left in the hands of private entrepreneurs wishing to offer listeners, it was claimed, what they wanted to hear. The market principles governing other business sectors were generally applied to broadcasting. Supply and demand was expected to serve the interests of both the audience and private broadcasters. Advertising as a means of financing broadcasting, it was believed, ensured that private broadcasters would seek to meet public demand at all times—after all, the rate paid by advertisers for commercials was linked to the broadcaster's ability to reach the widest possible audience. And if the audience tuned in, it was assumed that the public was satisfied overall with the programmes offered (CMRTV, 2001).

The public-service model, while it stems from the vision some had for radio, was also based on mistrust: mistrust of the ability of market mechanisms to fulfil certain goals, and mistrust of the state's ability to achieve the same objectives, generally grouped under the broad expectations that still apply to public broadcasting today, that is, to inform, educate and entertain. This vision of the role and importance of public broadcasting required a public organization, at the service of citizens, culture and democracy (CMRTV, 2001).

Some countries rejected the notion that public interest, in broadcasting, could be served by the interests of private entrepreneurs primarily looking for profit. At the same time, however, people were suspicious of the state as well. Because of broadcasting's social, cultural and political potential, it was felt that direct state involvement in a field related by and large to thought and expression was not desirable. This is generally the least obvious distinction between public and state broadcasting when the different models are compared.

Thus, the main categories of PSBs in operation today could be described as:

- *National public service broadcasting*
  These are national broadcasting services or networks which are largely independent of day to day editorial control by the government of the day, but funding and administrative structures are still subject to

17

political decisions. Funding could come from a licensing fee, direct government grants or commercial advertising or a combination of these. Such systems exists today mainly in Europe, Australia, Canada and Japan.

- *Alternative public broadcasting*
  These systems could be described as the spin-offs of the major PSBs, services set up to serve minority tastes and communities or a second public channel. Britain's Channel 4, Australia's SBS, French-German cultural channel ARTE, New Zealand's Maori Television and many ethnic language channels in Asia and perhaps India's Doordarshan development broadcasting channel could be classified as such.

- *Multiple ownership services*
  This is a new phenomenon in public broadcasting where the state owned channels may go into a joint venture set up with a privately owned broadcaster or media company. Recent examples of this are BBC's global broadcasting channel in partnership with Pearson PLC, Russia's conversion of Ostankino into a 51-49 joint venture with the state, French channel TV5 and ARTE. This could become an emerging trend in a new form of PSB.

- *Community broadcasting*
  Though community broadcasters prefer to see them as non-state, non-commercial, localized broadcasting, reflecting the community perspective and tastes, these latter objectives by themselves make community broadcasting reflect a public service objective. Yet, they do not receive state backing nor are they restricted by the mandate of PSBs. Community broadcasters have little access to government funding and limited scope for advertising revenue. Thus, these services are mainly dependent on community support and volunteer labour.

- *State broadcasting*
  These broadcasting systems are fully government funded, though they may also be commercial in nature, raising advertising revenue. But, they are directly answerable to the government of the day and are seen as purveyors of government policy. These services are not only national or regional broadcasting systems, but may also broadcast overseas as an instrument of government policy such as China's CCTV or US's Voice of America or Russia's Radio Moscow (during the Soviet era). Sometimes these systems of state broadcasting are easily confused with PSB.

Definition of PSB channels

Council of Europe's Independent Television Commission (2004) has described the definition of a PSB channel as which brings together most or all of the following elements:

1. Wide range of programmes catering for a variety of tastes and interests, taking scheduling into account.

2. High quality in terms of technical and production standards, with evidence of being well resourced and of innovation and distinctiveness, making full use of new media to support television's educational role.

3. Catering for minorities (cultural, linguistic and social) and other special needs and interests, particularly education including schools programmes and provisions for disabled people.

4. Catering for regional interests and communities of interest, and reflecting the regions to each other.

5. Reflecting a national identity, being a "voice of the nation", the place where people go on national occasions.

6. Containing a large amount of origin productions made especially for first showing.

7. Demonstrating a willingness to take creative risks, challenging viewers, complementing other PSB channels and those, which are purely market driven.

8. Strong sense of independence and impartiality, authoritative news, a forum for public debate, ensuring a plurality of opinions and an informed electorate.

9. Universal coverage.

10. Limited amounts of advertising (a maximum of seven minutes per hour across the day).

11. Affordability: Either free at the point of delivery or at a cost which makes it accessible to the vast majority of the people.

In understanding the role of PSB, the following factors could be taken into account in judging whether a PSB is playing the role it is expected to perform:

- *Universality*
  Public broadcasting must be accessible to every citizen throughout the country. This is a deeply egalitarian and democratic goal to the extent

that it puts all citizens on the same footing, whatever their social status or income. It forces the public broadcaster to address the entire population and seek to be "used" by the largest possible number. This does not mean that public broadcasting should try to optimize its ratings at all times, as commercial broadcasting does, but rather that it should endeavour to make the whole of its programming accessible to the whole population. This does not merely involve technical accessibility, but ensuring that everyone can understand and follow its programming. As well as democratic public broadcasting programming must be "popular" not in the pejorative sense that some give this term, but in the sense that the public forum it provides should not be restricted to a minority. Thus, public broadcasting, while it should promote culture, should not become a ghetto constantly frequented by the same group of initiates.

- *Diversity*

  The service offered by public broadcasting should be diversified, in at least three ways: in terms of the genres of programmes offered, the audiences targeted and the subjects discussed. Public broadcasting must reflect the diversity of public interests by offering different types of programmes, from newscasts to light programmes. Some programmes may be aimed at only part of the public, whose expectations are varied. In the end, public broadcasting should reach everyone, not through each programme, but through all programmes and their diversity. Finally, through the diversity of the subjects discussed, public broadcasting can also seek to respond to the varied interests of the public and so reflect the whole range of current issues in society. Diversity and universality are complementary in that producing programmes intended sometimes for youth, sometimes for older people and sometimes for other groups ultimately means that public broadcasting appeals to all.

- *Independence*

  Public broadcasting is a forum where ideas should be expressed freely, where information, opinions and criticisms circulate. This is possible only if the independence—therefore, the freedom—of public broadcasting is maintained against commercial pressures or political influence. If the information provided by the public broadcaster was influenced by government, people would no longer believe in it. Likewise, if the public broadcaster's programming was designed for commercial ends, people would not understand why they are being asked to finance a service whose programmes are not substantially different from the services provided by private broadcasting.

- *Distinctiveness*
  This requires that the service offered by public broadcasting distinguish itself from that of other broadcasting services. In public-service programming—in the quality and particular character of its programmes—the public must be able to identify what distinguishes this service from other services. It is not merely a matter of producing the type of programmes other services are not interested in, aiming at audiences neglected by others, or dealing with subjects ignored by others. It is a matter of doing things differently, without excluding any genre. This principle must lead public broadcasters to innovate, create new slots, new genres, set the pace in the audiovisual world and pull other broadcasting networks in their wake.

(CMRTV, 2001).

In a speech to the World Electronic Media Forum Workshop on Public Service Broadcasting in Geneva (2003), Dr Abdul Waheed Khan, UNESCO's assistant director general for communication and information, said that "only in the unrestricted pursuit of objective truth and in the free exchange of ideas and knowledge can we achieve international peace, understanding and sustainable development".

He argued that in today's world, in the interplay of major technological, commercial, political and cultural factors, when commercial interests and political interference fiercely challenge the field of broadcasting, public service broadcasting makes a landmark.

"However, the results that the world envisioned public service broadcasting to deliver are not exactly met due to the different factors surrounding its nature," added Dr Khan. "First and foremost the basic role of PSB is to provide an inclusive platform for a Public Sphere in which representative pluralism is reflected and nourished".

He went on to argue that the editorial purpose of the PSB should consistently show the ability to become the voice in the society, guaranteeing equal access for wide range of opinions by bringing together common conversation that shape the public will, and in particular should become a trendsetter in taking vital socio-political issues for discussions.

"To perform this function the public broadcaster should be accountable to the society under a regime of free expression and be free of political and economic pressures. This requires independent management structures devoid of sectarian political and private interests and sufficient public funds to function. This task cannot be achieved without autonomous, independent, competent and representative governance to ensure the public service of the broadcasting systems," he said.

"We are all conscious about how PSB serves as a channel where we can gain access to education and culture, developing knowledge and fostering interaction among citizens. PSB is most suited to meet the challenges of development faced by the developing countries: to address the problems of the rapid population growth, to fight illiteracy, the HIV/AIDS pandemic as well as working for poverty eradication. The use of audiovisual techniques, multimedia formats and the possibilities of interactivity that PSB offers highlights its role as an educational force alongside libraries and multipurpose information resource centres that we have today. For those committed to participatory democracy it is important to ensure that PSB play its pivotal role in the democratic processes. We not only need to get public resources and institutional protection for public broadcasting; we also need to reform it mightily so that it serves more directly as a purveyor of democratic ideals, helping to broaden horizons and enable people to better understand themselves by better understanding the world and the others," added Dr Khan.

A history of public service broadcasting

PBS systems originated in European democracies in the second quarter of the 20th century. At the core of each was a commitment to operated broadcasting services—radio and later television—for the public good. The principle model adopted was the establishment of a state-owned broadcasting service either functioning as a monopoly or at least as the dominant broadcasting system.

The beginnings—BBC model

The roots of public service broadcasting are generally traced to documents prepared in support of the establishment of the British Broadcasting Corporation (BBC) by Royal Charter on 1 January 1927. This corporation grew out of recommendations of the Crawford Committee appointed by the British Postmaster General in August 1925, included in those recommendations was the creation of a public corporation which would serve as a trustee for the national interest in broadcasting. It was expected that as public trustee, the corporation would emphasize serious, educational and cultural programming that would elevate the level of intellectual and aesthetic tastes of the audience.

The conception of the BBC was that it would be insulated from both political and commercial influence. Therefore, the corporation was a creation of the crown rather than parliament, and funding to support the venture was determined to be derived from license fees on radio (and later television) receivers rather than advertising. This made the BBC financially independent of the government of the day and on advertising revenue.

Under the skilful leadership of the BBC's first director general, John Reith, this institution of PSB embarked on an ethical mission of high moral responsibility to utilize the electromagnetic spectrum—a scarce public resource—to enhance the quality of life of all British citizens. He developed strong ideas about the educational and cultural public service responsibilities of a national radio broadcaster, which operated on a non-commercial basis, offered national coverage with centralized control and developed high quality standards of programming. These ideas were subsequently pursued by many broadcasting systems around the world.

From its inception in 1927 up to 1954, the BBC had a monopoly on broadcasting. In 1954, an independent television station was licensed but this station was under the same duties of providing a public service to disseminate education, information and entertainment as the BBC, until 1981. It was only in 1973 that local commercial radio was finally given the green light.

The BBC operates under both Royal Charter (RC) and a Licensing Agreement (LA). RCs are grants from the Sovereign to undertake certain activities, often on an exclusive basis. The BBC's Charter is drafted by the Secretary of State for National Heritage and is subjected to mandatory Parliamentary scrutiny. The LA between the Secretary of State for National Heritage and the Board of Governors of the BBC specifies in further detail the governance and public service obligations of the BBC.

These public service mandates include providing radio and television broadcasting programmes with educational, informational and entertainment value. It is spelt out in detail in the LA, which covers areas such as contents and editorial integrity. The current RC and the LA was renewed in 1996 for a 10-year period.

BBC is today one of the world's largest broadcasting organizations with a staff of over 25,000 and an annual budget exceeding US$4 billion. Bulk of BBC's budget is funded by a licensing fee, which is levied on every household with a television set. The price is fixed by negotiation between the BBC and the government, and the level of the fee has kept pace with the retail price index since the mid-1980s. But, since this period there have been many reviews of this funding arrangement beginning with the 1985 Peacock Committee on Financing the BBC.

With the establishment of the Independent Television Commission (ITC)—whose duties are set out in the Broadcasting Act of 1990—a system of commercial broadcasting franchises has been set up in Britain. Also, the birth of Channel 4 in 1982, with PSB objectives but structured as a facilitator rather than a producer of high quality educational and informational programmes, has created a network of professional independent production houses which provides healthy competition to the BBC.

Threats to the BBC

> Commentators tout the achievements of public service broadcasters—the drama, the culture—as if they were astonishing. But if you give someone 75 years of access to every home in the land and guarantee them billions of pounds every year, it would be truly astonishing if they didn't achieve a level of excellence, regardless of audience taste.
> – Rupert Murdoch, CEO, News Corporation, addressing the European Audio Visual Conference, Birmingham, April 1998

What is emerging today is a mixed system of broadcasting in Britain and hence, BBC's funding arrangement has been under attack by vested media interests and even politicians. In announcing an advisory panel for the review of the BBC charter, Labour government's Cultural Secretary Tessa Jowell said that everything was up for grabs including how the BBC "should be funded and regulated and whether it delivers good value for money" (Roddick, 2003).

In Britain's multi-channel broadcasting environment, the force of audience competition is shaping everything it touches. There is hot bidding for popular sporting events with commercial operators complaining about "unfair" competition from a "taxpayer" funded public broadcaster, while parliament has keenly debated proposals to guarantee access for free-to-air channels against exclusive satellite deals. With competition for viewers becoming a struggle to be noticed (rated), the BBC itself has been accused from time to time of drifting away from the PSB objectives to compete with popular commercial entertainment programmes. Recently the BBC was forced to shut down some of its websites (Malkani, 2004)—such as "Fantasy Football" and "Pure Soap"—when a government-commissioned report found that some of its internet services were "insufficiently distinct" from commercial websites.

The 2003 Communications Bill presented to parliament claimed to define PSB within the law for the first time. Holland (2003) criticized this bill as acknowledging all broadcasting services as having "public service" elements within the output of different channels with some broadcasters as PSBs and others less so.

The powerful government broadcasting regulator Ofcom (refer to Chapter 2 for more information) set up under the 2003 Communication Bill is now gearing up to review the BBC charter and LA and set up a new framework for PSB in Britain, which will involve a revamping of the license fee regime. At the time of writing, a heated battle has begun between the BBC and the ITV (trying to protect its funding source) and independent production houses and commercial media trying to pry open access to these funds.

Jowell (Indymedia, 2004) has signalled the Labour government's position when she said that reality television shows broadcast on commercial TV may well qualify for PSB status because "a reality-TV show that explored some particular aspect of human behaviour could be argued for as public service broadcasting, with an interest that extends beyond profits and high ratings". She also suggested some story lines on TV soap operas often had a strong public service value.

In a submission to the public consultation exercise on BBC's charter review, PACT (the British trade body for independent production industry) has argued that they should be allowed to access some of the funding under the licensing fee to produce programmes for the BBC (Martinson, 2004). They recommended that the BBC cut its in-house production from 70 per cent to 50 per cent and outsource the rest.

Ofcom has offered support for this view by its criticism of BBC's "centralized studios and vertically integrated broadcaster-producer" system. "A strong independent production sector is an important part of the mix to deliver effective PSB," it said in a blueprint laid out by the new regulator (Matinson, 2004).

In a report commissioned by the opposition Conservative Party, David Elsien the former CEO of Channel 5 argued that if the money raised by the license fee could be distributed to any broadcasting organization, which made a case for it. The committee of broadcasting experts, which drafted this report, has advocated phasing out the licensing fee over a 10-year period beginning in 2007 (Wells, 2004). This fee could be reduced, as BBC's digital channels move to subscriber funding, and gradually the other free-to-air channels also move to a subscriber base. Meanwhile, all broadcasters, including the BBC, could apply for money from a "public broadcasting authority" that would distribute up to one billion pounds (US$2.1 billion) a year of taxpayer's money to producers of public service programming. The BBC would also become a state corporation broadcasting programmes made independently.

As Yeo (2002) put it: "The television tax affects the behaviour not just of the BBC but other broadcasters too. It limits the power of consumers to determine what they are offered. It's a crude and undiscriminating way to charge for television. It wouldn't survive if consumers were used to paying for what they want and nothing else".

Thus, the battle is on to wean off the BBC and its supporters from the notion that the licensing fee is BBC's "birthright". Critics and supporters of the BBC model argues that such views reflects the American perspective on PSB and aims to reduce the BBC into US's PBS (explained later in the chapter) model, which has been proved to be an ineffective PSB.

The European experience

Public service broadcasting is a vital element of democracy in Europe. Across the continent, its future is challenged, by political and economic interests, by increasing competition from commercial media, by media concentrations and by financial difficulties. Some post-communist countries have not yet even started the transition from state-controlled to public electronic media. In other countries, public service broadcasting is in crisis.
– Report on PSB by the Committee on Culture, Science and Education of the Parliamentary Assembly of the Council of Europe, January 2004.

After the concept of PSB was born in Britain prior to World War II with the establishment of the BBC, this model became dominant in countries of Western Europe until the 1980s. Though there were a number of variations, such as PSBs coming under direct government control in France, Italy and Greece compared to more autonomy in Britain and Scandinavia, the essential form of PSB however was a national broadcaster operating as a regulated monopoly that broadcast for, and represented the views and culture of the population of the country in question.

McQuail (1994) has identified six major characteristics of this PSB model: (a) a strong notion of public service which sought to provide cultural, informative and educational programming catering for everyone in the community; (b) public accountability of public funds spent; (c) monopoly broadcasters licensed by the government; (d) politically linked to the state with varying degrees of politicization; (e) national in scope; and (f) non-commercial in nature with programming freed from the need to make profits.

From the mid-1970s when Britain and Italy allowed the establishment of private broadcasting, the monopolistic PSB model began to face competition from private broadcasters with the trend picking up steam in the 1980s. Subsequently, private broadcasters were able to open up the airwaves across Europe, which Blumler (1992) describes as the "commercial deluge."

During this period, there were new terrestrial TV channels, which were launched across Europe such as France's Canal Plus and Sky TV in Britain. Invariably the PSBs lost audience share as the new broadcasters began to fragment the market. In Italy, public broadcaster's share fell to 49 per cent by 1995, in the Netherlands commercials gained 28 per cent of the audience share by 1996 and in Britain commercial channels were getting 18 per cent of the audience by 2001 (ITC, 2001).

Thus by the 1990s, the PSB system in Europe has been transformed into a duel system, with commercial broadcasters along and in competition with PSBs. However, from its inception, broadcasting in Europe was seen as accomplishing an important democratic and cultural mission. Which was emphasized by the 1982, Council of Europe "Declaration on the Freedom of Expression and Information" which laid down that technological developments "should serve to further the right, regardless of frontiers, to express, to seek, to receive and to impart information and ideas, whatever their source" (UNESCO, 1995).

But, changes in the political set up in many European countries in the 1980s and 1990s, where governments committed to deregulation of markets (including broadcasting) paved the way for the privatization of broadcasting on the notion that deregulation of the media will lead to democratization. The big countries of Italy, France and Germany led the way, while the smaller ones followed.

In France however, this deregulation has not undermined the PSB role of the broadcasting media. The notion of even commercial broadcasting as a public service rather than simply a commercial exercise is still very strong (Mendel, 2000). The main elements of public service mandate are contained in Article 1 of the 1986 Law, entitled Article premier. This Article provides, among other things, for the main regulatory body Conseil Superioer de l'Audiovisual (CSA) to guarantee the independence and impartiality of public service broadcasting organizations and to ensure that all broadcasters promote quality and diversity of programming, national audio-visual production and the French language and culture. Many of the obligations established by this law are applicable to both PSBs and commercial broadcasters.

When commercial broadcasters came on board, there was a dramatic rise in prices for film and sports rights in the 1990s, and the competition for advertising money became harder. Private broadcasters thus started to argue that the financing system of public broadcasters is a violation of European competition law. The license fee would give public broadcasters an unfair privilege and would undermine the capacity of private broadcasters to compete under equal conditions.

To overcome this problem, the private broadcasters proposed that the license fee system (which would lead to the abolishment of the public broadcasting system) be abolished or a clear distinction be made between license fee financed public broadcasting and advertisement financed private broadcasting and a re-definition of "basic services" for public broadcasters which would exclude sports and films from basic services (which would lead to a marginalization of public broadcasting).

European Council after discussing these issues adopted as part of the "Amsterdam Treaty"[2], a special "Protocol on Public Broadcasting Services". The protocol says that a financing system based of license fees is legal and justified because public broadcasting is directly related to the "democratic, social and cultural needs of each society" and it is an important element to safeguard "pluralism". On the other hand, it says that funding of public broadcasting should not "affect trading conditions and competition". There should be a "fair balance" which should allow private broadcasters to compete under "fair conditions". At the same time, the protocol says, that, according to the principle of subsidiarity, the concrete practice is a sovereign decision of the member state.

In the 1990s in many parts of Europe, PSBs were subjected to attack. As private broadcasters provided more and more programming, the idea of a public license fee was questioned. Media moguls such as Silvio Berlusconi and Rupert Murdoch promoted deregulation as a part of a drive to launch commercial channels tapping into the European advertising revenues. As Blumler (1992) observed, the "new entrepreneurs were able to present themselves as the people's champions against entrenched and stuffy elites".

This issue of license fee subsidy for PSBs became a global issue when "trade in services" became a part of the mandate of the "World Trade Organization's (WTO) negotiations on global trade liberalization (Wolfgang, 2004). The issue here is that according to the WTO rules, there should be no national subsidies for the production of goods and services, which would distort competition. From a US perspective, the European license fee system for broadcasting is interpreted as such a "subsidy" which

---

[2] Adopted on 2 October 1997.

undermines and blocks the capacity of US broadcasting corporations to enter the European broadcasting market.

In Central and Eastern Europe, after the fall of communism, the introduction of PSB has either so far failed or has produced very uncertain results, as PSB organizations lack social embeddedness and the right democratic context in which to operate. The belief that one can transplant institutions as part of a process of "imitative transformation", especially in such a sensitive area as the mass media, has proved overoptimistic (Jakubowicz, 2004).

Jakubowicz (2004) points out that following the fall of communism in 1989, Central and Eastern European countries embarked on re-designing their media systems. In objective terms, that required:

- Creation of the guarantees of freedom of expression and of the media.
- Introduction of market forces into the media system.
- "Catching up" with the evolution that media systems in more developed countries had undergone in the 20th century.
- Incorporation of media systems into the global market and development of a response to the (conflicting) requirements of international organizations, as well as (at least in the case of EU candidate countries) to the 21st-century challenges of the Information Society.

There were three early media policy orientations, which contributed to shaping the path (or views) of a new media order in these countries. Jakubowicz describes these as "idealistic", "mimetic" and "atavistic".

- *Idealistic*
  This orientation was in line with the tendency of dissidents to think in terms antithetical to the Communist system itself, this orientation assumed the introduction of a direct communicative democracy as part of a change of social power relations. This was promoted by the intellectual and cultural opposition to the system, fascinated with western concepts of "access", "participation" and "social management" of the media.

- *Mimetic*
  This orientation was conceived as a way of achieving approximation to "the West", including full liberalization of the print media and creation of a balanced dual system of broadcasting. The "mimetic" orientation focused on the key objectives of the public service phase of media policy development in Western Europe.

- *Atavistic*

  This orientation was conceived by the "political society", which emerged after the fall of communism. This resulted in systems of political and public life dominated by political parties. The new power elites, while ostensibly accepting the "mimetic" orientation, in many cases sought to cling to whatever elements of the old command system they could still maintain. This, then, was a plan for a media system based, to differing degrees, on social responsibility, paternalism, development communication and authoritarian press theories.

Since the "idealistic" orientation was immediately rejected everywhere after the demise of the Communist system, the only choice for Central and Eastern European countries was between the other two orientations—or some combination of them.

In practically all post-Communist countries, commercial stations appeared before PSBs were created. Accordingly, the latter had to compete head on with commercial stations even as they were trying to establish themselves. At the same time, politicization of content, management and staff meant that restructuring and managerial reform could not in reality be carried through. This meant that newly created PSBs were not given enough time for the necessary institutional changes, the professional and cultural changes among staff (independence, impartiality, detachment from politics, dedication to public interest, commitment to quality, ability to refrain from pandering to the lowest common denominator), or the major managerial restructuring that would downsize the organizations, reduce staffing and promote cost-effectiveness and efficiency. The overall result of this combination of circumstances could be called a lack of social embeddedness of PSB in post-Communist countries, depriving it of its natural social habitat and cultural context. Even more seriously, all this is taking place against a background of increasing doubts in Western European countries as to the continued legitimacy of maintaining PSBs (Jakubowicz, 2004).

By 1996, many European institutions were concerned about the future of PSB and this materialized into two initiatives taken in September 1996. On 11 September, the Committee of Ministers of the Council of Europe (CE) adopted Recommendation No. R (96) 10 on the Guarantee of Independence of Public Service Broadcasting and on 19 September, the European Parliament (EP) adopted a Resolution on the role of public service television in a multimedia society.

The CE recommends 23 guidelines on desirable contents, legal frameworks and status, specific missions and structures of PSB. The EP Resolution passed by 213 to 140 votes emphasized the cultural importance of PSB, and demanded that, the European Commission (EC), as part of competition and internal market policy, lay down guidelines to promote PSB in Europe.

In October 2001, the EC issued a clarification on "state aid rules to Public Service Broadcasting" in which they said that States are in principle free to define the extent of the public service and the way it is financed and organized, according to their preferences, history and needs (more details on this later in the chapter).

Currently there is a huge variation in the situation with PSB across Europe. At one extreme, national broadcasting continues to be under strict government control and there is little prospect of introducing PSBs by legislation in the foreseeable future (Mooney, 2004), such as in Russia. Meanwhile in Bosnia and Herzegovina and in Kosovo, PSB regulations have been imposed from outside by the international community, in Czech Republic, Hungary and Slovakia PSB is facing severe financial difficulties and in Greece, Italy, Portugal and Spain political interference is still preventing PSBs from being fully emancipated from direct government control.

In summarizing the development of PSB in Europe, one could distinguish three waves beginning with the establishment of the BBC in 1927. The second wave was in the 1960s and 1970s when sweeping political change in Western Europe, such as in France and Italy, began to transform government service broadcasters into PSBs. The third is the political changes in Central and Eastern Europe since 1989, where media system changes are a part of the overall political transition to democracy after an authoritarian system was dismantled.

Three types of broadcasting organizations are emerging in Europe (UNESCO, 1995) thus:

- PSBs, which have to accomplish a cultural mission, laid down by law and which are supposed to provide programmes for the entire population.
- Commercial channels which have to comply with very few regulations concerning their programming, which are financed by advertising revenue.
- Pay-TV channels also subjected to very few regulations, with discriminating or more affluent audiences as their specific target group and funded by subscriptions only.

In such an environment, there would always be debate about the specific roles of PSBs and commercial broadcasters. Tongue (1996) argues that those who support PSB should resist the argument that PSBs should concentrate "only" on supplying the kinds of programmes, which are not provided by the commercial sector. By "ghettorizing" PSBs in such a way will reduce audiences, thereby reducing its legitimacy. She predicts in coming years, as commercial broadcasters become more similar in their mass-market appeal, it will be the PSBs who would have to provide the "widest range of accessible choice for the public".

The American experience and the PBS

> Non-commercial TV should address itself to the ideal of excellence, not idea of acceptability—which is what keeps commercial TV from climbing the staircase. I think TV should be providing the visual counterpart of the literary essay, should arouse our dreams, satisfy our hunger for beauty, take us on journeys, enable us to participate in events, present great drama and music, explore the sea and the sky and the woods and the hills. It should be our Lyceum, our Chautauqua, our Minsky's, and our Camelot. It should restate and clarify the social dilemma and the political pickle. Once in a while it does, and you get a quick glimpse of its potential.
> – New Yorker journalist E B White's letter to Carnegie Commission on Educational TV, 1996

In November 1967 the Public Broadcasting Act was signed into law by President Johnson. The Act established the Corporation for Public Broadcasting (CPB) as an independent, non-governmental body that would ultimately serve as the umbrella organization for public broadcasting in the United States. At that time 125 educational television stations reached six million viewers. Within the decade the number of public stations more than double and 30 million homes enjoyed access to public broadcasting.

The CPB was authorized to facilitate the development of educational broadcasting and finance interconnection facilities to link the independent public television stations, but was restricted from owning stations, systems, networks, or interconnection facilities. The CPB's Board of Directors are appointed by the President and confirmed by the US Senate.

The CPB established the Public Broadcasting Service (PBS) in 1969 to manage the interconnection of independent public and educational broadcasting facilities. To this day, PBS remains "owned and directed by its member stations, which are in turn accountable to their local communities" (Stevens, 1995).

There are 170 non-commercial, educational licensees who operate the 349 PBS member stations. Of the 170 licensees, 87 are community organizations, 57 are colleges/universities, 20 are state authorities and six are local educational or municipal authorities[3].

---

[3] PBS website www.pbs.org

THE PUBLIC BROADCASTING ACT SECTION 396
CORPORATION FOR PUBLIC BROADCASTING[4]

The Congress hereby finds and declares that:

(1) It is in the public interest to encourage the growth and development of public radio and television broadcasting, including the use of such media for instructional, educational, and cultural purposes.

(2) It is in the public interest to encourage the growth and development of non-broadcast telecommunications technologies for the delivery of public telecommunications services.

(3) Expansion and development of public telecommunications and of diversity of its programming depend on freedom, imagination, and initiative on both local and national levels.

(4) The encouragement and support of public telecommunications, while matters of importance for private and local development, are also of appropriate and important concern to the Federal Government.

(5) It furthers the general welfare to encourage public telecommunications services, which will be responsive to the interests of people both in particular localities and throughout the United States, which will constitute an expression of diversity and excellence, and which will constitute a source of alternative telecommunications services for all the citizens of the Nation.

(6) It is in the public interest to encourage the development of programming that involves creative risks and that addresses the needs of unserved and underserved audiences, particularly children and minorities.

(7) It is necessary and appropriate for the Federal Government to complement, assist, and support a national policy that will most effectively make public telecommunications services available to all citizens of the United States.

(8) Public television and radio stations and public telecommunications services constitute valuable local community resources for utilizing electronic media to address national concerns and solve local problems through community programmes and outreach programmes.

(9) It is in the public interest for the Federal Government to ensure that all citizens of the United States have access to public telecommunications services through all appropriate available telecommunications distribution technologies.

(10) A private corporation should be created to facilitate the development of public telecommunications and to afford maximum protection from extraneous interference and control.

– PBS website –

---

[4] The Public Broadcasting Act was signed into law by President Lyndon B. Johnson on 7 November 1967.

From its early stages, in spite of its privileged position as a government-supported entity, public broadcasting received little opposition from commercial broadcasters. The president of CBS, Frank Stanton, has once observed that public broadcasting "will do special things that we don't do in quantity at the present time" (Stevens, 1995).

Ronald Coase, a Professor of Economics at the University of Chicago went further in articulating additional benefits public broadcasting would create for commercial broadcasters. He observed that public television was bound to "result in the long run in a much less insistent demand from the intellectual community that the commercial television industry broadcast public service programmes and will therefore enable them to concentrate to an even greater extent than they do now on more popular (and more profitable) programmes" (Stevens, 1995).

PBS is well-known for its quality programming, which includes shows like *Sesame Street* and *Mister Roger's Neighbourhood*, favourite channel of many children. In addition to its pre-eminence in both educational and cultural programming throughout its first 20 years, PBS was also a technological leader. In 1978, PBS became the first American broadcast television system to distribute its programmes via satellite.

Today, the network of public television stations organized through PBS is watched by more than 100 million people each week. The PBS operating revenue has grown from US$262 million in 1998 to over US$320 million in 2003. Out of this, only US$62 million came from CPB and US Federal Government funds, while US$46 million came from educational product sales and another US$56 million from royalties, license fees and investment income.

Many of PBS's educational and cultural programmes have superseded those proffered by other networks in the past. Yet in an increasingly competitive television environment, it is unlikely that PBS can retain that comparative advantage. If demand for educational programming is high enough, commercial networks will begin to carry those programmes, as demonstrated by the growth and success of the Discovery Channel and The Learning Channel. Even in an environment in which unfaltering public support is behind attempts to improve educational materials, PBS is not likely to succeed solely on the merits of its programming. In a multi-channel environment, opposition to increased public funding for PBS may be realistic, as the public need for educational programming will be filled by commercial providers. PBS will be able to procure limited funding for a few types of programming that commercial organizations will not provide, but if the production and distribution of these programmes are retained as

PBS's main focus, the future for public broadcasting looks dim, especially if the current Congressional mood is taken into account (Stevens, 1995).

In 2004, with the US government looking to trim its budget, the PBS system faced its most complex battle to keep its share of government funding. With a market share of about three per cent of the television audience, PBS will be hard-pressed to defend its funding sources.

Thus, priorities for stations include the following:

- Defending the appropriations process that secures federal funding two years in advance.
- Preserving Commerce Department funding for digital conversion.
- Securing new funds from Education and Agriculture Departments for distance learning and rural digital conversion.
- Influencing possible legislation reauthorizing the Corporation for Public Broadcasting.

The re-authorization fight likely will include an examination of perceived commercialization of public broadcasting brought on by non-commercial stations' fundraising demands.

The Canadian experience—A different North American model[5]

Under the Canadian constitution, broadcasting is a matter of federal jurisdiction given its transcendent national significance. The broadcast regulatory regime was placed in proper context by the Federal Court of Appeal when it stated that, "the importance of broadcasting to the life of the country" is reflected in Section 3(b) of the Broadcasting Act, which [provides] that "the Canadian broadcasting system should be effectively owned and controlled by Canadians so as to safeguard, enrich and strengthen the cultural, political, social and economic fibre of Canada".

The cornerstone of the regulatory regime is the 1991 Broadcasting Act (BA) which defines the basic mandate and philosophy for broadcasting in Canada, and creates an independent administrative agency, the Canadian Radio-Television and Telecommunications Commission (CRTC) to implement and administer the nation's broadcasting policy. The BA also established the Canadian Broadcasting Corporation (CBC) as Canada's public service broadcasting organization.

In short the Canadian system consists of the CBC as public service

---

[5] Mendel, 2000, Article 19.

broadcasting organization, the CRTC as broadcast regulator and Parliament as the ultimate arbiter of broadcast policy and practice.

The Canadian Broadcasting Corporation (CBC) was first created by Parliament in 1936 to provide a national radio service, to some extent in response to fears of emergent American broadcasting growing to dominate the Canadian airwaves. The CBC is a crown corporation, wholly owned by the Canadian government, and by consequence the Canadian people. This means that the federal government controls the terms and conditions of the CBC's existence and operation through its legislative authority. Since it is a creature of statute, the CBC does not have a share structure, and its governance is based not on general companies' legislation, but rather on the specific terms of the BA which delineate its structures of corporate governance.

The CBC presently operates two main television networks, CBC Television in English, and *La Télévision de Radio-Canada* in French, which offer general and special interest programmes, two financially self-sustaining cable news and information television networks, CBC Newsworld in English, and RDI (*Le Réseau de l'information*) in French. In radio, the CBC operates four national network services: French and English AM networks offering information and general interest programmes, as well French and English FM systems, which specialize in classical music and cultural programmes.

The public service mandate of the CBC is set out at Section 3(1) (l) and (m) of the BA. The national public service broadcasting organization is established to, "provide radio and television services incorporating a wide range of programming that informs, enlightens and entertains". More specifically, "the programming provided by the Corporation should be predominantly and distinctly Canadian, reflect Canada and its regions to national and regional audiences, and reflect the multicultural and multi-racial nature of Canada".

In furtherance of its mandate to inform Canadians on matters of public importance, the CBC has formulated a Journalistic Policy Handbook which governs its news and current affairs programming, and is intended to guarantee that the corporation lives up to its "duty to provide consistent, high-quality information upon which all Canadians may rely".

The BA also explicitly provides for the CBC's freedom of expression, making the values of creative and journalistic independence paramount to political or financial interests. This affords the CBC a measure of protection from influence by its "owners" external interests, which private broadcasters, governed by traditional corporate law principles, do not enjoy.

Despite the extensive powers which the BA grants the government over the CBC, to say nothing of the broadcaster's substantial financial dependence on the public purse, the CBC is firmly independent, and operates what many argue is Canada's finest broadcast news service. CBC journalists pay considerable attention to domestic politics and are often at the forefront of critical investigations into the conduct of government. This independence is not merely a product of fortunate happenstance, but is clearly established in the BA. Most importantly, Section 46(5) states that, "The Corporation shall, in the pursuit of its objects and in the exercise of its powers, enjoy freedom of expression and journalistic, creative and programming independence".

As a matter of company policy, the CBC retains an internal Ombudsman, fully independent of the Corporation's management, to review serious unresolved public complaints related to the discharge of its mandate. Although the Ombudsman reports directly to the President, he or she does not possess any statutory or otherwise binding authority.

PSB in Asia

The situation with PSBs in Asia is as diverse as the linguistic and cultural spectrum of the continent. In the last decade with the rapid liberalization of broadcast regulations and enactment of new regulations, the broadcasting industry in most Asian countries have been rapidly privatized with many PSBs losing its monopolistic position in the market. Some have even been privatized themselves or have been put on a commercial footing.

At the first conference of Ministers of Information and Broadcasting in Asia-Pacific, held at Bangkok in May 2003, the declaration on public broadcasting called upon governments to encourage public service broadcasters to "create programmes that promote cultural diversity and bring positive effects of globalization to all communities". They are also urged to create rich and quality content for all, and in particular by and for women, youth and children that "counters the influence of violence, communal hatred and carry such content on prime time. The call includes public debate to counter negative effects of violence in media as well".

The host nation Thailand's predicament reflects the dilemma faced by many Asian countries on how to respond to the people's clamour for more independent non-commercial broadcasting services, which are accessible to them.

Permanent Secretary of the Office of the Prime Minister Yongyuth Sarasombath told the conference that public service broadcasting was one of the major concerns in Thailand, particularly since the promulgation of the

CHANNEL 11 SHOULD BE MADE THAILAND INDEPENDENT PUBLIC BROADCASTER
BY KAMOL SUKI

State-owned Channel 11 should be transformed into an independent public television station to break up media monopolies and better serve the public, a recent study on media reforms recommended.

Dr Somkiat Tangkitwanich of the Thailand Development Research Institute (TDRI) said the public station could rely on state and public subsidies instead of advertising revenue, similar to the BBC in Britain.

He said the station would broadcast only "quality" programmes that benefit society, unlike current offerings on commercial TV.

"An alternative is needed urgently," he said yesterday at the unveiling of his research study, funded by the Thailand Research Fund (TRF).

"There are two choices, Channel 11 or a new station," he said. "The first choice is better because less investment would be required and the equipment and network is readily available. Channel 11's initial aim was to be a public channel, before it was used as a government mouthpiece".

Somkiat's research also found that more public radio stations were needed. He said alternative use could be made of some of the 147 stations under the Department of Public Relations (DPR).

"Public broadcasting media would provide viewers with different types of programmes, more diverse content, neutral presentation and access to those individuals who are currently ignored by mainstream commercial media," he said.

"It would also help develop democracy and encourage a climate where more attention is paid to programme quality rather than audience numbers," he said.

A committee such as the National Broadcasting Commission could be established to oversee the administration of the new stations and ensure transparency, assessments and regulations.

He suggested that the budget to run the stations could be allocated from a special fund for the development of national telecommunications and broadcasting for public benefit. "That fund would generate income from the current concession revenue," he said, which would later be collected in the form of an approval fee after the reform.

Somkiat's research is the first of its kind on Thai media and possible reforms.

Somkiat expressed surprise that his suggestions were welcomed by media owners. "They seemed to be of the opinion that allowing Channel 11 to become a public channel was better than letting it fall into the hands of a competitive business group," he said.

– Nation, 30 January 2004 –

new constitution in 1997. Section 40 of the Constitution clearly states that all frequencies used for broadcasting and telecommunications are national communication resources for the public interest. "This section leads the country to work on a new concept for its communication and broadcast laws to ensure that the utmost public benefit in education, culture, state security, and other public interests, including fair and free competition, will be regarded", Sarasombath said.

Thailand's Deputy Prime Minister Wissanu Krea-ngam added that "Thailand has been working on a re-allocation of frequencies used for telecommunication and broadcasting to ensure that the use of such frequencies will best serve the interest of the public.

PSB in Japan[6]

Japan perhaps provides the best example of a PSB system in Asia. Japan's public service broadcasting organization, the Nippon Hoso Kyokai, (NHK), traces its roots to 1926, when it was created out of three city-based radio broadcasters. Since then it has grown into possibly the world's best-funded public service broadcasting organization, with a total expenditure in 1999 exceeding 625 billion yen (nearly US$6 billion). NHK currently operates as a classical public service broadcasting organization, as established pursuant to the Broadcast Law of 1950, as amended.

NHK operates five national television and three national radio services. It also provides a worldwide service, consisting of NHK World TV, NHK World Premium and NHK World Radio Japan. NHK operates two terrestrial television services: General TV and Educational TV. The former, the heart of NHK's television service, presents a balance of news, education, culture and entertainment programming. In 1997, the breakdown was approximately 41 per cent news, 19 per cent education, 29 per cent culture and 11 per cent entertainment. The other terrestrial channel, Educational TV, provides mainly educational (77 per cent) and cultural (20 per cent) programming. The three other television services are subscription satellite services, which, between them have attracted over nine million viewers. DBS-1 focuses on news, documentaries and sports, while DBS-2 is more oriented towards entertainment, the arts and culture.

Radio 1 is a channel of news, current affairs and practical information. Radio 2 is oriented towards educational programming, as well as broadcasting in foreign languages. FM Radio is NHK's music channel, focusing on classical music, as well as regional programming.

---

[6] Mendel 2000, Article 19.

NHK is subject to a number of obligations binding on all broadcasters in Japan, as well as specific public service broadcasting obligations. The general purposes of NHK, set out at Article 7 of the Broadcast Law, are to provide abundant, high-quality domestic programming for the public welfare, which can be received all over Japan, as well as to conduct international broadcasting. Article 44 elaborates the additional public service obligations of NHK, to supplement those binding on all broadcasters, set out at Article 3-2. These additional obligations include satisfying the wishes of the people, enhancing the level of civilization, providing local, as well as national, programmes and striving towards popularising modern civilization, as well as preserving excellent features from the past. The international service shall promote international friendship and economic interchange by promoting an understanding of Japan and Japanese culture, and provide entertainment to Japanese nationals abroad.

PSB in India[7]

India has had a public service broadcasting system for more than half a century. Radio broadcasting began in India in 1927, with two privately-owned transmitters at Mumbai and Calcutta. These were nationalized in 1930, and operated under the name Indian Broadcasting Service until 1936 when it was renamed to All India Radio (AIR). Although officially renamed again to Akashwani in 1957, it is still popularly known as "All India Radio".

Television came to India only in the 1970s and until the arrival of the satellite television revolution in the 1990s, Doordarshan—India's government funded national television broadcaster—had a monopoly in the market. With a network of over 600 transmitters across the sub-continent, Doordarshan is today the world's second biggest television network, but its audience share has shrunk tremendously due to the satellite television onslaught. With government funding dwindling, Doordarshan has gone on the commercial path to increase its audiences and raise funding, even to the extent of selling its airtime to foreign television companies.

Prasar Bharati (Broadcasting Corporation of India) was established on 23 November 1997 following a demand that the electronic media in India should be made free from government control and given autonomy in their functioning. The Parliament of India passed an Act to give autonomy to the media in 1990 but the said Act was brought into force as late as 15 September 1997. Thus, both Doordarshan and All India Radio were released from

---

[7] http://rdair.res.in/doc/dth.html

being a government broadcaster to the status of a true PSB. But, it also had its darker side. The two services were no longer fully subsidized and Doordarshan in particular, had to find the extra funding to fend off its private satellite competitors, especially ZEE-TV.

The Prasar Bharati Act gives a mandate to both All India Radio and Doordarshan Television to give adequate coverage to the diverse cultures and languages of the various regions of the country by broadcasting appropriate programmes. It also mandates them to provide appropriate programmes for children, youth, weaker and rural sections of society, people residing in remote and backward areas, and for minority communities and tribal communities.

Prasar Bharati Corporation (PB) has the largest radio and television network in the world. It has 213 radio stations and 50 television stations with 340 radio and 1358 television transmitters in every nook and corner of the sub-continent. Figures show that on an average, PB's daily audience is over 400 million.

There are two ways to influence a nation's broadcasting. The first is direct regulation; such as, for example, the intent of our proposed Broadcasting Bill. This would prevent broadcasters from offering programmes that (for example) offend certain sections of the community; or, require broadcasters to air certain number of news and education programmes. However, it has been the worldwide experience that such regulations, even if legally permissible, are not good enough to meet the public service objectives. Such regulations are primarily negative in nature and can, at best, prevent the undesirable, but cannot ensure the desirable.

The second, and perhaps the only meaningful manner in correcting the market deficiencies, is through the strong and dominant presence of a Public Broadcaster. Such a broadcaster would set programming norms and standards; and, provide leadership in this area. Experience shows that commercial broadcasting services follow the lead of such a broadcaster in order to compete for the viewership of such programmes.

Such an approach brings a clear concept of what constitutes public service broadcasting. It is a broadcasting service, which does not depend solely on market forces, but must take into account audience needs and requirements. Indeed, a public service broadcaster should primarily focus on influencing the programme quality and content of all broadcasting, including those by the private sector.

However, the broadcaster cannot take the audience for granted. If such programmes lack appeal, they will not have an audience. The challenge is to provide programmes that are meaningful and need-oriented, and yet achieve a reasonably high audience share.

– From the Report on the Review Committee on the Working of Pasar Bharati –

The committee set up by the Minister of Information and Broadcasting to report on the workings of Pasar Bharati noted, that in India, the process of large-scale commercialization of broadcasting began in the 1980s. Even though Doordarshan and All India Radio enjoyed a monopoly, a reduction in the proportion of budgetary support, combined with pressures to raise more revenues to fund rapid expansion, had forced the pace of commercialization.

"As Doordarshan sells airtime on the basis of the size of its viewership, it began to look for ways and means of increasing its share as the media market became increasingly more competitive. This resulted in a reduction in emphasis on public service programmes, as the prime time was reserved for commercial programming which earned the most revenue. Radio underwent a similar process, though to a lesser extent," observed the committee.

In its report, the committee warned that a problem has arisen because both services, particularly, Doordarshan, auctioned airtime slots, either by programmes and, more recently, in half-hour segments during the evenings, to private Producers in order to maximize revenue. Which has led to a quixotic situation that, increasingly, Doordarshan, a public service broadcaster, owns neither the programme content nor the marketing rights to the programme being shown on its channel.

The committee was strongly of the view that a need for a truly public service broadcaster was greater today than before. "The proliferation of channels has fuelled many wants and fulfilled some needs, but, has left gaps," argued the committee's report to the minister. "These should be filled by a public service broadcaster. This is because commercial television broadcasting conducted by privately owned satellite channels must target the relatively affluent urban market as they can only air their programme through a cable operator. Similarly, the private FM radio stations would target the up market, more urban radio listener. The private channel must primarily deliver an audience; rather than being a vehicle for delivering new ideas, information and education to its viewers and listeners".

The report went on to argue that a public service broadcaster must be concerned about a broader set of clientele and has a much larger mandate. "It has to meet the complete media needs of all, including those of a villager who has very few media options. Such a person is either watching television or listening to radio, on a community set, in an isolated part of the country. The public service broadcaster also needs to take into account the media needs of the minority audience, whether they be ethnic, religious or linguistic. Such a broadcaster needs to concern itself with developing taste,

---

MARKETING PSB IN ASIA
BY AFSAN CHOWDHURY (WORKSHOP FACILITATOR)

PSB is need based. Nature of broadcasting has changed. Radio has always been marketing products.

It sold colonialism during the British rule and the idea of the Nation State after they left. The dominant products in the market are consumables but it does know very well how to sell them. It has to tackle soaps and washing machines as well as PSB.

PSB marketing has to change too. Use contemporary marketing tools. Research audience analysis to package it. Radio is more PSB friendly because of the cost factor. There is higher mobility in production and cost optimization can be achieved more easily.

Basic message is identify your needs. Produce it in a way that people will listen. Whatever be the message, you have to tailor it to the audience. Otherwise, you will fall through the cracks of indifference.

If the package is good, they will buy it. The packaging has to change to meet but the process is general in all professional productions.

– Report on the workshop on Public Service Broadcasting, Patan, Nepal, May 2000 –

---

promoting understanding, spreading literacy and development, creating informed debate and empowering the disadvantaged—major issues that a commercial broadcaster rarely addresses. This, then, is the real *raison d'être* of a public service broadcaster," noted the report.

In 2005, Doordharshan is due to introduce India's first DTH (Direct To Home) satellite television service offering 29 television channels and 10 radio channels. In television 17 of the channels will be Doordarshan's own, while the others are mainly private Indian TV channels plus the BBC World. All the radio channels are AIR's and include seven regional language channels.

Doordarshan's "DD Direct+", as the service is named, is the first of its kind in the world meant for mass consumption mainly aimed as universal service which is free at delivery to the viewers with a minimal one-time investment, unlike other DTH services which collect a monthly subscription besides huge initial cost to the viewer. Doordarshan's DTH service will cost the viewer, besides his TV receiver, a one-time cost of about Rs.3000. There is an estimated 40 million households, which receive only one Doordarshan channel and are not hooked onto cable television because of the inability to pay monthly subscriptions. This segment may opt for Doordarshan's free DTH service since they could receive about 30 channels free of cost instead of just one channel with a one-time investment of Rs.3000.

The Australian model[8]

Australia has two separate public service broadcasting organizations, the Australian Broadcasting Corporation (ABC) and the Special Broadcasting Service Corporation (SBS). The ABC provides information and entertainment services of general interest on both radio and television, while the much smaller SBS provides specialized services focused on fulfilling the media needs of Australia's culturally diverse population. Both broadcasters are public corporations operating under Charters enacted by Australia's federal Parliament. While ultimately accountable to the government for the way in which they spend public funds, both the ABC and the SBS are independent of governmental control and enjoy substantial creative and editorial freedom.

Australian Broadcasting Corporation

The ABC provides a national television network (ABC-TV), available on terrestrial reception throughout the nation. The system has production facilities and transmission centres in all state capitals, as well as the national capital, Canberra, and the City of Darwin, and reception is available to virtually all Australians. ABC-Radio also operates six distinct audio-broadcast services. Metropolitan Radio, a network of nine stations, one in each state capital, as well as one in each of Darwin, Canberra and Newcastle, provides a core service of news, current affairs, talk, information, sport and entertainment programmes. Regional Radio, a national network of around 70 AM and 180 FM stations, as well as state and national satellite services, provides a mix of local, regional, state and national programming for audiences outside the capital cities. The ABC also operates four specialty radio networks. The Radio National network features programmes on the arts, religion, politics, the law, news and current affairs, science and technology, history, health, adult education and social change, economics and international affairs. Classic FM is, as the name suggests, dedicated to classical music. Triple J is a youth network featuring predominantly popular music, but also carrying news and current affairs, comedy and special features. Finally, ABC runs News Radio, a continuous news and current affairs service, with live broadcasts of both Houses of Parliament when they are sitting.

The Charter of the ABC, set out in Section 6 of the 1983 Australian Broadcasting Corporation Act (ABC Act), (30) establishes the functions of the Corporation, which are "to provide within Australia innovative and

---

[8] Mendel, 2000, Article 19.

comprehensive broadcasting and television services of a high standard as part of the Australian broadcasting and television system consisting of national, commercial and public sectors". More specifically, the Charter calls upon the ABC to provide broadcasting programmes that "contribute to a sense of national identity and inform and entertain, and reflect the cultural diversity of the Australian community", in part by promoting music, drama, and other performing arts in Australia. It also requires the ABC to provide educational broadcasts as a substantial component of its programming.

More specifically, several requirements in relation to programming are imposed on the ABC. Its enabling statute requires the ABC to develop and maintain an independent service for the broadcasting of news and information, and the ABC is required to broadcast daily, from all national radio and television stations, regular sessions of news and information relating to current events within and outside Australia. Section 4 of the Parliament Proceedings Broadcasting Act (1946), (33) requires the ABC to broadcast the proceedings of the Senate, the House of Representatives or a joint sitting of both Houses of the Commonwealth Parliament on such days and during such periods as the Joint Committee on the Broadcasting of Parliamentary Proceedings determines. The proceedings are to be broadcast from medium wave radio stations in each state capital city and Newcastle, and from such other radio stations as may be prescribed.

The federal government of Australia has jurisdiction over broadcasting, and therefore ultimate legislative control over the ABC. However, the terms of the ABC's Charter, mandating it to provide comprehensive and independent news and information broadcasting for all Australians, combined with the terms under which Directors of the corporation are

> The monopoly I have in mind when considering the ABC is its dominant position in what I reluctantly call "quality broadcasting". I realize this term is unsatisfactory, not least because the ABC does a number of quite different things for quite different audiences. However, for the purpose of this speech, I'm concerned with the Corporation's dominance of broadcasting to the better-educated, higher income Australians who live mainly in our capital cities. Such people comprise a majority of the Corporation's 15 per cent of the broadcasting audience. They like the ABC for its television news and current affairs, children's, cooking, gardening and British drama programmes, and for its genteel chat shows on the radio. What I'm describing, in other words, is broadcasting for the cultured upper-middle classes.
>
> – Michael Duffy, former Communication Minister of Australia (2001) –

appointed, ensure the ABC a large measure of editorial independence from the government.

Special Broadcasting Service

SBS is Australia's unique multicultural and multilingual public service broadcasting organization, founded in 1975 to serve Australians of diverse ethnic backgrounds and to promote cultural awareness. The Special Broadcasting Service Act (SBS Act) (44) establishes SBS as a corporation with a Charter, at Section 6, setting out what the Australian people through the Parliament require as a national specialty broadcaster. The SBS's Charter specifies that its principal function is to "provide multilingual and multicultural radio and television services that inform, educate and entertain all Australians, and, in so doing so, reflect Australia's multicultural society".

The SBS operates a television channel, SBS TV, which broadcasts a combination of purchased and specially produced programming. Half of the SBS's scheduled programming is in languages other than English, and its weekly viewership extends to some 4.6 million Australians. The SBS also operates five radio channels, which broadcasts programmes in over 50 different languages. All programmes start with news and contain a mixture of current affairs, talks, views, sports, community information and music.

The SBS's Charter states that its principal function is to provide multilingual and multicultural radio and television services that inform, educate, and entertain all Australians and, in doing so, reflect Australia's multicultural society. The Charter clearly specifies SBS's public service obligations in the performance of its functions. According to the Charter, the SBS must "contribute to meeting the communications needs of Australia's multicultural society, including ethnic, Aboriginal and Torres Straight Islander communities; and increase awareness of the contribution of a diversity of cultures to the continuing development of Australian society; and promote understanding and acceptance of the cultural, linguistic and ethnic diversity of the Australian people; and contribute to the retention and continuing development of language and other cultural skills; and as far as practicable, inform, educate and entertain Australians in their preferred languages; and make use of Australia's diverse creative resources; and contribute to the overall diversity of Australian television and radio services, particularly taking into account the contribution of the ABC and the public broadcasting sector; and contribute to extending the range of Australian television and radio services, and reflect the changing nature of Australian society, by presenting many points of view and using innovative forms of expression".

Evolving post-apartheid public broadcasting system in South Africa[9]

Like many public institutions in South Africa, the South African Broadcasting Corporation (SABC) has undergone a number of changes in recent years to bring it into line with the new democratic dispensation and to ensure that it serves the needs of all the citizens of South Africa. A completely new broadcasting act, the key legislation governing the SABC, was adopted in 1999 (the 1999 Act), replacing the former 1976 Act, and the changes introduced by the new law have yet to be fully implemented. Formally, under the 1999 Act, the SABC has been transformed into a limited liability company with a share capital and subject to the Companies Act, although Section 7 recognizes that the normal rules for companies will need to be modified to take into account the special nature of the SABC as a corporation. In particular, to begin with at least, the state will own 100 per cent of the shares of the SABC, a deviation explicitly authorized by Section 19(1) of the Act from the normal rule requiring at least seven shareholders. Section 9 provides for the effective division of the SABC into public service and commercial operations, to be separately administered under a single corporate structure. The latter is to be treated like any other commercial broadcasting operation while the former is subject to special statutory obligations.

The Independent Broadcasting Authority (IBA), established by a law passed in 1993 (the IBA Act). The IBA has broad regulatory powers over broadcasters, particularly in relation to licensing, and the 1993 law completely restructured the regulation of private broadcasting. The IBA also has some powers in relation to the SABC. As a result of these significant changes, the SABC is very much in a state of transition. The full effect of many of the changes remains to be seen. At the same time, financial pressures have meant that the SABC receives most of its funding from advertising, rather than the public purse. The longer-term goal is to divide the service into public and commercial operations, with the latter subsidizing the former. Whether this will be a success, and to what extent, remains to be seen.

South African Broadcasting Corporation

As noted above, the 1999 Act provides for the effective division of the SABC into commercial and public service operations. Indeed, Section 1 of the

---

[9] Mendel, 2000, Article 19.

1999 Act contributes to this confusion, defining "public service broadcasting" as any service, including a commercial service, operated by the SABC, while Section 9(1) provides for a distinction between the "public service" and "commercial service" operated by the SABC. In terms of licensing, the IBA is required to distinguish between "public", "commercial" and "community" broadcasting services.

The SABC currently offers three televisions channels, SABC 1, SABC 2 and SABC 3, providing over 80 per cent geographical coverage of South Africa, although a far smaller proportion of the population actually have access to television, due to low rates of television set ownership and lack of electrification in some rural areas. In 1998, the total daily SABC television audience was estimated at approximately 14 million viewers, out of a total population of over 40 million.

SABC also provides 19 radio stations through its national network. These include 11 stations—one in each of the 11 official languages—an international service, a couple of regional stations and a number of English language stations broadcasting primarily music. Together, the SABC radio stations attract about 14 million listeners daily, the bulk of which tune in to the nine African language stations.

Section 8 of the 1999 Act sets out the objectives of the SABC as a whole, which by-and-large govern both its public service and its commercial operations. Sections 10 and 11 set out more detailed obligations relating, respectively, to the public service and commercial operations. Pursuant to Section 8, and in line with obligations on many public service broadcasting organizations, the SABC is required to make its services available throughout the territory of South Africa, on a free-to-air reception basis, and to provide programming that informs, educates and entertains. Pursuant to Article 8, the SABC is also obliged to maintain libraries and archives of materials relevant to its objectives, to collect news and information, to establish and subscribe to news agencies, to carry out research on new technologies, and to nurture South African talent and train people in production skills.

Pursuant to Section 10, the public service must make services available in all official languages, reflect both the unity and cultural and multilingual diversity of South Africa, and enrich the country's cultural heritage, both traditional and contemporary. The public service must strive to be of high quality in all languages, providing significant amounts of news and public affairs programming that meets the highest standards of journalism, and is fair, impartial, balanced and independent from government, commercial and other interests. In addition, the public service must provide significant amounts of educational programming, national and minority sports programming, as well as services targeting children, women, the youth and the disabled. Finally, the public service must broadcast both its own programmes as well as those commissioned from the independent sector.

Call to action—PSB declarations

In recent years, there have been a number of conferences, workshops and seminars organized by UNESCO in particular, and many international media organizations and political bodies to address the question of public service broadcasting or more so, the declining standards of educational and information-oriented broadcasting due to the proliferation of commercial broadcasting around the world.

In this section we will examine some of the declarations and recommendation made by these gatherings to improve the quality of PSB and encourage its development in countries which are transforming its broadcasting systems away from state control.

Public broadcasting for all campaign[10]
The International Federation of Journalists (IFJ) launched a worldwide campaign in 2001 to defend public service broadcasting. The campaign aims to promote public service values, editorial independence, quality programmes and democratic and accountable systems of administration. The IFJ campaign builds union solidarity. It coordinates discussions with international organizations and other global groups dealing with media. This worldwide action programme is geared towards lobbying developing countries against accepting policies of international financial institutions—or their own governments—to privatize former state broadcasters. The IFJ Campaign supports journalists organizations and civil society in the transformation of state broadcasters in regions such as central Europe, West Africa or South Asia into genuinely public service institutions, that serves the public, not private, interest.

As part of this campaign, the IFJ has held a number of conferences around the world, such as "The Challenge of Public Broadcasting in Asia" conference held in Colombo in December 2003. Journalists' unions and associations from 13 Asian countries attended this conference at the end of which they issued a "Colombo Declaration" which recognized the need for strong, independent unions of journalists and media workers to play a vital role in the development of an independent public service media.

---

[10] www.save-public-broadcasting.org

The conference agreed on the following actions to implement a regional campaign to promote public service broadcasting:

- Each journalists organization in the region affiliated with the IFJ will work with the IFJ Asia office under the auspices of the IFJ's "Public Broadcasting for All" campaign to develop national action plans to promote public service broadcasting in that country.
- As part of this action plan, IFJ affiliates will work with civil society, political forces and other interested groups to promote public support for the structures and values of PSB.
- These action plans will examine ways of building and strengthening independent trade unions in public service media including trade union training, administrative skills support and organising around professional issues affecting PSB including editorial independence and other public service values.
- These action plans will also examine ways of assisting journalists and other programme makers in taking initiatives to establish editorial statutes and to draft their own ethical guidelines with proposals for self-regulation in both public and private media that reflect common values in order to ensure editorial independence.
- The IFJ will work with affiliates to eliminate all forms of corruption in the media such as bribes, gifts and "envelopes" which undermine the integrity and independence of journalism.

IFJ affiliate, the European Federation of Journalists (EFJ) at the end of their annual meeting in Prague in May 2003 issued a statement calling upon the drafters of the European Union constitution to include a strong legal framework "to control the threat of excessive concentration of (private) ownership in the media sector".

The EFJ noted its support for the Clement report in France, which outlines the need to include the principle of the coexistence of public television services alongside commercial channels in the European Constitution. They pointed out that this initiative gives the hope that there is scope for the establishment of a credible and effective Charter of Independence for public broadcasting in Europe.

The EFJ said that it "requests urgently that the ETUC (European Trade Union Congress), in defence of media pluralism and democracy, supports the introduction of standards to protect independence by appropriate rules to prevent political figures who are candidates for political office in government from holding substantial shares in the media, information and communication sector. Such conflicts of interests, especially in the media

and information area, compromise the balanced and professional development of media in democratic society".

European Commission Declaration on state aid

On 17 October 2001, the European Commission clarified its stand on state
aid to PSBs. It said that member states are in principle "free to define
the extent of the public service and the way it is financed and organized,
according to their preferences, history and needs". The Commission
however called for transparency "in order to assess the proportionality
of state funding and to control possible abusive practices". The Commission however reserved its right to intervene "in cases where a distortion
of competition arising from the aid cannot be justified with the need to
perform the public service as defined by the Member State". This statement was made in response to concerns on PSB funding, which has been
the subject of complaints to the Commission by private media operators
who see state funding of PSBs as anti-competition.

The Commission recognized the particular role of PSB as acknowledged
by the Protocol to the Amsterdam Treaty in the promotion of democratic,
social and cultural needs of each society. Yet, it said that public broadcasting can be defined as a service of general interest, but when funded by state
resources it amounts to state aid, which the Commission is empowered to
check for "abusive practices and absence of overcompensation".

African Charter on Broadcasting

On the occasion of the tenth anniversary of the *Windhoek Declaration on
the Development of an Independent and Pluralistic African Press*, UNESCO
organized another Windhoek Conference[11] *"Ten Years On: Assessment,
Challenges and Prospects"* from 3–5 May 2001, which declared that the
legal framework for broadcasting should include a clear statement of the
principles underpinning broadcast regulation, including promoting respect
for freedom of expression, diversity, the free flow of information and ideas,
as well as a three-tier system for broadcasting—public service, commercial
and community.

They reiterated the following principles in regards to PSB:

1. All state and government-controlled broadcasters should be transformed into public service broadcasters, that are accountable to all
   strata of the people as represented by an independent board, and that

---

[11] www.article19.org/docimages/1019.htm

serve the overall public interest, avoiding one-sided reporting and programming in regard to religion, political belief, culture, race and gender.

2. Public service broadcasters, like broadcasting and telecommunications regulators, should be governed by bodies that are protected against interference.

3. The public service mandate of public service broadcasters should clearly defined.

4. The editorial independence of public service broadcasters should be guaranteed.

5. Public service broadcasters should be adequately funded in a manner that protects them from arbitrary interference with their budgets.

6. Without detracting from editorial control over news and current affairs content and in order to promote the development of independent productions whilst enhancing diversity of programming, the public service broadcasters should be required to broadcast minimum quotas of productions by independent producers.

7. The transmission infrastructure used by public service broadcasters should be made accessible to all broadcasters under reasonable and non-discriminatory terms.

The Accra Declaration

From the 16 to 18 September 2002, a conference on Public Service Broadcasting in West Africa was held under the auspices of the Article 19 and the Media Foundation for West Africa (MFWA) in Accra, Ghana. Participants included Heads of PSB Organizations, Heads of Regulatory Bodies, regional media organizations, media specialists and other regional stakeholders. The meeting deliberated on the need for reform of public service broadcasting in the West Africa sub region to reflect and sustain the new democratic dispensation and to allow popular participation in public affairs.

The conference declaration included the following:

1. The status and mandate of Public Service Broadcasting Organizations should be provided by a legislation, which states and defines the mandate, powers, responsibilities, modalities of appointments, funding sources and accountability mechanisms. Public broadcasters should provide balanced, accurate and relevant information and programmes to the public and should strive to reflect the people's voice.

2. The independence of regulatory bodies should be guaranteed by law and respected in practice. Appointment of Members should be made within organizations reflecting a broad spectrum of stakeholders and the process for appointing members should be set out clearly in law.

3. The principle of editorial independence, whereby programming decisions are made by broadcasters on the basis of professional criteria and the public's right to know, should be guaranteed by law and respected in practice.

4. Public Service Broadcasters have an obligation to ensure that the public receives adequate, unbiased information, particularly, during elections.

5. While there is the need for continuous state funding of Public Service Broadcasting, the PSB organizations should explore other sources of funding such as Special Trust Funds and effective collection of licensing fees.

6. Cooperation and co-production of broadcast material should be encouraged among Public Service Broadcasting organizations in the sub-region under mutually beneficial and proper contractual framework.

Almaty Recommendations

Asian Institute for Broadcast Development (AIBD) and FES organized a seminar on public service broadcasting in the Central Asian republics in February 2003 in Almaty, Kazakhstan. The seminar was held under framework of PSB providing an important contribution to the development of democracy in Central Asia, with a means to building an informal civil society, which recognize pluralism and the importance of national identity and culture.

The seminar participants considered PSB as a necessary, powerful and effective means to support the educational and cultural potential of the people, as well as providing them with objective and reliable information. In this context some of the recommendations the participants came up with are as follows:

1. The idea of public service broadcasting should be encouraged, publicized and popularized among the people and the authorities.

2. Public broadcasters should be encouraged to provide a forum for public dialogue, knowledge sharing and deeper understanding.

3. Public broadcasters should develop pluralistic programme structure of interest to all groups of society, reflecting different cultures, tradi-

tional customs and religions to promote understanding, tolerance and peace.

4. The authorities may be requested to create a favourable legal, economic, administrative and financial climate for different systems of broadcasting.

5. A broadcasting council should be established with legal guarantees against government interference, and with minority government representation in the council.

6. An independent organ should be established to address complaints against broadcast standards and contents.

Bangkok Declaration[12]

The 1st Conference of the Ministers on Information and Broadcasting in Asia and the Pacific region was held in Bangkok from 27–28 May 2003. This was in the form of a Thematic Debate and a regional preparatory meeting for the World Summit on Information Society to be held in Geneva in 2003.

The conference adopted the following recommendations on public service broadcasting.

Public Service Broadcasters are encouraged to:

1. Promote and develop education—including community education, spread of information, empowerment and people's participation in society and development addressing all groups of society.

2. Create programmes which carry credibility with pluralistic groups and which promote cultural diversity and bring positive effects of globalization to all communities.

3. Create rich and quality content for all, and in particular by and for women, youth and children that counters the influence of violence, communal hatred and carry such content on prime time.

4. Initiate public debate and common ground talks between policymakers, academics and media professionals to counter negative effects of violence in media. Broadcasters can promote the culture of dialogue among civilizations with the view to promote understanding and peace.

5. Exploit new technologies to expand coverage and accessibility to information and healthy entertainment.

---

[12] www.mcot.org/specialevent/index2.html

6. Promote protection of copyrights of content by coming out strongly against piracy and unauthorized use of content.

   Authorities are encouraged to do the following:

1. Allow autonomy in content creation, management, finance and administration of Public Service Broadcasters.
2. Study and consider the following funding mechanism for public service broadcasting:
   a. One-time fee while buying a radio, television, electronic appliance or mobile phone
   b. Introducing a license fee: either as a stand alone or as an addition to the electricity bill
   c. Government grants for infrastructure
   d. Advertisement/commercial revenue. But it should not undermine the mandate of public service broadcasting
   e. Sponsorship
3. Contribute to production of programmes for clearly defined developmental needs.
4. Regularly review the mandate of Public Service Broadcasting in view of national, regional and global events in order to foster mutual understanding, tolerance and trust.
5. Allocate preferential frequencies to Public Service Broadcasters.
6. Create legal structures to allow independence of decision making to the public broadcasters.
7. Ensure allocation of adequate time by private networks for public service programmes and for pluralistic content for all groups of the society.
8. Ensure complete editorial independence.

Amman Declaration

A Regional Workshop on "Public Service Broadcasting and the Civil Society in the Arab Region", was organized by UNESCO[13] in Amman, Jordan, from 15 to 17 July 2003 with the main objectives of sharing experiences and expertise, to promote the concept of public service broadcasting.

---

[13] UNESCO website.

The workshop adopted the following declarations and recommendations:

1. Public Service Broadcasting (PSB) should be encouraged and further developed in all countries of the region as an important element of society and of citizen participation in the public life and sustainable democratic development.

2. PSB should first and foremost provide a service to the entire population, in particular balanced and impartial information needed for independent and informed decision-making; therefore, its functional autonomy must be guaranteed by law.

3. All countries of the region should further encourage the development of Public Service Broadcasting by providing the necessary legal framework, financial and human resources needed for this purpose.

4. National public broadcasters should develop content specifically addressed to all components of society, in particular children, women and youth, thus fulfilling its educational, cultural and social functions and contributing to further understanding of the needs and aspirations of the entire society.

5. To foster cooperation and partnership in the countries of the region within the civil society with a view of enhancing its relationship to the media, in particular PSB.

6. Follow-up action in the region to involve decision-makers, legislators, the sector and civil society.

Thus, with such clear-cut definitions and principles already in place on the role, function and funding mechanisms for public service broadcasting, the challenge for the international community is to find motivation and encouragement to set up, maintain and develop viable PSBs across the globe. The rest of the chapters in this publication would discuss some "good practices" in PSB which we hope would inspire others who are committed to establishing good public service broadcasting systems unhindered by commercial and government interference.

References

Blumler, J. (1992). Public Service Broadcasting before the commercial deluge. In J. Blumler (Ed.), *Television and the Public Interest* (pp. 7–21). London: Sage.

CMRTV. (2001). *Public Broadcasting: How? Why?* UNESCO, Paris.

Duffy, M. (31 March 2001). Eat your heart out Murdoch or, The ABC of Monopoly and Synergy. Speech to the Institute of Public Affairs ABC Conference held in Sydney.

EU. (17 October 2001). Commission clarifies application of state aid rules to PBS. Brussells, Belgium.

IFJ. (30 April 2004). Journalists in new protest as Berlusconi's grip on Italian media becomes a strangehold. Press release, IFJ.

International Television Commission. (2 May 2001). Television Audience Share Figures. Press Release, London.

Jakubowicz, K. (2004). Idea in our heads: Introduction of PSB as part of media systems change in Central and Eastern Europe. *European Journal of Communication*, 19(1), 53–74.

Holland, P. (2003). Conceptual Glue: Public service broadcasting as practice, system and ideology. Paper presented to MIT3 Television in Transition conference held in MIT, Massachusetts, USA.

Khan, A. W. (11 December 2003). Introductory remarks to the World Electronic Media Forum workshop on PSB held in Geneva.

Lindsey, D. (2004). Media Davids vs Goliath. Deutsche Welle. Retrieved from www.dw-world.de

Malkani, G. (2004). BBC cuts websites after inquiry attacks. *Financial Times*.

Martinson, J. (2004). Pact seek 50 per cent BBC quota. *Guardian*.

McChesney, R. (1997). The Mythology of Commercial Broadcasting and the Contemporary Crisis of Public Broadcasting. University of Wisconsin.

McConnell, B. (24 February 2003). PBS Fights for its Future. *Broadcasting & Cable*, 133(8), 30. USA.

Mc Quail, D. (1994). Western Europe: The mixed model under threat in drowning. J. et al Question the Media.

Mendel, T. (2000). Public Service Broadcasting Organizations, Article 19, London.

Mendel, T. (2000). Public Service Broadcasting, a comparative Legal Survey. AIBD, Kuala Lumpur, Malaysia.

Mooney, P. (2004). Public Service Broadcasting. Report by the Committee on Culture, Science and Education, Parliamentary Assembly of the Council of Europe held in Brussels, Belgium.

Murdoch, R. (April 1998). Speech to European Audio Visual Conference held in Birmingham.

Raboy, M. (1999). The World Situation of Public Service Broadcasting, Public Service Broadcasting in Asia: Surviving in the new information age (Ch 1). Singapore: AMIC.

Raboy, M. (Ed.) (1996). Public Broadcasting for the 21st century. *Academia Monograph* 17. UK: University of Luton Press.

Roddick, A. (2003). Rupert Murdoch vs the BBC. Alternet, Independent media institute, USA.

Stevens, V. (1995). Public Broadcasting Service: rebirth or demise? Retrieved from lucy.media.mit.edu/~vanessa/pbs/pbs.html

Tongue, C. (1996). "The future of public service television in a multi-channel digital age". Report to the Committee on Culture, Youth, Education and the Media of the European Union. Retrieved from www.poptel.org.uk/carole-tongue/pubs/psb_b.html

Tuazon, R. (2002). The Government Media: Rewriting their Image and Role. National Commission for Culture and the Arts, Philippines. Retrieved from www.ncca.gov.ph/culture&arts/cularts/others/communication/communication-government.htm

UNESCO. (1995). Public Service Broadcasting: Cultural and Educational Dimension. Paris, France.

Wells, M. (25 February 2004). 1 bn price tag to ending licence fee. *Guardian.*

Wolfgang, K. (2004). Public broadcasting in Europe, the EU. Amsterdam Protocol of 1997 and the GATS negotiations within the WTO. Retrieved from www.medialaw. ru/indep/en/k3-6.htm.

Yeo, T. (2002). Towards a 21st century model of Public Service Broadcasting. Retrieved from www.tory.org.uk

Websites

Amman Declaration on PSB in the Arab region, July 2003, Jordan (UNESCO website).

Features of Doordarshan's Free-to-air and free-to-view DTH system. Retrieved from rdair.res.in/doc/dth.html

Perspectives on PSB in Europe, Communication Policies project, The European institute for the Media. Retrieved from www.eim.org/ComPol/Projects/print.content. php3?ID=2

Proceedings of the first conference of ministers of Information and Broadcasting in Asia-Pacific, Bangkok. Retrieved from www.mcot.org/specialevent/index2.html in May 2003.

Public Broadcasting for All, International Federation of Journalists. Retrieved from www.save-public-broadcasting.org

Report on the workshop on Public Service Broadcasting, Patan, Nepal. Retrieved from www.panos.org.np/resources/reports/psb.htm in May 2000.

The Report on the Review Committee on the Working of Pasar Bharati. Retrieved from www.scatmag.com/govt%20policies/rcpb1.htm

Government allows crap TV to become public service, Indymedia 3.3.04. Retrieved from www. broadcastnow.co.uk

Gloves off as ITV and BBC slug it out over public service broadcasts. Retrieved from www.freeview-digital-tv.co.uk

Public Service Broadcasting. Retrieved from www.museum.tv/archives/etv/P/htmlP/ publicservicb/ publicserviceb.htm

Public Broadcasting Service of United States,. Retrieved from www.pbs.org

Public Service Broadcasting in Europe. Retrieved from www.mediator.online.bg/eng/ broadc.html

The 1st Conference of the Ministers on Information and Broadcasting in Asia and the Pacific region, 27–28 May 2003, Bangkok. Retrieved from UNESCO website.

Windhoek Charter on Broadcasting in Africa. Retrieved from www.article19.org/ docimages/ 1019.htm

Public Service Broadcasting
Theory and Reality—The Measurement Challenge

Chapter One traced the development of Public Service Broadcasting (PSB), setting out its main features as exemplified by PSB systems and arrangements in countries across all continents. Against that background this second chapter will try to identify the essentials of a framework for benchmarking PSB and evaluating its outcomes, bearing in mind that public service content will change, and be changed by, the multi-platform world. The parameters of PSB will be replaced by those of PSCP—Public Service Content Provision.

Identifying measurement benchmarks will involve some retracing of steps across PSB development. History holds out many pitfalls to the researcher—not least the danger of confusing the face of PSB with its essence or of mistaking linkages for cause and effect. Misidentifications must distort the search for valid benchmarks. PSB does not come about by being promoted as government policy, even of a democratic government. PSB is not signed into life at the stroke of a civil servant's pen, nor is it some sort of potion extracted from a pool of social or cultural wisdom. It cannot be assembled like a piece of carpentry from an instruction sheet or like recipe ingredients from a cookbook.

Two illustrations: A closer focus

A relevant preamble, even pre-condition, for identifying authentic benchmarks may, therefore, be to highlight what PSB is not. Two examples will illustrate this.

First the post-Communist media transition experience in Central and Eastern Europe shows that, although constitutions and texts are necessary, it is delivered content and how people perceive it which defines PSB; society and culture are the soil in which PSB grows, and they need to be fit for the purpose.

The second case study comes from the UK. Its point is that PSB is more than any single PSB player. This is highlighted by the current debate in the UK about the BBC and the evolution of a pluralistic PSB ecology. British society has proved suitable soil for growing PSB. There is, in Gellner's (1983) terminology, the required "congruence of polity with culture". The BBC, cornerstone of PSB in the UK, is one of the world's great cultural institutions. Yet the BBC is not synonymous with PSB in the UK. The future will depend on competitive offerings from varied players—public and commercial, large, small and medium-sized. "If we are to have any hope of conserving a splendid tradition, public policy has to maintain the existence of strong public service broadcasters and to promote effective competition between them" (Birt, 2005).

That "splendid tradition" is marked, as regards content, by two particular characteristics: quality and diversity. Quality, as will be seen later (where research into public attitudes is reviewed) defies simple definition. A number of strands can, though, be identified: integrity and the application of high-level professional skills; creativity and the use of original material: being counted on to cover major events—diaried or not (i.e. national elections, the UN Assembly, famines and floods, wars, terrorist attacks and revolutions, the funeral of a Pope, the winning of the (cricket) Ashes, the Olympic Games and the football World Cup): covering not just events but themes and trends.

As for diversity, it implies a commitment to serve not only majorities but minorities—whether defined by culture, geography, ethnicity, passion or taste. Evaluating the provision of diverse content is not easy (Tambini and Cowling, 2004). Are higher marks to be given for choice between programme types than between programmes of the same or similar type?

The premise has been suggested that competition among media should be used to satisfy the demands of consumers (Low, 2000). But how do consumers sensibly choose? Do they have a frame of reference or experience? Or are they like the cat in the Purina cat food advertisement, seated in front of one thousand licked-clean dishes and saying "Five million cats can't be wrong"?

What is clear from the deregulation experience on three continents in recent years is that pluralism in itself does not produce diversity or improve quality. A clutch of new private sector license-holders may well be motivated by putting on programmes which maximize revenue, steering clear of content which might offend power elites and jeopardize their licenses.

Even in developed democracies content choice—for reasons of both profit and distribution dynamics—often fails to reach the people. "Demassification of the mass media in the form of cable narrowcasting has resulted in a plurality of channels catering to different interests and tastes. However, because of the primacy of commercial interests, plurality of political and social views are not reflected in the diversity of channels" (Tehranian, 2002). "By not having to answer to monster media monopolies, the independent media has a life's work, a political project and a purpose: to let truth be known. This is increasingly important in the globalization process" (Abramian, 2001).

Constitutions and license provisions may be broadcasting's external face but satisfying cultural expectations is the core. John Reith, the BBC's founding Director-General, in his introduction to the BBC first annual handbook—only weeks after the British Broadcasting Company had been restructured to form the Corporation—wrote:

> The constitutional change-over from Company to Corporation status has for the moment drawn some attention to the administrative side, as it is change and not continuity that comes into the limelight. The outlook, though still developing by experience is essentially the same ... In order to avoid misunderstandings, let it be said now that public service ... means primarily a standard and an outlook, and only secondarily a form of administration (1928: 32).

Reith's comments were preceded by these from Lord Clarendon, the Chairman:

> The corporation, although it might be termed a state concern, is not under government control in the ordinary sense of the expression. Our broadcasting system in four years and a half has assimilated the British public service tradition, which it will be our privilege and duty to perpetuate and strengthen. ...that broadcasting in this country has been so comparatively free from errors of judgement ... (is) ... a tribute to the enterprise, vision, discretion and vigilance of those who have developed it, but one that carries with it the implication that the listeners themselves have an increasingly important part to play in future progress (1928: 29–30).

Clarendon's remarks are prophetic of the importance of a sensitively responsive relationship between programme commissioners and audiences, including opportunities for the public to air their views and question broadcasters in feedback programmes. Already in Clarendon's time the public was ready for the arrival of broadcasting. The BBC was established in the wake of a burgeoning of the British press, broadsheet and popular. The 20s witnessed a demand for media fare different and distinct from the fare served up by Lords Northcliffe, Beaverbrook and Rothermere. As press dominance made the BBC's arrival very timely, so the power of today's big media players, like the BBC itself and BSkyB, are increasingly perceived as a reason for shaking up the status quo, for nourishing a variety of players and utilizing new technologies for creating a fit-for-context broadcasting ecology (Hattersley, 2004 and Williams & Allan, 1960).

Reith described the BBC as "the nation talking to itself". Nations and communities differ, so judgements about PSB must, to some extent be relative and PSB institutions not "all of a piece". Conditionality does not mean, however, that no core or common principles exist or that the search for benchmarks is a waste of time; that, in truth, cross-country or trans-cultural comparisons are impossible. Conditionality means that that benchmarking is inevitably complex.

What the broadcaster does, according to Scannell (1997: 93) is to sort out a myriad communications entitlements; he puts these in two categories—opinion entitlements for decision-makers and influencers, and experience entitlements for other programme contributors. The public verdict on the broadcasters will depend on whether they are perceived as allocating entitlements in ways that are fair and sensitive, not patronizing or partial. Another way of looking at it is that of Karl Deutsch who has studied the relationship between communication and choice; he employs the analogy of an angler letting out a fishing line (Hoggart and Morgan, 1982: 100–108). It is a suggestive simile if not a perfect one: Societies and cultures will arrive at different judgements about the amount of line or when the boundary to arrogance or paternalism has been crossed.

Crossing the boundaries—PSB and transnational broadcasting

"The media" is used in different ways. In a value measurement context "the media" (in the sense of institutions driving output in line with organizational remits), should not be confused with the actual broadcast content—or web-based material. It is the content which holds the discourse where, if at all, public service values will be found.

Defining PSB requires a readiness to build into the definitional framework elements of flexibility, conditionality or relativism. Content may, for example, be acceptable in a society valuing originality, diversity, tolerance and critical challenge but not acceptable where there is a stronger cultural emphasis is on consensus, conformism and respect for age, tradition and authority (see box).

One can reflect, non-judgementally, on how a similar episode—involving issues of religion and ethics, taste and decency—might have played out in (say) Malaysia and what decision RTM would have taken about transmis-

The BBC received 47,000 complaints ahead of the scheduled broadcast of the musical "Jerry Springer" in a late even slot on BBC 2 (in January 2005). Hundreds of protesters gathered outside the BBC TV Centre in London, and a blasphemy prosecution was threatened. The musical portrays Jesus, the Virgin Mary and God as characters on the "Jerry Springer Show", with some three hundred swear words.

The BBC went ahead with the broadcast despite the protests. The BBC pointed out that the programme was scheduled for late in the evening on the second channel, and preceded by on-air warnings that it might offend some viewers. The BBC said the musical had artistic merit and the BBC remit involved airing original artistic work even if controversial.

Jana Bennett, Director of Television, said: "We are not running some kind of pop idol competition in which the greatest number of votes gets a programme pulled from the schedules"; she declined to answer a hypothetical question about whether the BBC would broadcast a musical causing comparable offence to Muslims.

[The High Court denied the Christian Institute permission to take the BBC to court and Ofcom turned down a post-transmission complaint, saying in its adjudication that the programme was an important commentary on a television genre and did not breach any of the currently valid Content Codes or Guidelines]

Jana Bennett said each programme, or situation, was judged on its merits weighing content quality and likely offence. A Sunday newspaper article for example, about Arabs by talk show host Robert Kilroy-Silk has been thought sufficiently offensive for Kilroy-Silk to be dropped.

On the other hand an earlier decision to pull [not transmit] "Popetown", a satirical animation, was not because of protests from Catholics but because the programme lacked artistic quality. An episode of "Spooks" had gone ahead, however, despite protests from Muslims about the fictional portrayal of a foreign Muslim extremist using a mosque as a cover.

– www.ofcom.org.uk/tv/obb/prog_cb/pcb61.34pdf –

sion, in the context of an officially Muslim country.

In a trans-national broadcasting environment major multi-platform media players are struggling to square the circle of being culturally congruent with diverse audiences, whilst preserving a coherent corporate identity. CNN's international schedules are not the same as those they run in the US. International broadcasters like the BBC World Service and the Voice of America strive to stay editorially consistent while catering for the diverse sensibilities of audiences to different language services.

Anshu Chatterjee (2004: 415), using organizational models from McQuail, notes the difficult judgement calls MTV India had to make when MTV in the US showed a programme, "Clone High", depicting

Mahatma Ghandi as a rock fan who uses drugs and wears an earring: MTV executives in India distanced themselves, explaining it was a US-conceived and produced programme for American audiences. Corporately MTV apologized for any offence to Ghandi's memory, explained that American audiences were familiar with this kind of social parody and "Clone High" co-creator, Phil Lord, said the show was meant to be "a social commentary … where adolescents deal with what their tensions are about". MTV did not, however, dismantle its "Clone High Yearbook" website accessible to surfers in India and round the world[1].

These editorial/managerial decisions go to the heart of PSB, registering the content and ambiance of the relationship between broadcasters and their public. This implies a requirement for PSB researchers to study levels of responsiveness and accountability, and to evaluate mechanisms for achieving interactivity and audience participation. Digital technology and non-linear formats are encouraging the tendency for broadcasting to be positioned increasingly "with" audiences rather than "at" them.

The search for congruence is now more complicated and more commercially driven than when Gellner formulated the notion half a century ago. Globalization, media deregulation and new technology have ratcheted up both risk and opportunities. A helpful way of understanding this process (Mansell & Jenkins, 1992) is to consider the media as a cogwheel in the interplay three systematic dimensions: social systems, information systems and computer/communications systems. In this context, the significance of convergence is two-fold: from the supply side through technological innovation, and on the demand society from the appetite for sharing and leveraging knowledge and information.

Understanding these drivers and their interrelationships is important for the establishment of a relevant framework for studying and measuring PSB.

CASE STUDY ONE
Former communist countries: The new Europe and old media—Learning the hard way

The lack of a PSB ambiance
The uncompleted post-1989 transition from state broadcasting to public service broadcasting well illustrates the difficult learning process about what PSB is, and what it is not. Participants learnt, and are learning, the hard

---

[1] www.eonline.com/News/Items/ 0,1,11218,00.html

way the difference between the theoretical conditions and the deliverable reality. Transition has been dogged by dilemmas and disappointments. The struggle to create independent media—with the inevitable drafts and re-drafts of constitutions, regulations and procedures—depended on a consensus among politicians, the very people whose eventual disengagement was essential to making PSB a reality.

Those difficulties should not cause surprise. Even in established Western European democracies parties keep a wary eye on senior appointments; in some countries this involves a more or less explicit sharing out of key managerial and programme-commissioning posts. This kind of expectation was inevitably stronger in countries where single-party control of the media had been institutionalized for decades. Implementing pluralism came to be understood as each party utilizing the system to place people it thought reliable. Without the buffer of civil society, a culture of diversity and the demands of a mature electorate, independence was too rarely a stimulus to creative programme leadership and too often a signal to politicians to taking a negative approach: preventing the media falling into the hands of political opponents.

No media executive could aspire to the power, time or creative scope which John Reith had at the BBC in the 20s and 30s or, two generations later, Jeremy Isaacs at Channel 4. "Not since the early days of the BBC and John Reith," wrote the biographer of Michael Grade, Isaac's successor (and now BBC Chairman), "had one man so stamped his personality on a particular broadcasting medium as Isaacs had on Channel 4. He saw it as his baby, and all those who worked for the channel held him in a mixture of love and awe that was truly remarkable" (Grade, 1992: 207).

The approach could hardly be more different from the norm in Central and Eastern Europe during the 1990s. Reviewing the situation a Hungarian media observer wrote:

> "One of the great illusions of the transformation of the media had to be abandoned. Although the passing of the broadcasting Acts was expected to create a "rule of law" in the sector and to put an end to the decades-long tradition of manual direction, practice has shown that political pressure persists ... Authoritarian reflexes die hard. Politicians in the region advocate outdated concepts of the media. The Soviet-type agitation and propaganda model which considers journalists to be "the party's soldiers" and "the architects of the soul" persisted with the political elites. Many think the media legitimizes those in power by advocating their policies—a concept which is contrary to the democratic idea that the media legitimizes power-holders by watching them.
>
> (Bajomi-Lazar, 2002)

Karol Jakubowicz, a senior Polish media regulator and Chair of the Council of Europe Steering Committee on the Mass Media (CDMM), attributes the prolonged difficulties to transition countries' failure to develop a set of mutually supportive institutions, attitudes and processes. Drawing on a framework developed by Linz and Stepan (1996), Jakubowicz (2002) identified five societal dimensions:

- Civil Society (freedom of association and communication)
- Political Society (free and inclusive elections)
- Rule of Law (constitutional process, independent judiciary)
- Public Administration (civil servants working to rational-legal norms or standards, sustained by citizens' expectations)
- Economic Society (a market system, institutionalized through public acceptance as well through a proper regulatory framework)

Jakubowicz emphasized that pre-empting dysfunctionalism required the five elements to be synergized through shared values and cooperative behaviour. PSB is not a wish or intention, expressed in documents, but actual institutions delivering content which fulfils—and is seen to fulfil—a PSB remit. A country may be considered ready for PSB when two factors co-exist: enforcement mechanisms for the media's own accountability alongside acceptance by the political classes of the media's role in enforcing that accountability (McNair, 1995: 18).

Constitutional factors and regulatory arrangements

The achievement of independent, impartial media was an obvious objective; but delivering it depended on top media executives who had to be a chosen by a transparent and legitimate process. Typically, the operational management board would be appointed by a supervisory board and that supervisory board by the National Broadcasting Council or Commission. This shifted the pressure point but did not eliminate it. Who would appoint the Council members? Since the organizations' remits and funding were public matters, appointments to supervisory or management posts had to be derived from a transparently legitimate source. This could only be found from within the constitution.

Whichever part or, more usually, combination of parts—Presidency, Parliament or Executive—were chosen, the appointments trail became entangled with party politics. According to the Czech formula[2] members

---

[2] Basic Broadcasting Law of 17.05.2001, Article 7 (1): www.rrtv.cz/zakony_en/broadcasting_act 2001.html

of the National Radio and Television Council (NRTC) are appointed by the Prime Minister, on the proposal of the Parliament (where the Prime Minster's party grouping might be expected to have a majority). In the mid-1990s the Chair of NRTC wrote how he was bitterly criticized by the Prime Minister, Vaclav Klaus, for awarding the first private TV license to Nova TV, put together by the Central European Broadcasting Group whom the PM believed had links to opposition politicians.

Under Polish law[3] the nine-member Council is composed of four members nominated by the Sejm (lower house of parliament), two from the Senate (upper house) and three, including the Council Chair by the President of the Republic[4].

However the rules were manipulated or ignored—less in fact by the former communists than by Lech Walesa who on two occasions secured the dismissal of chairpersons he had himself nominated despite parliamentary objections and the courts ruling his actions illegal.

The legacy of a totalitarian system was terribly hard to shake off. Ring-fencing appointments to supervisory and management bodies with eligibility exclusion clauses was one approach. There was common sense and prudence in seeking to isolate appointees from active party politics and from the civil service payroll. The Council of Europe (Chapter 1) has taken a special interest in media development as an indicator of good governance and the implementation of human rights. For instance a Council of Europe Expert mission to Croatia produced a critique of that country's draft media law (June 2000) in a consultancy report recommending tighter appointments rules for Supervisory and Management Boards as well as the added safeguard of a clearer demarcation between those two boards lest residual inappropriate influences or attitudes on the Supervisory Board seep through into the Management Board[5].

Drafting safeguards, though, was not easy. There was the added problem that a safety net too widely spread would disqualify many strong candidates, with appropriate knowledge and experience. Suspicion was an inevitable consequence of assuming that appointees' performance would be driven by a political affiliation, business connection or other interest, however vague or remote. Applied in the UK such provisions would have excluded some members (from the House of Lords, for example) from the BBC Board of

---

[3] Broadcasting Act of 29.12.92, Article 7: www.media-forum.si.sl.pravo-tujina-broadcasting-law-poland

[4] See also various websites and "Regulatory Powers in 35 European Countries", by Serge Robillard (European Institute for the Media: monograph no.19).

[5] www.osce.org/documents.mc/2004/02/2091_en.pdf

Governors. Tighter laws, leading to "safer" but less qualified appointees on media bodies, may be a price to be paid for isolating the past.

In some cases the attempt to achieve independent, apolitical bodies was virtually abandoned in favour of a formulaic council of government and opposition nominees and responsive, therefore, to the vagaries of the election cycle—militating against continuity, creativity and strong programme leadership. Hungary's 1996 Media Law (Chapter Three, Section 33(3) and (4)) provides that the Chairman of the National Radio and Television Commission should be nominated jointly by the President of the Republic and the Prime Minister, with the others, numbering not less than four, nominated by the parliamentary factions[6].

This short summary has focused so far on the politico-constitutional dimensions achieved the continuation of public funding without the political control, which previously went hand in hand with it.

Organizational, personnel and HR factors

There were, of course, other dimensions. One was intra-organizational. The attitudes and assumptions around the periphery of broadcasting penetrated the organizations themselves. Programme commissioners, editors, producers and reporters all worked in an engrained culture of censorship and self-censorship. Changing the mindset presented a huge psychological challenge. Options ranged—as in any regime change—from root-and-branch reorganization to a minimalist approach in which only a few senior posts changed hands. The tendency towards minimalism was reinforced by the costs, in human as well as financial terms, of being more radical. This meant that pockets of old-style thinking survived. Also in every organization there were some senior appointments—at channel controller or news department director level—where appointees' political affiliations were known—generating certain expectations both from staff inside the organization and from those outside who had a hand in the appointment (Sparks and Reading, 1998: 100).

A minimalist approach seemed more practical in two countries—Poland and Hungary where the Party had already conceded some ground in 1989.

- In Poland, Jerzy Urban, the minister handling cultural matters, had signed an agreement allowing media access to the Church and this was expanded when the Mazowiecki government took power after Solidarity defeated the Communists in the June 1989 elections.

---

[6] www2.essex.ac.uk/elect/electjp/hu_medl96.htm

- In Hungary, Imre Pozsgay, the leading reform communist in the last ruling politburo, had conceded that "the government does not consider the media exclusively its own political instrument". Reform communism came too late to avert defeat for the party in the first free elections of 1990 when a right wing (MDF) government came to power. The new Chairperson of Hungarian TV, a well-regarded academic and social scientist, Elemer Hankess, defined his personnel objective as "destroying the old power structure without running a witch hunt". In radio (Magyar Radio) producers and editors (inclining mainly to reform communists or the left-leaning Free Democrats) took an instinctive dislike to the Chairman, Laszlo Csucs, appointed after the MDF formed the government. This writer recalls, as an outsider, a conversation with that Chairman who described his staff as exercising not freedom (*szabadsàg*) but licentiousness (*szabadossàg*).

By contrast with Poland and Hungary, staff changes were far more sweeping in East Germany and in the Czech Republic. In Prague hard liners were still in charge of news reporting when the big demonstrations began on 22 November. "The Garage" group of rebellious journalists were so called because they had gathered in the garage basement of Czech Radio headquarters; by 24 November they had taken charge in the newsroom. Within weeks 60 per cent of the journalists had been replaced.

Secondly, and curiously, the old culture of control and the new culture of choice combined to produce a different sort of tension. Programme statements or positions which were patently political were justified or excused by the new freedoms and through the apparent belief that tendentious broadcasts were acceptable if set off against tendentious broadcasts from a different standpoint. When journalists and producers from transition countries attended courses in the UK and elsewhere, broadcasting trainers saw a tendency for liberation to be so relished that freedom was confused with license—endangering professional standards. According to one analysis (Balcerowicz, 2002: 49–50), years of imposed "positive bias" were replaced by rampant "negative bias" as journalists found themselves free to implement the "good news is no news" principle—an established part of the media discourse in many non-communist countries. However the extent of the negativity appalled many in a context of competitive greed and short-term advantage. A small minority (mainly incumbents, from the former *nomenklatura*) emerged with rich pickings from manipulating transition, without delivering improved programme choice to audiences.

Change was hampered not only by elites but by audiences.
It was no wonder that audiences hankered for the old state broadcasting and that, as Yeltsin handed over to Putin, research by the Philadelphia-based Pew Institute showed a majority of Russians favouring a stronger media role for government. State broadcasting had not been public service broadcasting, but nor was it its total opposite and it had contained some elements which would pass a reasonable PSB test. In the former Soviet Russian heartland, if not in the reprieved satellite countries, the schedules swept in by commercial influence repelled many if not most.

Michael Nelson (1997: xvi) in his survey of international broadcasting during the cold war, quotes the distinguished Paris-based Czech writer in exile Milan Kunderer as saying "the struggle of man against power is the struggle of memory against forgetting". Many Central (especially) and East or South-East Europeans liked to think of 1989 as the year, which opened their way back into the European family. A senior Czech politician, Prime Minister of the Czech lands within the still federal Czechoslovakia, said that there was a gap of two and half young generations who had grown up in ignorance of free speech. The truth, however, is that apart from inter-war Czechoslovakia, none of the Communist block countries had known a settled culture of democracy and transparency.

Economic and financial factors

The third element was economic and financial. The transition countries were not rich: but their state broadcasters could count on resources. Under the old regime media, especially news media, had a high priority. There was (excluding that part of the GDR where audiences could pick up West German television) no internal rival, either for funds or audiences. After 1989 the established broadcasters faced, alongside political and psycho-logical changes, a transformed economic environment. Competition was not just possible but encouraged. Commercial investment came in, as the iron curtain came down. Developments occurred at different speeds in different countries, depending on the regulatory bodies. Some regulators gravitated towards the notion of PSB outcomes being delivered by a fully-fledged commercial market; others, to ring-fence PSB, were more restric-tive towards commercial ventures (Robillard, 1995). There was a general pattern, however, of foreign media groups teaming their investment capacity with local or *émigré* players who had the culture and the contacts necessary to acquire licenses.

The diversion of audiences to commercial TV exacerbated the former state broadcasters' problems, as they struggled to retain resources in the face of decision-makers ready to leap on any rationale for reducing them. The climate change after 1989 had conveniently enabled the authorities to allow, indeed encourage, the former state broadcasters to take advertising. In the year after Nova TV started, however, Czech Television lost 60 per cent of its advertising revenue.

Through the late 80s and 90s technological advance—including platform multiplication through satellite, cable and new media—provided further arguments for reducing the resources of existing PSBs. Globalization made the winds of change blow stronger. Before 1989 political and industry players under late communism had believed they could have globalization "a la carte": technology and investment (Rantanen, 2002). After 1989 this proved illusory as formerly protected institutions felt the full blast of world competition.

The impact on content and ratings was dramatic. The new entrants became market leaders. Arguments about protecting the cultural heritage played quite weakly against the background of recent history. Nova TV's license required 40 per cent domestically-produced programming. Poland imposed a 35 per cent figure. In Hungary the government put two channels out to private tender retaining a 26 per cent ownership stake. Domestic content quotas were interpreted in a somewhat cavalier way; and some countries—Romania and Slovakia, for example—made little effort to impose them.

Summary

In the post-Communist transition countries, as indeed in many countries across the world, the territory of publicly funded and organized broadcasting institutions was roughly coterminous with the serious production of PSB content. The choice was a simple one—between PSB institutions with PSB content and commercial broadcasters subject to only very limited PSB obligations.

State broadcasters were seen to fail their audiences because they were unable to develop into independent and creative cultural institutions. The politicians were, in large measure, responsible for that. The arrival of commercial players, with strong foreign ingredients, in a sense added insult to injury. This trend also involved the politicians, it too failed to create an ambiance of respect and cultural congruence between broadcasters and audiences. Citizen expectations were again disappointed—from a different direction: a second failure to create cultural congruence and institutional trust between broadcasters and audiences. This sharply distinguished the post-Communist situation from the broadcasting landscape in several West European countries.

CASE STUDY TWO
The United Kingdom: Reconciling pluralistic PSB with the BBC "Big Beast"

Setting the scene

The United Kingdom is, perhaps, the paradigmatic example of a more varied landscape where public service broadcasting is not coterminous with publicly funded institutions. The UK has a long tradition of private broadcasters trading revenue-earning franchises against public service obligations. This history influences the current UK debate around PSB: how its values should be defined, its outcomes measured and its cost assessed, and then "who pays, and how?" History and experience have encouraged a general acceptance of a substantial public intervention in broadcasting with the BBC as its central feature. Substantial research for Ofcom, the media regulator in its first month's of operation, as well as for the government, clarified that[7].

Broadcasters and their environment: The requirement for congruence

The current debate focuses on the relationships between the publicly-funded BBC and commercially-funded PSB players; and how policy and practice can encourage a competitive complementarity between private and public sectors. In the years after its foundation the BBC quickly established itself in public favour because it was congruent with its environment in the first age of democracy (women got the vote in 1918) and as a counterweight to a potentially overweening press. Maintaining that congruence—the prerequisite of public acceptance—means the BBC re-positioning itself in a world where burgeoning choice among broadcast content-providers has become a given of the social and economic landscape.

As we shall see, the flurry around the establishment of Ofcom and the renewal of the BBC Charter has generated solid survey evidence on PSB as well as serious economic analysis around the value of public financial intervention in broadcasting. British data may provide pointers towards trans-national benchmarks for defining, measuring and evaluating PSB.

UK broadcasting: The principal players

There are six main groups of actors in the UK debate: (i) the government; (ii) Ofcom (the UK's first combined regulatory body established under

---

[7] Ofcom Review of Public Service Television, June and November 2004, Phases One and Two.

the 2003 Communications Act to cover both broadcasting and telecommunications); (iii) the BBC; (iv) commercial terrestrial broadcasters with specified PSB obligations—the ITV regional franchise-holders, Channel 4 and 5; (v) commercial satellite and cable companies (BSkyB is the biggest) whose operations are a mix of branded channel ownership and bouquet distribution; and (vi) lastly and more loosely—the aggregation of present and past politicians, government advisers, broadcasting executives, media academics and pundits what is often called "the chattering classes". These are the contributors to the discourse which, over time, drives or nudges policy on broadcasting.

Ofcom and the BBC

Ofcom's powers are different in relation to the BBC than to other broadcasters. Over the latter it has full regulatory authority covering programme content, distribution capacity (spectrum) and market context. Its powers over the BBC are limited, since it is the BBC Governors—shortly to be reformatted as the BBC Trust—who, according to the Royal Charter and License, approved by Parliament, are basically responsible for what the BBC transmits on radio, television and online. However,

- Ofcom is the final point of appeal for programme complaints (for example, about fairness and privacy), not resolved through BBC internal processes;
- Ofcom also has review powers over BBC programming through its statutory obligation to ensure certain public service needs are satisfied in the mix offered by the PSB players "taken together" to the viewing public;
- Under the market impact rubric and, alongside the Office of Fair Trading [OFT], Ofcom oversees the activities of the BBC's commercial arm (BBC Worldwide) where the interface of the BBC's publicly and commercially funded activities raises issues of financial transparency, unfair competition and state subventions under both national and European legislation; and
- Ofcom's remit gives it an across-the-board interest in media accountability. This gave it an entry point into BBC governance; where a series of events—including, most recently, the Hutton Enquiry and BBC coverage of Iraq—had increasingly called into question whether the BBC Governors could credibly be the BBC and regulate it.

The government and the BBC Charter

In the end, though, the big decisions about what the BBC was, how it functioned and was financed, fell within the terms of its Royal Charter and License. This is renewable every 10 years by Parliament, on terms proposed by the government. As Ofcom opened for business at the turn of 2003/2004, preparatory work was already under way on renewing the BBC's Charter. One of Ofcom's own first initiatives was a Review of Television Public Service Broadcasting; its findings were published in three phases, between June 2004 and February 2005 (15 June 2004, 24 November 2004 and 8 February 2005)[8]. In March 2005 the government published its own proposals, "Review of the BBC Royal Charter: A strong BBC, independent of Government"—prepared by the Department of Culture, Media and Sport (DCMS) working with other areas including the Department of Trade & Industry (DTI) and prime ministerial policy advisers in Number 10 Downing Street. Like Ofcom, the government had commissioned extensive opinion research to back up its ideas. The BBC did likewise when formulating its own response issued in May 2005: This developed themes from "Building Public Value", a core document submitted by the BBC to the government the previous year. In June 2005 Ofcom published its reactions "Ofcom Response to the Green Paper" (8 June 2005).

The intensifying debate

Early in the review process Culture Secretary Tessa Jowell had appointed an Independent Review Panel to advise on the BBC's future. It was led by Lord Burns, former top civil servant in the Treasury, now a major city figure as Chairman of the Abbey National Bank. After eighteen months' consideration—and within weeks of the government publishing its own proposals—the Burns Panel made known its own findings. Burns recommended (1) the establishment of a new Public Service Broadcasting Commission (PSBC) to regulate all PSB players (the BBC included) and allocate funding between them; (2) Ofcom to retain its existing ("Tier 2") powers over the BBC, in fairness and privacy issues and quotas for programme genres; and (3) Ofcom to take a lead role in regulating the BBC's commercial activities and their impact in the media market place.

These recommendations went counter to the plans of the BBC Chairman, Michael Grade, recently appointed to the job in the wake of the Hutton debacle. Grade's strategy was to persuade the government to reaffirm the BBC's independence—including the license fee monopoly and strictly limited external regulation—in return for offering major reforms of BBC Governance to reassure critics. It was being reliably reported that Grade and the BBC's new Director-General Mark Thompson had gone some

---

[8] www.ofcom.org.uk

way to persuading Jowell; so the conclusions of the Burns Panel—set up by Jowell herself—aroused intense speculation as Green Paper publication approached. Lord Burns' views, furthermore, were rumoured to be endorsed by Lord Birt, former BBC Director-General (1992–2000), later working as a Strategy Adviser to the Prime Minister. What, it was asked, did the PM himself think? On which side would the Green Paper come down?

Birt had been at the BBC helm during the last cycle of Charter Renewal—the first of the digital and Internet age. Alongside a programme of job cuts and efficiency improvements the BBC had then placed a bid for massive resources to meet the digital age. This might have misfired as an attempt to extend the BBC's dominance. In the event the bid succeeded. The government reaffirmed the license fee, raising it by more than the rate of inflation. The BBC geared up to deliver new digital radio and TV channels (some of which began controversially because of their very small audiences and subscription-only access). Along with this went an Internet investment strategy which, much less controversial, was the driver behind what was soon hailed as one of the world's great information websites.

There were two personal twists in the tail of this success story. Birt was followed at the BBC not by one of his reportedly preferred successors— from the home-groomed team—but by an outsider, Greg Dyke, Director of Television Channels at the Pearson media corporation (owners of the Financial Times and other titles) and formerly a force behind TV AM—a successful commercially-funded breakfast show. Dyke's style was almost the diametric opposite of Birt's: This produced disagreements and tensions long before they were blown into a storm by the saga around BBC Radio's *Today* programme reporting of Iraq and the subsequent Hutton enquiry. There was personal background to Birt's "more in anger than in sorrow" speech in the House of Lords criticising the BBC's reporting standards, editorial disciplines and review procedures, in the face of complaints from Number Ten Downing Street.

The economic and financial context

The second twist was economic. The 2000 license fee settlement handed the BBC an even stronger market position than had been anticipated. Not only was license income been set to grow above the rate of inflation, but social changes increased (by some 14 per cent over five years) the number of single households—and therefore license payers. The BBC benefited from this arithmetic boost at a time when the commercially-funded ITV companies (with PSB obligations attached to their regional franchises) were suffering from the "bust that followed the boom" across the ICT sector. The events of 11 September 2001 made things worse.

According to Luke Johnson, Channel 4's Chairman, within 30 days of the New York and Washington attacks, the company's advertising revenue had halved. Along with Channel 4, the commercial TV franchise-holders were also hit—which speeded the trend to industry consolidation. When two of the biggest companies (Granada in the North and Central England) and Carlton (London and the South East) merged, only three of the original 15 players remained in the terrestrial commercial market. A low point was the failed launch of ITV Digital—the commercial PSB broadcasters' attempt to compete with the BBC's digital expansion and with Rupert Murdoch's BSkyB which had made itself the market leader in satellite distribution—promoting, at the same time, its own branded channels. Sales flopped in a glare of bad publicity, as Britain's top football clubs witnessed the disappearance of a revenue stream they had been counting on for match broadcast rights through contracts with ITV digital.

Greg Dyke's BBC moved with some agility and ingenuity to set up Freeview, based on digital terrestrial technology (DTT) enabling viewers to receive up to fifty channels without signing up to a commercial satellite or cable package. Viewers needed only to buy a set-top box, with prices starting from around £30 (US$50) upwards, to place on the TV set. Very recently the ITV commercial companies themselves have (September 2005) teamed up with the BBC to announce the launch of a Freesat distribution facility as an alternative to BSkyB.

From spectrum scarcity to spectrum plenty: Pressures on commercial PSB

"Spectrum matters to society"

Spectrum is more than energy distributions from a radiant source, arranged by wavelength. It is more than a tradable commodity. Spectrum is a scientific corridor, a socially significant guarantee that content will pass unimpeded and unobstructed from a transmitting to a receiving entity The awareness of being able to receive, along with a finite group of others and on the same terms, unimpeded, unobstructed content may contribute almost as powerfully to the sense of community as understanding and appreciation of the actual content. The geometrical definition of the concept of the "public sphere" implies both free internal movement and the notion of a periphery or boundary. Spectrum distribution decisions are, therefore, a benchmark for evaluating PSB implementation.

In December 2004 the England and Wales Cricket Board awarded an exclusive contract for the coverage of Test Matches to pay-TV satellite broadcaster BSkyB. Apparently they had outbid the current rights-holder, Channel 4, and the BBC. There were mutterings from cricket fans but it was December—the middle of the football season, cricket was not on the front pages and England, although on the way to recovery, had turned in some lacklustre performances over the past decade.

"Fast-forward" to September 2005. England have beaten Australia, regained "the Ashes"; the team makes a triumphant tour through London, including Trafalgar Square and climaxing at the Lords cricket ground. Millions who knew nothing about cricket salute the heroes. Mutterings, serious mutterings, begin to be heard that, to follow the heroes next time, audiences will either have to be content with BBC Radio 4, or pay extra to watch Sky Sports. Some criticism is directed at Channel 4 and BBC TV for missing out; more criticism hits the England and Wales Cricket Board for accepting the Murdoch bid, and excluding those who cannot or will not pay the necessary subscription (US$40 monthly).

The currently fashionable culture of selectivity and consumer choice comes up against the country's call for universal access to the feats of their national heroes and a re-discovered national sport.

Has cricket breathed new life into the public service culture, and has it forced a decision on priorities between two kinds of freedoms—on the one hand the economic freedom to choose and, on the other hand, the social right to free access?

Spectrum history: The past fifteen years

Apart from the media market downturn and some individual misjudgements, a longer-term trend had been pressing on the balance sheets of terrestrial commercial broadcasters with PSB obligations. For more than four decades, since the start of commercial broadcasting in the UK, commercial franchises were based on an implicit deal. The TV companies had exclusive rights to advertising revenue, subject to a levy, in their allocated franchise areas. In return, they would supply specified PSB elements in their programme mix—especially programmes targeted at local audiences, as well as at national audiences reflecting the regions, produced with regional resources, using local skills. The trade-off for these PSB obligations was free access to terrestrial transmission capacity which—if the companies had to pay for it within the then prevailing context of scarcity—would have cost them some £2 billion by the late 1980s.

However it was precisely at this point in time that satellite and cable distribution kicked in; within a decade, spectrum scarcity was replaced by spectrum surfeit; the economic viability model for commercial PSB players, balancing obligations with incentives, no longer held good. This applied especially in a time of tumbling media stock prices, against a BBC with securely rising income and the entrance of new commercial players not saddled with PSB obligations and favoured by the falling price of digital spectrum.

The continuing cost to the commercial PSB broadcasters of fulfilling their public service remit (i.e. the "opportunity cost" of not delivering more advertiser-friendly, cheaper-to-produce programming) was estimated by the ITC (Ofcom's predecessor regulator) at £260m; Channel 4's estimate for their opportunity costs, which Ofcom thought reasonable, was £160m against a total programme budget of £400m. Then there was the "real money" cost of the regional franchises: £239 million paid to the government in 2003. Meanwhile, during the five year period 1998–2003 the BBC share of the total public subsidy towards television (including positive investment and spectrum subvention) rose from 85 per cent to 87 per cent. This figure will rise towards 100 per cent as the license fee becomes even more dominant in the armoury of public intervention weapons (the others are free or subsidized spectrum, the license fee and—for Channel 4—the waiving of the dividend payment obligation)[9].

The revival in media markets and industry rationalization has brought balance sheet relief to commercial PSB players. This has energized the discussion about how much support they really need to sustain adequate earnings levels and fulfil PSB obligations—with predictably different estimates coming from free market enthusiasts on one side and defenders of the traditional British PSB pattern on the other. What is beyond doubt is that the perceived failure of the model has been a major factor in Ofcom's analysis of the right role for different players in the UK broadcasting ecology.

Around broadcasting: A changing intellectual climate

The first 70 years of broadcasting politics
Through most of the broadcasting era—and certainly since television became a mass medium—broadcasting decisions have been premised on what British commentators often call "Butskellite"[10] principles: The premise of a market economy softened by substantial elements of public financial

---

[9] Ofcom Review of Public Service Television Broadcasting. Phase 2. November 2004. pp. 20–37.

[10] The conflated epithet "Butskellite" refers to R. A. Butler who led the modernization of the Conservative Party after its 1945 defeat and Hugh Gaitskell the Labour opposition's "centrist" leader from 1955 to 1963.

intervention in services and utilities provision. Broadcasting fell into this category—which justified the way the BBC was set up and supported—even after the Conservative government set up ITV as a commercial alternative in 1955.

There were audible rumblings against consensus during the Thatcher administration (stimulated, atmospherically, by the prime minister herself or perhaps by what people thought she thought). The critique of the BBC was, however, mainly confined to the radical right which tended to regard smaller as more beautiful and instinctively disliked large publicly funded organizations—especially ones which dealt in culture and ideas rather than commercial goods and services and whose staff gave the impression of being more than averagely avant-garde, negative or critical of the existing state of things.

The Thatcher government did indeed commission a report on future options for BBC funding, from Professor Sir Alan Peacock. Published in 1986, Peacock's radical and indeed prescient recommendations included making subscription to the BBC voluntary and a fund to subsidize PSB as a whole on a competitive basis. Peacock reiterated his ideas in "Public Service Broadcasting without the BBC?" one in a collection of essays published by the free market Institute for Economic Affairs[11]. The proposals probably appealed to Thatcher and her inner circle, but there were more pressing items on the government's agenda and, despite rumbling and hints, nothing had been done by the time Thatcher was replaced as prime minister by the more "butskellite" John Major. This and the first serious cost-reduction measures within the BBC reprieved the BBC reprieve through the 1990s. In addition the prime minister's difficulties with his party's Euro-sceptic "bastards" (Major's word)—the very people who would have had the BBC in their sights—probably did the BBC no harm.

The last decade: New Labour and the intensifying debate

It was not, in the event, the Conservative right which changed the intellectual and economic climate around broadcasting, but market conditions, new technology and New Labour.

The Blair leadership which swept Labour to power in 1997 has been the first Labour leadership not just to accept but really to welcome market forces. This Labour shift is hugely important for the tenor of the current broadcasting debate and for the behaviour of the new regulator Ofcom. Circumscribed though Ofcom may be by the detailed provisions of the

---

[11] By Profile Books, 2004.

2003 Communications Act, it has scope and a duty to make decisions, develop regulatory case law and feed an atmosphere. Avowedly (in view of its adopting the phrase "citizen consumer") Ofcom wants a middle way between free market forces and regulatory intervention; its actual record is studied by observers on all sides to see when and why it supports public intervention. This implies a continuation of the debate which surrounded the Communications Act becoming law, on controversial issues like the right of foreign companies to take over a UK commercial PSB player.

Two years of Ofcom: Discerning the regulatory approach

From a study of Ofcom's approach and intentions[12] certain basics emerge. First the current firm preference is for what is coming to be called "light touch" regulation—not a million miles from "the discreet regulatory focus" recently advocated by John Birt[13].

Ofcom expresses it like this: "Ofcom will operate with a bias against intervention but with a willingness to intervene firmly, promptly and effectively where required. Ofcom will intervene where there is a public statutory duty to work towards public policy goal markets alone cannot achieve. Ofcom will always seek the least intrusive regulatory mechanisms ..."[14]. It is interested in co-regulation in selected areas (e.g. broadcast advertising), seen by some as a sensible way of involving industry stakeholders and by others as potentially weakening public protection. This latter group justify their suspicions by reductions in PSB genre output which Ofcom has allowed commercial franchise-holders on the ITV network (Channel 3), and they are concerned Ofcom's emerging policy on spectrum trading and channel sponsorship.

Secondly, Ofcom favours entrepreneurialism as a stimulus to a varied competitive market and an outlet for the application of new technology. It proclaims that it wants to encourage new players and guard against dominance by incumbents. This is behind its proposal[15] for a Public Service Publisher (PSP). As a publisher the PSP would not deploy the production capacity or infrastructure which existing PSB players like the BBC have at their disposal. The PSP would, though, be designed avowedly as a counterweight to the BBC with a "critical mass" capacity to commission content widely and to distribute it through the full range of platforms—traditional and new media. The contract to run the PSP would be put out to tender with all players except the BBC free

---

[12] Ofcom's Annual Plan 2004/5 and 2005/6.
[13] MacTaggart Lecture at the annual Edinburgh Festival, 26 August 2005: www.mediaguardian. co.uk
[14] Annual Plan 2005/6, p. 9.
[15] Review of Public Service Television Phase Two, p. 81.

to apply. The PSP, incidentally, would be based away from London.

The PSP proposal reflects the growing consensus that between the two "big beasts", the BBC and Rupert Murdoch's BSkyB, a new aggregation of talent and resource is required; this should occupy PSB territory and be a guarantor of continued variety and pluralism on the UK broadcasting land-scape. There is a trail here back to the Communications Act where Section 256(7) requires that Ofcom's reviews of PSB outputs and programmes genres (individual companies or "taken together") will consider the costs to particular service providers and the sources of income available to each: a definite pointer towards a pluralistic PSB vision.

The government's proposals for the BBC's future

It was only a matter of weeks after Ofcom launched its PSP proposal and the Burns Panel (see (c) above) recommended a Public Broadcasting Commission—to run the BBC and other public service broadcasters—that the government published its own Green Paper proposals. They had been keenly

REVIEW OF THE BBC'S ROYAL CHARTER: A STRONG BBC, INDEPENDENT OF GOVERNMENT

Royal Charter to be renewed for 10 Years (till 2017)

License Fee system to be kept for 10 years, but with review around 2012–13, when digital switchover implications could be assessed. Review would examine alternative funding options and possible distribution of license fee income to other broadcasters.

Governance: BBC Board of Governors to be replaced by a BBC Trust (Michael Grade, current Chairman to be Chair of the Trust), accountable to license-payers. Executive Board, reporting to the Trust, will have some Non-Executive Directors (i.e. not drawn from BBC senior management) BBC Trust, with a firmer separation than the Governors from the BBC management, to hold BBC, through Executive Board, to its distinctive public purposes, using Service Licenses to authorize funding.

New BBC programme service proposals will be subject to market impact studies by Ofcom which will be the external regulator for the BBC's commercial businesses.

Other BBC obligations, linked to continued license-fee funding, are: a lead role in "building digital Britain"**, and support for a strong independent production sector—"venture capital for a creative Britain".

**A sixth public purpose along with sustaining citizenship and civil society , promoting education and learning, stimulating creativity and cultural excellence, representing the UK—its nations, regions and communities, and bringing the UK to the world and the world to the UK.

awaited—not least because of quite recent tensions (linked, in particular, to Iraq coverage) between the BBC and the government, especially 10 Downing Street and cabinet ministers close to the Prime Minister. The word had gone out that the Charter Renewal process would not be used to punish the BBC, and the Review's title sheet indicated that word would be kept.

Reaction to the government's proposals for the BBC

Substantial responses to the Green paper came from the BBC and from Ofcom. The BBC was, on balance, the more content having achieved its main aims: a renewed, if modified, Royal Charter and continued hypothecation of the license fee, for a 10-year period. They conceded that the government's governance reform proposals were more thoroughgoing and certainly more formal than those envisaged and set in train by Michael Grade after his appointment as Chairman in the (for the BBC) traumatic environment of early 2004. The BBC took the opportunity trenchantly to restate its opposition to funding "contest-ability" (i.e. other PSB players being free to compete with the BBC for license fee income). The Governors said[16] that "contestability or "top-slicing" would break the direct and clearly understood line of accountability between the BBC and the UK public, at a time when there are demands for stronger links between the BBC and license-fee payers". May be this was a warning shot ahead—a long way ahead—of the funding options review announced in the Green Paper for a point midway in the life of the new Charter (i.e. around 2012).

Ofcom zeroed in on the same issue—but with, of course, a different slant. They categorized their "key messages"[17] into "agree", "further analysis" and "disagree". First item of disagreement was the proposed timing for the funding options review; "it was too late", said Ofcom, considering the stage digital switchover would by then have reached (2012 the just-announced completion date) and the huge implications for all market players from the accelerated pace of technological change.

The Green Paper proposals may suggest that the BBC has held the line. Informed opinion, though, decreasingly sees it like that. It seems likely that pressures on the BBC will mount to cooperate in a reappraisal of funding options at an earlier date than the Green paper envisaged.

The House of Lords report

The (at the time of writing) most recent critique[18] of the Green Paper came from the upper house of the legislature in December 2005. The House of Lords can delay but ultimately cannot (since the 1910 Parliament Act)

---

[16] BBC Response May 2005, p. 4.
[17] Ofcom Response, June 2005, p. 7.

resist the democratically-elected House of Commons. However during a decade when large majorities and discipline within New Labour ranks have reduced the chances of effectively opposing government proposals in the House of Commons, the House of Lords has won recognition as a reviewing body where there is less adversarial politics and a greater willingness to seek empirically-based "middle ground" solutions. The Lords Report proclaims essentially the same PSB objectives as the government's Green Paper but, in several areas comes up with different—sometimes radically different—ways of achieving them. The Report reopens—for the first time since the BBC's foundation 80 years ago—key issues about PSB implementation: a reopening redolent of the raw discussions which have taken place in countries seeking to move from a publicly funded state broadcasting system to a mixed funding public service broadcasting system. With clever minds focussed on satisfying core public service broadcasting values, it is instructive to see how, as between the government and the House of Lords Committee, the "shared objectives, different solutions" scenario shapes up.

BROADCASTING INDEPENDENCE

The Lords say:
- Charter details are negotiated bilaterally between Government and the BBC, only being put to Parliament for final approval.
- The same applies to setting the license fee level and ultimate decisions on service changes.
- Despite professionalization of selection procedures, final power of appointing BBC Chairman and Trustees rests with the government.
- The Royal Charter is an arcane instrument, non-transparent to the public and disliked by other major players in the broadcasting industry.
- So instead the BBC be established by a Statute: Thereby it would, automatically, be subject to parliamentary scrutiny involving all political parties. The Statute would enshrine essentially the same autonomy, programme values and financial security as the Charter.

The Government says:
- Surveys show the public even keener to keep parliament away from the BBC than to keep government away.
- Risks of political interference would not be removed—might indeed increase—with parliamentary involvement. The issue of one party potentially dominating the House of Commons would remain.
- The Royal Charter system has proved itself over time. Potential problems have been addressed by new codes of practice.

---

[18] Select Committee on the BBC Charter Review, First report. December 2005.

Governance Model

The Lords say:

- The BBC Trust cannot have ultimate management control of the BBC Executive Board and have credibility as its regulator. There should, therefore, be one Board (containing a Management Committee). It should be regulated by Ofcom—as are all other broadcasters (although this would pre-suppose Ofcom strengthening its programme regulatory capacity, its Content Board).

The Government says:

- The BBC Trust has been devised to face both ways, and can do so. Distinct governance arrangements are needed because the BBC is different from other broadcasters, in terms of the public's expectations of what it will get for the BBC license fee and of the public's perceptions of what the BBC represents in British life and culture.

It should be noted however that "the BBC is different" argument was accepted in part by the Lords Committee, who rejected the Burns Panel idea to subject the BBC, along with all other PSB players, to a Public Service Broadcasting Commission with powers over governance, programme sand resources (including slicing license fee funds away from the BBC to other PSB players). The Lords agreed with the Burns Panel on the unitary board principle and on enhanced Ofcom regulation of the BBC. They felt, however, however, that the full Burns proposal would weaken the accountability link between the BBC and license-payers/audiences as well as creating a substantial new body which might overlap with or duplicate Ofcom's own.

There were two other areas emphasized in the Lord Report—not marked by particular conflict with Government:

(i) The Public Value Test to precede the introduction of new BBC Services or major changes to existing one. The Lords wanted a stronger role for Ofcom to safeguard the interest of other market players than that envisaged by the BBC itself in "Preparing for the New BBC Trust: Service Licenses and the Public Value Test".

(ii) The so-called Window of Creative Opportunity (WOCC). The Lords wanted to reinforce this suggestion which had come from the BBC itself in order to optimize chances for independent producers in the market place.

In spite of that serious divergence of opinion with the House of Lords, it appeared—as the New Year opened—that the government would stand by its Green Paper proposals and table them as a White Paper in the House of Commons by February or March 2006.

Some issues around the BBC and defining PSB

The BBC, confirmed as the cornerstone of PSB in the UK, is not the sole identifier of the genre. It would be absurd if a programme were to be classified as public service simply because it came out of the BBC stable. On the other hand, there is a forceful argument that it is the BBC's particular place, within the wider PSB ecology, not just to fill gaps left by market failure but to offer programming across the range, for all classes, to "make the good popular and the popular good"[19]. That assumption drives, for example, the BBC's seeking strongly to make its BBC Radio 1 (pop music station) distinctive and different from a commercially funded channel targeting a similar teenage/youth audience.

There are also scheduling and contextual dimensions. Can it be said that, through being "hammocked" between programming with a lower or zero PSB factor, PSB can attract wider and different audiences—which would imply essentially non-PSB programmes acquiring social value points through scheduling. Public service stalwarts say that disaggregating genres within a BBC schedule would dilute or desiccate the mix, and generate a downward spiral in audiences and funding, eventually breaking the BBC's critical mass and undermining the public service character of British broadcasting. Sceptics say this is the sort of self-regarding argument the BBC has served up for years to justify its hold on massive resources. The government, in its Green Paper, endorsed the BBC's own view that it "should be big enough deliver the services audiences demand, but as small as it mission allows"[20]. This begs, amongst other things, the question whether, in an environment where the BBC has traditionally played so wide a role, audiences can make a reasonable and reasoned judgement about which services the public and/or private sectors can be counted on to provide.

Public investment and PSB content outcomes
Ofcom estimates actual BBC TV production costs at £2.3 billion[21]. It is fair to ask how much of this budget is required (in the public interest): What would be the programme consequences of certain levels of cuts (via top-slicing the license fee or in other ways); whether a given content cut would be made good by other players (PSB or non-PSB) and, if not, whether that would matter. These questions persist because of the live debate around PSB pluralism and because the BBC share of the roughly £3 billion public intervention in broadcasting is 85 per cent and (for reasons explained earlier) rising. Because the answers to the questions depend on imponderables, the public's hunch about them will be significant. Public acceptance is bound to be a major ranking factor in the health and strength of PSB.

---

[19] Huw Weledon, former BBC TV Managing Director.
[20] Green Paper, p. 7.
[21] Review Phase Two, p. 22.

A specific issue will be the relationship between "money in" and PSB delivered outcomes. That relationship is less easy to determine for the BBC than for Channel 4 which has a less widely-spread more focussed public service brief some recent allegations notwithstanding that reality shows like Big Brother and some other recent programme commissions have been driven by the need to boost audiences for advertisers. Channel 4's programme budget (around £200 million) and viewing share (just under 10 per cent across all platforms) are on the record. Aside from cost concessions on spectrum and the waiving of a dividend requirement, Channel 4's balance sheet is like that of a commercial company: the income comes from the advertisers.

The regulator Ofcom gave a notably complementary report to Channel 4 for "an on-screen performance which has exceeded most industry expectations ... achieved during a time of significant internal change and despite continued pressure from increasing digital penetration"[22]. In governance terms, moreover, Channel 4's model of a single unitary board has been finding increasing favour, edging ahead (with informed, hitherto uncommitted opinion) of the BBC's model of governance responsibility split between a Trust or Board of Governors and a Management or Executive Board (see below *House of Lords Select Committee on BBC Charter Review*).

In the BBC case, the trail from PSB content outcomes back to cost is more complicated, and in which the public, which foots the bill, inevitably takes a major interest. The BBC2 programme budget is just slightly larger than Channel 4's and alongside that must go substantial parts of the BBC1 £1.2 billion budget—not to mention corporate overheads; BBC1 and BBC2 together deliver a 36 per cent audience share, across all channels: three times Channel 4, but on a budget six times as large. The radio budget contains a higher (than TV) genuine PSB component. News and current affairs spending is thoroughly PSB. The public will not calculate in detail which budgets deliver which outcomes but they will have a shrewd idea about PSB value for money, and that will almost certainly, in the longer term, affect their readiness to pay.

PSB and the people's view

When Ofcom started its research into public thinking about PSB, they did not ask the public to come up with definitions—which would have been perhaps over-ambitious. Instead they adopted a "box-ticking" approach inviting people to rank and evaluate a number of PSB programme genres.

---

[22] Review Phase 3, p. 54ff.

Section 264 (4) of the Act specifies programmes which "meet the purposes of public service television broadcasting in the United Kingdom".

These are required to:

(a) deal with a wide range of subject matters;
(b) be offered at viewing times to meets needs and interests of as many different audiences as practicable;
(c) be relevant and properly balanced in terms of nature and subject matter; and
(d) maintain high general standards of content, production and applied editorial and other professional skills.

Section 264 (6) further specifies programmes should be assessed by the regulator, Ofcom, in terms of whether (taken together) they:

(a) disseminate information, and provide education and entertainment;
(b) reflect, support and stimulate UK cultural activity and its diversity;
(c) in news and current affairs, facilitate civic understanding and fair well-informed debate, as well as providing comprehensive authoritative coverage within—and in different parts of—the UK, and from around the world;
(d) satisfy a wide range of sporting and other leisure interests;
(e) contain suitable quality and range of programmes on educational matters;
(f) [also] on science, social issues, matters of international significance/specialist interest, and religion—including therein information about the history, beliefs and practices of different religions;
(g) contain a suitable quantity of high quality and original programmes for children and young people;
(h) contain sufficient programming to reflect the lives and concerns of different communities and cultural interests and traditions within the UK, and locally in different parts of the UK; and
(i) for UK-produced programmes, an appropriate range and proportion are to be made outside the M25 [i.e. Greater London] area.

They also tested the public's readiness to continue paying money, through the license fee or otherwise, to guarantee a supply of PSB programmes.

They hooked their research onto Article 256 of the 2003 Communications Act (see box) which required Ofcom to report on the fulfilment of the public service remit.

This was the statutory remit and these the criteria against which Ofcom was required to report. Members of the public, responding to Ofcom's enquiries, were aware of this framework as well as of the "boxes" they were ticking in relation to concepts like output genres, objectives and impact. Various PSB elements were put to participants who were asked to rank their importance for themselves personally and societally, and score their satisfaction with delivered

content. There was, therefore, solid experiential value in the data. By implication the ranking process, by the audience, (as evidence of perceptions and
priorities) contributed to the task of defining PSB (see box).

In summary, a picture emerges of a public with a shrewd and solid sense
of what it understands by PSB. The public wants a broad and balanced
programme mix, with a top priority on news, a preference for home-made
programming, first runs rather than repeats and excluding material not
appropriate for family viewing.

The BBC's positive qualities are perceived as being continuity and
reliability, in particular being counted on to broadcast major national and
international events. On the negative side, though, are the impressions of

The main findings of the "Ofcom Review of Public Service Television Phase
1" (p. 48) were as follows:

1. News is considered the most important element of PSB: equally so
    personally and societally (mentioned by 87 per cent).
2. That high importance rating is matched by an almost equally high
    performance satisfaction rating on News output.
3. Protecting children from unsuitable content was mentioned by 85 per cent
    [with only 28 per cent satisfaction].
4. The next highest priority was for a balanced varied programme mix in
    peak hours [84 per cent] and at all times of day [82 per cent importance,
    only 44 per cent satisfaction on delivery].
5. This next two prioritized items were an expectation of high professional
    skills in programme-making [82 per cent] and request for first-run
    programmes (i.e. not repeats) [80 per cent importance, only 37 per cent
    satisfaction on delivery].
6. General factual programmes scored highly on importance [82 per cent],
    with a slightly lower [69 per cent] satisfaction score.
7. Lowest scores on importance ratings went to programmes for minority
    groups [perhaps inherently not a surprise number of mentions may be
    low—< 50 per cent—but intensity behind them high].
8. Interestingly, higher importance ratings went to programmes promoting
    awareness and understanding of different communities [59 per cent] or
    reflecting the needs/concerns of different regional communities in the UK
    [65 per cent].
9. Other high-scoring programme genres (for importance) were specialist
    educational programmes for children and adults [76 per cent], protecting
    national heritage and traditions [71 per cent] and promoting social action
    (e.g. crime-stoppers) [68 per cent].
10. Highest genre discrepancies between personal and societal evaluation
    were: education, regional, consumer affairs, children's programming—
    personal rating < [lower than] societal arts, classical music, films, comedy,
    drama—personal rating > [higher than] societal.

taking audiences for granted and of being oversized. The BBC's presence across platforms (radio, TV, online, books and magazines) and vertically (commissioning, production, distribution, sales rights) has long been a double-edged sword. Economic considerations argue for synergizing assets but expensive multi-faceted promotion can weary the public—sometimes giving an impression of institutional narcissism.

The public's willingness to pay

How ready is the public to pay? In response to the question: "Do you support the general idea of the license fee?" 46 per cent said "yes" and 32 per cent said "no"—from a sampled 6,000 households across the country. Support for the license fee seemed to be somewhat stronger in the London area, the South and the West of England, possibly because they have a higher proportion of ABC1 viewers who are more likely to watch PSB content.

The data do not, however, convey an impression of overwhelming support. When the question was put somewhat differently, as to whether the license fee offers good value for money, the outcome was much closer—with 42 per cent saying "no" and 46 per cent "yes".

The figures suggest a state of public opinion, which could be turned by market and technological changes over the coming years. There may be continuingly wide support for the publicly funded provision of PSB content and the idea that it should be generally accessible and available. But do people believe that the public purse should bear the burden of providing the same PSB choices to everyone, with equal accessibility and equal quality? (Echoes perhaps of the parallel argument about universal access to broadband).

Differentiation of PSB provision already exists, with people opting into discretely-priced satellite or cable subscription "bouquets" at various levels—and including BBC digital channels not otherwise available. There may well be support for extending this trend over the next decade—through, for example, HDTV reception (high definition television) being available for viewers willing to pay for this extra[23]—without this option being rejected as violating notions of social equality.

In the long run, will the public lose patience? Will the BBC have to make a choice between becoming a much smaller organization, retaining its public funding to handle market failure needs only or stay at its present size and move towards becoming commercial?

---

[23] As suggested by Barry Cox, (former Deputy Chair of Channel 4 and Chair of Switchco, the company tasked with leading digital switchover—also a close friend of Prime Minister Tony Blair) in a speech to the European Media Forum 12 July 05, reprinted in "Television"—Journal of the Royal Television Society, September 2005, pp. 17–21.

The answers will depend on the choice of products and services in the market as well on subtle intangibles in the broadcasting environment. Important elements, as we have seen, in the PSB culture are quality, diversity and community, along with continuity. In the public mind public investment tends to be associated with continuity of provision: with reliability and reduced risk. Markets offer opportunity and more risk. These imponderable are very much "cause and effect", "chicken and egg" questions. Has the BBC been sustained by a society that inherently and instinctively favours PSB and believes that only public funding can be counted on to deliver it? Or is the relationship more pragmatic—that the public has grown to like most of what it gets, and doesn't want to lose that programming?

Both answers are probably true; decision-makers and the public at large will have to assess risk. The BBC will not be dismantled overnight, the big questions will be about proportionate impact and risk.

PSB VIEWING LEVELS

International data from a number of developed countries show the UK having the highest proportion of TV viewers watching PSB genres, around 42 per cent, with France in a close second place. Next come Sweden, the United States and the Netherlands.

Broadcasting spend in relation to total GNP

The relatively high number of US viewers watching PSB-type content is interesting (assuming the data do refer to authentic PSB content) in view of the miniscule role of public funding in overall broadcasting spend: around one per cent. The US shows a total broadcasting spending which represents a higher proportion of GDP than any other country apart from the UK, provoking the question of whether public money may sometimes dis-incentivize private investment. Other countries to spend a relatively high proportion of GDP on broadcasting are Canada, Portugal and Japan.

Public funding as share of total broadcasting spend

Only in Germany does public funding account for a bigger share of totalling broadcasting spent than in the UK. The figures for France are interesting: not a particularly high total spend nor a particularly high public funding element within it yet this delivers a PSB viewing share second only to the UK among countries surveyed (each over 40 per cent). Perhaps this has some link with the French public emphasis on national and European-originated content. France also scores highly in terms of peak output produced from the home market, higher than any non-English language country except Japan.

– Ofcom Report Phase 2, p. 47 –

- What would particular funding cuts mean for specific programme outputs?
- How far would these cuts affect various PSB genres?
- To what extent would commercial broadcasters fill the gap?
- If they do not, could lost PSB-type provision be reinstated?

CASE STUDY INPUTS TO AN UPDATED MEASUREMENT FRAMEWORK
From PSB to PSCP (Public Service Content Provision)
The global and the national dimensions

Future measurement and analysis will be focused on the more embracing concept of PSCP rather than on PSB alone. This is reflected in changing media regulation models as exemplified by the pending conversion of the EU 1989 Television Without Frontiers Directive into the Audiovisual Media Services Directive which will be submitted by the EU Commission to the Council of Ministers and the Parliament this year [2006]. Subjective policy responses to the objective situation are, however, not uniform. The UK Secretary for Culture, Media and Sport has voiced opposition to EU plans for regulating the internet, saying further measures should be based on self-regulation models—thereby endorsing the light-touch approach deployed by Ofcom since its inception in 2004[24].

Divergent policy and regulatory responses do not, however, obscure the essential facts around the new media platforms, and the links of these distribution systems or infrastructures with converging information flows— local/community, national, regional and global. Globalization is unfolding both economically and technologically. Content is being dragged along in the process, giving globalization a third, thematic, dimension. Global-scale markets offer new scope for corporate multinational players to "colonize global public space. Simultaneously, new technology and ripening consumer and audience choice are offering new market entrants unprecedented opportunities to build the "thousands to millions" information environment.

It is an open question among scholars how far global information flows, and the channels which carry them, have created a global public sphere in the way that for decades—in some cases centuries—such public spheres have existed inside nations or other societal entities (Habermas, 2001).

---

[24] Tessa Jowell, in a speech at the Oxford Media Convention (19 January 2006) said: "If we want further regulation, then I believe the best approach is to rely as far as possible on self-regulation", www.business.timesonline.co.uk/article/0,,13130-2001048,00.html

Recent revolutionary changes notwithstanding, significant elements of continuity with past structures remain. Inputs to the global public sphere—whether from publicly or commercially funded players, corporate giants or entrepreneurial minnows—are still influenced by the legislation of the countries or (in the EU case) supranational entities where they are anchored and, in theory, accountable. Nation states themselves are, like corporate media players, involved in colonizing the global public space.

Although an embryonic information ambiance is opening out in the global public sphere, PSB/PSCP measurement should commence in the national environment. Indeed, as Boyd-Barrett (2002) argues, there is a configuration of political, economic, social, and cultural forces such that twin processes of globalization and national consolidation are advancing side by side.

Benchmark measurements of PSB will need to cover content delivered to audiences, the reputation and resilience of deliverer-organizations, and the environment in which both content-providers and audiences function. Data will include the following:

1. Legislative texts, supervisory provision and regulatory remits, offering significant initial data.

2. Evidence of how the ruling classes—as reflected in regulation and generally—treat public service content providers.

3. The shape of public service content provision—in terms of pluralism, funding and other factors—as a resilience indicator for PSB values and institutions. (Views differ considerably about the ideal balance between major and minor players; and around how far free markets underpin content quality and diversity and how far they threaten them.)

4. Criteria by which—in a particular environment—media players, publicly or commercially funded, make investment decisions. How effectively and efficiently do different players convert public support (financial or otherwise) into PSB content?

5. The prominence and range of PSB genres within content available to a given society or community.

6. The accessibility of those genres, measured by reception capability, ease or clarity of choice—for example, electronic programme guides—and cost.

7. Audience share, reach and appreciation indices as pointers towards utilization levels and readiness to pay. New technology, with enhanced interactivity and participation, adds sophisticated tools for evaluating utilization.

References

Abramian, D. (2001). *The Decline and Fall of Public Service Broadcasting.* Massachusetts: Cambridge.

Balcerowicz, L. (2002). Post-Communist Transition: Some Lesson. Institute of Economic Affairs, London.

Bajomi-Lazar, P. (2002). Public Service Television in East Central Europe: A study for the International Federation of Journalists.

Boyd-Barrett, O. (2002). Global News Wholesalers. In Sreberny et al. (Ed.), *Media in Global Context* (Ch. 13). Arnold, Hodder.

BBC. (1928). Annual Handbook. London.

Birt, J. (28 August 2005). MacTaggart Lecture, Edinburgh Festival. Retrieved from www.mediaguardian.co.uk

Briggs, A., & Burke, P. (2001). *A Social History of the Internet Polity*, Ch. 5 ans 6. UK: Cambridge.

Chatterjee, A. (2004). In M. Castells (Ed.), *The Network Society: A cross-cultural perspective* (Ch. 18). Edward Elgar Publications.

Gellner, E. (1983). *Nations and Nationalism.* Oxford: Blackwell.

Grade, M. (1992). *Screening the Image.* Virgin Books.

Habermas, J. (2001). The Public Sphere. In Durham & Kellner (Ed.), *Media and Cultural Studies:Key Works* (pp. 102). Blackwell.

Jakubowicz, K. (February 2002). What Prospects for Public Service Broadcasting in Central and Eastern Europe? Remarks at the International Federation of Journalists Conference held in Budapest.

Roy Hattersley, L. (2004). *The Edwardians.* Time-Warner Books.

Hoggart, R., & Morgan, J. Ed. (1982). *The Future of Broadcasting.* London: Macmillan.

Linz, J., & Stepan, A. (1996). *Problems of Democratic Transition and Consolidation: Southern Europe, South America and post-Communist Europe* (Ch. 15–21). Baltimore and London: Johns Hopkins U.P..

Low, L. (2000). *Economics of Information Technology and the Media* (pp. 66). Singapore University Press.

Mansell, R., & Jenkins, M. M. (1992). Forecasting Multimedia Markets. CICT/SPRU pamphlet.

McNair, B. (1995). *Introduction to Political Communication.* London & New York: Routledge.

Nelson, M. (1997). *War of the Black Heavens.* Brasseys.

Rantanen, T. (2002). *The Global and the National: Media and Communications in Post-Communist Russia* (Ch. 1 & 5). Rowman & Littlefield.

Robillard, S. (1995). Television in Europe: Regulatory Bodies: Status, Functions and Powers in 35 European Countries. *European Institute for the Media: monograph,* no. 19. John Libbey.

Scannell, P. (1997). *Radio and Television in the Modern World.* Blackwell.

Sparks, C., & Reading, A. (1998). *Communism, Capitalism and the Media. Sage.*

Tambini, D., & Cowling, J. (2004). From Public Service Broadcasting to Public Service Communications (pp. 138). IPPR, London.

Tehranian, M. (2002). In E. Aksu & J. A. Camilleri (Ed.), *Democratizing Global Governance* (Ch. 3). Palgrave Macmillan.

Williams, F., & Allen, W. (1960). In John Raymond (Ed.), *The Baldwin Age.* Eyre & Spottiswoode.

Keep the Essence, Change (Almost) Everything Else: Redefining PSB for the 21st Century

Not a month has passed in the past decades without a major new report, book, conference or study about public service broadcasting in one country or another. One constantly hears of new laws being adopted, or of reforms of public service broadcasting (PSB) organizations being launched somewhere. All this attests to the importance of this broadcasting institution, recognized, after all, as one of "the most invaluable socio-political inventions of the western democracies in the 20th century" (Silvo, 2003).

However, it also provides evidence of the sensitivity, indeed vulnerability, of the concept of public service broadcasting to changing circumstances, requiring constant readjustment, redefinition, reaffirmation of its legitimacy and adaptation to a new context. If PSB is to serve the public interest, then any change in how it is defined and understood in a particular society must have a knock-on effect on PSB itself.

According to the Parliamentary Assembly of the Council of Europe, PSB is under threat. It is challenged by political and economic interests, by increasing competition from commercial media, by media concentrations and by financial difficulties. It is also faced with the challenge of adapting to globalization and the new technologies. More than that—we may be coming up to a make-or-break moment in the history of PSB, one that will decide whether it can have a future. If, as Siune and Hulten (1998: 36) maintain, PSB needs "support from the political system as well as the audience for its services", then we may be coming to a time when these twin pillars on which PSB rests may erode and crumble. Within a decade or two, it may have to fight for its life.

Let us not be misled about the nature of the PSB debate. It is not a debate about a form of broadcasting, but about the values and principles governing society and social life. It is, in reality, primarily an ideological and axiological discussion about the kind of society we want to live in. At the same time, it is not possible to make a convincing case for PSB without correctly identifying its axiological underpinnings and the nature of the public interest it should be dedicated to serving.

Support for continuation of PSB proceeds from the view that whatever the market may offer, the community still has a duty to guarantee provision of broadcasting services free from the effect of the profit motive, offering the individual a "basic supply" of what he/she needs as a member of a particular society and culture, and of a particular polity and democratic system. Proponents of this approach cherish more values than just those related to the market, and more motivations than just the profit motive. The case

Resolution No. 1 on the future of public service broadcasting adopted at the 4th European Ministerial Conference on Mass Media Policy (Prague, 7–8 December 1994)

Participating States agree that public service broadcasters must have principally the following missions:

- To provide, through their programming, a reference point for all members of the public and a factor for social cohesion and integration of all individuals, groups and communities. In particular, they must reject any cultural, sexual, religious or racial discrimination and any form of social segregation.
- To provide a forum for public discussion in which as broad a spectrum as possible of views and opinions can be expressed.
- To broadcast impartial and independent news, information and comment.
- To develop pluralistic, innovatory and varied programming which meets high ethical and quality standards and not to sacrifice the pursuit of quality to market forces.
- To develop and structure programme schedules and services of interest to a wide public while being attentive to the needs of minority groups.
- To reflect the different philosophical ideas and religious beliefs in society, with the aim of strengthening mutual understanding and tolerance and promoting community relations in pluriethnic and multicultural societies.
- To contribute actively through their programming to a greater appreciation and dissemination of the diversity of national and European cultural heritage.
- To ensure that the programmes offered contain a significant proportion of original productions, especially feature films, drama and other creative works, and to have regard to the need to use independent producers and cooperate with the cinema sector.
- To extend the choice available to viewers and listeners by also offering programme services which are not normally provided by commercial broadcasters.

for PSB should rest on a vision of society animated by more than market forces and on our definition of ourselves as more than just consumers and of our societal interactions as more than mere commercial transactions.

However, this is not the only school of thought on this matter. According to the neo-liberal approach, the proper mechanism for the satisfaction of individual and social needs is the market where required goods or services can be purchased. The law of supply and demand, together with the profit motive, will ensure provision of these goods and services. State or public sector involvement in meeting these needs is unnecessary and unwelcome, as it interferes with, and distorts the operation of, market forces. Therefore, PSB should be dismantled.

Then, there is also the market-failure rationale for PSB. The market should indeed predominate, but since it does not meet every need, there is room for the public sector to supplement what the market has to offer. Nonetheless, public institutions should, under no circumstances, compete with private enterprise, nor engage in any kind of activity that private entrepreneurs might wish to pursue. So, what is needed is "pure PSB" as a niche broadcaster, offering only broadcast content and services which private broadcasters find commercially unrewarding.

The result of this running ideological confrontation concerning PSB will decide whether there will be the political will to develop forms of public service provision for the Information Society.

Defining PSB: A high-stakes game

The original motivation behind the birth of PSB was, of course, paternalistic; it emerged as "a typical modernist project of the cultural elite" (Van den Bulck, 2001: 54). Successive waves of PSB development were associated with advances of democracy in particular countries.

In most Western European countries, PSB emerged during the "public service" phase of media policy development in Western European countries (McQuail, 2000). It was dedicated to the achievement of cultural and social goals (mainly in broadcasting) and to the provision of "communication welfare", also by ensuring the social responsibility of the print media and limiting the power of monopoly owners of the media. The ultimate goal was protection of the public interest and enhancement of democracy.

In most cases, PSB was originally a product of what might be called collec-tivistic, social-democratic social arrangements (the Welfare State), assigning an important role to the public sector in providing for the satisfaction of the needs of the individual. An important element of this was the culture of "non-commercialism". "The political and cultural forces ranged against private exploitation of broadcasting were strong and the main available model of commercialism, that prevailing in the USA, was not viewed with much favour by most social and political elites." (McQuail, 1986: 153)

Moreover, PSB originally emerged at a time of spectrum scarcity and, to begin with, as a monopoly broadcaster. It was thus natural to develop a public service remit for broadcasting and a generalist orientation for its programme services, as well as to impose on it a universal service obligation. Naturally, a PSB organization, as a country's only broadcaster, also needed to be a producer of its own programming, with all the organizational, technical and financial consequences of this fact.

All too often, the shape and remit of PSB as developed in these contexts are erroneously (but sometimes also deliberately so) represented as the defining features of public service broadcasting. If this view is accepted, then it will be easy to draw the conclusion that changing circumstances spell the doom of public service provision in the broadcast media.

This is the purpose of a long-term campaign pursued by commercial broadcasters, vis-à-vis national and EU policymakers (Association of Commercial Television in Europe et al, 2004; VPRT, 2003). It encompasses a number of strategies.

- An "arrested PSB evolution" strategy (ultimately leading to the marginalization and obsolescence of PSB, culminating in its disappearance), comprising:

  (a) A "semantic" strategy, arguing that public service broadcasting should remain precisely that—broadcasting—and PSB organizations should not be allowed to move into the new technologies (seen by commercial broadcasters as their next frontier and growth area, where they would like to see as little competition as possible).

  (b) A "clear and precise definition of the remit" strategy, designed to obtain a detailed legal definition of PSB in its traditional form (generalist, universally accessible broadcast channels) which could then be used to block any change of the remit and means of delivering it (e.g. move into thematic channels, use of new technologies which may not be immediately accessible to all, and would in any case be used only by a part of the audience).

- A "harmless PSB" strategy, comprising:

  (a) Demands that PSB be reduced to redressing market failure by providing programming commercial broadcasters find unattractive, and thus turn into a niche broadcaster (the so-called "monastery model" of PSB).

(b) Demands that PSB be prevented from running advertising.

(c) Demands that production of "PSB content" be financed by a special fund and commissioned from all comers, so PSB organizations do not monopolize funds or production capacity.

- A "PSB no longer needed" strategy, following on from the last one, based on the argument that so much "PSB content" can be found in the programming of commercial broadcasters, or is/can be produced by others (the so called "distributed public service model"), that PSB organizations as such are no longer necessary for the audience to have access to it.

All this could be called an "attrition model" of PSB, representing, as it were, Darwin's theory of (un)natural selection in reverse, in that survival of the fittest would result not from ability to adapt to the environment, but from the ability to prevent others (in this case PSB) from adapting to a changing environment,

Associated with this last strategy is a tendency to define PSB in terms of particular programme genres, so that the commercial sector could claim that it, too, is performing a public service by scheduling "PSB genres". Not surprisingly, PSB broadcasters oppose this approach. As noted by Collins (2003), what counts is the entire schedule: "The public service character and obligations are of the essence and must inform the very fabric and texture of the broadcaster. It also follows that the public character is reflected in the overall schedule and is not something which inheres in individual programmes which are then distributed across a schedule, somewhat like sultanas in a fruitcake". Also the BBC (2004: 7) notes that "the public continue to define public service broadcasting (PSB) not as a narrow set of particular programme categories which the market may fail to provide, but as a broad and integrated system of programmes and services. To them, PSB includes soaps, drama, sport, comedy and natural history just as much as (and in some cases, even more than) the traditional "public service" categories of current affairs, arts and religion".

Paradoxically, what the commercial sector may not realize is its campaign may be counter-productive in two ways:

- It forces some policymakers to come to the defence of PSB.
- It prevents some governments and public-service broadcasters from doing what they might otherwise do of their own accord, i.e. from developing concepts of PSB that might go some way towards meeting the expectations of commercial media establishments.

This is shown by the debate within the EU, resulting in part from the many complaints lodged by commercial broadcasters with the European Commission in pursuit of the strategies described above (Ward, 2002, 2003; EBU, 2004), as well as from the EU's own problems with PSB in the context of state aid and competition issues (see Harrison, Woods, 2001; European Commission, 2001; Jakubowicz, 2004). The European Commission would have been quite happy to embrace a view of PSB strikingly similar to that proposed by the commercial sector, but yielded to pressure from member states and adopted a different approach.

The Council of Europe is committed to the existence and continued development of public service broadcasting, stressing that its role in modern democratic societies is to "support the values underlying the political, legal and social structures of democratic societies, and in particular respect for human rights, culture and political pluralism". That is why it has called on member countries to "guarantee that public service broadcasting, as an essential factor for the cohesion of democratic societies, is maintained in the new digital environment by ensuring universal access by individuals to the programmes of public service broadcasters and giving it inter alia a central role in the transition to terrestrial digital broadcasting" and to "reaffirm the remit of public service broadcasting, adapting if necessary its means to the new digital environment" (Committee of Ministers, 2003). This shows how high the stakes are in deciding the future of PSB and in developing a definition that will legitimize it in changed circumstances.

THE EUROPEAN UNION VIEW OF PSB

- PSB is directly related to the democratic, social and cultural needs of society and media pluralism.
- PSB has a comprehensive mission and must deliver a wide range of programming in order to address society as a whole.
- PSB must provide a suitable balance of entertainment, culture, spectacles and education; there is natural overlap between its programme offer and that of commercial broadcasting in popular genres—sport, comedy, drama, news and current affairs.
- PSB can legitimately seek to reach wide audiences.
- PSB is important in promoting new audio-visual and information services and the new technologies.

PSB is a key element for the development of an information society for all, ensuring that the largest possible number of citizens benefit from the potential offered by new digital applications and services.

– Compiled by the author –

It has been noted that governments, under pressure from the commercial sector and also (in the case of EU members) from the European Union, are imposing more and more accountability systems on PSB organizations (Jakubowicz, 2003a, b). At the same time, however, public service remits in force in particular countries (see Betzel, forthcoming) show that little has changed in terms of the very traditional definition of PSB obligations. As concerns national policies with regard to the use of the new technologies by PSB organizations (see Aslama, Syvertsen, forthcoming), it is clear that no clear pattern is emerging and very different policies apply, with some countries not yet willing to accept PSB use of anything but traditional broadcasting technology.

These twists and turns of national policy may in fact be exacerbating the problem, as pointed out by Atkinson (1997): "Public television is in the throes of a crisis. It is expected to do better than the private channels in embodying the public service ideal of which it is no longer allowed the monopoly, and in order to achieve this it is expected to adopt a mode of operation which no longer distinguishes it from the commercial channels. It is expected to be productive, efficient, capable of generating its own income and able to attract "consumers". It is also expected to differ from the private channels in its programming. So it is expected to be similar and different at the same time".

We have already noted that the concept of public service broadcasting has often had to be readjusted and adapted to changing circumstances. The nature of the main challenges facing PSB over the course of its history is outlined in Table 1.

Today, it is time to take stock of the situation of PSB against the background of social and technological change and to develop a vision of PSB suited to the conditions of the Information Society.

Changing circumstances of PSB operation

PSB and convergence

Convergence is the takeover of all forms of media by one technology: digital computers, capable of handling multimedia content. This will naturally change patterns of communication almost beyond recognition.

One thing is certain: Convergent digital communication system will no longer provide a natural habitat for traditional public service broadcasting. Table 2 shows what the situation would be like if PSB failed to change and modernize, or if the commercial sector's strategies were successful.

If that is not to happen, the concept of PSB must be extended in a technological sense involving presence on all significant platforms, since

Table 1
PSB in the context of evolving electronic communication[1]

	1st generation broadcasters (PSB)	2nd generation broadcasters (commercial)	3rd generation broadcasters (thematic)	4th generation communicators: Non-linear, on-demand communication, "pull technology"
Funding	Public Advertising	Advertising Subscription	Subscription Advertising	VOD, Pay-per-view, micro-payments, commission on transactions, etc.
Output	Generalist	Generalist (more entertainment); Premium Pay-TV	Thematic	No, or few "flow channels", most content available on demand
Licence conditions	Strong	Moderate	Weak	Unknown at this stage
Programme expenditure	Mainly originated	Mainly originated, but also acquired	Mainly acquired	Unknown at this stage
Challenge to PSB	None, PSB monopoly or domination	Loss of monopoly on audience. Need to compete for it and for advertising.	Loss of monopoly on most "PSB genres"	Channels, schedules disappear. No more need for public service broadcasters? Should they evolve into something else?
Effect of challenge	None	At first, PSB identity, funding and legitimization crisis. Then, as growing competition drives commercial broadcasters to abandon PSB commitments. New prospects may open.		Need to reinvent institutional and financial form of public service provision.

PSB "has to follow its audiences wherever they tend to look for content" (Thomass, 2003: 34, see also Wessberg, 2000), and in terms of its relationship to its audience (e.g. provision of a "personalized public service" via online delivery).

Thomass (2003) argues that the typical PSB aim of social integration can

---

[1] Adapted from The Impact of Digital Television on the Supply of Programmes, 1998.

DESCRIPTION OF CONVERGENT COMMUNICATION

- Multimedia communication
- Interactivity: interchangeable sender/receive roles
- Pull technology (non-linear, on-demand communication and access to content gradually replaces push technology (linear communication)
- Asynchronous communication: Content can be stored and the user's decision to access it.
- Individualization/personalization (customization): Sender can address individual users with content selected according to different criteria, or users can select content from what is on offer.
- Portability of terminals and mobility
- Disintermediation (elimination of intermediaries, e.g. media organizations, as anyone can offer information and other content to be directly accessed by users and receivers) and "neo-intermediation" (emergence of new intermediaries, especially on the Internet, capable of offering new services or packaging content in new ways)
- "Anyone, anything, anytime, anywhere"—the ultimate goal of access to anyone from any place and at any time, and to all existing content stored in electronic memory

– Compiled by the author –

Table 2
Digital television service packages[2]

Service packages	Who will be able to offer them
Basic programmes (channels) that are more diverse than the current analogue television world	Both PSB and commercial broadcasters
• Thematic programmes (channels) targeted at a special audience • Interactive programme services • Online programme services of standard programmes • Online services of archives etc • A pay-TV environment • More advanced device management (including time transfer capability)	Commercial broadcasters alone

no longer be supported only by the means of broadcast media, with their ability to reach millions, but also must include all the new possibilities of

---

[2] Adapted from Wiio, 2004.

online transmission. The Internet, digital distribution, interactive services and wireless services—all of these are means wherein a public-service orientated content must be available for users.

This view is supported in the Council of Europe: "The means to fulfil the public service remit may include the provision of new specialized channels, for example in the field of information, education and culture, and of new interactive services, for example EPGs and programme-related online services" (Committee of Ministers, 2003).

Accordingly, the image of PSB as a medium offering universal and universally accessible content must change. To keep abreast of changes in electronic communication and in user behaviour, it must offer the full gamut of services—from national, generalist channels, through thematic channels, to an Internet-delivered "personalized public service".

This calls for a re-definition of some of the main features of PSB as traditionally understood:

- Universality of content can no longer be understood as one-size-fits-all programming on one or more broadcast channels, but as both universality of basic supply on generalist channels (including mass appeal, entertainment programming), which will be central to what public service broadcasters offer to the public, and universality across the full portfolio of services, some of them specialized or tailored for specific audiences, adding up to a more extended and comprehensive range of services.

- Universality of access can no longer be understood as a couple of terrestrial channels available to the entire population, but as presence on all significant media and platforms with significant penetration, but also the ability to deliver a "personalized public service" in the "pull", online and on-demand environment (see EBU, 2002).

Hence calls for a new name for PSB—in keeping with this process, but also to counter the "semantic strategy" referred to above. One proposal comes from Kearns (2003): "Social and technological change means facing the challenge of renewal—from public service broadcasting to public service [online] communications the entire Public Service Communications community needs to move away from the broadcast paradigm of content delivered to a mass public and towards the usage and participation paradigm of the network age" [emphasis is author's]. Another proposal is to use the term "public service media" (Nissen, 2005), or perhaps to speak of public service content provision.

In this new context, the idea of "basic supply" programming, delivering everything on two or three channels, must also be revised. The answer to that may be the concept of "portality", serving to describe the role of the PSB organization as offering access via different programme and service formats as well as different delivery methods (including the online media) to a wide-ranging universe of content (Silvo, 2003).

As we note in Table 1, the consequences of convergence for PSB will be paradoxical. So far, it has brought on a crisis of identity and legitimization. On the other hand, it is already apparent that the commercial sector may

---

THE SIX PROMISES OF PUBLIC SERVICE DIGITAL TELEVISION

1. **Knowledge and culture**
   Public service digital television is society's most central provider of knowledge and cultural services. It provides citizens with trustworthy and significant cultural and knowledge contents.
2. **The self and identity**
   Public service digital television offers a wide range of programming. It supports the citizen in the development of identity, independence and the self.
3. **Citizenship and community spirit**
   Public service digital television supports both local identity and living as a member of national and international communities.
4. **Expertise and cooperation**
   Public service digital television is competent. It supports expertise and cooperation both in its own activity and within society. The points of departure of expertise and cooperation are the viewer's development as an individual and support for national competence.
5. **Audiences and participation**
   Public service digital television comprehends audiences as groups of citizens with different needs, and not merely as customers. Public service digital television uses different distribution channels in such a way as to support and increase citizens' opportunities for participation.
6. **The equality and availability of the knowledge society**
   Public service digital television provides the knowledge contents of the knowledge society and, through its programming, supports the development of new easy-to-use and interactive knowledge society services as well as the equal development of the knowledge society's service structure. The objective is the availability of knowledge society services through public service digital television in every home.

One option of how public service digital television could perhaps fulfil these promises is the division of the services to be supplied into three sub-categories: services for large audiences, services for special audiences and personal services.

– Wiio, 2004 –

not, due to growing competition, persist in providing PSB content for much longer. In the UK, it has been made clear that neither Channel 3 nor Channel 5 would probably be able to "deliver PSB in the longer term, well beyond digital switchover"[3]. Also OFCOM identifies a period of declining PSB obligations: "This period will start once the scarcity value of the analogue spectrum has fallen close to the opportunity cost of the PSB obligations on ITV1 and Five. It could occur well within five years. We should expect great pressure to reduce the PSB obligations alongside increasingly credible threats from these companies to hand back their digital licenses. To avoid this threat becoming a reality, Ofcom would have to consider reducing PSB obligations on ITV1 and Five. Channel 4 would face increasing difficulty in cross-subsidizing challenging PSB programming from other parts of its schedule" (OFCOM, 2004b: 33).

Thus, convergence may actually help provide arguments in favour of retaining and modernising PSB. On the other hand, the growing profusion of programming delivered to the individual in more and more ways may weaken the popular support for the continuing existence of PSB, and even more of the licence fee system, required to finance it.

PSB, globalization and "cultural decolonization"

Kofi Annan, UN Secretary General is quoted as saying: "Globalization is a fact of life. But I believe we have underestimated its fragility". The reason for this fragility is hinted at in a definition of globalization formulated by Anthony Giddens:

> Globalization can be defined as the intensification of worldwide social relations which link distant locations in such a way that local happenings are shaped by events occurring many miles away and vice versa. This is a dialectical process because such local happenings may move in an obverse direction from the very distanciated relations that shape them. Local transformation is as much a part of globalization as the lateral extension of social connections across time and space.
>
> (cited after Waters, 1996: 50)

Thus, globalization is an internally contradictory process. Its "fragility" derives principally from the fact that many elements of globalization produce "local happenings" or transformation running counter to globalization, weakening or negating its effect.

Thus, globalization is said to involve such contradictory developments such as the following.

---

[3] Refer "ITC Consultation on Public Service Broadcasting" (2000: 8–9), www.itc.uk.org

- Erosion of the nation-state, with the supra-national or global level seen as the most appropriate for tackling many important problems, a process promoted by international integration; at the same time the sub-national or regional level acquires more importance as the proper framework for dealing with other issues.
- Economic globalization and concentration, accompanied by renewed attention to local markets and customers' individual taste, especially in e-commerce.
- Spread of a "global culture", leading in part to renewed attention to national and regional culture, or indeed to the birth of national, religious or cultural fundamentalism in many areas as they respond to the threat to their identity arising out of globalization, attesting to the continued vitality of the issue of national and cultural identity.
- "Globalization" of the media and communication patterns, as they both concentrate at the European and global level and at the same time progressively localize. Some of the global television players (e.g. MTV or CNN) respond to this by a process of "regionalization", introducing new channels for particular regions or countries, involving specialized content originating from, or tailored specially for target audiences.

In recent decades, another historic process is challenging globalization: It is the rising assertiveness of non-European cultures, recognized by some as a process of "cultural decolonization". After political decolonization in the 1950s, and the (failed) economic decolonization of later years, "At the end of the 20th century we entered the third phase—that of cultural decolonization, as Third World countries rediscover their own identities and roots. Full decolonization will also entail the dethronement of Europe after half a millennium of its rule in the world" (Kapu ci ski, 2005).

Huntington (1993; see also Huntington, 2000) goes further and posits "the clash of civilizations as the new stage of human conflict". Whether or not Huntington's thesis should be accepted without reservation, there is no question that anti-Westernization pressures are gathering momentum in many parts of the world (see Maisami, 2003; Monshipouri, 2005), contributing to increasing international tensions and a rising tide of terrorism. All this may have profound long-term consequences for nation-states and cultural and national identities and for social cohesion.

One of the strengths of PSB has been its close ties to, and identification with, the nation-state it serves. The EBU (2002) points out that PSB must serve the obligations of citizenship and be a force to enable the effective working of a pluralist democracy. It must also include media content which preserves and develops national culture and identity. Public service broadcasters must be aware of the role they can play to ensure social cohesion. That is likely to continue to be its main characteristic.

Still, globalization and "cultural decolonization" re-define political and cultural citizenship and thus require a considerable change in the way PSB obligations should be understood and pursued. Otherwise, PSB will fail to provide an adequate response to globalization.

Accordingly, public service broadcasters should re-orient their programming in order to achieve the following.

- Spread awareness of the additional (both supra- and sub-national) dimensions of political citizenship, as well as individual and societal co-responsibility for developments at these other levels.
- Provide of more in-depth information on the situation prevailing on the international scene and in individual countries, helping develop the international/global public sphere and serving as a watchdog of international bodies and organizations; this job will be made extremely important and difficult, given that Keane (2001) describes the current situation at the global level as a case of "New Medievalism", "a *mélange* of political and legal structures, ... a clutter of nation states and regional and local governments; intergovernmental agencies and programmes ... a hotchpotch system of global governance also includes global accords, treaties, and conventions; and new forms of public deliberation and conflict resolution". Today, fully informed citizenship requires considerable effort to understand and become involved in the processes of global governance, affecting everyone's life.
- Engage, where appropriate, in "peace broadcasting" and promotion of post-conflict reconciliation; in any case, promote cultural diversity and intercultural dialogue, so as to promote the peaceful existence not only of the nation-state, but also of the larger international community.
- Reflect the increasingly multi-ethnic and multicultural societies, without unduly accentuating differences or "ghettoising" different social and ethnic groups by locking them into "walled gardens" of programme services, dedicated solely to them.

Unless PSB organizations can do so, they will not be able to equip their audiences with the knowledge and skills need to operate with ease in a globalized, multicultural context. Moreover, country-bound PSB organizations will be at a disadvantage when competing on a globalized market with multinational media corporations, though no one has yet come up with a practicable vision of how to provide PSB at a trans-national level.

PSB and marketization

The "public service" phase of media policy development, which was highly conducive to the operation of PSB is being replaced by what McQuail (2000) calls a "new paradigm" of media policy emerging in Western European countries since the 1980s. It is oriented more to economic goals than to social and political welfare. Policymakers and regulators accept the *de facto* commoditization and commercialization of mass media in the hope that this will set the stage for the media's expected contribution to economic and technological growth. The principle of non-commercialism has been effectively transformed into one particular minority value.

What is behind this change is the general ideological evolution of society, expressed i.a. in what Murdock and Golding (1999: 3) call marketization, i.e. "all those policy interventions designed to increase the freedom of action of private corporations and to institute corporate goals and organizational procedures as the yardsticks against which the performance of all forms of cultural enterprise are judged". Marketization thus comprises privatization, liberalization and corporatization (i.e. encouraging or compelling organizations still within the public sector to pursue market opportunities and institute corporate forms of organization) (see also Murdock, 2001).

With the old social-democratic social arrangements now increasingly a thing of the past, and with the media seen as crucially important for technological and economic development, policy in this area has been redefined sharply, with primacy given to the market as the driving force of media development.

Ideological change has been accompanied by cultural change. Bardoel and Brants (2003) note that the Dutch policy discourse on role and functions of public service broadcasting has displayed four general tendencies and shifts:

- From political to cultural motives.
- From collectivism to individualism.
- From ambiguous to positive assessment of economic and market forces.
- From purely national to also minority cultures, with more attention to minority groups and different cultures.

In short, the old, modernist paradigm is being replaced by a more post-modernist approach. There is more room for individual cultures, styles, and tastes. Accordingly, PSB is re-conceptualized from broadcasting in the service of the public sphere to broadcasting in the service of the listener/viewer, whose prime purpose is to satisfy the interests and preferences of individual consumers rather than the needs of the collective, the citizenry (Syvertsen, 1999).

The result is a serious crisis of legitimation for PSB broadcasters. Much more than convergence and globalization, ideological and cultural change may over time undercut the political will needed to redefine PSB and its remit.

An indication that this may already be happening is provided by the apparent willingness of the Dutch government to reduce the functions of the main national public service broadcasting organization to provision of news, with programming devoted to opinion-shaping and public debate to be provided by the broadcasting organizations, while the provision of education, arts and culture will be "subject to further decision-making". Entertainment, on the other hand, "cannot be a goal in itself, but will be permitted as a format" ("Easter Agreement", 2005; emphasis added).

Rationale for PSB: Continuity and change

There seems little doubt that the distinctiveness of PSB derives from two of its key features:

- The way it defines its audience, and its needs and interests.
- Its dedication to serving the public interest.

All other functional or institutional features of PSB can be traced back to these two constitutive axiological elements, either as a means of their implementation or as a prerequisite of their preservation (e.g. institutional autonomy and editorial independence; freedom from political and commercial pressures; method etc.).

We could attempt to formulate the way PSB defines its audience in the following way—it perceives its audience as composed of complete human beings, with a full range of needs and interests (as citizens; members of different social groups, communities, minorities and cultures; consumers; and seekers of information, education, experience, advice and entertainment), also seeking to broaden their horizons and enrich their lives.

Other broadcasters—whether commercial, community, alternative or "civic"—may also deliver worthy, high-quality programming. However, none of them addresses the audience as composed of "complete human beings" and seeks to meet every need, as PSB broadcasters should do in the totality of their programming.

All other types of broadcasters may also serve the public interest in one way or another, but again, usually only by concentrating on selected aspects of it. PSB cannot pick and choose: It must serve it in as comprehensive a way as possible. Moreover, PSB broadcasters must provide such content free at the point of reception, while elsewhere it may be available for additional payment. In addition, PSB programming should largely be domestically produced and operate within the cultural, historical and other frames of reference within which the audience actually lives. This is not always the case in commercial broadcasting.

In this context, mention might be made of the way the BBC (2004) defines the way it serves the public interest by "building public value", consisting of three components:

- Value to people as individuals. The BBC aims to inform, educate and entertain.
- Value to society as a whole—to people as citizens—by contributing to the wider well-being of society. Citizen value often rests on the availability of a service to all on equal terms. The BBC aims to contribute to the wider social, democratic and cultural health of the UK through the range and quality of its broadcasting.
- Impact on the performance of the wider commercial market—its net economic value. The BBC's market impact can have a positive element, such as through its impact on training and creative investment, and also a negative element in cases where it reduces demand for commercial products.

On this last point, it could be added that the rationale for PSB today and in the future will also encompass the fact that it acquires growing importance as an element of "structural regulation" oriented to shaping the broadcasting and electronic media system as a whole (McKinsey & Company, 1999: 16). It can keep audience demand for high-quality programming alive in the market and thus produce a "demonstration effect" by encouraging commercial broadcasters to imitate PSB distinctiveness and emulate programme genres and formats successfully pioneered by public service broadcasters.

The BBC adds that it contributes to public value in five main ways:

- *Democratic value*
  The BBC supports civic life and national debate by providing trusted and impartial news and information that helps citizens make sense of the world and encourages them to engage with it.

- *Cultural and creative value*
  The BBC enriches the UK's cultural life by bringing talent and audiences together to break new ground, to celebrate our cultural heritage, to broaden the national conversation.

- *Educational value*

  By offering audiences of every age a world of formal and informal educational opportunity in every medium, the BBC helps build a society strong in knowledge and skills.

- *Social and community value*

  By enabling the UK's many communities to see what they hold in common and how they differ, the BBC seeks to build social cohesion and tolerance through greater understanding.

- *Global value*

  The BBC supports the UK's global role by being the world's most trusted provider of international news and information, and by showcasing the best of British culture to a global audience.

Smith (1989: 23) has said that "public interest implies the invocation of social purpose in all matters in which there remains a territory of discussable collective policy within society". Accordingly, different needs and issues may predominate in different countries and collective policy may be directed to solving different problems. This suggests potentially considerable differences between PSB organizations serving different notions of the public interest, with these differences being reflected in varying degrees in the organization and structure of a PSB broadcaster, programme content and so on.

However, what is important is that these fundamental features of PSB should not be lost, as nothing can replace them. Here is where the ideological and axiological considerations forcefully come into play. Just as PSB must continue to exist as a guarantor that whatever other broadcasters and content providers may be doing, content of sufficient range and quantity, serving the fundamental needs of society and various groups within it, will always be universally available, so the preservation of this institution should provide a guaranteed supply of programming serving the complete human being and serving the public interest and building public value, as a counterbalance to other sources of programming dedicated to private interest and private value.

This is not to say that PSB organizations must always remain in their present form: With a wide diversity of content offers and methods of delivery, institutional frameworks and schemes for producing this content may change.

It might be argued that if the ideological and cultural change described briefly above is as profound as might appear, then societies (or their governments acting for them) should be free to decide whether or not they want to preserve societal institutions governed by a social philosophy that is different from the mainstream. Moreover, some might claim that a fatal flaw exists in the whole concept of PSB. As Collins et al (2001: 7–8) maintain, echoing many other voices, "There is little point to public funding of merit goods if they are consumed by few. Public service broadcasting cannot succeed unless it is popular (and) cannot be consigned to a ghetto at the margins of the market, filling the gaps disdained by profit-maximizing broadcasters". Therefore, it could be said, in order to be popular, PSB must offer many of the same types of mass-audience programming as commercial broadcasters, so it must go down the road of "programme convergence" with them and thus cannot remain true to its fundamental vocation.

Part of the answer to this is that PSB organizations which maintain their distinctiveness do well on the market. This is as true of BBC2 and Channel 4 in the UK, which have maintained their market shares in a multi-channel environment (OFCOM, 2004a), as of Finnish PSB television (Aslama, 2004) as indeed of German public service television (Meier, 2003). Secondly, as the television market fragments further, the pressure on PSB to maintain high market shares will make less and less sense, especially if PSB is present on many different platforms, some of which can never control a large part of the market, anyway. Moreover, digital technology will, by boosting the number of channels and other outlets available to PSB, facilitate the strategy of "multiple selves", whereby these organizations fulfil the remit on some channels, while using others to defend their share of the market.

Conclusion

We have seen that re-definition of PSB broadcasting must begin with dropping or modifying what may appear to be an inalienable part of its name, i.e. broadcasting, and should allow far-reaching change in its methods of operation, programme obligations and methods of delivery. At the same time, its fundamental features (its definition of the audience and its dedication to serving the public interest, as defined in a particular country) should remain the same.

However, public service organizations are demoralized, insecure, beleaguered and confused. Many have lost their nerve and with it their creativity, and ability to find an answer to the dilemmas of today and tomorrow. Nothing poses a greater danger to the future of PSB than this situation.

Picard (2004) argues that if license fees and support for public service broadcasting are to survive, viewers and listeners must not have to ask the question "why should I pay the license fee?" Public service broadcasters

---

TEN CENTRAL MISSIONS FOR PSB IN A DIGITAL COMMUNICATIONS SYSTEM

1. PSB has to serve as an "island of credibility" in fragmented media markets.
2. PSB guarantees participation by everybody in the advantages of the digital revolution.
3. PSB has to serve as an independent and credible provider of information.
4. PSB guarantees the based on nationwide provision of perspectives information and interests.
5. PSB serves as [a] nation[']s voice in Europe and in the world.
6. PSB guarantees quality standards.
7. PSB corrects the supply shortages of the commercial sector.
8. PSB serves as a guarantor of cultural identity.
9. PSB encourages national and European productions.
10. PSB is a motor for innovation.

– Holznagel, 2000 –

---

must work to ensure that viewers and listeners know what they get for the license fee, how it serves their interests, and why it is important. They must clearly know why they should pay the fee—but more importantly—they must want to pay it. The motivation for paying the licence fee should be based on individual choice and loyalty to the PSB broadcaster, not one of compulsion or necessity: "In the contemporary broadcasting world real bonds and relationships between audiences and broadcasters—not merely lip service to those relationships—must be nurtured and solidified if license fee funding and the role and functions of public service broadcasting are to be maintained".

Collins et al (2001: 11) similarly point to the important role of the PSB broadcasters themselves in safeguarding their own future: "People should be able to feel that public service broadcasting is theirs. New media, as several public service broadcasters have recognized, provide striking opportunities to break out of (the) "take what you are given" mode. But organizational changes also offer public service broadcasters to build new relationships of partnership, identification, and sense of shared ownership which involve viewers, listeners and Web surfers—indeed, which make receivers into senders".

If Picard and Collins et al are right, and it seems they are, then this passive stance of PSB organizations will indeed spell their doom. They must fight back, for it is up to them to reinforce—or regain—the loyalty, identification and partnership of their audience. If they can do that, and this can only be done by remaining true to their vocation, they will have gained a powerful ally, one that will prevent governments from adopting policies designed to marginalize, weaken or eliminate PSB. Under pressure from public opinion, policymakers will find ways of working new definitions and remits of public service provision into the laws, and will find answers to the questions of financing and institutional change affecting public service broadcasting organizations.

If, however, PSB fails to re-invigorate public support for its own continued existence and modernization, and if consequently public opinion reacts with indifference to the practical implementation of the "attrition model" of PSB, then we can expect it to be played out in full.

References

Aslama, M. (2004). Convergence or Diversification? Changing Markets and Finnish Televisual Programme Culture, 1993–2002. Paper delivered at the RIPE 2004 Conference, Denmark.

Aslama, M., & Syvertsen, T. (forthcoming). Public Service Broadcasting And New Technologies: Marginalization Or Re-Monopolization? In E. de Bens, C. Hamelink, K. Jakubowicz, K. Nordenstreng, J. Van Cuilenburg & R. van der Wurff (Eds.), *Media between Culture and Commerce*. Bristol: Intellect Books.

Association of Commercial Television in Europe, et al. (2004). Safeguarding the Future of the European Audiovisual Market. A White Paper on the Financing and Regulation of Publicly Funded Broadcasters, Brussels.

Atkinson, D. (1997). Public Service Broadcasting: the Challenges of the Twenty-first Century. UNESCO, Paris.

BBC. (2004). Building Public Value. Renewing the BBC for a digital world. British Broadcasting Corporation, London.

Betzel, M. (forthcoming). Public Service Broadcasting in Europe: Distinctiveness, Remit and Programme Content Obligations. In E. de Bens, C. Hamelink, K. Jakubowicz, K. Nordenstreng, J. Van Cuilenburg & R. van der Wurff (Eds.), *Media between Culture and Commerce*. Bristol: Intellect Books.

Bardoel, J., & Brants, K. (2003). From Ritual to Reality. Public Broadcasters and Social Responsibility in the Netherlands. In T. Hujanen & G. Lowe (Eds.), *Broadcasting and Convergence: New Articulations of the Public Service Remit Gothenburg* (pp. 167–186). NORDICOM.

Collins, R., et al. (2001). Public Service Broadcasting Beyond 2000: Is there a Future for Public Service Broadcasting? *Canadian Journal of Communication*, 25, 3–15.

Collins, B. (2003). A New Future for Public Broadcasting. Speech at the conference in Wellington, New Zealand. Retrieved from www.newfuture.govt.nz/docs/SpeechByBob CollinsAtWellington.doc

Committee of Ministers. (2003). Recommendation Rec 9 on Measures to Promote the Democratic and Social Contribution of Digital Broadcasting, Strasbourg, Council of Europe. Retrieved from www.coe.int/T/E/Human_Rights/media

Easter Agreement. (June 2005). HilverSummary, Number 2. Hilversum: Netherlands Public Broadcasting. Retrieved from www.ebu.ch

EBU. (1998). The Public Service Broadcasting Remit: Today and Tomorrow.

EBU. (2002). Media with a purpose. Public Service Broadcasting in the digital era. The Report of the Digital Strategy Group of the European Broadcasting Union. Retrieved from www.ebu.ch

EBU. (2004). EBU contribution. Conference on The Key Role of Public Service Broadcasting in European society in the 21st Century" held in Amsterdam on 1–3 September. Retrieved from www.ebu.ch

European Commission. (2001). Communication from the Commission on the application of state aid rules to public service broadcasting. *Official Journal of the European Communities*, C 320, 5–11.

Harrison, J., & Woods, L. M. (2001). Defining European Public Service Broadcasting. *European Journal of Communication*, 16(4), 477–504.

Holznagel, B. (2000). The Mission of Public Service Broadcasters. Paper distributed at EU Colloquium on European Public Television in an Age of Economic and Technological Change held in Lille on 19–20 July.

Huntington, S. P. (1993). The Clash Of Civilizations. Foreign Affairs, 72(3), 22. Retrieved from www.alamut.com/subj/economics/misc/clash.html

Huntington, S. P. (2000). *Zderzenie cywilizacji I nowy kształt ładu wiatowego. Warszawa: Muza.*

Jakubowicz, K. (2003a). Bringing Public Service Broadcasting to Account. In T. Hujanen & G. Lowe (Ed.), *Broadcasting and Convergence: New Articulations of the Public Service Remit*. Gothenburg: NORDICOM.

Jakubowicz, K. (2003b). Endgame? Contracts, Audits and the Future of Public Service Broadcasting. *Javnost/The Public*, X(3), 45–62.

Jakubowicz, K. (2004). A Square Peg in a Round Hole: The EU's policy on Public Service Broadcasting. *Journal of Media Practice*, 4(3), 155–175.

Jakubowicz, K. (forthcoming). Public Service Broadcasting: a Pawn on an Ideological Chessboard. In E. de Bens, C. Hamelink, K. Jakubowicz, K. Nordenstreng, J. Van Cuilenburg & R. van der Wurff (Eds.), *Media between Culture and Commerce*. Bristol: Intellect Books.

Kapu ci ski, R. (6–7 August 2005). *Detronizacja Europy. Gazeta Wyborcza*, pp. 17–18.

Keane, J. (2001). Global Civil Society? In H. Anheier, M. Glasius & M. Kaldor (Eds.), *Global Civil Society 2001* (pp. 23–47). Oxford: Oxford University Press.

Kearns, I. (2003). A Mission to Empower: PSC. From Public Service Broadcasting to Public Service Communications. Speech presented on behalf of the Institute for Public Policy Research, Westminster e-Forum. Retrieved from www.ippr.org/research/files /team25/ project61/ WMFSpeech.doc

Maisami, M. (2003). Islam and Globalization, Fountain. Retrieved from www. fountainmagazine.com/articles.php?SIN=6c0bd092ca&k=33&1355021942&show=par t1 in August 2003

McKinsey & Company. (1999). Public Service Broadcasting Around the World. London.

McQuail, D. (1986). Commercialization. In D. McQuail & K. Siune (Eds.), *New Media Politics. Comparative Perspectives in Western Europe* (pp. 152–178). London: Sage Publications.

McQuail, D. (1998). Commercialization and beyond. In D. McQuail & K. Siune (Ed.), *Media Policy. Convergence, Concentration and Commerce. Euromedia Research Group* (pp. 107–127). London: Sage Publishers.

Meier, H. E. (2003). Beyond Convergence. Understanding Programming Strategies of Public Broadcasters in Competitive Environments. *European Journal of Communication*, 18(3), 337–366.

Monshipouri, M. (2005). "Identity and Human Rights in the Age of Globalization: Emerging Challenges in the Muslim World. Zaman Online. Retrieved from www. globalpolicy.org/globaliz/cultural/2005/0502identity.htm on 2 May 2005.

Murdock, G. (2001). Digital Divides. Communications policy and its contradictions. *New Economy*, 8 (2), 110–115.

Murdock, G., & Golding, P. (1999). Common Markets: Corporate Ambitions and Communication Trends in the UK and Europe. *Journal of Media Economics*, 12(2), 117–132.

Nissen, Ch. (2005). Public Service Broadcasting in the Information Society. Strasbourg, Council of Europe.

OFCOM. (2004a). Review of public service television broadcasting: Phase 1 – Is Television Special? London.

OFCOM. (24 November 2004b). Review of public service television broadcasting. Phase 2 – Meeting the digital challenge. London.

Picard, R. G. (2004). Why Should I Pay the License Fee? Issues of Viewers and Listeners as Customers in the Twenty-First Century. Paper delivered at the RIPE@2004 Conference in Denmark.

Silvo, I. (3 November 2003). Securing Access to Diverse Services and Content on Digital TV Platforms: Experiences of a Public Service Broadcaster, YLE of Finland. Paper delivered at a conference on Digital Television in Europe: What Prospects for the Public? held in the Council of Europe, Rome.

Smith, A. (1989). The Public Interest. *InterMedia*, 17(2), 10–24.

Siune, K., & Hulten, O. (1998). Does Public Broadcasting Have a Future. In D. McQuail & K. Siune (Eds.), *Media Policy. Convergence, Consolidation and Commerce* (pp. 23–37). London: Sage Publications.

Syvertsen, T. (1999). The Many Uses of the "Public Service" Concept. *NORDICOM Review*, 20(1), 5–12.

The Impact of Digital Television on the Supply of Programmes. (1998). A Report for the European Broadcasting Union. Arthur Andersen.

Thomass, B. (2003). Knowledge Society and Public Sphere. Two Concepts for the Remit. In T. Hujanen & G. Lowe (Eds.), *Broadcasting and Convergence: New Articulations of the Public Service Remit* (pp. 29–39). Gothenburg: NORDICOM.

Van der Bulck, W. (2001). Public service television and national identity as a project of modernity: the example of Flemish television. *Media, Culture and Society*, 23(1), 53–69.

VPRT., et al. (2003). Broadcasting and Competition Rules in the Future EU Constitution – a View from the Private Media Sector. Retrieved from www.vprt.de/dateien/ sn_020503_verbaende_zu_eu_konvent.pdf

Ward, D. (2002). The European Union, Democratic Deficit and the Public Sphere. An Evaluation of EU Media Policy. Ohmsha, Amsterdam: IOS Press.

Ward, D. (2003). State aid or band aid? An evaluation of the European Commission's approach to public service broadcasting. *Media, Culture & Society*, 25(2), 233–250.

Waters, M. (1995). *Globalization*. London: Routledge.

Wessberg, A. (2000). "Public Service Broadcasting, Information Society and Small Markets Paper". Presented at a conference on "Public Service Broadcasting. The Digital and Online Challenge", London, 28–29 February.

Exploring a Conceptual Model for Public Service Television Programming

In this chapter I will first explore the promise and problems of Public Television before laying out a conceptual model for Public Service Television. As discussed in earlier chapters, public service television programming can be broadly interpreted to categorize all television programming content (irrespective of point of origin), that is created and delivered in the interest of the general public/common audience without any necessary profit motives. The purpose of such programming is usually enrichment, information, entertainment or education of the audiences. Public Service programming can be of two kinds on any television channel. The first is where a separate network exists for such programming. The existing models of this type are usually government owned in most developing countries and autonomous corporations under indirect government regulation in other countries. A concept of such an exclusive network dedicated to public service broadcasting usually limits the free market model.

The second kind of public service broadcasting (PSB) is where such programming is embedded in private channels that operate on the free market model—public service programming is encouraged on such channels through government subsidies, policy regulations and other concessions. Such models create more problems than they solve.

For the purpose of this chapter, the assumption of PSB is of a separate dedicated network that is devoted exclusively to such programming. An ideal public television network, (by virtue of its lacking the profit-making "requirement" unlike "commercial" television), conjures up images of pristine, television content, on the "socially" right path, uncorrupted by any common biases inherent in privately-owned, commercial television. Public service television is in the "public interest" and so is usually on the opposite end of the spectrum from "commercial" television that works overtime to maximize its programme ratings to attract the most money (usually from advertising).

Almost every country has experimented with some form of public television. In India (as discussed in chapter six), public television conjures up images of social development and nation-building programming on Doordarshan (especially since the SITE days to the pre-satellite television era). In the United Kingdom, public service broadcasters like BBC, ITV and Channel Four cater not only to British and European audiences with well-appreciated current affairs programming but are also well known to global audiences with their enriching programming.

In the United States of America, public television brings to mind images of classical music, the Lehrer News hour and award winning programming like Nova, Nature, Scientific American and Frontline. However, public television also brings to mind hours and hours of pledge drives soliciting contributions to make possible the programming it brings to its audiences in the USA while in India, it is replete with instances of bureaucratic interference, political pressures and boring programming. The biggest problem of a subsidized network that is propped up with government or subsidized support is that of sustaining viewer interest.

The promise of public service programming

In the parlance of economics, a good television programme is a "merit" good, similar to education, training and health services. Left to the market forces, it is possible that purely commercial broadcasting will not meet the full needs of public service broadcasting. This is because commercial broadcasting regards the audience as consumers, and not as citizens.

In a poor and developing country like India, this distinction has considerable implications, since the market power or purchasing power of a large segment of the population is small. Moreover, the information and education needs of this segment of the population may not be met by commercial broadcasting. Hence the need for public service broadcasting.

– Report of the Review Committee on the Work (Clause 2.1.6)

– www.scatmag.com/govt per cent20policies/rcpb1.htm –

Public service television promises a lot in an "ideal" context. Most of it seems utopian but is in the realm of possibility. The lofty goals of television content presented, most of the time with a non-profit motive, are seemingly unsustainable if not unattainable in an era of corporate privatization, commercial globalization, competitive greed, capital-intensive infrastructure needs and audience narrowcasting.

However, with the right mix of political intention, programming autonomy, public participation and availability of funding, public service television does have the potential to live up to the promise of providing rich entertainment that is informative, educating and above all enriching in the public interest. In addition, in an era of trans-national corporate dominance and the decline of the powerful nation-state, it does have the capacity to act as a community watchdog and provide a forum (global/national/local) for public activism and public participation.

The promise of public television especially lies in its potential to engage the common audience in the larger political process. The basic purpose of public television should be to enrich, entertain and empower the audience by generating debates and activism in the public sphere. By setting in place a three or four-tiered television network/s, at the nation-state-city and community levels, public television can make the political process transparent by acting as a watchdog (a role earlier demarcated to the Fourth estate); providing access to government policy generation processes and promoting public participation and debate in its channels. A number of television channels from Australia's ABC TV, India's Doordarshan, USA's C-SPAN and local access TV and Britain's BBC have channel time devoted to telecast senate/parliamentary proceedings. One of the best examples, that I have seen, of public television facilitating public participation and acting as a watchdog, was the "Mukyamantri tho Mukhamukhi" (Face to face with the Chief Minister) television programme in Telugu on Hyderabad Doordarshan when Naravarapally Chandrababu Naidu was the Chief Minister[1] of this southern state in India[2].

This question and answer session was live with the Chief Minister of Andhra Pradesh answering questions of viewers every week (Mondays at 7 p.m.) for half an hour. Any viewer from any part of the state could dial into the programme with their questions and the Chief Minister would answer it live on air. Viewers usually would call in with their problems and/ or complain about inaction of bureaucrats in their particular case and the Chief Minister would try to act on it immediately or get back to the caller with action taken in that instance. This prompted a positive public reaction

---

[1] Equivalent to the elected head of the state government.
[2] This very successful programme was discontinued after Mr Naidu's party, the Telugu Desam, lost the elections and the Congress party came to power in the recent elections in the state in 2004.

and forced the slow government machinery to deal with people's issues faster for fear of being bought to the attention of the Chief Minister.

For any public television to facilitate public participation, there will be crucial issues to determine—especially of political and programming autonomy, professional training, acquisition and maintenance of infrastructure, existence of an independent regulatory authority/framework, provisions for annual funding/auditing process and the most important—allowing for free access and voluntary public participation.

Problems of public service television

Such promise (as laid out above) is not without its perils. The potential and promise of public television can only be realized if the possible problems and pitfalls are acknowledged and tackled. These differ from country to country and network to network.

In India, for instance, television made its beginning for the express purpose of social programming and nation building. From SITE to INSAT to EduSat, the goals are still expressly stated in Doordarshan's policy even though the ground realities in practice are much different. In an arena where private players outnumber the public networks, the odds are still stacked in favor of Doordarshan by sheer virtue of its free-to-air reach to nearly 100 per cent of the geographical area that is India (read also chapter six).

However, various scholars have pointed out the problems in Doordarshan's programming—from promoting certain points of view over others (including of its own notion of national identity); constant bureaucratic interference; excessive political pressures; lack of professional training and code of ethics; and holistically lack of a larger vision and policy itself. Trying to compete with commercial, private players for advertising share of the markets only takes away from Doordarshan's stated purpose of nation-building and social development.

Instead of trying to compete for advertising dollars, Doordarshan should stick to what it does best and that is television programming for nation building. While the SITE[3] programmes in the 1970s were a big step forward in this direction, a number of instances exist of other development programming on Doordarshan that served its nation-building purpose. The best examples I can think of are the various agricultural, health and social programmes shown on Doordarshan. The Educational Multimedia Research Centres (EMMRC's) also do a good job with producing the educational programming required for the University Grants Commission's (UGC) educational channel.

---

[3] Satellite Instructional Television Experiment.

Model for public service television programming

In an era of globalization, when media saturation (irrespective of the country of origin) is fast becoming the norm rather than the exception, it is important to delineate certain standards for Public Service Programming. The specific model for all countries cannot be the same. The below model (see figure) can be the broad basis of implementation of an effective and viable programming standard for Public Service television but only if it is contextualized to the specific needs of each nation based on its own socio-political-economic-cultural idiosyncrasies.

The three key players in this model are the state, the public and the autonomous regulatory body created to oversee the public service broadcasting setup. These are obviously overseen by the constitutional framework of the particular nation and hence are all subject to the laws of the land. In this model these three players are shown in a symbiotic relationship with each other but at the same time each is tasked with at least one aspect of the 3 P's of programming—Policy, Process and Participation that are again influenced by each other[4].

The state

The state is obviously the key player in this process and it is only if it has the political will to implement such a process that this model can be implemented. Once put into place, the state will continue to be a key player in determining the future direction of the television environment in the nation.

In this model, the state is tasked with determining and setting the future national communication policy of the nation (including television). It includes policy planning and investment in infrastructure and technology that will enable the dissemination of television across the nation and make it easily accessible to all its citizens. The policy should be periodically revised to keep pace with national, global and technological changes and be done in consultation with the other key players—the Regulatory body and the Public.

Indian television is a good example of how a futuristic communication policy is very important for successful public television. Indian television was in the forefront of using programming for nation building and social development when it conducted the SITE experiment in the 1970s (refer to chapter six). However, in subsequent years, it lost track of its goals when

---

[4] Private, for-profit, television channels are deliberately kept out of this model as they are out of the scope of this discussion.

Figure 1
3 P's Model for Public Service Programming – Muppidi

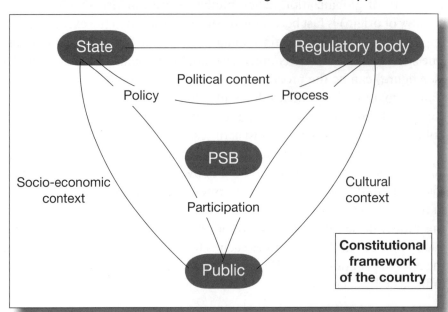

a communication policy (or lack of it) focused exclusively on hardware (in setting goals of number of transmitters per year) and didn't plan much for programming. However, things seem to be on an upturn after Doordarshan became autonomous with the formation of the Prasar Bharati Corporation. The commercial revenue earned by Doordarshan has been substantial (see Table 1).

The Prasar Bharati Corporation has been putting in place different acts and policies for the television industry in India that lay down rules and regulations for all television players (domestic and foreign) operating inside the national boundaries. Apart from restoring some order to the cable television industry, a new division called the "development communication division" was formed within Doordarshan to make social development programmes and cater to the programming needs of all public service agencies in the country. In addition the proposal to implement Direct-to-Home (DTH) satellite television in the country is also a step forward in the right direction for putting in place a visionary communication policy.

One big caveat is that the state should not interfere directly or exert control over the PSB network on a day-to-day basis or else this model is doomed to fail.

Table 1
Commercial Revenue by Network and Major Kendras in India
1995–1996 to 2002–2003 (Rs. in Million)

Networks/Kendras	1995 –1996	1996 –1998	1997 –1998	1998 –1999	1999 –2000	2000 –2001	2001 –2002	2002 –2003
Networks								
National Network	1879.7	2835.5	2638.8	2115.5	3175	2591	3305.5	2699.6
Metro Network	795.4	1027.4	937.9	735.1	461.8	872.9	823.2	227.7
DD Sports	—	—	—	—	896.8	719.9	698.3	923.4
DD India	—	—	5.4	4.7	14.7	12.1	14.9	6.8
Kendras								
Delhi	241.8	180.4	49.3	58.1	81.1	67.2	95.2	122.3
Lucknow	41.1	35.3	28	31	41.4	32	41	32.6
Jaipur	5.2	9.3	9.2	12.1	17	19.3	32.2	33.6
Jalandhar	26.6	24.6	25	50.2	43	47.3	70.4	86.3
Mumbai	184.3	261.7	144.9	142.5	147.6	143.4	181.9	180.3
Ahmedabad	40.1	31.4	19	27.8	28.9	38	40.8	55.5
Bhopal	8.9	8.9	9.7	18.1	14.8	17	24.7	22.9
Chennai	404.5	428.3	276.4	147	185.2	72	75.1	101.9
Hyderabad	183	241.3	181	146.2	194.4	128.7	90.8	122.5
Bangalore	189.6	262.8	219.7	137.3	167.6	84.3	136.2	136.2
Thiruvananthapuram	144.1	167.1	166	153.1	201.7	162.4	148.1	131
Calcutta	140.9	177.5	155.8	168	258.4	299.2	277.4	217.9
Bhubaneshwar	8.5	23.7	20.5	20.1	18.3	27.3	31.9	37.8
Guwahati	4.8	9	7.6	9.8	10.7	15.8	21.7	46.7
Patna	1.5	3	6.4	12	8.6	18.4	22	11.7

Source: Doordarshan India 2003, Prasar Bharati, Broadcasting Corporation of India & Past Issue.

Regulatory body

The regulatory body is proposed as an autonomous entity that will directly oversee the television environment in the nation and will be responsible for the larger regulation and licensing of all television-related matters within the country. It will oversee the functioning of the private players also in matters of licensing and implementing the code of ethics. I see this entity as a combination of the Federal Communications Commission (FCC) and the Corporation of Public Broadcasting (CPB) in the United States of America with all their responsibilities.

The FCC is an independent United States government agency, directly responsible to Congress. The FCC was established by the Communications Act of 1934 and is charged with regulating interstate and international communications by radio, television, wire, satellite and cable. The FCC's jurisdiction covers the 50 US states, the District of Columbia, and US possessions. The FCC is directed by five Commissioners appointed by the President and confirmed by the Senate for five-year terms, except when filling an unexpired term. The President designates one of the Commissioners to serve as Chairperson. Only three Commissioners may be members of the same political party. None of them can have a financial interest in any Commission-related business. As the chief executive officer of the Commission, the Chairman delegates management and administrative responsibility to the Managing Director. The Commissioners supervise all FCC activities, delegating responsibilities to staff units and Bureaus. In a two-party system like the US has, this is easy to implement but still runs into controversies[5].

The CPB is also a private, non-profit corporation created by Congress in 1967. The basic goal of the CPB in the US is to enhance the value, utility and effectiveness of Public Television to the masses. All its goals and objectives strive to enhance that in every way. As per the mission statement of the CPB adopted in July 1999:

> The mission of CPB is to facilitate the development of, and ensure universal access to, non-commercial high-quality programming and telecommunications services. It does this in conjunction with non-commercial educational telecommunications licensees across America. The fundamental purpose of public telecommunications is to provide programmes and services which inform, enlighten and enrich the public. While these programmes and services are provided to enhance the knowledge, and citizenship, and inspire the imagination of all Americans, the Corporation has particular responsibility to encourage the development of programming that involves creative risks and that addresses the needs of unserved and underserved audiences, particularly children and minorities. The Corporation is accountable to the public for investing its funds in programmes and services which are educational, innovative, locally relevant, and reflective of America's common values and cultural diversity. The Corporation serves as a catalyst for innovation in the public broadcasting industry, and acts as a guardian of the mission and purposes for which public broadcasting was established[6].

---

[5] As per the FCC website. Retrieved on 27 December 2004 from www.fcc.gov/aboutus. html

[6] As per the mission statement of the CPB. Retrieved on 27 December 2004 from www.cpb. org/about/corp/mission.html

The funding for public television comes from membership fees (the largest chunk); appropriation funds from the federal government; and corporate sponsors like local businesses and foundations. The licensing and all regulations are overseen by the FCC. The model I am suggesting calls for the integration of both these entities into one single body. This is more effective in societies outside the US especially because they cannot hope to have the large membership resources and donor support from corporate houses that public television has in the USA.

The Indian model of the Prasar Bharati Corporation, as an autonomous corporation, to oversee television policy and programming in the country is ideal except for two things. First, it needs to move away from having political appointments at the top decision-making levels which is the norm now. This only leads to each political party in power stacking the board with its "own" people thereby discouraging independence.

Secondly, it needs to have its own employees instead of borrowing from the Indian bureaucracy. The process of having administrators appointed from the Indian bureaucracy discourages innovation and motivation among the employees. Also, most of these appointments are on a fixed-term basis after which they are reverted back to other government organizations. This does not encourage anyone to take a long-term interest in the growth of this organization.

IN "TRANSITION", PBS FORGES AHEAD

I do not think we're in crisis, and I certainly don't think we're in peril. I think we're in transition. But I'm very optimistic and bullish about our future ... I know what the threats are ... but I just sort of think it's an incredibly defendable brand. PBS, on the most feeble of budgets, produces what is more or less generally accepted to be the best public affairs, the best science, the best nature, the best children's and, I'm told, the best history programming out there. That's pretty terrific.

– Pat Mitchell, President, Public Broadcasting Service (2004)

– USA Today, 9 July 2004 –

Programming

In this proposed "integrated" model the regulatory body is also tasked with overseeing the process of day-to-day implementation of the policy and production of public service television programming. The ideal structure for Public Service television in this model is seen as four-tiered at the national, state, city (or province) and the local community levels. This body will have the programming autonomy and will be tasked with developing the infrastructure and resources for the network. While composition of this regulatory body will be through a panel of experts selected/nominated equally by the state, the public and the press, care should be taken to keep the panel professional and unbiased[7]. The employees for this organization should constitute a separate cadre that is limited to this organization. The specifics can be worked out on a country-by-country basis. Funding for this body can be derived from annual licensing fees, government funds, and from a percentage of the annual tax revenues on private television players in the same markets. The regulatory body should also be subject to an independent auditing process.

The production of programming can be a combination of in-house programming, sponsored programming and commissioned programming from a list of qualified professionals. This programming should cater to the diversity in the nation and be archived in an appropriate, readily accessible manner. Again the specific details need to be worked out on a country-by-country basis.

The content of the programmes should be decided on two criteria—the demographic composition of the population and the programming objectives of the network. Based on demographic criteria, there should be a certain percentage of mandatory programming for linguistic, religious and social minorities and other sections of society that need special attention. As part of their licensing requirements, the private players in the market can also be mandated to provide a certain percentage of their programming to cater to specified sections of society. The specifics can be worked out based on the society and its idiosyncratic needs. While I have not seen any national network that presently follows this model, an indirect version of this is where the government funds public television through federal grants using taxpayer money. A big criticism of FCC in the USA is that it does not auction spectrum space and instead just collects a license fee. This option can be explored as a viable alternative in other countries.

The BBC in UK, Doordarshan in India, public television in the USA represents all examples of how this works. A look at Doordarshan's programming structure reveals regional, language, socio-cultural, age and gender diversity in programming content aimed at different demographics of the national audience in India.

A more recent example is that of Maori television in New Zealand. Initially a lot of hue and cry was raised about public taxpayer money being

---

[7] Steps should be especially taken to avoid all conflict of interest.

MAORI TV REPORTS SUCCESSFUL FIRST YEAR

Auckland: Maori Television has reported a successful first full year as a New Zealand broadcaster, meeting its objectives and posting a surplus of $3.2 million.

In its annual report, released today, Chairman Wayne Walden said it was the leading broadcaster in terms of local programming content.

Locally-made programmes comprised more than 90 per cent of its schedule and the production Pepi won best information programme in the Qantas Awards.

Walden said *te reo* Maori was at the core of Maori TV's purpose, and 71 per cent of its programmes were in Maori, with 67 per cent during prime time.

At the end of the 2005 financial year there was a surplus of $3.2 million and its bank loan repayments were two years ahead of schedule.

"We enter 2005/06 still in our infancy but nevertheless in a strong position and with a clear and relevant strategy for a sustainable, successful future," Walden said.

Chief executive Jim Mather said a significant achievement was the creation of a cultural advisory team of 10 kaumatua.

"We are able to receive independent guidance on how we are operating the channel from the perspective of many of those who contributed to its establishment."

He said "an obvious measure of customer satisfaction was ratings".

The number of viewers increased from a monthly cumulative average of 327,800 in July 2004 to a peak of 426,300 in April this year.

Cumulative averages count viewers who have tuned in at least once over a period, and are not comparable with rating figures used by the other channels.

– NZ Herald Online/Pacific Media Watch –

allocated to fund a public television regional channel[8] but recent reports have suggested that Maori television is more popular with non-Maori viewers (more than 65 per cent of its viewers are non-Maoris)[9].

The public

The common people in any nation are/should be the ultimate beneficiaries of any Public Service Television Network. What the public desire should be an important consideration in programming but with reasonable limits to avoid pandering by the network. It is with that reason that the public

---

[8] See press release of the New Zealand National Party "Taxpayers funding second Maori TV Channel" dated 23 March 2004.

[9] See "Maori TV has widespread appeal" dated 24 June 2004 and accessed from tvnz.co.nz/ view/news_national_story_skin/432629

has been accorded an equally important role in this process. At every tier of the four-tiered structure of public television there are avenues built in for public participation. While public participation is assumed directly and indirectly in composition of the state and the regulatory body, it is important (especially at the community level) to ensure not only the transparency of government and public officials but also community involvement and public activism. At the community level, local non-profit and educational organizations should be encouraged to get involved in programming and community volunteers can help to staff most of the non-core positions on a day-to-day basis. I see this as a combination of the C-SPAN and community channels in the United States.

The C-SPAN (Cable Services Public Affairs Network) was created by the cable television industry in the USA as a public service to their viewers. The stated goal of C-SPAN was to provide open access to their audiences to the live proceedings in both houses of Congress without any form of censorship or editing. In addition, the network provides elected and other "Public" officials a direct channel to reach audiences in a similar manner. Some of the popular programmes on C-SPAN include call in shows where audiences call in to express their opinions and ask questions to featured public policymakers and officials. This practice is now also seen in other nations wherein parliamentary proceedings are broadcast live.

In addition, the local access channels in the USA are local community based channels that are usually staffed and run by volunteers in each community. Most everyone is allowed to make programmes and broadcast them on the local access channels. These channels are also used to relay the live proceedings of all town and public meetings in the community. The videotapes of such programming are later made available (for anyone interested) at the local public libraries.

This is an especially important feature of public television, as by involving the local communities in day-to-day programming, public television will not only ensure that it is catering to the needs of the community but also encourage the people to get involved in community issues. This will only empower and encourage public activism and ensure an independent community watchdog that is so essential in the present age of corporate dominance.

Conclusion

While my intention is not to give excessive credence to the notion of media centrality, I do wish to point out that within a certain socio-cultural-political context; public television can still be effectively harnessed to achieve its goals—Entertainment, Enrichment, and Empowerment.

Even in a country like India that has witnessed a phenomenal media explosion and has numerous private channels today, Doordarshan still reaches the most number of the people in the country compared to any other channel (see Table 2).

While most of the private channels concentrate on programming for the Indian, educated, middle class that can afford to pay for consumer products and thereby increase each channel's advertising revenue, Doordarshan is more the "common man's" television network reaching everyone alike. It still continues to enrich and entertain but has a long way to go before it can make really thought provoking and empowering programmes. Its main problems are the lack of a vision to make a difference and the lack of a will to be the best.

Some of the suggested strategies should explore and incorporate solutions to the following, as a starting point.

1. Allow freedom from "political" authority

The term "political" here is intended to mean freedom from all "vested" interests that might control. While there is a feeling that public television in the USA is independent, critics of the Corporation for Public Broadcasting (CPB) do feel that there is an inner coterie that makes money while the real "independents" are left out in the cold. The recent controversy with "political" appointments to the CPB only adds to the muddle and prevents an independent functioning of the network.

2. Build in sources of "independent" revenue

In a country like India, a percentage of the profits of all private channels can be used to sustain and fund a public service channel, possibly on the lines of C-SPAN, in the USA. The idea can be further extended to allow infrastructure development at the local community levels too. One of the models that the Indian government is exploring is to provide Doordarshan with tangible assets like transferring ownership of the real estate on which its offices and studios are located. This could be used by Doordarshan as collateral to raise needed revenue or loans from banks, etc for development purposes. However such a revenue generation model depends a lot on the "vision" of the administration which has historically been a major problem with Doordarshan. However, such a model does hold promise in other societies.

3. Community television

Infrastructure needs to be provided to local communities to encourage participation in public forums and bring in transparency to the political

Table 2
TVR and Share of DD and Private Satellite Channels in India
(as at 11–17 January 2004)

Channel	All 4+ YRS			CS 4+ YRS		
	000's	TVR %	Share %	000's	TVR %	Share %
(2100–2300 h: all days)						
DD1	13085	9.06	33.18	850	0.99	3.46
Sony Entertainment TV	1771	1.23	4.49	1771	2.06	7.2
Star Plus	5485	3.8	13.91	5485	6.39	22.3
Zee TV	630	0.44	1.6	630	0.73	2.56
Sun TV	1779	1.23	4.51	1779	2.07	7.23
DD Bharati	16	0.01	0.04	16	0.02	0.06
DD News	799	0.55	2.03	142	0.17	0.58
Watching Other Channels	15867	10.99	40.24	13922	16.23	56.6
Watching Any Channel	39432	27.31	100	24595	28.67	100
(0700–2300 h: all days)						
DD1	3490	2.42	17.29	240	0.28	1.78
Sony Entertainment TV	483	0.33	2.39	483	0.56	3.59
Star Plus	1775	1.23	8.79	1775	2.07	13.18
Zee TV	361	0.25	1.79	361	0.42	2.68
Sun TV	1171	0.81	5.8	1171	1.36	8.7
DD Bharati	8	0.01	0.04	8	0.01	0.06
DD News	521	0.36	2.58	79	0.09	0.59
Watching other channels	12378	8.57	61.32	9348	10.89	69.42
Watching any channel	20187	13.98	100	13465	15.69	100
(Sun: 0900–1300 h)						
DD1	5327	3.69	30.9	483	0.56	4.24
Sony Entertainment TV	256	0.18	1.49	256	0.3	2.25
Star Plus	353	0.24	2.05	184	0.41	1.61
Zee TV	184	0.13	1.07	951	0.21	8.35
Sun TV	951	0.66	5.51	1	1.11	0.01
DD Bharati	1	0	0.01	80	0	0.7
DD News	329	0.23	1.91	9086	0.09	79.74
Watching other channels	9842	6.82	57.08	11394	10.59	100
Watching any channel	17243	11.94	100	13.28		
Universe in '000	144,376	85,800				

Source : Lok Sabha Unstarred Question No. 3355, dated 5 February 2004

process. This is a process that takes time but is important to nurture and sustain. UNESCO's concept of developing "knowledge societies" is one such step that will enable a lot of community networks to be set up and they can be integrated to provide relevant participation in this process. However, governments that have gone out of their way to encourage private, corporate players (domestic and foreign) to start private channels have shown an odd reluctance to allow local citizen communities to start their own community radio and television networks.

4. Regulatory framework

An independent regulatory authority, with its own code of ethics, its own powers to penalize, and which is truly independent of the political and bureaucratic process is important to make this process sustainable. It is also important for this authority to have its own "employee recruitment system" independent of any outside influence. This "independence" will also allow employees to be motivated and objective and be interested in the proper functioning of this authority.

5. Community empowerment

This should be the stated objective irrespective of the shorter goals or objectives of every programme. An empowered community and a transparent political process are the best bets in a globalized world. After all, community activism in the public sphere is the best antidote to trans-national globalization.

This model assumes an environment that has the larger political intention to see such a process take place effectively. Any model is only as successful as the intention of those who have the power to ultimately implement it and this is no exception.

References

Agrawal, A. (15 April 1994). Opening up at last. *India Today*, pp. 108–119.

Ang, I. (1990). The nature of the audience. In J. Downing, A. Mohammadi & S. Mohammadi (Eds.), *Questioning the media: A critical introduction* (pp. 155–165). Newbury Park, CA: Sage.

Karp, J. (1994). TV Times. *Far Eastern Economic Review*, 157 (50).

Kumar, K. J. (2004). *Mass Communication in India.* New Delhi: Jaico Books.

Kumar, K. (1998). History of television in India: A political economy perspective. In S. R. Melkote, P. Shields & B. C. Agrawal (Ed.). *International broadcasting in South Asia: Political, economic and cultural implications* (pp. 17–46). New York: University Press of America.

Luthra, H. K. (1986). *Indian broadcasting.* New Delhi: Publications Division.

Malhan, P. N. (1985). *Communication media: Yesterday, today and tomorrow.* Meerut, India: Link Printers.

Melkote, S. R., Sanjay, B. P., & Ahmed, S. A. (1998). Use of STAR TV and Doordarshan in India: An audience-centered case study of Chennai city. In S. R. Melkote, P. Shields & B. C. Agrawal (Eds.). *International broadcasting in South Asia: Political, economic and cultural implications* (pp. 157–179). New York: University Press of America.

Melkote, S. R., Sanjay, B. P. & Kumar, D. (1996). Relative impact of STAR TV and Doordarshan in India: An audience-centered case study of Madras, India. Paper presented to the participatory communication division of the International Association for Mass communication Research at Sydney, Australia in August 1996.

Mitra, A. (1993). Television and the nation: Doordarshan's India. *Media Asia*, 20(1), 39–44.

Mody, B. (1988). The commercialization of TV in India: A research agenda for cross-country comparisons. Paper presented at International Communication Association, Intercultural and Development Communication Division.

Muppidi, S. R. (1998). The Uses and Gratifications of Doordarshan and Eenadu TV: A Study of a Regional Indian Television Audience. Doctoral Dissertation, Bowling Green State University.

Pathania, G. (1994). Ambivalence in a STAR-ry eyed land: Doordarshan and the satellite TV challenge. *South Asia Graduate Research Journal*, 1(1).

Pendakur, M. (1990). A political economy of television: State, class, and corporate confluence in India. In G. Sussman & J. A. Lent (Eds.), *Transnational communications: Wiring the Third World*. Newbury Park: Sage.

Rahman, H. R. (Fall 1998). Uses and gratifications of satellite TV Egypt. TBS Archives, 1, 2. Retrieved from TBS Archives Database.

Rajagopal, A. (1993). The rise of national programming: The case of Indian television. *Media, Culture and Society*, 15, 91–111.

Rao, S. (1998). The New Doordarshan: Facing the challenges of cable and satellite networks in India. In S. R. Melkote, P. Shields & B. C. Agrawal (Eds.). *International broadcasting in South Asia: Political, economic and cultural implications* (pp. 47–59). New York: University Press of America.

Rao, S. (1999).The rural-urban dichotomy of Doordarshan's programming in India: An empirical analysis, *Gazette*, 61(1), 23–37.

Rao, S., & Melkote, S. R. (1998). Viewing of Doordarshan by cable subscribers in Bangalore, India: Is there a difference with non-subscribers? In S. R. Melkote, P. Shields, & B. C. Agrawal (Eds.), *International broadcasting in South Asia: Political, economic and cultural implications* (pp. 181–203). New York: University Press of America.

Rao, S., & Muppidi, S. R. (2005). Impact of Cable on Network Television in Liberalized India. *Journal of Communication Studies*.

Shields, P., & Muppidi, S. R. (1996). Integration, the Indian state and STAR TV: Policy and theory issues. *Gazette*, 58(1), 1–24.

Singhal, A., & Rogers, E. (1989). *India's information revolution*. New Delhi: Sage.

Skinner, E. C., Melkote, S. R., & Muppidi, S. R. (1998). Dynamics of satellite broadcasting in India and other areas: An introduction. In S. R. Melkote, P. Shields & B. C. Agrawal (Eds.). *International broadcasting in South Asia: Political, economic and cultural implications* (pp. 1–18). New York: University Press of America.

Vilanilam, J. (1989). Television advertising and the Indian poor. *Media, Culture & Society*, 11, 485–497.

Yadava, J. S., & Reddi, U. V. (1988). In the midst of diversity: Television in urban Indian homes. In J. Lull (Ed.), *World Families Watch Television* (pp. 25–34). Newbury Park: Sage.

Legal and Regulatory Aspects of Public Service Broadcasting

It would be no exaggeration to say that the success and viability of any system of public service broadcasting depends decisively on the regulatory regime within which it is allowed to operate. Recent years have seen a welter of alternative approaches being mooted in this area, and the discussion has, not surprisingly, been influenced by multiple considerations, including those of a political, economic, technological, and social nature. The advent of globalization, with the consequent decline of statist ideologies worldwide, has also cast a shadow on this discussion, with increasing scepticism being expressed about the usefulness of conventional, government-dominated, models of public service broadcasting. This chapter will examine some of the regulatory challenges which face contemporary policymakers and campaigners alike, and assess the impact they might have on the changing media landscape.

Definitional issues

A debate about public service broadcasting (PSB) is in reality a debate about the philosophical, ideological and cultural underpinnings of society and about the role of the state and the public sector in meeting the needs of individuals and society as a whole. This, rather than technological developments, may be the decisive factor in determining the future of PSB. In many European countries PSB is still the major broadcaster and audiovisual producer, performing its proper role defined in the many documents on the subject. The challenge today is how to preserve what has been described as one of the key socio-political and media institutions developed by Western European democracies in the 20th century in a form suited to the conditions of the 21st century.

– *Public service broadcasting, report of the Committee on –*
Culture, Science and Education, Parliamentary Assembly,
Council of Europe, January 2004

At the outset, it is worth turning our attention to an important preliminary issue, which has sometimes confounded policymakers and media practitioners alike, and which, if left unclarified, has the potential to skew regulatory thinking on public service broadcasting. This relates to the meaning of the term "public interest" which, as will be widely accepted, is inextricably linked to the concept of PSB. The matter goes well beyond a question of semantics; its importance has been underlined, among others, by media scholars Monroe Price and Marc Raboy (2003: 167) in their recent work on PSB:

> Much has been written about the idea of public interest. It is intriguing to try to determine the relationship between the phrase "public service" and the phrase "public interest". It may well be that the term public interest exists, primarily in the US discourse, to describe those activities which are imposed upon private broadcasters in their partial function as trustees of the public airwaves. In this sense, the term "public interest" could be said to be a marker for what we call … a system of "distributed public service" where the functions are performed by public, private and mixed entities. The term "public interest" is also deceptively bland. It bears within it the mark of being readily defined, decent and generally acceptable. It is, however, culturally specific, contentious and disguises important possible areas of debate about the range of dissent, questions of pluralism, gender and the allocation or redistribution of resources.

A number of elements, which comprise the public interest in relation to broadcasting have been identified over the years. Price and Raboy (2003: 168) cite the following principles contained in a list compiled in Ireland.

- Broadcasting is expected to serve the "public interest" or "general welfare" by carrying out tasks that contribute to the wider and longer-term benefits of society as a whole.
- Broadcast programmes should be available to the whole population.
- Broadcast programmes should cater for all interests and tastes.
- Minorities should receive particular provision.
- Broadcasters should recognize their special relationship to the sense of national identity.
- Broadcasting should be distanced from all vested interests and in particular from those of the government of the day.
- The public guidelines for broadcasting should be designed to liberate rather than restrict the programme maker.

While many of these principles will find widespread acceptance, the list is not without contention. At a policy level, it begs the question, for example, as to how far broadcasters should be required to go in ensuring provision for minorities—an issue which is devilishly difficult to answer in conflict-ridden societies. At the level of semantics, there can be a wide—even mutually irreconcilable—range of opinions on what is "designed to liberate rather than restrict" a programme maker.

The situation is made more complicated by the fact that even the continuing relevance of the word "public" in relation to PSB has begun to be called into question in recent times. Werner Rumphorst (2003), the author of a "model" PSB law, bemoans the fact that, over the years, public broadcasting has become synonymous in many minds with "state-funded" broadcasting, "with the underlying assumption that it must be close to, if not a mouthpiece of, the government". This, he argues, would be a fallacy given that PSB is "anything but "state", "government" or "official" broadcasting".

Holland (2003) has argued that the traditional notion of the "public" as comprising a national public, i.e. citizens of a nation, needs to be re-thought, given the increasingly trans-national character of broadcasting. Speaking in the British context, she points out that:

> The media giants who will be buying into UK television as the Communications Act becomes law, are not confined to nations. They seek out high profile programming which aims to appeal to publics much wider than the national ... The attempt to address smaller publics within a nation becomes more difficult in the face of this sort of pressure.
>
> (2003: 9–10)

She also notes, pertinently, that "the public of the Internet is both dispersed and trans-national, often building on cultural, linguistic and kinship links which reach well beyond national boundaries" (2003: 10). "Public service" therefore needs, she urges, "to address trans-national forms of citizenship and participation".

These are but a few examples of the definitional problems that bedevil public service broadcasting. Not surprisingly, the lack of a consensus on some the fundamental issues has meant that it is impossible to reach agreement on a global template—or even a set of global guidelines—for the legal regulation of PSB. Each country will, therefore, have to be left, at least for the foreseeable future, to determine the parameters and the details of its own regulatory regime, based on a number of local factors.

Even so, it is arguable that there are at least three essential features of PSB which distinguish it from other forms of broadcasting. In the words of Graham (2005: 10), they are as follows:

> First, (PSB) has purposes that are different from those of the market. Second, these purposes—in particular, to inform, to educate and to

entertain—apply across genres rather than being restricted to a particular genre. Third, it must be free at the point of use to everyone.

These elements find reflection in national and international law, including Resolutions and Declarations passed at inter-governmental forums in recent years, as will be described below.

Compatibility of PSB and commercial media

The traditional dichotomy between public sector, i.e. state-sponsored, broadcasting and commercial broadcasting in relation to PSB is fast disappearing. There is an increasing realization that PSB is best promoted by a combination of—including partnerships between—public and commercial broadcasters, and this has meant some important changes to the regulatory approaches adopted by governments. The European Union has, for example, accepted that that while EU member-states "value highly public service broadcasting as a main guardian of freedom of information, pluralism and cultural diversity ... public broadcasting must respect the basic ground rules of a market economy that ensure a healthy development of the dual system"[1].

A recognition of the "public-private" partnership therefore forms the centrepiece of European governments' endeavours to promote PSB. Unsurprisingly, a plethora of laws, including strong antitrust laws, have been put in place in recent years to ensure that a proper balance is struck between support for public broadcasting and fairness to commercial broadcasters. The basic principle finds clear statement in the, annexed to the EU Treaty:

> The provisions of the Treaty establishing the European Community shall be without prejudice to the competence of Member States to provide for the funding of public service broadcasting insofar as such funding is granted to broadcasting organizations for the fulfilment of the public service remit as conferred, defined and organized by each Member State, and insofar as such funding does not affect trading conditions and competition in the Community to an extent which would be contrary to the common interest, while the realization of the remit of that public service shall be taken into account.
>
> (Ungerer, 2003: 6)

It is worth noting that in a recent judgment, the European Court of Justice laid down certain strict conditions under which PSB is to operate, so that there is a level playing field for all broadcasters. PSB should, said

---

[1] Example: Articles 81 and 82 of the EC Treaty.

the court, adhere to substantial transparency requirements, its mandate should be clearly specified, and an independent regulator should oversee its performance. The court was also keen to emphasize that, in its promotion of PSB, governments should not allow New Media to be unduly circumscribed[2].

In practice, the dual system has worked reasonably well. In the United Kingdom, for instance, despite the proliferation of satellite TV and Internet broadcasting, public service broadcasters still command 61.6 per cent of the total audience in multi-channel homes—a figure which increases to 70 per cent at peak times[3].

It has even been argued that the dual system has actually enriched PSB through continuous cross-fertilization and mutual challenges between "popular" and "serious" programming. As Holland (2003: 8) has noted, "Diversity of types of funding and ownership (licence fee next to advertising funded, next so subscription funded) has encouraged competition for quality and audience appeal, rather than for profits and audience size".

Regulatory challenges

What, then, are the challenges that face governments today in relation to public sector broadcasting? Leaving aside concerns that may be specific to particular countries, it is possible to identify a number of generic issues of near-universal concern. There can be no serious argument, of course, that broadcasting needs to be treated differently from other mass media in the matter of regulation. This is dictated both by the immediacy of its impact on audiences (which is qualitatively different from the impact that, say, the written word might have), and by the reality of spectrum scarcity.

The main challenges may be summarized as follows.

1. The need to provide a universal service which meets all the desired objectives within the society in question without imposing impossible burdens on broadcasters.

2. To ensure adequate independence for broadcasters from interference in editorial/programming matters, whether from governmental or commercial sources.

---

[2] *Altmark Trans GmbH et al v. Regierungspräsidium Magdeburg*, case C-280/00, Judgment dated 24 July 2003.

[3] "A New Future for Communications", White Paper published by the UK Government, 2001, cited in Price and Raboy, supra note 3, pp. 105.

3. To determine the best possible "fit" of public/private structures and processes.

4. To determine the best possible funding strategies without, on the one hand, compromising on core PSB values and, on the other, distorting competitive fairness in the market.

5. To meet the ever-increasing demands imposed by advancing technology, i.e. the need for the law to stay one step ahead of technological innovation.

6. To strike a fair balance between light touch and prescriptive regulation.

7. To ensuring adequate accountability to the viewing/listening public, including sufficient responsiveness to their changing needs and aspirations.

8. To achieve the right degree of flexibility and technological neutrality.

How a government meets these challenges is, obviously, dependant on a number of factors, and it would be difficult to suggest a single, "one-size-fits-all" regulatory model. The best that can be said is that whatever approach is adopted, it should be as "responsive" at possible—a concept which embraces three features:

> One is that the regulators should have the power to respond in a variety of ways with the strength of the response increasing with the seriousness of the issue. The second is that the stronger the response, the less it would be used—the philosophy is a big stick, but a big stick held in the background, hardly ever used. The third is that the actual legislation—that is the words enshrined in an Act—should for the most part restrict themselves to the core principles with the implementation of these principles being left to the regulatory bodies.
>
> (Graham, 2005: 12)[4]

The European experience suggests that the regulatory outlook should be informed by certain broad principles of universal applicability and the widest possible public appeal. A document put out by the European Commission in 1999 (Doc.COM 657) lists the following as useful principles: the need for a truly independent regulator who will act evenly as between the government and broadcast operators; a framework under which regulation will only be activated where it is necessary to achieve any of the agreed public objectives; and regulatory rules which will undertake a dynamic assessment of actual

---

[4] See also, in this context, Ayres and Braithwaite (1992).

audience and market power rather than separate sectors and technologies in a rigid manner.

In terms of specifics, it has been suggested, among other things, that the regulatory framework should insulate public service broadcasters from the civil service of governments and from unwarranted interference by public authorities in their operation; provide a clear, detailed and verifiable definition of the PSB remit which, while making public service programmes distinct from their commercial counterparts, do not consign them to a neglected niche; encourage and promote self-regulatory schemes in the area of programme standards and journalistic ethics; and offer sufficient incentives to PSB operators to serve as repositories of the nation's audiovisual heritage[5].

Regulation: Some fundamental issues

There are a number of regulatory matters of fundamental importance which are generic in nature and which will therefore have to be faced by policymakers around the world.

One such issue is whether it is desirable for the law to regulate content and carriage together or separately. By "content" is meant the words, pictures, images, sound effects and other tangible manifestations of the information being imparted by a broadcaster. "Carriage", on the other hand, relates to the mode by which such information is transmitted, viz. the cables, fibre optic networks, satellite dishes and associated paraphernalia. Quite clearly, there are different considerations at play in the regulation of each, and those differences cannot be lost sight of by the legislator and/or regulator.

In the case of carriage, the foremost consideration is economic efficiency, namely the ability to deliver, to the consumer, a reliable service of the highest possible quality as cheaply as possible. Economies of scale would inevitably play an important part in achieving this objective, so it may be that the best results come, not from small, local enterprises, from a large conglomerate, or a group of large conglomerates, who may end up exercising a dominant position in the market. Although competition laws can, to some extent, deal with the problem of market dominance, the compulsions of economic efficiency may, in some cases, require a toler-

---

[5] See, e.g. Recommendations of a conference organized at the instance of the OSCE Representative on Freedom of the Media, Ljubljana, 11 March 2003, OSCE Doc. FOM. INF/1/03 dt. 21 March 2003.

ance of large, even monopolistic entities, at least in the short to medium term.

By contrast, an altogether different approach would normally be favoured in relation to content. Here, economic efficiency is not as important as the promotion of certain social goals and values, such as the need to offer the consumer an wide choice of serious educative and informative programming, the need to allow creative artistes maximum freedom to exercise their talents for the benefit of the community, the need to ensure that vulnerable groups (e.g. children) are protected from corruption by unsuitable programmes, and the need, above all, to make the broadcasts available to everyone free at the point of access.

The regulatory framework should be tailored to reflect these different requirements. Where it is deemed desirable to have separate regulators to deal respectively with content and carriage, rules and protocols should be put in place to ensure that they work cooperatively, especially in relation to problems where a joint solution is called for.

A second issue relates to the distinction between what are usually referred to as "negative" and "positive" regulation. Put simply, negative regulation involves banning or restricting certain types of activity or content, e.g. obscenity in broadcasts. Positive regulation, on the other hand, involves the encouragement or promotion of activity or conduct that is deemed desirable, e.g. programmes involving civic education. By its very nature, positive regulation forms an integral part of public service broadcasting, and therefore deserves much greater attention that would be accorded in relation to commercial broadcasting. The point that is often made in this context is that it is not enough simply to give formal recognition to measures of positive regulation, but to provide the legal and infrastructural back-up to ensure that the objectives of such regulation are achieved in practice.

A third issue concerns supra-national regulation. Given the fact that many of the new technologies employed in broadcasting—whether public service or commercial—are such that their effects cannot realistically be confined within national boundaries, the need for international regulation will become more keenly felt in the coming years. This will call, not only for greater cooperation between regulatory policymakers in individual countries, but also for due deference by national law-making authorities to global (or regional, as the case may be) bodies. Judges and other adjudicatory functionaries, too, will have to pay greater attention to supra-national norms and standards to ensure that domestic laws and regulations are applied harmoniously with such norms and standards.

Global support for PSB

The growing importance attached to public service broadcasting worldwide is reflected in the focused attention that has been paid to this concept by national governments, non-governmental organizations, and inter-governmental bodies in recent decades. PSB has also been the subject of close scrutiny and much support from judicial and other adjudicatory bodies, both domestic and international.

At a general level, the Universal Declaration of Human Rights (UDHR) contains a strong guarantee on freedom of expression, which has been seen as supportive of PSB:

> Everyone has the right to freedom of opinion and expression; this right includes the right to hold opinions without interference and to seek, receive and impart information and ideas through any media and regardless of frontiers[6].

This right has been reaffirmed in the International Covenant on Civil and Political Rights (ICCPR)[7], a multilateral treaty under which signatory governments—some 145 of them around the world—are legally obliged to ensure that people within their territories are able to enjoy the rights laid down therein. Similar guarantees of freedom of expression are also contained in regional human rights instruments, such as the European Convention for the Protection of Human Rights and Fundamental Freedoms[8], the American Convention on Human Rights[9], and the African Charter on Human and Peoples' Rights[10]. Despite the general terms in which the right to freedom of expression has been couched in these documents, its relevance to the promotion of public service broadcasting has been underlined time and again by the strong support that the mass media have derived from judicial decisions in which the right has come up for interpretation[11].

Among the specific obligations highlighted by the courts of direct relevance to PSB are the principles of diversity and pluralism. The European Court of Human Rights has noted, for example, that "(Imparting) information and ideas of general interest ... cannot be successfully accomplished

---

[6] UDHR Article 19.
[7] Article 19.
[8] Article 10.
[9] Article 13.
[10] Article 9.
[11] See, e.g. the observation of the Inter-American Court of Human Rights in *Compulsory Membership of an Association Prescribed by Law for the Practice of Journalism*, Advisory Opinion OC-5/85, 13 Nov 1985, Series A, No. 5, para. 34, that "It is the mass media that make the exercise of freedom of expression a reality".

unless it is grounded in the principle of pluralism"[12]. The Supreme Court of India has held that, in order to fulfil its constitutional obligation of guaranteeing the free speech rights of its citizens, the state had a positive duty to ensure plurality and diversity of views, opinions and ideas through the airwaves[13]. The Federal Constitutional Court of Germany has ruled, more explicitly, that public service broadcasting organizations have a duty to ensure that they offered their viewers and listeners a wide and comprehensive range of programmes[14].

POLICY FRAMEWORK FOR PUBLIC SERVICE BROADCASTING
PUBLIC SERVICE REQUIREMENTS

Participating States agree that public service broadcasters, within the general framework defined for them and without prejudice to more specific public service remits, must have principally the following missions.

1. To provide, through their programming, a reference point for all members of the public and a factor for social cohesion and integration of all individuals, groups and communities. In particular, they must reject any cultural, sexual, religious or racial discrimination and any form of social segregation.
2. To provide a forum for public discussion in which as broad a spectrum as possible of views and opinions can be expressed.
3. To broadcast impartial and independent news, information and comment.
4. To develop pluralistic, innovatory and varied programming which meets high ethical and quality standards and not to sacrifice the pursuit of quality to market forces.
5. To develop and structure programme schedules and services of interest to a wide public while being attentive to the needs of minority groups.
6. To reflect the different philosophical ideas and religious beliefs in society, with the aim of strengthening mutual understanding and tolerance and promoting community relations in pluriethnic and multicultural societies.
7. To contribute actively through their programming to a greater appreciation and dissemination of the diversity of national and European cultural heritage.
8. To ensure that the programmes offered contain a significant proportion of original productions, especially feature films, drama and other creative works, and to have regard to the need to use independent producers and cooperate with the cinema sector.
9. To extend the choice available to viewers and listeners by also offering programme services which are not normally provided by commercial broadcasters.

– "Media in a Democratic Society", Council of Europe (1994). –

---

[12] *Inforationsverein Lentia & Ors. v. Austria*, Judgment dt. 24 November 1993, 17 EHRR 93, para. 38.
[13] *Secretary, Ministry of Information & Broadcasting v. Cricket Association of Bengal* (1995) 2 SCC 161.
[14] *The Fourth Television Case*, 73 BverfGE 118 (1986).

There is evidence of strong support for public service broadcasting in inter-governmental resolutions such as the UNESCO-sponsored Declaration of Alma Ata (1992) which urged governments to encourage the development of public service broadcasters within their respective territories. A Resolution of the Council and of the Representatives of the Governments of the Member States of the European Union, noted the close connection between PSB and democracy, and underlined the need for media pluralism. Even more pointedly, a 1994 Resolution on the Future of Public Service Broadcasting, passed under the auspices of the Council of Europe, called for the establishment of at least one comprehensive PSB organization in each country[15].

AFRICAN CHARTER ON BROADCASTING. 2001

Part I: General regulatory issues

1. The legal framework for broadcasting should include a clear statement of the principles underpinning broadcast regulation, including promoting respect for freedom of expression, diversity, and the free flow of information and ideas, as well as a three-tier system for broadcasting: public service, commercial and community.
2. All formal powers in the areas of broadcast and telecommunications regulation should be exercised by public authorities which are protected against interference, particularly of a political or economic nature, by, among other things, an appointments process for members which is open, transparent, involves the participation of civil society, and is not controlled by any particular political party.
3. Decision-making processes about the overall allocation of the frequency spectrum should be open and participatory, and ensure that a fair proportion of the spectrum is allocated to broadcasting uses.
4. The frequencies allocated to broadcasting should be shared equitably among the three tiers of broadcasting.
5. Licensing processes for the allocation of specific frequencies to individual broadcasters should be fair and transparent, and based on clear criteria which include promoting media diversity in ownership and content.
6. Broadcasters should be required to promote and develop local content, which should be defined to include African content, including through the introduction of minimum quotas.
7. States should promote an economic environment that facilitates the development of independent production and diversity in broadcasting.
8. The development of appropriate technology for the reception of broadcasting signals should be promoted.

---

[15] *Resolution No. 1, Future of Public Service Broadcasting*, Fourth Council of Europe Ministerial Conference on Mass Media Policy, Prague, 1994.

Part II: Public service broadcasting

1. All state and government controlled broadcasters should be transformed into public service broadcasters, that are accountable to all strata of the people as represented by an independent board, and that serve the overall public interest, avoiding one-sided reporting and programming in regard to religion, political belief, culture, race and gender.

2. Public service broadcasters should, like broadcasting and telecommunications regulators, be governed by bodies which are protected against interference.

3. The public service mandate of public service broadcasters should clearly defined.

4. The editorial independence of public service broadcasters should be guaranteed.

5. Public service broadcasters should be adequately funded in a manner that protects them from arbitrary interference with their budgets.

6. Without detracting from editorial control over news and current affairs content and in order to promote the development of independent productions and to enhance diversity in programming, public service broadcasters should be required to broadcast minimum quotas of material by independent producers.

7. The transmission infrastructure used by public service broadcasters should be made accessible to all broadcasters under reasonable and non-discriminatory terms.

– www.misanet.org/broadcast.html –

The need for broadcasters in general, and public service broadcasters in particular, to enjoy a high degree of independence, especially from government pressures, so that they are able to discharge their obligations to the public effectively has been emphasized in a number of international documents. The 1996 Recommendation on the Guarantee of the Independence of Public Service Broadcasting, issued by the Committee of Ministers of the Council of Europe, urged strong guarantees to PSB operators on freedom from interference in programming matters, against arbitrary dismissals from employment, and against potential conflicts of interest[16]. The management of a PSB operator should, said this document, be given exclusive responsibility for the day-to-day running of broadcasting operations and it should be properly shielded from any form of political interference[17].

---

[16] Recommendation No. R(96) 10 – see esp. Arts. 9–13.
[17] Ibid., Arts. 4–8.

Another document, put forth by UNESCO in 1996, viz. the Declaration of Sana'a went so far as to state that any provision of international assistance for state-funded PSBs should be made contingent upon the state guaranteeing the necessary independence to these entities. The Declaration of Sofia, issued a year later by UNESCO, hoped that state-funded PSBs would gradually transform themselves into truly independent organizations enjoying real editorial freedom.

The link between the independence of a public service broadcaster and the sufficiency of its funding has been recognized in many of the published international standards. The Resolution of the Council of Europe on the Future of Public Service Broadcasting, for example, underlines the pivotal importance of financial independence for PSBs, as do a number of other documents issued by that body in recent years[18]. Funding for PSBs should, it has been noted elsewhere, not only be commensurate with their obligations, but also insulated from arbitrary increases or decreases at the whim of whoever controls the purse-strings[19]. The need for stability and security of funding was underlined in a paper published by the European Broadcasting Union in 2000:

> To be stable and secure, such funding needs a clear legal basis (apart from a law approving the state budget), which projects the level of funding for an appropriate period of time. Dependence on annual decisions (on the state budget) or on ad hoc measures would create a climate of insecurity and would undermine a public broadcaster's ability to plan ahead and invest.
>
> (EBU, 2000: 16)

The issue of autonomy for public service broadcasters has also engaged the attention of courts in a number of countries. The Indian Supreme Court, for example, ruled that, the airwaves being public property which belonged to the people as a whole, it was not permissible for the government of India to exercise a monopoly over broadcasting[20]. Equally robust views were expressed by the Supreme Court of Ghana, in a judgment delivered in 1993[21]:

---

[18] See, e.g., Res. 428 of 1970 and Rec. 748 of 1975 of the Parliamentary Assembly, CoE. See, also, Res. 2 (Fifth conf., 1997) of the Ministerial Conference, CoE.

[19] See, e.g. Rec. R(96)10, Council of Europe, supra note 26, Arts. 17–19.

[20] *Secretary, Ministry of Information & Broadcasting v. Cricket Association of Bengal*, supra note 25.

[21] *New Patriotic Party v. Ghana Broadcasting Corpn.*, Writ No. 1/93, Judgment dt. 30 Nov. 1993.

The state-owned media are national assets. They belong to the entire community, not to the abstraction known as the state; nor to the government in office, or to its party. If such national assets were to become the mouthpiece of any one or (a) combination of the parties vying for power, democracy would be no more than a sham[22].

The Supreme Court of Sri Lanka in 1997 struck down a law which allowed the government to influence the appointment of Directors to the country's broadcasting regulatory authority. The court expressed the opinion that, were the law to stand, it would lead to the authority being deprived of "the independence required of a body entrusted with the regulation of the electronic media which, it is acknowledged on all hands, is the most potent means of influencing thought"[23].

As for the mode of funding PSBs, the contemporary consensus of opinion seems to be strongly weighted in favour of mixed funding, i.e. funding from both public and private sources. The reasons why this is preferred are not far to seek:

Firstly, there is normally no single source of funding available which, on its own, would be sufficient to provide the necessary financial resources. Secondly, reliance on one particular source of funding creates quality and efficiency of the fulfilment of the public service remit. Thirdly, as each of the different sources of funding has particular advantages and disadvantages ... the combined use of the sources can maximize the advantages while limiting the disadvantages, provided that this is done in an intelligent way, i.e. adapted to the different legal, political and economic situations of the individual countries and markets. Last but not least, a mixed system is more robust in a rapidly changing environment, where certain sources may suddenly dry up while others grow and new ones may appear[24].

PSB and multimedia

Some fears have been expressed about the future of public service broadcasting in the emerging multimedia environment around the world. The advent of the Internet, in particular, has been seen as a potential threat to the continuing viability of PSB. Such fears may, however, be exaggerated. Indeed, public service broadcasters may actually be able to turn the challenges presented by the Internet into advantages, as many PSB campaigners have pointed out.

---

[22] Ibid., at p. 17.

[23] *Athokorale & Ors. v. Attorney-General*, S.D. No. 1/97–15//97, Judgment dated 5 May 1997.

[24] *The Funding of Public Service Broadcasting*, supra note 32, at p. 22.

The potential offered by the Internet for interactive local broadcasting to small communities is a case in point. Public service broadcasters can use this resource beneficially by putting out programmes which would be of local importance. This would, among other things, be a very tangible contribution to the democratic process. The legal and regulatory framework should recognize this fact and provide the necessary space and the necessary incentives for such synergy between the Internet and broadcasters.

Conclusion

There is, quite clearly, a wide diversity of approaches to the legal regulation of public service broadcasting around the world. Significant differences in structures and processes are evident even among leading jurisdictions. Whatever the nature—and nomenclature—of the regulatory mechanisms adopted, the ultimate test for their effectiveness would have to be whether the regime, as a whole, ensures enough independence and adequate resources for the PSB organizations as well as the requisite degree of public accountability to command the confidence of the vast majority of viewers and listeners within a given country.

Public sector broadcasting organizations, generally speaking, tend to be "vulnerable and fragile constructions", as a veteran Swedish broadcaster (Rydbeck, 1990) once put it, and while the law can go some way in ensuring that they meet the ever-growing challenges thrown at them, their long-term health depends on the willingness of ordinary men and women in any society to protect and nourish them.

References

Ayres, I., & Braithwaite, J. (1992). *Responsive Regulation*. UK: Oxford University Press.

Council of Europe. (1994). Media in a democratic society, resolutions and political declaration. 4th Ministerial Conference on Mass Media Policy held on 7–8 December in Prague.

European Parliament. (14 December 1999). Principles and Guidelines for the Community's Audiovisual Policy in the Digital Age. Communication from the Commission to the Council, the European Parliament, the Economic and Social Committee and the Committee of the Regions, Doc. COM, 657.

European Broadcasting Union. (9 November 2000). The Funding of Public Service Broadcasting, Doc DAJ/MW/mp.

Graham, A. (2005). The Future of Communications: Public Service Broadcasting. Discussion document. Retrieved from www.communicationswhitepaper .gov.uk/cwp_ Consultation/psb.pdf

Holland, P. (2003). Conceptual Glue: Public service broadcasting as practice, system and ideology. Paper presented to the MIT3 Television in Transition 2003 Conference. Retrieved from cms.mit.edu/mit3/papers/holland.pdf

Mooney, P. (12 January 2004). Public service broadcasting. Report of the Committee on Culture, Science and Education, Parlimentary Assembly, Council of Europe. Retrieved from assembly.coe.int/Documents/WorkingDocs/doc04/EDOC10029.htm

Price, M. E., & Raboy, M. (2003). Public Service Broadcasting in Transition: A Documentary Reader. Kluwer Law International, The Hague.

Roddick, A. (23 October 2003). Rupert Murdoch vs the BBC. Mediachannel.org, London.

Rumphorst, W. (2003). Model Public Service Broadcasting Law. Retrieved from www.ebu.ch/CMSimages/en/leg_p_model_law_psb1_tcm6-14334.pdf

Rydbeck, O. (1990). *I maktens närhet* [Close to power]. Stockholm: Bonniers.

Ungerer, H. (2003). Legal and Regulatory Aspects of Public Service Broadcasting – Panel Contribution. Paper presented at a conference on Public Sector Broadcasting held in Bucharest on 19–20 September 2003. European Commission document COMP/C2/HU/rdu.

India
Public Service Broadcasting and Changing Perspectives

In this chapter, our aim is to examine and analyse how public service broadcasting in India has been re-defined and refined in a historical perspective. The major focus will be to cover post economic liberalization public broadcasting scenario. For the purpose of presentation, broadly three major historical periods will be taken into consideration. These are:

- Broadcasting in British colonial India.
- Government-controlled broadcasting in independent India.
- Free media after economic liberalization.

Broadcasting in British India

Undivided India is among the first British colonies to have privately owned experimental broadcasting stations as early as 1923. The same was taken over by the then government of India and designated as the Indian State Broadcasting Service. The British Broadcasting Corporation was the model around which the British colonial government fashioned the Indian radio and gave it a new identity, which continues to be called by the same name, All India Radio (AIR). Since 1937, AIR continues to be a public broadcasting service even after the partition of India in 1947, until today. At the time of India's independence in 1947, there were only six All India Radio stations, which also began to be referred as Akashvani. Since then, all English programmes are broadcast by All India Radio and all Indian language programmes are broadcast by Akashvani. This duality of the public broadcasting system continues to haunt the split personality of the Indian Broadcasting service.

Public Service Broadcasting (PSB) in British India meant propaganda, controlled information dissemination and promotion of colonial interests. Also, expansion of All India Radio was considered unnecessary since information dissemination could have endangered the British interests in India. Registration and licensing of radio receivers remained in force during the entire British period. More than anything else, political news, views and editorial comments were carefully controlled and often manipulated to help maintain law and order and subjugate the Indian citizens.

Due to technological limitations, radio remained an urban phenomenon, having limited reach. Also, due to non-availability of radio receiving systems, its access was extremely limited. It was not uncommon to have just one radio set for a couple of 100,000 families; that too owned by the literate urban, white-collar or rich households. In the wake of the second world war, the popularity of radio increased a great deal as listeners were keen to know war news in which India contributed the largest number of soldiers to fight for the allied forces.

Public service broadcasting in independent India

In independent India, the political leaders recognized the value of information and its use for accelerating the process of development and for democratizing an ancient country rising out of the ashes of colonialism, feudalism and a caste-ridden society. The framers of the Indian constitution also recognized the value of independent, impartial and innovative public broadcasting to meet the aspirations and expectations of its citizens. However, it was also felt that in the newly independent nation that lacked maturity in democratic values, the public broadcasting system could not survive without the full support and control of the government. Besides, there were fissiparous tendencies trying to take advantage of the conflict in the newly created countries in South Asia. The feudal forces too were still very strong.

The then Prime Minister of India, Jawaharlal Nehru, opted to have full government control over public service broadcasting for the time being and defended the decision to create an independent broadcasting service. In retrospect, many observers feel that the colonial hangover and fear of the unknown did not allow bringing about change in the broadcasting policy, or for that matter, regulate the free flow of information within the country. It took another 45 years in 1992 when the same could be followed; that too by default at least in the case of television. For radio, it had to wait for half a century before the same could be done. Even then it was without full freedom to broadcast news.

It took several committees and commissions, national level debates and discussion before AIR could be freed from governmental control. The Parliament of India, during this period, must have debated and discussed the desirability to have free broadcasting—without success. Each successive government was accused by the opposition for using public broadcasting to manipulate, suppress and suffocate the voice of the people.

History of Indian radio broadcasting

Radio broadcasting, which came to India experimentally in 1923, started operating first from Calcutta and then Bombay and Madras. Lionel Fielden, a senior producer of the BBC takes the credit of renaming the Indian State Broadcasting Service as All India Radio, laying the foundation for public service broadcasting in India with the goal of providing information and education (ICFAI, 2005: 22). During that time, administrative control of broadcasting was placed under the Department of Industries and Labour and was transferred to the Department of Communications in 1937 and later to the Department of Information and Broadcasting in 1941. All India Radio began expanding in terms of geographical and linguistic coverage and transmission hours, becoming a major broadcasting service in Asia.

However, it was during the 1962 Chinese aggression that certain inadequacies of radio reception and its informational role came to light, with listeners in the border areas receiving Radio Peking. For the first time since public broadcasting began, the government of India felt the need to review the information and broadcasting policy and operations. The government of India constituted the Chanda Committee in 1964 to evaluate the functioning of All India Radio. The Chanda Committee found that "It is (was) not possible in the Indian context for a creative medium like broadcasting to flourish under a regiment (sic) of departmental rules and regulations. It is only by an institutional change that AIR can be liberated from the present rigid financial and administrative procedures of the government"[1]. However, the Cabinet decided to hold the decision for conversion of AIR into an autonomous corporation in December 1969.

Television was introduced in India as an experimental service with a small transmitter and a makeshift studio with just three days of transmission a week in 1959. In 1965, television, as a wing of All India Radio, began regular telecasts. Television as an independent entity was separated, though it remained under the Ministry of Information and Broadcasting and re-christened as Doordarshan.

---

[1] Refer to *Ministry of Information and Broadcasting Annual Report 1978*, p. 5.

The sender's approach to communication in broadcasting institutions of India

In the early 1950s, radio was considered a public service. In this newly independent country, radio was remodelled to achieve a nationalist image, a countrywide broadcast of national programmes and the promotion of Hindi as the national language. On July 1952, the first national programme of music went on air. In January 1958, an unusual but short-lived experiment in the use of folk media for social communication was launched as an annual festival of "Songs of Nation Builders", in which folk musicians and dancers from different parts of India presented songs with developmental content. (Baruah, 1983, as quoted by Kumar 2003). B. V. Keskar, India's earliest and longest serving Minister of Information and Broadcasting, patronised Indian classical and folk music. While AIR's classical music broadcast rose to nearly 50 per cent, Indian listeners, tired of such music, switched to Radio Ceylon that played all the film songs. It was years later, in 1967, that listeners could finally tune in to music and entertainment programmes of their choice on All India Radio.

Television too, having started out as an arm of the All India Radio, relayed programmes on the basis of its national mandate, not showing much sensitivity to the stark contrasts and cultural diversity that is the unmistakable reality of the Indian Civilization. One shortcoming that Doordarshan faced was its "Delhi-centric view of India", especially of news coverage. This was because each successive central government treated India as a single coherent civilization while formulating media policy. They argued that mass media cater to a large majority, promote cultural uniformity and draw the marginalized people into the national mainstream. (Agrawal, 1997). Yet, with such linguistic diversity, the language of programming was bound to become a core issue. For a country with more than 18 officially recognized languages and hundreds of dialects, how does the public broadcaster "serve the nation"—so to speak? With its initial telecasts in Hindi and English, Doordarshan soon felt the need to cater to the millions of regional viewers who would not understand Hindi or English. With this objective, it launched a three-tier service, consisting of the national service, the regional service and the local service by late 80s of the last century.

The problems of language and cultural context were well reflected in *The Working Group on Software for Doordarshan* report (1985), chaired by P. C. Joshi. From the report it was evident that a large number of viewers in almost all parts of India, including the remote northeast, could not relate to television content. Since then it has been a long road for Doordarshan to telecast in all parts of India including the northeast region, where it expanded by the year 2003–2004. In this way, Doordarshan, as a public broadcaster, could reach beyond mainstream regions of the country.

Public service to commercial radio (Vividh Bharati)

At a time when All India Radio took over the Indian Broadcasting Services, it had given up its commercial revenue, citing that broadcasting was primarily a public service. This view continued even after independence. However, The Chanda Committee in 1966 recommended acceptance of advertisements on a proposed Vividh Bharati channel "for additional resources for expanding the network and improving the programmes"[2]. Commercial radio service was thus inaugurated in 1967 from 28 Vividh Bharati Stations. The same year, All India Radio introduced advertising in 1967 to make up part of its revenue, while the government was to pool in any deficit in operating expenses.

In more recent times, Prasar Bharati, the Broadcasting Corporation of India formed in 1997, while fulfilling its mandate as a PSB, has also tried to generate revenue by aggressively marketing its in-house programmes and also by producing customized programmes. In the global market economy, this step has been extremely significant, leading to the creation of Marketing Divisions within AIR in the major cities of India. The marketing division reaches out to clients, prepares media plans, executes their publicity campaigns, and produces spots and jingles when necessary. Today, commercial revenue has come a long way; and with several ministries of the government and major companies as their clients, the gross revenue earned up to the end of December 2004 was 90 crores[3].

Leapfrog of public radio and television

The journey of television took a new turn when Satellite Instructional Television Experiment (SITE), the world's biggest techno-social communication experiment, was launched in 1975–76. It was India's great visionary, scientist Dr Vikram Sarabhai, who advocated the use of satellite communication to reach out to remote areas. To him, it was a system for social transformation for the underprivileged (Dave, 2002). He did not penalize remote rural viewers. It also marked 50 years of technological advantage and leapfrogging from the bullock era to the satellite era. Programmes on education, health, family planning, agriculture and other developmental issues were

---

[2] Refer to *Ministry of Information and Broadcasting Annual Report 1978*, p. 5.
[3] Refer to *Ministry of Information and Broadcasting Annual Report 2004–2005*.

beamed across 2,400 villages in the six states of Rajasthan, Bihar, Orissa, Karnataka, Madhya Pradesh, Andhra Pradesh and selected villages of Gujarat. Television sets, known as community TV, were installed in the *panchayat* (community hall) or school buildings for the villagers to watch the daily transmission.

Most importantly, it proved India's capability of using advanced technology and adapting it to the socio-economic needs of the country. It was a precursor to the INSAT satellite system today, which has taken television to all corners of the country.

Kheda Communication Project

As a part of SITE, in Kheda district of Gujarat, the Kheda communication project was extended beyond 31 July 1976, until 1991. Initially known as Pij TV, it had a one-kilowatt transmitter. The Pij transmitter could be received in a radius of about 30 km from Pij village. In this respect, the Kheda Communication Project was India's first local rural television telecast. Research studies have indicated limited positive gains from Kheda television (Agrawal, 2000).

Expansion of AIR

Parallel to television, All India Radio also expanded, becoming one of the world's largest radio networks. Today, AIR boasts of 336 transmitters, including 143 Medium Frequency (MW), 54 high frequency (SW) and 139 FM transmitters. Some 214 radio stations cover 91.37 per cent of India and reach 99.13 per cent of the population (ICFAI, 2005). In all, AIR broadcasts in 27 languages and 146 dialects—an impressive record by any standards. Programmes range from news and features to special bulletins on sports, youth, agriculture and family welfare. Music—classical, folk, light, devotional and film-based, is another major pillar of AIR. Radio had grown into such a powerful medium with extensive reach across India.

National emergency and public broadcasting

The national emergency brought in a new phase into the history of Indian broadcasting, with censorship being imposed on all mass media. "The then Prime Minister told a Conference of Akashvani Station Directors in September 1975 that she did not understand what the concept of "credibility" of radio implied, since there was no doubt that All India Radio (Akashvani) was and is (was) going to remain a government organ"[4].

The AIR code, which had been finalized with Cabinet's approval in 1967, was therefore scrapped, stating that it was not feasible under the changed circumstances. This served as the backdrop when the opposition parties made freedom of expression a major plank during the Parliamentary elections in March 1977, pledging "genuine autonomy" for Akashvani and Doordarshan[5].

The Verghese Committee, set up in the wake of the Emergency, addressed issues of how state-owned broadcasters could be liberated from restrictive governmental control and censorship. Its recommendations led to the introduction of the Prasar Bharati (Broadcasting Corporation of India) Bill in the Lok Sabha in May 1979. With the dissolution of the sixth Lok Sabha and the emergence of a Congress (I) government, which made no secret of its hostility to autonomous broadcasting, the Bill was allowed to lapse (*Frontline*, 1997).

Public broadcasting deregulated

Technological innovations, more than policy and governance forced public broadcasting to be deregulated, privatized and personalized. In the wake

---

[4] Refer to *Ministry of Information and Broadcasting Annual Report 1978*, p. 5.
[5] Refer to *Ministry of Information and Broadcasting Annual Report 1978*, p. 6.

of economic liberation, two major steps that extensively contributed to this process happened to be de-licensing of radio and television equipment and the sudden large-scale availability of audio and video cassettes, and video cassette recorders. These two factors brought about an unprecedented but silent communication revolution in the country by way of creating access at the cost of public broadcasting. Studies conducted in the mid-80s had predicted doom for both radio and television, along with public viewing of cinema. While access to Indian music and Indian cinema in almost all languages grew rapidly, the listenership of radio saw a decline; so did cinema and public television.

The arrival of cable television further accentuated the size of depleting public television viewers and public radio listeners. Punctuated by economic liberalization, rapid expansion of cable network with limited access to international television and public television created a gulf between those who could view cable television and those who could only view public service television. This was followed by an ongoing privatization of television and radio stations meant purely for entertainment and devoid of news.

Public broadcasting in India must be understood within this historical perspective, though it provides a glimpse of only 15 years (1990–2005) of the current ongoing competition between private and public broadcasting. Radio and television public broadcasting will be separately discussed.

Television

The country's only public service television, Doordarshan, has had to battle numerous challenges in the last three decades. Globalization and economic liberalization had revolutionized the television scenario in India. Doordarshan responded with several changes in its strategies, both in technology and software, while the debate over the role of public service television continued to rage.

India had opened its doors to trans-national satellite broadcasting. CNN footage marked the beginning of this era, with the live telecast of the Gulf War 1991. Since a large number of cable television networks were in existence at this point in time, especially in urban India, CNN telecast was quickly integrated into the existing cable television network. Further, when urban Indians learnt that they could watch Gulf War on TV, many rushed to buy dish antennae for their homes. "Others turned entrepreneurs and started offering the signal to their neighbours by flinging cables over tree tops and verandahs" (ICFAI, 2005). From large metros, satellite TV delivered via cable moved into smaller towns, spurring the purchase of TV sets and even the upgradation from black and white to colour TV. Other satellite channels soon followed—at first Rupert Murdoch's Hong Kong based Star TV, which began telecasting in English, and later India's home-grown Zee TV, which largely had its programmes in Hindi, which it considered as the language of the masses in large parts of South Asia. From the mid-90s began an era of several private satellite channels, with both national and regional bases, mushrooming in quick succession. These newly established television channels brought a fresh lease of life to television viewing in India. They experimented with material, and tried out several new and racy formats and met with much enthusiasm from the viewers. It also brought serious competition to public broadcaster, Doordarshan, which was rapidly growing with the advent of INSAT across India.

At this juncture in the history of public broadcasting, Doordarshan, after decades of being a monopoly, had to rethink its strategy in the face of unprecedented competition. Doordarshan began responding to these changes by cashing in on its own major strength: accessibility or reach. It quickly grew to have 403 programme production centres and 792 transmitting stations of varying powers. Doordarshan thus became accessible to 85.8 per cent of the population, covering approximately 68.4 per cent of the area of the country. Doordarshan channels were terrestrial, and telecast through INSAT satellite system, except for the Movie Club and DD international, which are telecast through PAS-4 satellite (ICFAI, 2005: 85). Private satellite channels began opening up in regional languages, and this hastened the process of Doordarshan launching regional language satellite channels on 1 October 1993, airing programmes in 10 languages, reaching out to almost every part of India. Though the satellite channel boom is continuing, no single private television network satellite channel has yet acquired the capacity to operate in so many regional languages as Doordarshan.

In the midst of all these developments, to face the challenges brought about by private broadcasting, AIR and Doordarshan became autonomous in the form of a corporation named as Prasar Bharati, the Broadcasting Corporation of India on 23 November 1997, as India's public service broadcaster. The coming into force of the Prasar Bharati Act marks the end of a prolonged struggle that revealed the enormous political and social importance attached to public broadcasting in India. One of the most important fallouts of the autonomy has been the relegation of the responsibility of public broadcasting to the backburner, to a large extent, and the increased stronghold of advertisers in shaping public broadcasting.

Programming content

- ### The nature of news

  Some of the changes that are most salient include 24-hour television news and large-scale talk shows, game shows and soap operas, popularly known as serials. Private Satellite television channels have brought with it a new era of news broadcasting. Private satellite channels have studied operating 24-hour news channels, which put much pressure on the available time and resources. Earning their own revenue in a market economy alongside several other channels would obviously take its toll. In media circles, the debate on the nature and content of news programmes of satellite channels had begun receiving both attention and criticism. The nature of news had started bordering on the frivolous and sensationalist. These channels also put in much of their resources in packaging, apart from other aspects. "One of the latest features that puts news channels in an advantageous position and building a brand image and identity is its ability to relay breaking news. Every accident is viewed as an opportunity for newscasters, as it provides 24-hour channels with footage that can be repeated several times. The Television Audience Meter (TAM) dictates nearly all television ratings. Even Doordarshan, a public service broadcaster, is continuously worried about TAM ratings, because it is this crucial figure that forms the focus of many media planning decisions" (Agrawal, 2003). Yet, in the face of all these changes, public broadcasting continues to broadcast its low-key news bulletins, albeit with emphasis on political news. It still largely remains devoid of glamour and hype, maintaining its journalistic integrity, for the most part.

It seemed that public broadcasting needed a new face to survive the private satellite and cable boom. "If Doordarshan is to reinvent itself as a public broadcaster, it needs to pay more attention to its arts programming and audience's needs rather than regulation and precedent. In India, despite its immense potential, the issue remains something of a non-starter. Jaipal Reddy, the Minister for Information and Broadcasting, started his term in the year 2004 with an ambition—to make Prasar Bharati function autonomously, like the BBC. But the crucial difference is that viewers of BBC pay up a monthly subscription (license) fee, apart from governmental funding (*Frontline*, 2004).

It was public broadcasting's turn to begin experimenting with new innovative programming. As part of this effort, it launched Doordarshan-3 (DD-3) as a "thinking person's channel" with attention to theatre and art, and discussions and analyses of books and ideas. As this channel could not recover the costs of programming, it was soon wound up. It could still not be ascertained if this formula continues to hold out against the new age racy formats of some of the private channels. Doordarshan continued its trial with another channel, DD-Bharati, very different from DD-3, with niche programmes in areas of health, children, art and culture. After years of tried and tested methods, it was now a phase of trial and error.

As in the case of other democratic countries, where public service television sets the trend that private channels have inevitably been forced to adopt, India too had a similar experience, though it seems the trend is reversing. Prasar Bharati, while stating that AIR and Doordarshan are a historical reality whose existence cannot be questioned, also admits the need to look for its basic purpose in the context of public service broadcasting. It takes the view that "The need for public service broadcasting has never been greater. The proliferation of private channels has fuelled many wants and fulfilled some needs, but has left gaps. These should be filled by a public service broadcaster. This is because commercial television broadcasting conducted by privately owned television channels must target the relatively affluent urban market as they can only air programmes through a cable operator"[6].

Cable television, once the preserve of India's biggest cities, has expanded to smaller towns and villages, with television emerging as the preferred mode of entertainment, information and news because of its affordability and wide programming range. Television channels have started making inroads into the rural areas as well. Yet the fact remains that public television broadcasters' reach and access to important state resources remain unmatched. But it does have to use precisely this unique selling proposition to wake up to the huge challenge brought by the private satellite channels boom. With a mandate that no channel can hope to fill single-handedly, Doordarshan is still in an advantageous position to be a responsible public service broadcaster, but with its own wit and ingenuity.

Not to be left out of the technology bandwagon, the government approved Doordarshan's pilot project of Ku-Band transmission "Free-to-air DTH (Direct to Home)" in November 2003. Its scope included setting up of a satellite earth station for uplinking TV channel bouquet and installation of a receiving system in villages over a dozen States, where television coverage is less than the national average[7]. In order to increase the reach of educational telecasts, the Ministry of Information and Broadcasting, in collaboration with the Ministry of Human Resource Development and the Indira Gandhi National Open University (IGNOU), introduced a satellite channel—Gyandarshan, in January 2000, dedicated to education.

---

[6] Refer to mib.nic.in/informationb/AUTONOMOUS/nicpart/pbservc.htm
[7] Refer to *Ministry of Information and Broadcasting Annual Report 2004–2005*, p. 39.

DD'S DTH TARGETS ONE MILLION SUBSCRIBERS BY END 2005

New Delhi: A delay in the formal launch—or dedication to the nation, as Prasar Bharati would like to put it—of pubcaster Doodrashan's DTH service notwithstanding, it is going ahead with great gusto and marketing the service to subscribers.

"Some 200,000 (set-top) boxes have already been sold and we are targeting a million subscribers by the end of 2005," Prasar Bharati CEO KS Sarma told indiantelevision.com today.

DD Direct Plus, as the KU-band service is known as, is, probably, a unique experiment undertaken by a media company. For the first two years or so, beyond a one-time investment of approximately Rs. 2,500, a subscriber would have to pay nothing.

According to Sarma, the feedback from dealers of set-top boxes in recent times has been encouraging. Demand for the boxes for this free DTH service has increased with the addition of some private satellite channels.

Private sector TV channels that are being carried by DD Direct Plus include Zee Music, Smile TV and ETC Punjabi (from the Zee stable), Sun TV, Kairali TV, CNN, BBC, Star Utsav, Aaj Tak and Headlines Today, among the 30-odd channels being part of the service at the moment, according to Sarma.

"We are optimistic that we would be able to meet our target of one million subscribers by end 2005," Sarma said, adding that the demand is building up because it's a free service, unlike an existing service, Dish TV, which is 20 per cent owned by Zee Telefilms.

For example, in South India, the price of boxes were jacked up by dealers to about Rs. 3,500 as demand upped with the surfacing of South Indian language channels like Sun TV.

If Prasar Bharati's assertions are to be taken on its face value, then DD Direct Plus has notched up more subscribers in about 75 days than what Dish TV has managed to do since its launch in October 2003. Dish TV's claimed present subscriber base is approximately 160,000.

Though DD's DTH service is primarily aimed at those places where cable or terrestrial TV's penetration is low, it is banking heavily on the inclusion of private sector channels, especially the popular entertainment ones (like Star Plus, Sony, Sahara One and Zee TV) on the platform, which has not happened as of yet.

But DD is optimistic that a proposed initiative of the sector regulator would help it net most private sector channels on its DTH platform. At the moment, the Telecom Regulatory Authority of India is in the process of fine-tuning the interconnect regulations, which envisage a controversial clause on making available all TV channels to all types of platforms on a non-discriminatory basis.

Industry sources point out that this particular clause is designed to help DD more than anybody else as it would necessarily mean all pay channels also being made available to a free non-encrypted DTH service—a scenario that has not gone down too well with pay broadcasters who have been lobbying hard against the clause likely to be finalized before the commencement of next session of Parliament that begins from first week of December.

However, industry sources also point out, DD has become the first defaulter of the must-provide clause being debated as part of the interconnect regulations by Trai. The moment DD bagged the telecast rights of some of the cricket matches played in India last month, it sent a missive to Dish TV asking it to discontinue showing DD channels telecasting cricket. Dish TV complied with DD's request, but not before expressing to Trai its concern over this development.

There are over 900 dealers in 212 cities and towns attempting to push STBs for DD Direct Plus. A basic box for the costs approximately Rs. 2,500 (slightly over $54) and can access all free to air channels without the help of any smart card.

– Indiantelevision.com, 27 November 2004 –

Gyandarshan, as a public service broadcaster, could be considered India's first truly educational channel. It offers interesting and informative programmes of relevance to specialized categories—pre school kids, primary and secondary school children, college and university students, youth seeking career opportunities, housewives, adults and many others. In addition to educational fare, programmes from abroad are also broadcast to offer viewers a window to the world (IGNOU, 2005). In 2004–2005, Gyandarshan went completely digital and expanded into a bouquet of four channels. To make educational programmes more attractive and commercially viable, Doordarshan has made collaborative arrangements with other ministries and government departments for the production of programmes in diverse fields[8]. No matter how the analysis is carried out, it is clear that true public broadcasting television as conceived by the founders of the Indian constitution is largely like a private entertainment channel, devoid of its social responsibility. Just like in private channels, profit and revenue dictate programming philosophy and content, and it has turned pro-urban and rich.

FM Radio

For a long time, liberalization and globalization did not seem to have brought much change to public service radio as compared to television.

---

[8] Refer Ministry of Information and Broadcasting annual report 2004–2005, pp. 42–43.

It was much later, in the early years of this century that competition and commercialization crept into radio as well. Yet, in retrospect, radio in India has grown in two different directions—the private FM music channels and the public service education channels, while news remained conspicuous by its absence. This reality was reflected in the Review Commission on Prasar Bharati, which noted "private FM radio stations would target the up market, more urban listener. The private channel must primarily deliver an audience; rather than being a vehicle for delivering new ideas, information and education to its viewers and listeners"[9].

Educational broadcasts began since 1992, when AIR collaborated with Indira Gandhi National Open University (IGNOU) to telecast the university's educational programmes. In 1998, it also started the IGNOU-AIR Interactive Radio Counselling for students of Open/conventional Universities; this project aimed to bridge the gap between institutions and learners by instantly responding to their queries and providing academic counselling in their subject area. These programmes are relayed from 186 radio stations across India.

FM radio too came into the field of education with the launch of Gyan-vani, the educational FM radio channel of India. *Gyan* meaning knowledge and *vani* meaning aerial broadcasting, this channel is a unique concept of extending mass media for education and empowerment, suited to the local needs of the community (IGNOU 2001, as quoted by Vyas et al). Today, it operates from 40 FM stations, which has a localized coverage of about 60 km radius. The real challenge for Gyanvani is to develop language-specific, area-specific programmes with the help of local expertise, and involving the local listeners in the educational and developmental endeavour. In the present first phase of Gyanvani, 50 per cent of the country's population is expected to be covered.

In December 2002, the government of India decided to grant Community Broadcasting licenses to well-established educational institutions/organizations recognized by the central government or the state government. Thus, the country's first community radio station became operational on 1 February 2004 at Anna University, Chennai, in the southern state of TamilNadu, and later at two more stations at Erode (TamilNadu) and Pondicherry.

Meanwhile, a network of private FM radio channels known as Radio Mirchi was launched in seven cities. Mirchi is the Hindi word for chilli; and the station beams music programmes through the day. All India Radio had

---

[9] Refer http://mib.nic.in/informationb/AUTONOMOUS/nicpart/pbservc.htm

a single FM radio music channel, FM1, which was later renamed Rainbow (The Hindu, 2000–2005). A similar phenomenon that was earlier played out in the case of television is now happening on radio.

The styles and formats on private and public radio are just as contrasting, as it is in the case of television. Subsequently, All India Radio launched a second FM radio channel, FM Gold, to be carried on 35 radio stations across the country. The need of the hour for All India Radio may well be to market itself more prominently, as Doordarshan had done.

Conclusion

Historical analysis of public broadcasting in India shows distinct use of radio towards political ends since its inception in colonial India. It was to serve the political masters attain political power and control the subjects. In the initial years of independent India, no major changes in broadcasting philosophy were visible. In the post economic liberalization phase, it seems the profit motive determines the end use of radio for entertainment more than information and news.

Television arrived in India more than a decade after independence. Like radio, it remained under the direct control of the government to serve the political purposes.

Repeated efforts have been made to create independent public broadcasting system that would maintain a high degree of objectivity and autonomy, the public service radio and television continued under government control until the economic liberalization.

Economic liberalization and arrival of cable television was a turning point in public broadcasting. In this phase, radio appears to be largely losing its listeners to television and somewhat lost its direction. The reason is that while FM radio acts as an entertainment channel, the AM radio continues to be the information and news channel. The growing number of private satellite television channels, both of Indian and foreign origin, has made the role of public service broadcasting more significant in addressing the diverse needs of viewers, whom private television channels do not address. Today, public broadcasting has been placed in a highly market-driven economy; therefore public service has been taken over by profit driven broadcasting and indirectly controlled by advertisers.

References

Agrawal, B. C. (2003). "Reporting News or Creating News: The Everyday Dilemma". Paper presented at the Seminar on Media as Vehicle of Change organized by AMIC-India and Institute of Mass Communication held in Pune on 8–9 August.

Agrawal, B. C. (2000). Culture, Communication and Development: An Indian Perspective. In M. S. Gore (Ed.), *Third Survey of Research in Sociology and Social Anthropology*. New Delhi: Indian Council of Social Science Research and Manak Publications Pte. Ltd.

Agrawal, B. C. (1997). Television Policy in India: Future Directions. Paper presented at AMIC-India National Conference on Television: Beyond 2000 held in Chennai on 14–15 November.

Baruah, U. L. (31 May 1983). This is All India Radio. Publications Division, Ministry of Information and Broadcasting. As referred by Kachan Kumar in Mixed Signals: Radio Broadcasting Policy in India. *Economic and Political Weekly*. New Delhi.

Dave, B. (2002). Redefining the Idiot Box. Development and Educational Communication Unit, Indian Space Research Organization, Ahmedabad.

Gopalakrishnan, A. (19 June – 2 July 2004). Doordarshan's Dilemma. *Frontline*, 21(13). India.

Swami, P. (20 September – 3 October 1997). Autonomy in Prospect. *Frontline*, 14(19). India.

Gyanvani Gyandarshan (2005). Gyanvani Educational Radio Network of India, Gyandarshan Educational TV Channel of India, Indira Gandhi National Open Univeristiy, New Delhi.

ICFAI. (2005). TV-Radio-Film Journalism, pp. 22. ICFAI University, Hyderabad.

Kumar, K. (31 May 2003). Mixed Signals: Radio Broadcasting Policy in India. *Economic and Political Weekly*. India.

The Hindu. (2000–2005). The FM War by Sevanti Ninan. Retrieved from www.thehindu.com/thehindu/mag/2003/05/11/stories

IGNOU. (2001). Gyan Vani: The Educational FM Radio of India. As referred by R. V. Vyas, R. C. Sharma & A. Kumar in Educational Radio in India, Turkish Online Journal of Distance Education-TOJDE July 2002, 3(3).

Publications Division, Ministry of Information and Broadcasting, India. (1985). An Indian Personality for Television, Volume I and II. Report of the Working Group on Software for Doordarshan.

Ministry of Information and Broadcasting, Government of India, New Delhi. (1978). Akash Bharati National Broadcast Trust. Report of the Working Group on Autonomy for Akashvani and Doordarshan.

Websites

Doordarshan: www.ddindia.com

All India Radio: www.allindiaradio.com

Pasar Bharathi: www.vigyanprasar.com

Public Service Broadcasting Trust: www.psbt.org

Australia
The ABC and Public Value— Public Service Broadcaster in the Age of Competition

Australia has had public broadcasting since the ABC[1] was founded in 1932. It has always existed in a dual system with both commercial and public broadcasters operating in both radio and television. Television was introduced as a dual system in 1956 and in 1980 a second public service broadcaster, SBS[2], was introduced. Up to the time of the introduction of increased competition in radio in the mid-80s and the advent of multi-channel television in the mid-90s, the Australian broadcasting system was fairly stable with a clear sense of the different purposes of the public and the commercial sectors. As has happened in many other countries with traditional public service broadcasters, the advent of increased competition in the communications landscape has created problems for the traditional public broadcasters. The most notable are the fact that public funding has not kept pace with

---

[1] The Australian Broadcasting Corporation (ABC) is Australia's national public broadcaster. Originally created in 1932 as a radio network, the Corporation has gradually expanded and diversified into all forms of mainstream media, providing television, radio and online services throughout metropolitan and regional Australia, and overseas via its Asia-Pacific Television service and Radio Australia. The Corporation also runs a chain of ABC Shops selling books and audio/video recordings related to its programs, and publish its own magazines. The ABC is non-commercial, and is funded almost entirely by direct annual grants from the federal budget (en.wikipedia.org).

[2] The Special Broadcasting Service (SBS) is one of two government funded Australian public broadcasting radio and television networks, the other being the ABC. The stated purpose of the SBS is "to provide multilingual and multicultural radio and television services that inform, educate and entertain all Australians and, in doing so, reflect Australia's multicultural society". SBS began as a non-commercial network, but more recently has begun accepting and broadcasting television. It is notable, however, that advertisements are generally shown between programs; the network shows most its programs uninterrupted by "commercial breaks" (en. wikipedia.org).

increased costs and this, together with the imperative to move on to new platforms such as the internet and digital television, has put a great deal of pressure on public broadcasters' ability to maintain quality, diversity and audiences as well as to respond to the changing technological and regulatory pressures.

With the introduction of new platforms (cable television, the Internet and especially digital TV) and the consequent proliferation of channels and viewing and interacting opportunities, there is an increasing threat to the viability of the argument that the ABC and the SBS, as just two options among a plethora of choices, ought to have exclusive access to government support.

Economists have often argued the need for public service broadcasting (PSB) in terms of so-called "market failure". This means that the market is structured in such a way that some services, which are considered to have social value, are not supplied.

In this case, some form of intervention is justified to remedy this lack (Collins & Murroni, 1996: 7–8; Graham et al, 1999: 37–38). Before the multi-channel universe, it was possible to argue quite convincingly that certain broadcasting services—programmes for cultural minorities, programmes for children, education programmes, arts programmes—were not delivered by the market, as the ratings and the buying power of the audiences were not sufficient to provide them through a market mechanism.

But in the situation where 200 channels will be, or are available, many of which are able to ensure their financial viability by being able to reach transnational audiences, it is much harder to argue that these various minority audiences are not catered for. After all, pay TV and/or digital TV, which offer the technical possibility of hundreds of channels necessarily address niche audiences of taste or culture—that is, after all their *modus operandi*. Furthermore, much of the specialized information previously the preserve of the public service broadcaster—for example, science, health, technology, arts—is available via the Internet and via specialized TV channels such as the Discovery Channel or National Geographic. In such a situation, it appears that much of what has been considered the special mission of the ABC, is covered by other marketplace providers. Critics of the ABC and the SBS, in particular its television service, argue that in any case they are mostly providing for an affluent audience who are well able to pay for the services now being provided courtesy of the taxpayer (Jones, 1997: 257).

In this situation PSB has been forced to do two things: Firstly, it has had to ensure that it does not lose audiences, which would further undermine its argument for government funds; secondly, it has had to devise programming

---

ABC AND ITS ELITE AUDIENCE

My concern is that working-class taxes are being spent in order that the middle classes can watch The Vicar of Dibley and Ballykissangel without ad breaks. I think there is an element of snobbery or social distinction in Australia according to whether you like English or American popular culture. Many middle-class people's sense of social identity comes in part from the fact that they like British shows rather than American ones. It's a mark of intellectual distinction.
    – Michael Duffy, conservative columnist quoted in The Age (21 April 2001)

It's quite demeaning to talk about programmes on the ABC being a middle-class enclave when the diversity of the programmes appeal to everybody, What he is saying is that other Australians don't deserve these kinds of programmes without the burden of commercials.
    – Lee Burton, Lecturer in Media Studies at RMIT, quoted by the Age (21 April 2001).

What they (ABC supporters) demand is more money to do more of the same with the same people for a narrow and shrinking audience. Taxpayers are not going to fork out more money for the ABC unless it caters more thoroughly and distinctively to their needs ... The ABC has increasingly catered to a well-to-do elite that has other options available to it and has the wherewithal to pursue these options.
    – Mike Nahan, Executive Director, Institute of Public Affairs.

– Friends of the ABC –

---

strategies which appeal to broad audiences, not just so-called "elites", in order to address the claim that only affluent audiences use it, and ought to be forced to pay for it via subscription. In this chapter, I examine what one of the Australian public broadcasters, the Australian Broadcasting Corporation (ABC) is doing to respond to current conditions in the Australian broadcasting landscape.

The Australian context

The broadcasting sectors

Broadcasting in Australia consists of three main sectors—commercial, public service (called "national" in the Broadcasting Services Act 1992) and community. In the last 10 years the commercial sector has become very centralized with a virtual national networked system in both radio and television. In radio, there are four major networks and each of them cover between 50 per cent and 58 per cent of the Australian population (Communications Update, 2003: 24). The rest of the population (mainly in rural areas) is covered by a myriad of small stations with a large number of small owners, but some of their programming is syndicated from the larger networks. In commercial television there are three major networks, the Seven, Nine and Ten networks. Each of them owns around four capital city stations around Australia, but via a system of virtual syndication, they control the programming of all of the 56 commercial free to air (FTA) TV stations in the country.

Pay television was introduced in 1995. At first there were three different services. The biggest, Foxtel, was owned (and still is) by a consortium consisting of Telstra (the main telecommunications carrier), News Limited (Rupert Murdoch's company) and Kerry Packer's Publishing and Broadcasting (PBL), the owner of the most popular FTA network, Network Nine. The two others were Optus Vision, operated by the second telecommunications carrier, Optus (now owned by Singtel of Singapore) and Austar, which operated via MDS and satellite in regional Australia. Foxtel and Optus Vision both operate in cities via cable. In the last two years there has been a virtual amalgamation of these three separate services into one. At this time and in the foreseeable future, Pay TV will be running at a loss. Currently about 20 per cent of Australian homes subscribe but this figure seems to be stuck, in spite of the recent introduction by Foxtel of digital Pay TV.

Community Radio in Australia must be counted as a success in spite of miniscule ratings for any single station. There are currently 337 community radio stations operating and they fall into two categories, general geographic area (GCA) with 158 stations and Special Interest (SI) which includes educational, ethnic, indigenous and religious (Communications Update, 2003: 20). They are supported by volunteer labour, sponsorship and advertising, and a tiny amount from the federal government to support a national community radio news service, which is beamed around the country via satellite. This sector brings a welcome injection of diversity into the broadcasting landscape, with a huge variety of music, of cultural and community news, of languages and of political points of view.

Community television, unlike radio, has had a very troubled history with on-again, off-again patterns of broadcast on very low power transmitters. At the moment a new service is due to begin in Sydney next year, but there is very little investment available to start it up and, without government money (unlikely) its viability is questionable.

Indigenous broadcasting

Australia's indigenous population (Aborigines and Torres Strait Islanders) comprises about two per cent of the total population. There has been special provision for indigenous broadcasting since the mid-80s. There is one commercial TV station, Imparja Television, operating out of Alice Springs in Central Australia, which is owned and controlled by an indigenous group, the Central Australian Aboriginal Media Association (CAAMA). There are 97 indigenous radio stations operating around the country, in cities, towns, rural and remote areas. In addition there are 80 low power television services operating in remote Australia. The latter are the successors of what was called the BRACS (Broadcasting to Remote Aboriginal Communities) scheme, established in the 80s. These installations consist of re-transmission facilities for radio and television and basic production and switching equipment which permits local insertion of video and audio material.

Mainly via the radio sector, 50 indigenous languages are covered (Meadows, 1999). These broadcasting outlets exhibit a huge variety of content, and they provide material very tailored to the needs of local indigenous communities, with important community and government information, as well as a variety of musical forms and indigenous cultural maintenance and expression. They also provide training for indigenous media workers. They were funded by government through ATSIC (the Aboriginal and Torres Strait Islander Commission) but this was abolished. However, their funding has continued on an interim basis, and no doubt will be taken over by whatever body succeeds ATSIC.

As part of its current review of current broadcasting arrangements, the government is presently conducting an inquiry into the feasibility of creating an indigenous broadcasting service on a bigger scale than the small and scattered services that already exist (DOCITA, 2004).

Digital broadcasting

Officially Australia has entered the digital era with digital radio having been on the agenda for about 10 years and with the planning process endlessly ongoing, but as yet, there are no digital radio services in operation. Digital television began at the beginning of 2001, having been mandated by federal government legislation, including the requirement, unique to Australia, to broadcast a certain amount in HDTV. Under the 2000 digital legislation both the commercial and national sectors were required to simulcast analogue and HDTV digital services until 2007 at which time the analogue service would be "turned off". In addition, the two public service broadcasters,

ABC and SBS, were permitted to "multi-channel" although under very constrained conditions, being forbidden to broadcast on their extra digital channels, drama, sport, news or entertainment.

Digital television has not had a high level of take-up in Australia. By mid 2003 a total of 75,000 digital TV sets had been sold in a TV household population of about six million (Schulze, 2003). At time of writing (2005) a series of inquiries are being conducted by the federal government into the viability of the government's digital broadcasting strategy. Some of the issues to be examined are whether the requirement to simulcast and analogue and digital service should continue or whether multi-channeling should be allowed immediately; whether a fourth commercial television service should be introduced; and, as indicated earlier, whether an indigenous service would be viable.

Although not acknowledged as such, these inquiries amount to an admission that the original digital strategy was fatally flawed. This was predicted by many commentators (and by the Productivity Commission) at the time. They saw the digital strategy as being in the grand tradition of media policymaking in Australia—keeping the owners of the three powerful commercial TV networks protected and happy. The requirement to simulcast analogue and digital services and the requirement for HDTV, together with the exclusion of new entrants to the market were a way of allowing the existing networks to maintain their dominant position while at the same time giving them the space to make the large investment to make the transition to digital. The ban on their multi-channeling was to placate the pay operators (including, of course, Rupert Murdoch, who owns 60 per cent of the newspapers in Australia). A gesture was made in the direction of multi-channeling by the introduction of a new category of service, unique to Australia, called datacasting, but the limitations on this were so onerous that, when the government called for bid for licenses, no one applied.

Ownership and control changes

At time of writing the government is reviewing the ownership and control regime within the Australian communications sector. At present the sector is quite heavily regulated with prohibitions limiting ownership of more than one of newspapers, television and radio in a single market. There are also limits on foreign ownership of Australian media (Barr, 2000: 14–15). The government's desired outcome is to remove all the formal limits on cross—and foreign ownership, arguing that such regulation is outmoded in the age of convergence and places limits on the ability of Australia's media enterprises to grow and to become major world players.

The government does acknowledge that there needs to be some kind of regulation to ensure "diversity of voice" but its preferred outcome is to do this via trade practices legislation rather than specific broadcasting legislation. At the same time the government is preparing to complete the privatization of the major telecommunications carrier, Telstra, and there are signs that this might be accompanied by a weakening of its community service obligations.

In such a situation it might be expected that the public service sector of broadcasting would have an even more important role that at present, with the rest of the communications sector becoming so marketized. However, the political problems faced by the ABC (see below) might simply mean that it is left even more unprotected in an era of greatly intensified competitive pressures.

Current shape of the ABC

The ABC currently operates six radio networks, which operate out of capital city and 50 regional radio studios, and are carried to all parts of the continent via 931 transmitters. It operates one television network and an online service. Radio has 99 per cent coverage of the Australian population and TV has 98 per cent. The six radio networks are shown in Table 1.

The television service provides only one channel, which has presented a historic difficulty for a broadcaster that is obliged to provide programming which is at once comprehensive and specialized. Traditionally, and to varying extents this has persisted, it has emphasized high quality, in-depth and independent news and current affairs, programmes for children, both pre-school and schools programmes, specialized programmes in science, religion and the arts, documentary, "quality" drama, and some sport (in recent years, "minority" sport like women's netball). It endeavours to maximize its Australian content, but in reality, is heavily dependent on the BBC, Channel 4 and sometimes ITV for much of its programming, especially in drama, sitcom and comedy.

ABC television's ratings are reasonably stable, having moved between roughly 13 per cent and 16 per cent share over the last 15 years, but for the most part hovering around 15–16. For comparison, the national TV ratings for the week 15–21 May 2005 are shown in Table 2.

ABC also runs an online service called ABC Online with content available via both narrowband and broadband. It was started in 1995 "on the smell of an oily rag" and has prospered ever since, with it being one of the consistently most visited sites in Australia (Martin, 1999). Its function is

Table 1

Network	Description	Share
Radio National	News and current affairs, documentary, radio features, drama, specialized programming (science, religion arts etc.)	1.8%
Metropolitan/local	Lighter news and current affairs, sport, talk-back, comment, part national material with local announcers and local content	8% in cities, often large share in rural areas, with at most only one commercial competitor
Classic-FM	Classical music.	2.5%
Triple J	Youth network, mostly music with some comedy and youth-oriented news	5% Covers 95% of Australia.
News Radio	Rolling news and current affairs and broadcast of Parliament	2%
Radio Australia	International service with heavy footprint in Asia-Pacific	N.A.

largely to promote and enhance its radio and TV services but it has also introduced new types of content with special sites for children, youth, arts spaces, a science site called The Lab, and a regional site called The Back Yard. Online forums on a range of political and community issues are a

Table 2

	Free to air	All TV	Percentage loss to Pay TV
Network Nine	28.8	23.0	17.36
Network Seven	26	21.8	16.1
Network Ten	24.4	20.3	12.7
ABC	15.5	12.9	16.7
SBS	5.3	3.6	32.0
Pay TV	15.7		

feature and opportunities are provided for online discussion with journalists and programme makers and special guests.

The transition to digital television (digital radio has still not arrived) has proved particularly difficult for the ABC. Digital television came into being at the beginning of 2001. As outlined briefly above, the government's digital settlement involved a requirement for all FTA channels to simulcast a digital and analogue service until 2007, a requirement for a certain amount of HDTV and a prohibition on using the digital capacity to multi-channel. This prohibition on multi-channeling was also intended to apply to the ABC and SBS, but after a series of representations to government on the issue, an amendment to the relevant act in the Senate saw the public broadcasters being allowed to multi-channel with some fairly tight restrictions. As Jock Given explains:

> (The) new amendment proposed no national news, sport or drama programmes (other than "occasional stand-alone drama programmes"), although it did include a laundry list of programme areas where the national broadcasters would be able to multi-channel. These included education, science, religion, arts, culture, history, public policy, foreign language news, subtitled foreign language programmes, children's programmes, the proceedings of parliaments, courts and tribunals ...
>
> (Given, 2003: 179)

Commentators saw these restrictions as excessively onerous, as they prevented the national public broadcasters from broadcasting material likely to appeal to a significant audience.

Nevertheless, and in spite of the fact that the ABC received no significant extra funds for the conversion to digital (it did receive a small one-off injection for some aspects of the technical conversion), let alone for the increased production or acquisition it would have to undertake, in 2002 the ABC did establish two digital channels. These were FlyTV, a channel for young people, and Kidz, a new channel for children. Kidz was aimed at primary school kids and Fly at 13 to 18 year olds. FlyTV consisted of music, games, interactive drama, special kinds of information programmes, educational features disguised as fun. There was much excitement among the ABC's innovators about the prospect these channels offered for experiments with interactivity, via both the digital service itself and the internet.

In the 2003 budget process the ABC made a submission to the government that, without an increase in its annual appropriation, it could not continue to offer all the services it was currently offering. This fell on deaf ears and in the 2003 budget, the ABC received no extra funds. The ABC announced the immediate cancellation of its digital multi-channel service, and also of a very popular programme for schools called "Behind the News". The latter decision provoked a storm of protest from school kids, teachers and parents.

In March 2005, the ABC relaunched a digital television channel, ABC2. It is subjected to the multi-channeling restrictions outlined above and, at the moment, consists mainly of time-switched repeats from the main channel or the archive, with a small amount of new information programming, with an emphasis on regional Australia. The review of the digital television regime, and of the whole broadcasting system, is likely to see the removal of the multi-channeling restrictions on the public broadcasters, but of course, without new funding, they will not be able to take full advantage of new channel capacity.

Shape of schedules and programming

If we examine the actual programming on ABC radio and television, it is possible to see significant changes in the last five years, changes which reflect the ABC's response to increased competition and to the demand to remain relevant. For some critics, the introduction of more popular programming has led to the charge that the ABC is "dumbing down", an accusation that has also been leveled at the BBC.

Radio

Due to limitations of space, I will make my coverage of radio brief. Of the six radio networks described above, the only one that creates much controversy is Radio National. Rather like Radio 4 in the UK, it is a virtually all-talk network (it carries some specialist music programmes, e.g. opera and world music). All of its content is highly produced and of a "specialist" nature, and includes magazine programmes on science, medicine, law, media, religion, and many areas of the arts. It also carries radio drama, book readings, commentary programmes, radio documentaries etc. and of course serious news and current affairs. It has major news bulletins morning, midday and early evening, each followed by half hour current affairs programmes which are the flagship programmes of their kind, and are immensely influential. It also has a one-hour national talk-back forum, called Australia Talks Back, in which serious issues of the moment are discussed by experts and callers.

The problem comes because Radio National has a miniscule audience—1.8 per cent share, but uses a large proportion of the radio budget. From time to time it is accused of being elitist, both from outside the ABC, and also from within, when jealous programme-makers from other areas eye its budget longingly. By contrast, Local Radio has a eight to nine per cent share in the cities, but uses far fewer resources. Radio National's news and current affairs is hated by politicians because it is probing, so attacks on it for being elitist are often pretexts for something else.

It is in the area of radio that the arguments for continuing to support a public broadcaster are strongest because ABC Radio is so strongly differentiated from commercial radio. In Australia, there are really only two kinds of commercial radio styles—mainstream pop music on FM (with comedy breakfast announcers), and talk-back on AM (with usually right-wing radio shock-jocks). Radio National, Classic FM and JJJ (with its alternative rock) present a real alternative. Local radio is less clearly differentiated because its style and commentary is a bit more populist. However, sports fans generally acknowledge that ABC sports commentary (carried on local radio) is superior to most of commercial radio, except for the Rugby League specialists on the Southern Cross Network (2UE, 3AW etc.).

One of the best arguments for the continuing need for public broadcasting was a scandal that broke in commercial radio in 2001—the so-called "cash for comment" affair. It was revealed that the two leading shock-jocks, Alan Jones and John Laws, were accepting secret payments of millions of dollars for making favourable comments on air about major corporations (Telstra and the big banks), and passing it off as their independent commentary. This story was revealed by ABC TV's programme, "Media Watch", and it led to a major inquiry by the regulator and an attempt—so far unsuccessful—to curtail the practice. In such a situation the presence of an independent media outlet, not funded by advertising, is critical (Turner, 2003).

Radio Australia is a highly valued service in our region. It has a special remit for broadcasting about and to the Asia Pacific area and broadcasts in Chinese, Vietnamese, Indonesian, Khmer and Tok Pisin (for Papua New Guinea, the Solomon Islands and Vanuatu). In the past it was been important to populations in China and Indonesia at times when the media in those countries was more restricted than it now is. And it is an extremely significant source of news and comment about local and international news issues in the Pacific Islands, many of whom are too sparsely populated and poor to be able to mount adequate news and information services of their own.

Television

On weekdays there are pre-school children's programmes from 6 a.m. until 10 a.m. They are a mixture of local (The Wiggles, Playschool) and imported

(Basil Brush). From 10 a.m. until midday there are programmes for schools. At midday there is a half hour news and current affairs programme, followed by a repeat documentaries or features from the night before, which last till 3 p.m. Then there are children's programmes till 6 p.m. From 6 p.m. to 6.30 p.m. there is usually a UK sitcom or serial (e.g. reruns of the original Dr Who), at 6.30 p.m. a magazine programme showcasing interesting people and their activities. At 7 p.m. there is the main news broadcast, followed by the prestigious and influential current affairs programme at 7.30 p.m., The 7.30 Report, compered by the highly respected journalist, Kerry O'Brien. 8 p.m. to 8.30 p.m. sees a science programme or documentary, 8.30 p.m. is the drama or major documentary slot. From 9.30 p.m. to 10.30 p.m. there is a mixture of comedy, arts, magazine, followed by another half hour current affairs programme. From 11 p.m. on parliamentary question time is broadcast followed by repeat dramas, movies, etc.

Saturday is dominated by kids programmes, sport and popular programming like wildlife, comedy and drama; Sunday includes religious programming, arts (three hours), gardening and the Sunday night prime drama slot, almost invariably a BBC costume drama.

The only indigenous programming currently available anywhere on mainstream Australian TV is the half hour programme, "Message Stick", which occupies the 6 p.m. slot on Fridays and is repeated on Sunday.

As already indicated above, ABC TV is comprehensive and includes programmes from across the range of contemporary TV genres. The only exception is reality programming. The only kind of reality programme which the ABC permits itself is the high-brow version of it like the "Edwardian Country House", which comes from the UK.

ABC TV is differentiated from the commercial sector by having a range of specialist programmes in the classic sense, e.g. in arts, religion, social history; it is also the case that only the ABC and SBS broadcast documentaries. As might be expected, these are not the ABC's most popular programmes. This honour falls to programmes which could, arguably, find a home on the commercial channels, e.g., "The Bill", "Agatha Christie", "Red Cap" (all British imports).

An unkind commentator might cynically observe that the only difference between the ABC and the commercial channels is that on the latter you get American programming and on the former, British programmes. Under Australian TV regulation, 55 per cent of the hours on commercial television must be Australian. As well as that there are minimum requirements in relation to drama and documentary (documentary definition is rubbery and the requirement low). The ABC is morally though not strictly bound by these quotas, but it struggles to maintain its Australian content. In the area of Australian drama, it is doing much worse than the commercials, who admittedly can keep up their quotas via long-running soaps like "Home and Away" and "Neighbours".

Virtually all of the ABC's bought-in programmes come from Britain. You might get one programme from another English-speaking country like Canada, New Zealand and South Africa in a year. And this programming is by and large very conservative. It reflects the demographic of the ABC TV audience, which is middle-aged, middle-class and white. However, there are pockets of prime-time programming which are designed for younger and more diverse audiences—the most popular programme among my students is the 10 p.m. Friday programme, "The Glass House", which is compered by three well-known young radio personalities and is an extremely irreverent combination of comedy and biting current affairs commentary. My students tell me this is where they get their news!

The ABC's funding problems have produced a crisis for its Australian drama production. From being leader in the field up to 10 years ago, it is now very hard to recall an ABC originated drama production of any distinction. In 1986 the ABC broadcast 100 hours of drama; now it is down to about 14. In 2005 the Managing director of the ABC, Russell Balding, announced that unless the ABC received increased funds, it would not be able to produce Australian drama at all. This fell on deaf ears in Canberra.

As already indicted, the "special interests" of pre-school and school age children are very well served by the ABC. Other communities—indigenous, NESB (Non-English Speaking Background migrants), youth—are not particularly well-served. Of course it is the special mission of SBS to cater to NESB audiences, although by 2005, it was debatable whether it was fulfilling this function (see box). Indigenous communities are being well-served by the community radio sector, as are various other communities of interest. With only one TV channel, as mentioned above, it is difficult for the ABC to be both comprehensive and specialized.

This tension has recently manifested itself around the issue of arts programming. ABC TV has been much criticized by the arts community for its dumbing down and neglect of the arts. ABC management has introduced a conscious policy of "arts by stealth", smuggling in arts in the guise of documentary (a reality type programme about taking opera into the outback), competition (an amateur competition to find the best singing truck driver), etc. Arts lovers scream that the ABC is neglecting the charter; management replies that arts programmes are of minority interest and the audience for them is well able to pay for their arts access through pay TV

ETHNIC GROUPS FIND SBS'S SEX AND SOCCER A TURN-OFF
BY CHRISTOPHER KREMMER

Ethnic communities are on the brink of divorce with SBS Television. Tired of a service they say is increasingly irrelevant to their needs, the Federation of Ethnic Communities Councils of Australia is considering throwing its weight behind community-based television instead, posing a direct threat to SBS's $137 million annual budget allocation.

"The only people who like SBS TV now are the cappuccino crowd—well-educated, middle-class people," said Abd Malak, chairman of the federation. "It's mainly sex and soccer, I think."

But the former Prime Minister Malcolm Fraser, whose government established SBS-TV in 1980, warns ethnic communities are playing with fire by criticizing it. "Given half a reason, this government will say "SBS has served its purpose" and save money by abolishing it," Mr Fraser said. "They [the federation] won't get restructuring, they'll get abolition. If the ethnic communities' councils want to capture SBS and make it their plaything, then it's wrong. It's not about Arabic programmes for Arabs, or Indonesian programmes for Indonesians, but programmes of interest to all Australians".

Grievances came to a head this month when a Vietnamese group succeeded in having a programme of news from Vietnam's state-run broadcaster VTV removed from the SBS schedule. They claimed the programme "Thoi Su" (Current Affairs) was propaganda. SBS admitted it had not honoured a pledge to consult the community, apologized, and withdrew the programme.

A leader of the Vietnamese campaign, Dr Tien Nguyen, said their victory had opened the gates to other groups. "Now, they must consult with us before deciding what to show," he said.

But Mr Malak said the federation was "very close to giving up on SBS-TV ... In the last three or four years, they have separated themselves from ethnic communities, they don't come to our functions or religious festivals".

The managing director of SBS, Nigel Milan, said: "We're not going to cover clog dancing from Brisbane Town Hall. We'll cover issues, rather than events".

In the course of representations on the Vietnamese issue, the federation wrote to SBS outlining its concerns about television in particular: decreasing foreign language programmes; a management and board whose composition fails to reflect the communities they serve; airing of material produced by dictatorships; and a lack of close ties with ethnic communities.

Mr Milan agreed to a series of national consultations suggested by the federation. His TV managers will be led around the country to face their critics.

Lobbying by the federation was instrumental in the original decision to establish SBS-TV, which attracts more than seven million viewers a week.

Federation insiders speak of Plan B, in which the organization would lobby Canberra for more funds for local ethnic stations, possibly at the expense of SBS.

The Minister for Communications, Information Technology and the Arts, Daryl Williams, said the Australian Broadcasting Authority was considering granting community television licenses in several cities, and the government encouraged ethnic communities to get involved.

– *Sydney Morning Herald, 20 December 2003, page 5* –

or DVD or other specialist sources. Management argues that its primary duty is to bring the arts to a wider audience, and if that means using populist genres, that's what they will do.

Aside from some examples like arts programming, I would say that the ABC is not dumbing down as much as its counterparts in Europe and New Zealand. It maintains a real distinctiveness from the commercial sector. However, as indicated above, this may simply depend on the fact that it sources its programmes from the UK not the US and that its real problem is the conservativeness of much of its programming and it appealing to a very narrow demographic.

A few years ago, the ABC as more of an innovator than it is now. Its drama was among the most interesting and challenging made in Australia. It ability to develop high quality drama was for a time assisted by the fact that it could source large pre-sales from the UK and access local funding assistance. Changes in the UK television market have pulled the rug out from under this. The ABC was also an innovator in programme genres, especially comedy. A number of comedians who have migrated to bigger salaries at commercial stations were trained and developed at the ABC.

The ABC used to operate special units for indigenous and NESB programming. Both of these ventures have been abandoned, not for lack of commitment, I believe, but because of funding constraints. Rightly or wrongly, the ABC believes it must improve its ratings. It believes that as competition increases in the broadcasting arena, it becomes more and more vulnerable to the argument that it does not serve enough of the Australian population to deserve funding from the public purse. So whereas in the past, ratings of six or seven (or even lower) could be tolerated for programmes which fulfilled the charter but were not mass audience programmes (arts, science, religion), nowadays such ratings put the ABC at risk. It is now necessary to maximize audiences in every timeslot, at least in prime time.

The price does not seem to me to have been a high one in terms of adherence to the charter. The high rating programmes are the News, which has made no concessions at all to populism and is valued because it isn't populist, "The Bill" (twice a week), "Australian Story" (a personality-centred

AUSTRALIAN BROADCASTING CORPORATION ACT 1983
SECTION 6: CHARTER OF THE CORPORATION

(1) The functions of the Corporation are:

    (a) To provide within Australia innovative and comprehensive broadcasting services of a high standard as part of the Australian broadcasting system consisting of national, commercial and public sectors and, without limiting the generality of the foregoing, to provide:

        (i) Broadcasting programmes that contribute to a sense of national identity and inform and entertain, and reflect the cultural diversity of, the Australian community.

        (ii) Broadcasting programmes of an educational nature.

    (b) To transmit to countries outside Australia broadcasting programmes of news, current affairs, entertainment and cultural enrichment that will:

        (i) Encourage awareness of Australia and an international understanding of Australian attitudes on world affairs.

        (ii) Enable Australian citizens living or traveling outside Australia to obtain information about Australian affairs and Australian attitudes on world affairs.

    (c) To encourage and promote the musical, dramatic and other performing arts in Australia.

(2) In the provision by the Corporation of its broadcasting services within Australia:

    (a) The Corporation shall take account of:

        (i) The broadcasting services provided by the commercial and public sectors of the Australian broadcasting system.

        (ii) The standards from time to time determined by the Australian Broadcasting Authority in respect of broadcasting services.

        (iii) The responsibility of the Corporation as the provider of an independent national broadcasting service to provide a balance between broadcasting programmes of wide appeal and specialized broadcasting programmes.

        (iv) The multicultural character of the Australian community.

        (v) In connection with the provision of broadcasting programmes of an educational nature—the responsibilities of the States in relation to education.

    (b) The Corporation shall take all such measures, being measures consistent with the obligations of the Corporation under paragraph (a), as, in the opinion of the Board, will be conducive to the full development by the Corporation of suitable broadcasting programmes.

(3) The functions of the Corporation under subsection (1) and the duties imposed on the Corporation under subsection (2) constitute the Charter of the Corporation.

(4) Nothing in this section shall be taken to impose on the Corporation a duty that is enforceable by proceedings in a court.

– www.abc.net.au/corp/charter.htm –

documentary programme), the Sunday night UK bonnet drama. The rest of the time the ABC pursues its diverse programming strategy, which still maintains a clear enough differentiation with respect to the commercial channels.

As might be expected, pay services in Australia are very dependent on overseas sources. Australian regulation does mandate a five per cent expenditure requirement for pay channels which are primarily drama or documentary channels, but given the differential between the costs of imported and locally produced programmes, this does not buy very many hours overall. So the pay channels are the familiar ones seen all around the world—several movie channels, The History Channel, Nickelodeon, National Geographic, Discovery, Disney, ESPN, UK TV, BBC World, CNN, Fox News etc. There are locally packaged channels but they are overwhelmingly dependent on overseas sources, mainly American and British.

It could be argued that some of the Pay TV channels are offering alternatives to the ABC. For example, the locally packaged arts channel, Ovation, includes a large number of arts performances (operas, ballet, theatre, concerts) as well as arts documentaries. Perhaps that should mean the ABC's premier role in the arts is superseded since arts audiences should be affluent enough to pay. You might also argue that the diversity of documentary on Pay TV makes the ABC's role in this area superfluous too. But quite apart from the recognition that not everyone who wants to watch documentary can afford to subscribe, what Pay TV does very badly is present programmes of local relevance. Its Australian content, outside of the one area of the various football codes, is very poor. This is unlikely to change and perhaps shouldn't. But it does mean that services specifically designed for Australian audiences will continue to be needed. Commercial TV in Australia does a pretty good job of addressing local audiences, but as argued above, it does not cover the wide range of topics and specialist interests that the ABC does. So at the moment, and in spite of increased competition and the resulting increased exposure to a diversity of sources, the ABC is still very much needed in the Australian media landscape.

Relationship with audiences

In spite of the real pressure on the ABC to consider ratings more than in the past, officially, especially when talking to government, the ABC lays emphasis on reach, not ratings. Research usually quoted has ABC TV with a weekly reach of about 80 per cent, good enough one might have thought, to allow some toleration of low ratings for some programmes, but in today's environment, seen as not enough to guarantee the ABC a secure future.

It also regularly commissions "appreciation research" and this routinely demonstrates a very high level of support for the ABC within the Australian community. A survey undertaken by the professional polling firm, Newspoll, in 2005 reported that 90 per cent of the Australian community believed that "the ABC provides a valuable service to the community" (ABC, 2005). There was actually an increase in the numbers in country and regional areas of Australia who rated the services as valuable, up from 88 in 2004 to 92 in 2005. For television, the demographic group, which showed the biggest increase in appreciation for the ABC was teenagers, with the figure increasing from 51 per cent to 71 per cent. The report does not tell us what prompted this increase, but it is very likely due to ABC Television's emphasis on innovative programming for young people, such as the local satirical news-oriented programme, "The Glass House", the music quiz, "Spicks and Specks" and some UK comedy imports, such as "Dead Ringers".

The ABC's relationship with audiences can also be judged by examining the intimacy and intensity of the engagement with the ABC's website, ABC Online. More will be said about this below. And finally, the ABC has a vociferous and sizable community support group, known as The Friends of the ABC (FABC). Though often lampooned as being middle-aged, middle-class and opposed to change, this group is very effective at times when the ABC is threatened, as it was during the unfortunate tenure of a former Managing Director, Jonathan Shier (2000–2002). The FABC's very prominent campaign against Shier's plans for the ABC was one factor in his removal.

Funding issues

PSB in Australia is funded mainly from direct government appropriation. This makes it very vulnerable to political pressure and to short-term budget and political exigencies. The ABC is prohibited from taking advertising, unlike SBS, which is permitted to do so, and which now derives about 20 per cent of its television budget from advertising.

The ABC's funding has been falling steadily for many years. In 1985–6 the ABC received $868 million in operational appropriation from the government, in 2004–5 $614 million. It has also received some one-off expenditure to assist with the conversion to digital, although this does not cover extra programming costs, only the technical conversion. It has also received a small amount of extra funding to foster regional production, most of which has been used for radio. The ABC's counterparts in other countries are funded at more than ten times its level. For example, the German system (ARD and ZDF) receive £4,757 per head of population, NHK (Japan) £3,471 and the BBC £1,981. By contrast the ABC receives £306.

Economist, Glen Withers, has compared the ABC's efficiency with its commercial counterparts, and has demonstrated that it has become more and more efficient over time. In 1961 its TV expenditure ratio against the commercial sector was 1.78; in 1998 it was 0.42 (Withers, 2002).

What is the reason for this apparent government neglect of the ABC? One reason is certainly a bias within the (Prime Minister John) Howard government, in power since 1996, towards a neo-liberal agenda, coupled with a relative indifference, compared with the preceding Keating Labor government, towards arts and culture. However, many commentators have also seen a connection between the ABC's political independence and funding decisions.

There has in fact been a long history of government antagonism towards the ABC, with governments of both hues resenting its critical edge when it comes to reporting political issues. (Prime Minister) Bob Hawke's Labor government had a major dispute with the ABC over its coverage of the 1991 Gulf War (Dempster, 2003: 56 ff.) and the 2003 Iraqi War led to an even more extraordinary attack on the ABC from the then Minister of Communications, Senator Richard Alston (Jacka, 2005). This was the culmination of a series of virulent attacks, both from the government and from the right-wing "commentariat" about left-wing bias and "elitism" within the ABC.

In 1996, the then opposition leader, John Howard, refused to allow the ABC to carry the debate between him and Prime Minister Keating because of his perception that the ABC moderator, Kerry O'Brien would be biased in favour of Keating. As soon as the coalition was elected it began a sustained attack on the ABC, which has not abated to this day, and this was accompanied by severe funding cuts, notably in 1996 when a serious $55 million was taken away from the ABC. The terms of the attack included continuing complaints about bias, but also included reference to how bloated and badly managed the ABC was, and also to its "political correctness", and its capture by liberal elites.

In 1997, Howard spoke about how the ABC that it:

> Had uncritically accepted the dominant values and understandings of the reformist left and was too concerned with minority and social concerns. Multiculturalism, reconciliation, anti-discrimination and environment concerns were some of the issues involved.
>
> (Petersen, 1999: 49)

Since the controversy about the Iraqi war coverage, the ABC has tied itself in knots to make sure it is seen to be "objective", but so far, there is no improvement in its funding outlook.

ABC Online

Because of the high cost of maintaining a television service, compared with the cost of radio and online media, the ABC's funding problems affect its television service most visibly. In contrast, the last five years have seen a renewal and refreshment of the public service mission in both radio and online media, due in no small part to the synergies between them.

In the early period, between 1995–2000, and in common with many media websites, the ABC adopted a gateway structure, with prominent pathways into the site via content gateways (e.g. science (the Lab), arts (The Space), Education, Indigenous, News, Public Affairs, Rural, Asia Pacific, Sport, Kids, Youth, Local (The Backyard)) and station gateways (each outlet in both radio and TV has a home page). These gateways added value to pre-existing content, promoted content on radio and television, and in many instances, added new content as well. Thus those in the "old media" who had initially seen ABC Online in a purely promotional way could easily see its greater potential when all ABC science content, for instance, could be accessed from the science gateway. One way in which Online enhanced the content of television, for example, was through online forums after particular TV programmes.

Some of the prestige News and Current Affairs programmes, e.g. "Four Corners" and "Foreign Correspondent" conducted forums in which the investigating journalist would go online and respond to questions and comments about the material in the programme. Some of these were extremely intense with real-time discussion continuing for two or more hours after the end of the programme. The journalists found these very exacting, and moderating them consumed a large amount of resources. Often the allocation of resources was disproportionate to the small numbers of participants, and real time forums have recently been largely replaced with "guest books", which are less resource intensive.

The BBC's charter manifesto, "Building Public Value", (BBC, 2004), talks about five kinds of public value that are essential to the public service vision in the communications landscape: (i) democratic value; (ii) cultural and creative value; (iii) educational value; (iv) social and community value; and (v) global value. While keeping a sense of these in mind, I would like to repurpose them and invoke a concept of digital public value. These values are:

- Interactivity
- Community
- Access
- Information
- Education
- Usability
- Citizenship/participation
- Diversity

What is striking about ABC Online (and this is undoubtedly true of other PSB websites around the world) is its immediate accessibility and usability compared with say, ninemsn. The oft-repeated opposition between citizen and consumer is starkly illustrated by the contrast between the ease of accessing ABC Online—even the ABC Shop Online—a commercial part of the site—and the convoluted registration process on ninemsn, where the long pathway to be traversed before the user is in makes it obvious what you are giving them (your consumer profile) before they give you the free E-mail service (Martin, 2004: 202).

In various ways, the ABC site has a particular brief for community and diversity, not matched by commercial media websites. Local/regional—the Backyard gateway offers an extraordinary diversity of material that is especially relevant to particular communities. A cross-platform project (local radio, online and TV) recently conducted a survey of wildlife in backyards across the country. Regional/global—via Radio Australia and the Asia-Pacific gateway ABC Online achieves a significant international audience for many programmes that have quite a small Australian audience. And at least until recently, when funding shortfalls have constrained them, the ABC site has sought interactivity, emphasizing real-time forums.

As Fiona Martin noted in her analysis of ABC Online (Martin, 2004: 201), the ABC website is the only one which is not dependant on a specific operating system for premium usability (ninemsn works better with Windows than with other operating systems), has forums (at least until their use was limited by resource constraints) and guest books, and a long window of access to free news. This demonstrates its adherence to the digital values of access, usability and information. Its embrace of the digital values of community, diversity and citizenship is illustrated by the regional site, The Backyard, devoted to coverage of regional and rural Australia (Martin and Wilson, 2002), and the indigenous gateway, "Message Stick".

In March 2005 the ABC began "podcasting", making available virtually all of its Radio National content as downloadable MP3 files. This was a huge success, with accesses exceeding all expectations. This phenomenon, plus the multiplicity of other repurposing of content being done through ABC Online, has given the ABC a new lease on life. There is evidence in 2005 that younger audiences are returning to ABC "old media" services, and one can only conjecture that they are being led there via new media.

References

Australian Broadcasting Corporation. (31 August 2005). Media release: Community sentiment towards public broadcasting remains strong.

Barr, T. (2000). *Newmedia.com.au*. Sydney: Allen and Unwin.

BBC. (2004). Building Public Value: Renewing the BBC for a Digital World. London: The BBC. Retrieved on 8 May 2005 from www/bbc.co.uk/the future/pdfs/bbc_bpv.pdf

Collins, R., & Cristina M. (1996). *New Media, New Policies: Media and Communications Strategies for the Future*. Cambridge: Polity Press.

Communications Update. (2003). *Media Ownership Update*. Communications Law Centre, UNSW, Sydney.

Dempster, Q. (2000). *Death Struggle: How political malice and boardroom powerplays are killing the ABC*. Sydney: Allen and Unwin.

Department of Communications Information Technology and the Arts. (2004). A discussion paper on A Review of the Viability of Creating an Indigenous Television Broadcasting Service and the Regulatory Arrangements that Should Apply to the Digital Transmission of such a Service Using Spectrum in the Broadcasting Services Band: Discussion Paper. Retrieved from www.docita.gov.au/

Given, J. (2003). *Turning off the Television: Broadcasting's Uncertain Future*. Sydney: UNSW Press.

Graham, A. (Ed.) (1999). *Public Purposes in Broadcasting: Funding the BBC*. UK: University of Luton Press.

Jacka, L. (2005). The Elephant Trap: Bias, Balance and Government-ABC relations during the Second Gulf War. *Southern Review*, 37(3), 8–28.

Jones, R. (1997). Does Australia really need the ABC? *Agenda*, 4(2), 253–263.

Martin, F. (1999). Pulling together the ABC: the Role of ABC Online. *Media International Australia*, 93, 103–118.

Martin, F. (2004). Net Worth. In G. Goggin (Ed.), *Virtual Nation: The Internet in Australia*. Sydney: UNSW Press.

Martin, F., & Wilson, H. (2002). Beyond the ABC's Backyard: Radio, the Web and Australian regional Space. *Convergence*, 8(1), 43–61.

Meadows, M. (2000). The indigenous broadcasting sector. *Productivity Commission*.

Petersen, N. (1999). Whose news? Organizational conflict in the ABC 1947–1999. *Australian Journalism Monographs*, No. 3 & 4. Department of Journalism, University of Queensland, Brisbane.

Schulze, J. (2003). A Digital Dead-end. *The Australian: Media*, 5–11 June, pp. 3.

Turner, G. (2003). Ethics, Entertainment and the Tabloid: The case of talkback radio in Australia. In C. Lumby & E. Probyn (Eds.), *Remote Control: New Media, New Ethics*, (pp. 87–99). Melbourne: Cambridge University Press.

Withers, G. (2002). Funding Public Service Broadcasters. *Southern Review*, 35(1), 107–119.

9

Malaysia
Broadcasting, Public Culture and Ethnic Spheres

"Western" discourse on Public Service Broadcasting (PSB)—modelled after the BBC in particular—has not only been challenged in recent times in most of Europe and the United States amid changing media technology and rising privatization fever, but also bears little or no resemblance to its original conception in Asian countries such as Malaysia.

Since the Second World War and for a long time as compared to other media forms, television is believed to have had a great impact on audiences, despite research arguing that the forces influencing society are beyond television. Because of its ability to reach large numbers of people, it has been contended that television must be regulated in such a way that it is accountable neither to the state nor to the market but to the public alone. In other words, it is argued that a civil society can best be developed through the mechanism of public broadcasting detached from all forms of vested interest. As explained by Syvertsen (2003) and Tracey (1998), this means providing states "with the power, both technical and economic, to ensure that what's aired is morally, culturally and intellectually valuable to the general public". This privilege comes with obligations and the authors maintain these include principles of pluralism, diversity, universality, non-commercialism and independence (see also Collins, 2004).

To what extent is the public interest represented through television's central nation-building role in Asian countries such as Malaysia? Does public interest from an "Asian" journalistic standpoint mean, inter alia, taking preventive measures to avoid conflict and tension by "highlighting the positive and not the negative" (Moses, 2002: 105), as described by the news editor of *The New Straits Times*, a leading English language newspaper in Malaysia? Theorists on Asian media such as Kitley (2003: 12) contend that institutionalized relationships between bureaucratic authorities and private corporations in strong states block "the mediation of matters of public interest championed by civil society". He explains,

> In modern western political philosophy, civil society is premised on a clear distinction between the government and non-government spheres. To extend this distinction to the political culture in many Asian states is to misunderstand grossly the dynamics of what Linda Weiss and John Hobson call "governed interdependence".
>
> (Kitley, 2003: 7)

Thus, using Malaysia as a case, I argue that public service broadcasting has not been conceived in the traditional Western European sense and its current state is in effect a far cry from what is theorized. It was not born out of an Act of Parliament or by a Royal Charter but via the power of the ruling Barisan Nasional—the national coalition party (Nain, 2002: 119). Some of the transformations taking place today in the realm of public service broadcasting in the US and Western Europe are not comparable to the scenario in Malaysia. While Western Europe and the US may lament over the commercialization of the public domain, developing countries like Malaysia are hacked by a doubled-edged sword—commercialization and indigenization (Malayismization) in the wake of globalization.

As a state privilege, television in post-colonial Malaysia has hardly ever been delegated to the citizenry. For example, those who control operation and content creation tend to assume that the people must be guided, and television, especially in the context of a rapidly decolonizing and modernizing society, must protect the nation's "public culture" and for this the state knows better. Cultural protectionism through state television tends largely to refer to the sifting and discarding of "foreign" elements in the smooth institutionalization of a Malay(sian) national culture. However, despite such an ambition, programme content tends to continue to reflect large portions of importation, though no longer entirely and purely from the "western world". Where such importation takes place as in the case of popular game shows like the British "Who wants to be a Millionaire" or the American "Wheel of Fortune" local actors and icons replace the foreign making them as culturally specific and appropriate as possible. While in Egypt a fatwa was issued calling "Who wants to be a Millionaire" a sinful form of gambling (Banerjee, M. 2002: 109), it is of popular taste in modern Malaysia drawing large audiences and large numbers of Muslim contestants.

Indrajit Banerjee (2002), in his critique of the cultural imperialism thesis, explains how cultural production has been pluralized and in particular regionalized, in the context of liberalization and deregulation in most of Asia since the 1980s. Explaining this further, Mandira Banerjee points out:

> ... as the Western world is English centric, the pattern in Latin America, as in Asia and the Middle East have proven to be geo-linguistic regions as well. Each becomes dominated by one or more centres of audio-visual production. For instance, Mexico and Brazil for Latin America; Hong Kong and Taiwan for Chinese-speaking people; Egypt for the Arab world; India for the Indian populations of Asia and Africa.
>
> (2002: 109)

While the West may seem decentralized through the ongoing and simultaneous process of globalization, regionalization, multiculturalism and decolonization, the notion of asserting national identity based on the superiority of the "Malay race" continues to suture media representations and discourses in modernizing Malaysia. The national broadcast industry as a whole is a Malay business corporation built on Malay national values for a Malay national family in multi-ethnic Malaysia. Minorities, by accident of birth, shall remain a peripheralized national mediated symbol (cf. Morley, 2004) until independent and fair-minded programme producers are born.

The *bangsa* (race) essentialized characteristic of state policies such as the New Economic Policy[1] and Vision 2020[2] perpetuates and deepens group identity and firmly underwrites media discourses and images. Malays, Chinese and Indians[3] are represented as though no differences prevail within each group and as if no other ethnic groups exist. Ethnic communities in Sabah and Sarawak and the Orang Asli in peninsula Malaysia, for instance, are often excluded. This exclusion is taken for granted and naturalized in politics, employment, religion and education. The naturalization of *bangsa*, hence, makes it a determining element of culture, politics and economics in modern Malaysia.

---

[1] The New Economic Policy (NEP) was implemented in the 1970s, immediately following the 1969 ethnic conflict, to help uplift Malays who were seen as economically backward in comparison to the Chinese and Indians. Under an affirmative action programme, Malays were given special privileges such as quotas allowing them to enter universities and gain employment even if less qualified than applicants from other races. It also allocated 30 per cent of the equity in local companies to Malays. news.bbc.co.uk/1/hi/world/asia-pacific/886337.stm

[2] Malaysia's Vision 2020 to become an industrialized First World country was launched by Mahathir Mohamed in February 1991. It prescribes inter alia that Malaysia ... must be a nation that is fully developed in terms of national unity and social cohesion, in terms of social justice, political stability, system of government, quality of life, social and spiritual values, national pride ... (Goh, 1998: 170)

[3] Malaysia's 25 million people are largely multi-ethnic made up of 58 per cent Malays (*bumiputera*), 24 per cent Chinese, eight per cent Indian and 10 per cent other (including indigenous) ethnic groups.

The paper attempts to explore how the state strategizes public and private television in manufacturing a public culture, arguing that the Vision 2020 desire to create a public Malay(sian) culture for poly-ethnic and multi-religious Malaysia seems nothing more than a myth mediatized through polarized spheres.

News media debacle

Television—born as a state instrument in 1963—seen universally as a forceful mechanism capable of manufacturing common symbols and significations, continues to remain government apparatus, despite private television in the 1980s and the ushering of, other than cable (Mega TV in 1994), satellite television (Asia Satellite Television and Radio Organization—ASTRO—in 1996). Thus, the notion of "high culture" traditionally linked to PSB, does not seem to ring a bell nor commensurate with multiple meanings given to it in controlled and constricted environments where public television really means state television (*penyiaran kerajaan*). For example, although one might have the opportunity to witness the nationally televised Olympics as world citizens and the pilgrimage to Mecca as Ummahs, one may not be fortunate enough to be presented with the ethnic conflict in Sri Lanka, the Falun Gong persecution in China, death (by food poisoning) of activist Munir Said in Indonesia, the atrocities in East Timor prior to independence, and at home, the Kampung Medan ethnic conflict. Indeed, problems and issues confronting several minority communities around the world and indigenous groups like the Orang Asli in the homeland seem so distasteful to producers that they have hardly ever been aired. This absence of ethnic minority stories and images is in contrast to what Gabriel (1998) contends with regard to British racialized ideas of the nation where there has often re-emerged narratives of otherness that take ethnic minorities as "visible explanations" for social problems such as crime and through such regular articulation of "difference" causing moral panics (see also Hall et al 1978). Although minorities tend to be criminalized this way in western media, I contend it is through such moral panics and problematization that injustices and irregularities are brought to the fore and rectified. Moral panics do occur from moment to moment in Malaysia but these mostly problematize the Malay and seem deliberated to stabilize and normalize Malay culture and politics.

The sexuality-centred news narratives of the Anwar Ibrahim trial from 1998 to 2000 with media headlines such as "Sodomized: Two jailed six months for sex with Anwar" (*The Sun*, September 1998), "We had Sex in the Car, says Munawar" (*The Sun*, September 1998), and the satanic-centred Muslim youth deviance reports in 2001 with media headlines such as "black metal focuses on Satanism" (*The New Straits Times*, July 2001) and "Muftis want black metal music decreed 'haram' " (*The New Straits Times*, August 2001) are two Malay-centred episodes of moral panics in Malaysia—orchestrated mainly to stabilize Malay culture and hegemony.

Negative reporting of national events and people is not a principle of Malaysian journalism, contends Moses (2002), a veteran journalist. How could reporting approximate truth, when through the routine reliance on institutionalized sources such as government officials, media privileges their definition over events at the expense of counter-hegemonic minority voices (Cottle, 2000a: 432–3)?

Through framing and agenda-setting, issues are played out to guard the "national culture" and shoeshine national politics. Moses (2002) presents two useful examples in his article—first, the Kampung Medan ethnic conflict in early 2001 (primarily between disadvantaged Indian and privileged Malay communities in a Kuala Lumpur ghetto) which was not reported with journalistic responsibility to citizens who had the right to know; and second, the drastic downfall in the intake of poor Indian students into public universities used by the Malaysian Indian Congress (MIC)[4] leader to lobby for the perpetuation of an ethnic-based quota system which had in fact disadvantaged Indians and other minorities and over the last 30 years debased and ethnically mutinied higher education in Malaysia.

The Indian politician nor the media asked not why Indians and other indigenous minorities were socio-economically backward as this was asked of the Malays three decades ago and justified through the New Economic Policy and legitimatized through stringent laws and regulations[5] that forbid the questioning of such a policy. Hence, instead of reporting conflicting views, unearthing root causes through in-depth ethnographic reporting and providing fair space for debate, blanking the powerless, forgetting and/or burying them, seems the preferred position under the pretext that Malaysian audiences are recalcitrant.

---

[4] The Malaysian Indian Congress (MIC), headed from 1979 to date by Samy Vellu, is a coalition partner with the Malaysian Chinese Association (MCA), United Malays National Organization (UMNO) and 10 other parties mainly from Sabah and Sarawak, in the ruling Barisan Nasional (BN), formed in 1973 as a successor to The Alliance (Parti Perikatan) and has ruled since independence.

[5] For example, the Internal Security Act of 1960 sees as offensive speech or publication about traditional Malay rulers, Islam (the official religion), the Malay language (Bahasa Melayu/Malaysia) or that which may incite ethnic conflict.

Place, memory and identities

Insofar as various ethnic groups are not represented as differentiated elements of the national culture, their exclusion from the public sphere can be seen as contributing to a hegemonic discourse, which seeks to assimilate differences providing mythical account of the public national culture (Hall, 1980; Jakubowicz, 1994). In the context of ethnic minorities and the media in Australia, Jakubowicz (1994) contends that the media "in all their diversity are deeply implicated in the formulation of our understanding of what the range of meaning behind the label "Australian" might be". For most Malaysians who do not meet most of their fellow country people, in the consciousness of each, imaginatively, they exist in communion and herein lies the essence of the "national imagined community" (Anderson, 1983). In proposing a definition of the nation, Anderson says:

> It is an imagined political community ... It is imagined because the members of even the smallest nation will never know most of their fellow-members, meet them, or even hear of them, yet in the mind of each lives the image of their communion.
>
> (1983: 15)

Despite ethnic identifiers such as "I am Chinese" or state privileged ethnic positions such as "I am *bumiputera*"[6], the nation remains a cultural unit of identification, at least when one travels abroad and is confronted with the question, "Where are you from?" Thus, the answer, "From Malaysia" will most often be followed with the question, "Are you Malay?" Alas "who am I?" becomes a necessary question for ethnic minorities and diasporas whose identities have become de-territorialized, hybridized and fluid. The media thus remain central to our conception of "who we are" and "where we belong" particularly in the context of diasporas and cross-cultural communities (see Barker, 1997; 1999). With increased movement of population and the transfer and transplant of differing cultures within one nation, the method of identifying who we are through geographical location seems increasingly irrelevant (Sinclair and Cunningham, 2000). As argued by Indrajit Banerjee (2002: 524), globalization theory spells out "the need to understand cultural interactions and change through processes of cultural hybridization and the articulations between various cultural identities and forms, ranging from the patrimonial and local to the trans-

---

6 *Bumiputera* is a Malay term which means son or prince of the soil. It has been normalized in Malaysia to refer to indigenous communities such as the Malays and communities in Sabah and Sarawak. It however excludes the Orang Asli, an indigenous community in Peninsula Malaysia.

cultural and international". The nation as such is not the primary cultural identification for a citizen. Like most other nations in an interconnected world, the Malaysian cultural nation is a fiction, an imaginative construct, seeking to unite its dispersed and diverse multicultural citizenry. This fiction, mythologized for instance via state television campaigns tends to present at the political nation-building level, public culture as mostly Malay and masculine underpinned by Islamic mores and topped by Malay ceremony, while at the global-commercial level public culture frequently appears pluralistic, feminine and secular filled with lyrics such as "Malaysia truly Asia". Not only do these images, at national and global levels, conflict, they are constructed on narrow premises and as such fail to capture and deliver the wholesome and diverse history and culture of a Malaysian world.

The official interpretation of history, art, people and language, contends Benjamin (1968) always serves the interests of the contemporary ruling elite. Most modern states today tend to be characterized by conflict and unlikeness rather than by likeness and cohesion. However, in haste to create new decolonized nations, through convergence and identification among heterogeneous national population, the modern state commonly seeks to impose a standardized national culture. The state as such, selects elements from the pre-existing cultural wealth within its territory and radically transforms them into homogenizing national high culture (Gellner, 1983: 55–58). This involves a rigorous process of screening, sifting, selecting and excluding in the process of writing the national history and culture.

In a globalized world, shifts and transformations in interactions have led to the forging of trans-national cultural communities, the rethinking of notions of place and the compressing and collapsing of time and space, public and private (Meyrowitz, 1985). Mass communication technologies, in Bhabha's words (1990: 300) "transform the "difference of space" into the "sameness of time" by replacing the lack of physical interaction among a national population with an imagined bond". Thus, media technologies facilitate the development and the imagination of the modern nation and it is the modern (strong) state which dictates the content of this process. Cultural institutions such as the media are often used by the state to facilitate the process of "normalizing, rendering natural, taken-for-granted, in a word, "obvious" what are in fact ontological and epistemological premises of a particular and historical form of social order" (Corrigan and Sayed in Johnson 1994: 184). States ambitiously scheme and relentlessly strive to render natural and obvious "national culture" and "national history" due to their central positionality in fostering a sense of cohesion among people over space and time.

Nationally mediatized communities, hitherto, need to be re-conceptualized and re-imagined in light of the rapid flow of people, ideologies, technologies and in the process the trans-nationalizing, hybridizing and de-territorializing of communities. This re-conceptualization needs to be underwritten by a fair account of the nation's many people and their cultural substance. With a stringently guarded and regulated migration policy, close to zero migration other than through cross-national marriages, Malaysia is not experiencing the dynamics of an ever-increasing and changing flow of migrant communities. Nevertheless, Malaysia has historically been dominated by a majority immigrant population made up of Malays, Chinese and Indians and has since the 1980s re-witnessed the arrival of large numbers of new immigrants (legal and illegal) mostly from neighbouring Indonesia. Through the importation of foreign workers, in the main from Indonesia, she is being offered and confronted by a new "Malay" community—neither Malaysian nor *bumiputera* yet easily absorbable into either or both. Malaysia is estimated to have some 1.2 million foreign workers and an equal number of undocumented ones. More than 83 per cent of the workers are from Indonesia while the rest are from Philippines, Thailand, India, Cambodia, Laos, China, Vietnam, Bangladesh, Sri Lanka and Pakistan (*Asian Labour News*, 16 May 2005). Why, one may ask, are the bulk of migrant workers from Indonesia? Is this privileging of foreign workforce also a significant part of the imagining of the Malaysian nation manifested via modern architectural icons such as the world's tallest Petronas Tower (1, 457 feet), laboured by Indonesian workforce for their Malaysian brethrens? Goh (1998: 173) in referring to Malaysia's fetish for loftiness quotes an advertisement which reads, "At 500 feet above sea level, you can't help but look down on others".

Thus as large numbers of Indonesians become assimilated into the Malay culture and as Malaysian Chinese and Indian minorities shrink and continue to remain outside the Malay public culture, a mythic sense of "national cultural unity" and homogeneity becomes highly problematic. The "outsiders" (immigrant Indonesian workers) are made to belong while the "insiders" (Malaysian Chinese, Indian and other minorities) are left to remain outside because they do not belong to a "traditional (mythical) "way of life"" (Cottle, 2000b: 5). The national public is "usually constructed in the language of some particular ethnos, membership of which then effectively becomes the prerequisite for the enjoyment of a political citizenship within the nation-state" (Morley, 2000: 118). Anderson (1983: 30) and Bhabha (1990) both contend that "the imagining of a national communion is made possible by the development of mass media technologies which provide the technical means for representing the kind of imagined community that is the nation". Although Bhabha and Anderson present a non-essentialist understanding of the nation, Bhabha examines how difference is articulated moving on as such from Anderson's concern with how sameness is imagined within national boundaries.

Television typically organized as a centralized national broadcaster is a symbolic institution vital in mediating the contemporary national fiction to the public. Hall (1996) describes how the media functions as an important site of cultural production where the meaning of race (ethnicity) is articulated and re-presented. As van Dijk (1991: 39) argues in the context of western media "… if the press endorses the ideology that legitimates white group dominance, it may be expected that it will discredit, marginalize or problematize anti-racist positions and groups".

How and why does (not) the media in Malaysia, and in particular television, problematize ethnic minorities? How is television used by the state in the (re)construction of public culture and national identity? First, some understanding of Malaysia's broadcast history.

History in mind

Before television, radio played a territorializing role in the formation of independent Malaya (1957) and the Federation of Malaysia (1963). Significantly, in the period between 1948 and 1960 (known as the Emergency) in the propaganda offensive against communist insurgency and during confrontation with Indonesia in 1965, radio played a determining role. Glattbach and Balakrishnan (1978) identified the Communist insurgency of 1948 and the confrontation with Indonesia in 1965 as key factors that spurred radio expansion in the formative years of Malaysia. Kitley and Nain (2003) likewise maintain that "the emergency had a major impact on the infrastructure and ideology of broadcasting in Malaysia". Following commercial radio broadcasting in 1962 and the external service Suara Malaysia a year after, television broadcasting saw its entry into the Malaysian multi-cultural fabric on 28 December 1963 (Glattbach & Balakrishnan, 1978), approximately six years following independence from British rule, and since has been a state monopoly, perpetuating the British set up dating back to 1946 when the first Department of Broadcasting was established in Singapore (part of Malaysia until 1965). In other words, its purpose since inception has been to propagate state ideology.

A second emergency, following the bloody ethnic riots of 13 May 1969, led to a second television network being set up in November 1969. In the same year, and following the riots, major structural and ideological changes took place importantly the integration of radio and television (Radio Television Malaysia—RTM) into the Department of Broadcasting under the Ministry of Information and Broadcasting. The primary role of RTM has since been the promotion of national consciousness, national unity and a Malaysian culture aligned to *Rukunegara*—the state ideology.

At policy level, broadcasting is regarded as a major tool in developing national unity in a multiracial society (Kitley & Nain 2003; Glattbach & Balakrishnan 1978). Although broadcasting has been and continues to be carried out in four languages (Bahasa Malaysia, English, Tamil and Mandarin), catering to the linguistic needs of multi-ethnic Malaysians, Bahasa Malaysia became the "national language" of the broadcast industry, following the 1969 ethnic riots, supposedly to eliminate a divisive sphere (McDaniel, 1994) and premised on the assumption that strategic delivery of developmental information to the *kampung* (Malay) folks would be eased through the Malay language.

Clearly, Malaysia's broadcast history has been shaped by the need to counter foreign ideology like Communism, Indonesian-ism and British-ism. In fact radio and television functioned as key weapons in the cultural territorialization of Malaya/sia. This part of history is not forgotten; in fact it overarches the industry today which seems ethnically divisive and culturally protective in its programming.

FTA television today

The air space thus, has been the domain of the state. Every Prime Minister, in every election campaign since 1957 following independence from British rule, has been known to extensively utilize state-run radio and television to reach and win the electorate. If at all space was accorded to opposition parties such as the secular Democratic Action Party (DAP) or the Islamic Parti Seislam Malaysia (PAS) it has mostly been in detrimental light. This in effect explains the continued rule of the Barisan Nasional (known as The Alliance from 1957 to 1969), since independence to date. While Malaysians have hardly had the privilege to view the flipside to any issue, nor witness national televised debates, Prime Minister Abdullah Badawi, in his desire to unite the Malaysian people, had recently allowed such a debate among opposing political parties on state television.

Furthermore, in a post-Mahathir, freed-Anwar[7] climate, the Malaysian media appears to cautiously attempt to decriminalize Anwar Ibrahim. While the face of national television may seem to change under different leaderships and may seem fairer in Malaysia's modern times, it will tend to continue to serve the ambitions and aspirations of the state.

As discussed earlier, Malaysia's public (and private) free-to-air television is a state institution; a significant arm that has the potential to reach 90 per cent of households owning at least one television set. TV1 the prime channel (*saluran perdana*) and TV2 the golden channel (*saluran emas*) together with a website boast of providing Malaysians with an agora of infotainment and of achieving 80 per cent local programme content. In 1984, the first free-to-air privatized TV station (TV3) arrived under Mahathir's privatization and liberalization policy. This was followed by Metrovision in 1995 (stopped broadcasting in 1999), Natseven TV (NTV7) in 1998, 8TV (previously Metrovision) in January 2004 and channel 9 (started in September 2003, stopped in 2005, expected to resume in early 2006). This has been complemented with the arrival of cable (Mega TV) in 1994, Malaysia's first subscription television network, offering eight channels 24 hours a day, and satellite TV (ASTRO) in 1996 offering 32 channels of TV with a further 16 radio channels using a Ku-band beam to reach subscribers. These private networks (TV3, 8TV and channel 9) are said to be owned by Media Prima Berhad (MP) which is reported to be currently negotiating the purchase of NTV7[8]. Hence, private television seems a single-handed monopoly no different from state television (see box story). In fact what seems a duopoly in the form of state (RTM) and private (Media Prima = TV3 + NTV7 + 8TV + channel 9) is indeed a monopoly as the key stakeholder, directly or indirectly, remains UMNO. Despite privatization, as argued earlier on, foreign programmes (not necessarily "Western") continue to occupy close to 40 per cent of broadcast time mainly catering to the multi-ethnic and multilingual characteristic of the Malaysian population (Karthigesu in Goonasekera, 2001: 295).

---

[7] Anwar Ibrahim was sacked from his position as Deputy Prime Minister and from UMNO in September 1998 by the then Prime Minister, Mahathir Mohamed, and imprisoned for nine years on charges of sodomy and corruption. Following Mahathir's resignation in October 2003, and under the premiership of Abdullah Badawi the charges against Anwar were reversed by the appeals court and he was freed in September 2004.

[8] See www.aliran.com/charter/monitors/2005/07/tv3-8tv-channel-9-owner-gobbles-up.html

MALAYSIA: MAKING MEDIA MONOPOLIES

Visitors to Malaysia would be bewildered by the wide variety of newspapers, TV channels and radio stations that cater to most of the country's several language groups.

But as reality sinks in, it would become apparent that despite the deceptively wide range, mainstream media is becoming consolidated in the hands of a small number of privately-owned conglomerates with close links to the political establishment.

And amidst this small number, one media giant looms large over the others, quietly gobbling up television and radio stations as it tries to maximize its advertising revenue and overwhelm the competition.

"Media Prima", the new kid on the block, sort of rose like a phoenix out of the rubble of the 1997 Asian financial crisis, being the creation of a de-merger exercise involving Malaysian Resources Corporation Berhad (MRCB), owner of the politically well-connected TV3 private television station and the New Straits Times Press (NSTP) group, in 2003.

The main aim of the exercise was to re-structure the debts of the heavily-levered TV3 and MRCB and, as part of it, Media Prima acquired a 100 per cent stake in TV3 and a 43 per cent stake in NSTP and assumed the listed status of TV3 on the Malaysian stock exchange.

In January, last year, the group launched a second television channel under the brand of "8TV", offering a mix of Chinese and English-language programmes. This year, Media Prima has been busy again. In June, the company announced that it had acquired a 98 per cent stake in "Ch-9 Media Sdn Bhd", which operated the now-defunct free-to-air television station, Channel 9. The station is expected to be relaunched next year.

Then, last month, the firm revealed that it had entered into a "collaboration and assistance" agreement with the owners of the popular private television station "NTV7" and the radio station "WowFM".

If the deal with NTV7 goes through, the Media Prima stable of firms could control some 85 per cent of discounted advertising revenue from the country's free-to-air television stations. And it would command 46 per cent of all television (including pay television) viewership, leaving its closest rival pay-television satellite operator, Astro, trailing at around 20 to 30 per cent of viewership.

If the past is any guide, the range of views on offer among the various private television stations is unlikely to be wide, more so, if these stations come under the same conglomerate.

Media Prima not only dominates the television sector, it also has sizeable interests in the print media. The conglomerate has the largest combined circulation of newspapers, amounting to about 50 per cent of Malay and English newspapers, and controls two of the top three best-selling newspapers in Malaysia, the Malay language Berita Harian and the fast-rising Harian Metro. These two newspapers are read by close to three million Malaysians out of a population of 26 million.

– Inter Press Service, 30 August 2005 –

As state-funded RTM abolished licenses since April 2000 (Balraj, 2003), it became more dependent on advertising revenue, further marginalizing ethnic minorities as programmes concentrate on the wealthiest segments of society, which is often the Malays and Chinese. Fundamentally, television's potential to serve as a national public sphere, to create a national family, to brand national culture and to build the imagery of good government and good people is nowhere to be denied as we see it being harnessed and exploited in myriad ways by ruling elites whether in Communist or Democratic environments. For example, while CCTV in China, broadcasting mainly in Mandarin, is controlled by the Communist Party, in democratic India, Doordarshan, using Hindi in the main, remains a government instrument central to cultural hegemony (Pashupati et al 2003). In Japan, where the NHK is people-funded and free from commercial impositions, control over programme content, in the spirit of nationalism, is said to be a monopoly of the managerial elite (Yoshimi, 2003). Nations, in other words, are branding and positioning themselves via state-run television, creating a hyper reality of national culture, and this process seems enabled by commercialized public television in most of Asia which now has a three-fold purpose—perpetuating state ideology, strengthening public culture while profiteering. Hence the traditional notions of PSB remain a utopia, whether in India, Japan, China or Malaysia.

Privileged culture

Given the above, I contend that in modern Malaysia public broadcasting deviates from traditional democratic ideals and represents mythical images of public culture in ethnic sphericules and attempts to make normal and acceptable the following:

- Privileging one group over several others, one language and one set of values over others.
- Promoting the vested interest of the main component ruling political party, i.e. United Malays National Organization (UMNO).
- Representing a polarized Malaysian society, i.e. Malays and non-Malays or *bumiputera* (prince of the soil) and non-*bumiputera* (ethnic minorities or colonial immigrants).
- Mediatizing two public spheres—one sacred and the other non-sacred and within each enabling several circuits of discourses and practices, yet denying diversity and differences to prevail.

PRIME CHANNEL, TV 1

TV1 began its maiden broadcast on 28 December 1963 as its studio at Jalan Ampang. Known as the First Channel, it initially transmitted in black and white. On 6 October 1969, TV Malaysia began its broadcast from the Angkasapuri Complex on Bukit Putra. Fifteen years later on 28 December 1978, "The First Channel" changed its name to RTM1 and transmitted in colour. RTM1 then introduced the slogan "Teman Setia Anda" on 27 December 1987. On 1 February 1990, RTM1 became known as TV1—Your Prime Channel (Saluran Perdana).

Vision
That TV1—the Prime Channel will be competitive with the best in the Asia Pacific region.

Mission
- To uphold the nation's vision.
- To broadcast programmes that satisfy viewers taste.
- To provide high quality broadcasting service.
- To make TV1, the channel with the potential to succeed.
- To be sensitive and reactive to current domestic and foreign activities and issues

GOLDEN CHANNEL, TV2

Malaysia's second television channel began its maiden telecast on 17 Nov 1969 in its studio at Angkasapuri Complex. Known as the Second Channel, it began its telecast in colour and its initial coverage was for Peninsular Malaysia only. On 31 August 1984, its transmission also covers East Malaysia (Sabah & Sarawak). On 1 February 1990 the Second Channel was known as TV2, The Golden Channel.

Vision
To create programmes with a progressive and contemporary concept.

Mission
- To telecast, televise or air programmes suitable for Malaysian audience of all ages, race and religious beliefs.
- To upgrade or increase the percentage of local contents.
- To increase the total number of viewers and revenue by airing quality programmes.

Clients' Charter
- We pledge to televise, screen or air programmes to cater to our audience.
- We pledge to fulfil our advertisers' requirement.
- We pledge to disseminate information to our viewers and public.
- We pledge to deliver messages and policies of the government.
- We pledge to be always ready and open to views and constructive criticism for continuous improvements.

– www.rtm.net.my –

Clearly, a privileged Malay public sphere is evident in TV1 and a non-Malay public sphere in TV2. It seems, in other words, the sacred and the non-sacred are being nationally mediated. The former is filled with purity; it is non-penetrable by foreign cultural elements and seems beyond "the nons" (colloquial reference to minorities). The primary language is Malay and the values are Islamic. The latter, however, is typically like the Malaysian hawker food, *rojak*. It seems free for all, with a potpourri of Chinese, Tamil and English news and entertainment programmes whether from home or abroad. TV2 airs programmes for the Chinese largely imported from Hong Kong; for the Indians imported from India and for the English-speaking viewers imported from Singapore and the US in the main. While on the one hand, RTM may point out that it is providing fair content for all minority groups via TV2, on the other, knowingly or not, it is guilty of perpetuating a deeply wedged pure and impure public sphere, and in the process stumbling the state's (Mahathir's) vision of creating a single Malaysian race (*bangsa Malaysia*) come 2020.

Within the Malay public sphere itself, there prevails a form of subtle dualism—one for the *rakyat* (urban Malays) and one for the *Ummah* (kampong Malays). Ironically the *ummah* tends to refer to the kampong masses that are constantly bombarded with Islamic genre because they are presumably seen as an important constituent of the opposition Islamic party (PAS) and therefore must be won over by the ruling coalition party. The *rakyat*, referring to the citizenry and by such virtue inclusive of all people, tends, in practice, to denote the Malay-*bumiputera*, privileged middle class, who are an important constituent of the ruling Malay party UMNO whose undivided loyalty must be preserved and nurtured. Thus, while the *ummah* and the *rakyat* are the chosen audiences for TV1—the prime channel and the first channel, all the rest of the audiences, albeit the nons, are fed with *rojak* by a second (class?) channel. Differences within the *ummah* and within the *rakyat* are simply ignored because each as a group represents a political affiliation—the former towards PAS and the latter towards UMNO. To be inclusive in a divisive manner is but a reflection of the Malaysian ethnic-based political party system where the ruling Barisan Nasional is made up of the UMNO (a Malay party) representing the *rakyat*, while MIC (Indian component party) and MCA (Chinese component party) represent the nons. Indeed, state broadcasting in Malaysia reflects how one ethnic group is privileged over several other ethnic groups. If at all public broadcasting is to be realized in any meaningful sense, Malaysia's race-essentialized politics must change to accord such a privilege to all Malaysians.

Conclusion

While western scholars have said much about the "whiteness" of western media (cf. Hall, 1996; Hartmann and Husband 1974; Cottle, 2000b; Fiske, 1994; Allan 1999; van Dijk, 1991, Turner, 2000; Sinclair and Cunningham, 2000), nothing really has been said about the "blankness" of Malaysian media. Whatever is counter-hegemonic is blanked in the Malaysian media and minorities have been absent and under-represented for a long time. Their presence, insofar as they are subordinately positioned, has been rather unpleasant.

In all forms of home-made genres—commercial advertising, public campaigns, films, dramas, news, documentaries and sitcoms—for ideological and ringgit (Malaysian dollar) reasons, state television blanks minorities, in particular Indians and other indigenous minorities. According to Oorjitham (2001) about 54 per cent of Malaysian Indians work on plantations or as urban labourers on low wages with limited access to housing, education and jobs. Being eight per cent of the Malaysian population, Indians make up 41 per cent of Malaysian beggars, 63 per cent of those arrested for violent crimes and less than five per cent of successful university applicants (Oorjitham, 2001). It is not surprising that no single public campaign has thus far been designed to help improve the lot of the minority Indians. In fact, in most state campaigns, designed to improve the lot of the already affluent urban Malays, Indian-looking characters have often been depicted as "sick" or as destructive. For example, in a healthy lifestyle television campaign, an Indian-looking male is represented as a diabetic patient being advised by a Malay-looking medical doctor and in a public property campaign, an Indian looking male is depicted as vandalizing public property (Khattab, 2004). As Hall argues: "Even the dominant, colonizing, imperializing power only knows who and what it is and can experience the pleasure of its own power of domination in and through the construction of Other" (1996: 342).

While the normalization and universalization of whiteness through media representation is being challenged extensively, is it worth imagining the normalization of "Malayness" in the construction of Bangsa Malaysia?

Malaysian audiences are resisting such mediatization in alternative spaces such as via *Malaysiakini*, the only alternative (online) newspaper. Blogs and websites to some extent fulfil the notions of the public sphere and provide cyber avenues for critical debate. Stringent laws, however, retard the growth of rich alternative forms of discourses and articulations. Emulating western forms of media, the ethnically polarized public spheres in Malaysia seem further corrupted by the disappearance of citizenry and in its place a burgeoning consumerist middle class advanced by commercial television and boosted by an ICT state agenda privileging one group over several others. Through mediatized essentialist perspectives of "race" and "capitalism", Malaysia's cultural purse is being emptied and it's national narration made blank and bland. As communities within the national territory are subjugated to the same rhythms of national broadcast service, notions of equality and commonality seem promoted (Moran, 2004; Morley, 2004) creating as such false consciousness and a misplaced sense of reality and security.

References

Allan, S. (1999). *News Culture*. Buckingham and Philadelphia: Open University Press.

Anderson, B. (1983). *Imagined Communities: Reflections of the Origin and Spread of Nationalism*. Verso, London and New York.

Asian Labour News. (2005). Southeast Asia: Images of Migrants Often Negative – Critics, p. 2. Retrieved from www.asianlabour.org/archives/003278.php on 16 May 2005.

Balraj, S. (2003). Malaysia. In A. Goonasekera, et al (Eds.), *Asian Communication Handbook* (pp. 168–175). Singapore: AMIC.

Banerjee, I. (2002). The Locals Strike Back? Media Globalization and Localization in the New Asian Television Landscape. *Gazette: The International Journal for Communication Studies*, 64(6), 517–535.

Banerjee, M. (2002). Trends in International TV Broadcasting. *Media Asia*, 29(2), 107–110. Singapore: AMIC.

Barker, C. (1997). Cultural Identities and Cultural Imperialism. In *Global Television: An Introduction* (pp. 182–206). Oxford: Blackwell Publishers.

Barker, C. (1999). Audiences, Identities and Television Talk. In *Television, Globalization and Cultural Identities* (pp. 108–140). Buckingham: Open University Press.

Benjamin, W. (1968). *Illuminations*. H. Arendt (Ed.) & H. Zohn (Trans.) New York: Harcourt Brace & World.

Bhabha, H. K. (1990). DissemiNation: Time, Narrative and the Margins of the Modern Nation. In H. K. Bhabha (Ed.), *Nation and Narration*. London: Routledge.

Bhabha, H. K. (1999). Arrivals and Departures. In H. Naficy (Ed.), *Home, Exile, Homeland: Film, Media and the Politics of Place* (pp. vii–xii). New York: Routledge.

Bhabha, H. K. (1996). Cultures In-Between. In S. Hall & P. Du Gay (Eds.), *Questions of Cultural identity* (pp. 53–60). London: Sage.

Chua, B. H. (1998). Racial Singaporeans: Absence after the Hyphen. In J. S. Kahn (Ed.), *Southeast Asian identities: Culture and the Politics of Representation in Indonesia, Malaysia, Singapore and Thailand* (pp. 28–50). Singapore & London: ISEAS.

Collins, R. (2004). "ISES" AND "OUGHTS" Public Service Broadcasting in Europe. In R. C. Allen & A. Hill (Eds.), *The Television Studies Reader* (pp. 33–47). London and New York: Routledge.

Cottle, S. (2000a). Rethinking News Access. *Journalism Studies*, 1(3), 427–448.

Cottle, S. (2000b). Introduction: Media Research and Ethnic Minorities: Mapping the Field. In S. Cottle (Ed.), *Ethnic Minorities and the Media: Changing Cultural Boundaries* (pp. 1–29). Buckingham and Philadelphia: Open University Press.

Fiske, J. (1994). *Media Matters: Everyday Culture and Political Change*. Minneapolis: University of Minesota Press.

Gabriel, J. (1998). *Whitewash; Racialized Politics and the Media*. London and New York: Routledge.

Gellner, E. (1983). *Nations and Nationalism*. Oxford: Basil Blackwell.

Glattbach & Balakrishnan (1978). Malaysia. In J. A. Lent (Ed.), *Broadcasting in Asia and the Pacific: A Continental Survey of Radio and Television* (pp. 142–153). Philadelphia: Temple University Press.

Goh, B. L. (1998). Modern Dreams: An Enquiry Into Power, Cityspace Transformations and Cultural Difference in Contemporary Malaysia. In J. S. Kahn (Ed.), *Southeast Asian identities: Culture and the Politics of Representation in Indonesia, Malaysia, Singapore and Thailand* (pp. 169–202). Singapore and London: ISEAS.

Goonasekera, A. (2001). Ethnicity in the Global Village: Media and Ethnic Relations in Multicultural Societies of Asia. In A. Goonasekera & C. W. Lee (Eds.), *Asian Communication Handbook 2001* (pp. 278–298). Singapore: AMIC.

Hall, S., Critcher, C., Jefferson, T., Clarke, J., & Roberts, B. (1978). *Policing the Crisis: Mugging, the State and Law and Order*. London: Macmillan.

Hall, S. (1980). Encoding/Decoding. In S. Hall et al (Eds.), *Culture, Media, Language* (pp. 128–138). London: Hutchison.

Hall, S. (1996). Race, Culture and Communication: Looking Backward and Forward at Cultural Studies. In J. Storey (Ed.), *What is Cultural Studies? A Reader* (pp. 336–343). London: Arnold.

Hartmann, P., & Husband, C. (1974). *Racism and the Mass Media*. London: Davis Poynter.

Jakubowizc, A. (1994). Australian (dis)contents: film, mass media and multiculturalism. In S. Gunew & F. Rizvi (Eds.), *Culture, Difference and the Arts* (pp. 86–107). Sydney: Allen and Unwin.

Johnson, M. (1994). Making Time: Historic Preservation and the Space of Nationality. *Positions: East Asia Cultures Critique*, 2(2), 177–249.

Khattab, U. (2004). Wawasan 2020: Engineering a Modern Malay(sia): Sate Campaigns and Minority Stakes. *Media Asia*, 31(3), 170–177.

Kitley, P. (2003). Introduction: First Principles – Television, Regulation and Transversal Civil Society. In *Television, Regulation and Civil Society in Asia* (pp. 3–34). London and New York: RoutledgeCurzon.

Kitley, P., & Nain, Z. (2003). Out in Front: Government Regulation of Television in Malaysia. In P. Kitley, *Television, Regulation and Civil Society in Asia* (pp. 80–96). London and New York: RoutledgeCurzon.

McDaniel, D. O. (1994). *Broadcasting in the Malay World*. Norwood. NJ: Ablex Pub.

Meyrowitz, J. (1985). *No Sense of Place: the Impact of Electronic Media on Social Behaviour*. Oxford: Oxford University Press.

Moran, A. (2004). Television Formats in the World/the World of Television Formats. In A. Moran & M. Keane (Eds.), *Television Across Asia: Television Industries, Programme Formats and Globalization* (pp. 1–8). London and New York: RoutledgeCurzon.

Morley, D. (2000). The Whiteness of the Public sphere. In D. Morley (Ed.), *Home, Territories: Media, Mobility and identity* (pp. 118–127). London and New York: Routledge.

Morley, D. (2004). Broadcasting and the Construction of the National Family. In R. C. Allen & A. Hill (Eds.), *The Television Studies Reader* (pp. 418–435). London and New York: Routledge.

Moses, B. (2002). Ethnic Reporting in the Malaysian media. *Media Asia,* 29(2), 102–106.

Nain, Z. (2002). The Structure of the Media Industry: Implications for Democracy. In K. W. F. Loh & B. K. Khoo (Eds.), *Democracy in Malaysia: Discourses and Practices* (pp. 111–137). UK: Curzon Press.

Oorjitham, S. (26 January 2001). Forgotten Community: Many of Malaysia's Poor are Indians. *Asiaweek,* 27(3).

Pashupati, K., Sun, H. L., & McDowell, S. D. (2003). Guardians of Culture, Development Communicators or State Capitalists? *Gazette: the Internaitonal Journal for Communication Studies,* 65(3), 251–271.

Sinclair, J., & Cunningham, S. (Eds.) (2000). *Floating Lives: the Media and Asian Diasporas.* Brisbane: University of Queensland Press.

Sparks, C. (2004). The Global, the Local and the Public Sphere. In R. C. Allen & A. Hill (Eds.), *The Television Studies Reader* (pp. 139–150). London & New York: Routledge.

Syvertsen, T. (2003). Challenges to Public Broadcasting in the Era of Convergence and Commercialization. *Television and New Media,* 4(2), 155–175.

Tracey, M. (1998). *The Decline and Fall of Public Service Broadcasting.* Oxford: Oxford University Press.

Turner, G. (1997). Media Texts and Messages. In S. Cunningham & G. Turner (Eds.), *The Media in Australia: Industries, Texts, Audiences* (pp. 293–347). St. Leonards, Sydney: Allen and Unwin.

Van Diyk, T. (1991). *Racism and the Press.* London: Routledge.

Yoshimi, S. (2003). Television and Nationalism: Historical change in the National Domestic TV formation of postwar Japan. *European Journal of Cultural Studies,* 6(4), 458–487.

South Africa

Public Service Broadcasting in the Post-Apartheid Era—The Struggles and Tribulations of Turning a State Broadcaster into a Public Service Broadcaster

The tradition of public service broadcasting is strongest in Britain, embodied in the BBC under the direction of the first Director General, John Reith (Reith, 1924). Reith also wrote the founding documents for the South African Broadcasting Corporation in 1933, as well as the Charters for the Canadian, Australian, Indian and Kenyan broadcasters, among others. Thus there is a strong formalist similarity among these broadcasters, and public broadcasting principles are still referred to as "Reithian principles".

Reith argued that the radio wave spectrum, or Hertzian radio waves, was a scarce resource, and therefore should be developed and regulated in the interests of the nation. This implied a monopoly situation, which would only be acceptable if it were publicly owned and stood equally free from political forces—the government in particular—on the one hand, and various private economic interests on the other. Consequently, he was of the opinion that it should be financed by a licence fee, and not by advertising, since this would imply that broadcasters would have to pander to commercial interests, something that was an anathema to him. The British Broadcasting Corporation (BBC) to this day has no advertising, while in South Africa; broadcasting was advertising-free, depending entirely on licence income, until the advent of Springbok Radio in 1956.

Ancient history of the SABC

National broadcasting in South Africa was inaugurated in 1936, when the South African Broadcasting Corporation (SABC) was formed. At first, only radio services were provided, divided along language and racial lines, which both reinforced and served to draw the contours of a segregated apartheid society and social attitudes.

The year 1976 saw a profound change in South African leisure time activity when television was introduced into South Africa. Initially, only one channel was in operation for five hours an evening, and the broadcast time was equally divided between English and Afrikaans languages. A second channel was introduced in 1982. This channel carried TV2 and TV3 as split signals between were introduced. TV2 broadcast in Nguni languages—Zulu and Xhosa, while TV3 broadcast in the Sotho family of languages—North and South Sotho and Pedi. Both carried a predominance of English as a common language. The two channels shared a frequency, but were beamed to different geographical parts of the country.

In the late 1980s, the television structure was changed. TV1 remained purely English and Afrikaans, while TV2/3/4 became a signal integrated channel, named Contemporary Cultural Values (CCV). Although there was still a significant amount of African language programming, with a transmitter split to accommodate the news in different languages to different parts of the country, the "glue" which held the programming of CCV together was English, since, in the sentiments of the station's manager, English was the only common bond between all the peoples of South Africa.

In the 1980s the SABC explicitly supported the then government in its effort to combat what was represented as the "Total Onslaught" of "revolutionary forces", supposedly spearheaded by the African National Conference (ANC) in exile (Teer-Tomaselli & Tomaselli, 2001).

With the general transformation of South African political imperatives, being perceived as the voice of the government was no longer an option: It was a political and commercial liability. Thus, from the late 1980s, a process of restructuring began in which pragmatism, rather than propaganda, became the dominant ethos. This transition period was driven by forces both internal and external to the SABC. Internally, the SABC under the leadership of Wynand Harmse the SABC became increasingly commercially driven. At present, the SABC receives approximately four-fifths of its income from commercial advertising, and the rest as a combination of licences, programme sales and government grants towards educational programming. This is a very different situation to half a century ago.

By the end of the 1980s, the SABC was feeling the competitive effect of M-Net, the subscription television channel, which with its wealthier viewership was beginning to draw advertising away from the SABC. The response of the SABC was to introduce what Harmse referred to as the "most extensive process of change in the Corporations hitherto 56 year history" (SABC Annual Report, 1991: 9–10). The Corporation was divided into business units with a system of internal cost recovery, and the top-heavy administration of human resources and financial management was decentralized to each of the business unit. At the management level, remuneration was linked to performance, while at all levels significant staff reductions were implemented. In the financial year between 1990–1, the surplus was doubled, an achievement which was marred by a major industrial conflict in 1992. More serious even, was the realization that the Corporation was chronically schizophrenic: in its attempt to be a fully fledged public broadcaster, it was forced to rely more and more on commercial logic, which meant providing inexpensive programming that appealed to the largest possible segment of the attractive high-end audience. This seriously compromised the public mandate of the Corporation.

In 1991, the SABC set up a Task Group to study the issue of broadcast regulation. The report published in August of that year, was popularly known as the "Viljoen Report", covered the role of the national broadcaster, local programming, educational broadcasting, the liberalization of broadcasting through the issuing of new licences, and most significantly, the establishment of a regulatory body for broadcasting (see Louw, 1993 for further details). Despite the criticisms levelled against the Task Group, particularly over the manner of its appointment and composition, many of the recommendations made were similar to those made by more radical bodies.

External pressure on the SABC came in the form of numerous pressure groups, headed by the Film and Allied Workers Organization, (FAWO) and the Campaign for Open Media (COM). For three years, from the beginning of 1991 to the end of 1993, numerous workshops, seminars, position papers and public protests brought together a very catholic collection of interests from students, media workers, and political activities inside the country together with sectors of the ANC in exile. This "moment" in the popular struggle for the ownership of the media and its contents have been well documented elsewhere (Currie, 1991; 1993; Louw, 1993; Jululani, 1991).

Policy development and implementation (1993–1998)

The direct result of the popular campaigns was the appointment of the first democratically nominated Board of Governors, after a lengthy process of public hearings. This rapidly was followed by the passing the Independent Broadcasting Authority (IBA) Act (RSA, 1993), and further public nominations and hearings to select the inaugural five Councillors. The installation of the new SABC Board, and the reorganization that it was able to drive, was the beginning, rather than the end of the process. Ivy Matsepe Casaburri, then Chairperson of the SABC, now the Minister of Communication, opined:

> The old SABC is not yet dead, and ... the new broadcaster we want to be, is not yet born. The SABC has to "reinvent" itself: It is a vision of the SABC as the national public broadcaster, to deliver services of value to all South Africa's people in more creative and unique ways than ever before[1].

Triple enquiry

One of the first tasks of the new IBA was to undertake the Triple Enquiry, by convening hearings into, and formulating policy on the viability of the public broadcaster; local content, and cross-media ownership and control. A year of national and regional public hearings resulted in the report to Parliament. The triple enquiry attempted to present the broadcasting landscape as a whole, rather than looking simply at the SABC. The outcome was "a tightly argued ecological approach to broadcasting with shared opportunities and obligations on all broadcasters" (Gillwald, 2002: 178). A primary purpose of the Enquiry was to break the monopoly of the SABC and to open up the airwaves to a multiplicity of voices and economic opportunities. A three-tier system of broadcasting licences was advocated: public, private and community. In order to stimulate the "private" category, and counteract the criticism of unfair advantage of the SABC receiving both licence-fee monies as well as advertising revenue, the Enquiry Report recommendation to Parliament included the paring down of the SABC to two television channels, and the licensing of an independent commercial channel.

It also advocated selling off eight of the regional commercial stations. In its response, the SABC argued forcefully that all three television channels were required in order to fulfil the onerous mandate of serving public interests in all 11 official languages (SABC: Delivering Value). The SABC also insisted that two of six commercial channels—Radio Lotus in Natal and Radio Good Hope in Cape Town—were required to remain as part of the SABC stable in order to fulfil the mandate of providing for minority populations.

In respect of the other six regional stations, it was envisaged by both the IBA and the SABC that the revenue derived from the sale of these

---

[1] Refer IBA, 1994: Hearings towards the Triple Enquiry.

channels would be ploughed back into the SABC in order to contribute to the financing of heavier public service obligations. On this basis, the SABC agreed to the sale. However, when the stations were sold, the money raised was not returned to the SABC, but claimed by the Department of Finance, as capital realized on the sale of state assets, went back into the fiscus. It was seen as the "first round of privatization of state assets in the New South Africa"[2].

In terms of the recommendation, the stations should be made available to consortia bidders. The sale of the stations included four stages: the determination of price; a process of bidding by various interested parties; the awarding of the licence; and, finally, the sale and transfer of licence. The licence transfer took place after a complex process of public hearings, during which the various offers were assessed in terms of their bid prices, as well as public interest considerations[3]. The competitive environment was further advanced with the licensing of seven "greenfields licences" (i.e. licences without existing stations attached to them) by the IBA in late 1997. These are also commercial regional radio stations, often with quite distinct niche audiences[4]. In addition, 80 community radio stations were licensed throughout the country, of which more than a quarter are inoperative at present.

The Independent Broadcasting Authority (IBA) Act (1993) failed to provide specifically for satellite broadcasting. The IBA was responsible for the regulation of all terrestrial broadcasting. While aspirant entrants to the

---

[2] Refer IBA press release, 20 September 1996.
[3] The radio stations which changed hands in this way were:
- Radio Oranje in the Free State.
- Radio Algoa in the Eastern Cape.
- Highveld Stereo in Gauteng.
- Jacaranda Stereo in the Pretoria region.
- KFM Stereo in the Western Cape was acquired by Crescent Consortium at a price of R65 million.
  Some of the latter included the following: the bidders should be persons from the province of the coverage area; be persons from diverse groupings; not own a substantial portion of other media interests in the area of broadcasting. The new owners needed to indicate they were capable of catering for the language needs of the area, and of meeting the requirements local content imposed by the IBA.
[4] Kaya-fm (township youth—Gauteng).
- Classic FM (Classic and Jazz, Gauteng).
- YFM (youth—Gauteng).
- Punt Geselsradio (Afrikaans talk radio—Gauteng).
- P4 Radio Cape Town (Jazz—Western Cape).
- 567 Cape Town (Music/talk—Western Cape).
- Punt Geselsradio (Afrikaans talk radio—Western Cape).
- P4 Radio Durban—Jazz—KwaZulu-Natal).

satellite sector waited in vain throughout the 90s, the terrestrial subscription broadcaster, M-Net, used the opportunity and the gap in policy prescription to declare itself exempt from the need to apply for licence for satellite activity and established a Direct to Home digital satellite service, DStv (Gillwald, 2001: 179). The terrestrial pay channel, M-Net, as the holding company of both, MultiChoice, encouraged the migration of its considerable subscriber base from M-Net to DStv. The SABC's own attempt to establish an analogue satellite service initiative under the project name of Astrasat, failed miserably, and was scrapped at great expense.

The most significant source of competition has come from the free-to-air terrestrial commercial channel, e-tv[5], which after protracted negotiation and threatened litigation, was licensed in 1998, and now commands around 10 per cent of audience share, and 23 per cent of television adspend (SAARF, 2002).

The McKinsey process

The years between 1994 and 1996 were the golden season of public broadcasting in South Africa, and saw significant changes to internal organization of the SABC, as well as the programming fare broadcast. In its submission to the Triple Enquiry, the SABC argued, inter alia, that "SABC programming can deliver value by nurturing and reflecting cultural identity, meeting basic needs, developing human resources, building the economy and democratizing the state and society" (Delivering Value Vol. 1), and to a large extent the Corporation made good on this promise. The Charter to the SABC, which is found as an Appendix to the Broadcasting Act (RSA, 1999), provides a neat outline of the SABC's public service mandate. The Corporation is required to:

- make services available to South Africans in all official languages;
- reflect the country's unity, diversity and multilingualism;
- ensure quality across all services;
- provide significant news and current affairs programming, which is fair, unbiased, impartial and independent from government, commercial and other interests; and
- enrich South Africa's cultural heritage; strive to offer a broad range of services targeting, particularly, children, women, the youth and the disabled.

---

[5] e-TV is jointly owned by a local empowerment consortium, dominated by Hoken's and trade union interests, with a 20 per cent foreign ownership by Time Warner.

- Include both in-house and commissioned programmes; include national sports programming, including developmental and minority sports.

The reorganization following on the heels of the Triple Enquiry included a "relaunch" of all three television stations. SABC1, with the largest footprint, broadcast most of its prime-time programming in the Nguni group of languages—Zulu and Xhosa, with some additional Pedi and Ndebele—alternating with English; while SABC2, with the second largest footprint, carried Sotho, Tswana and Afrikaans during prime time. This policy saw the significant downgrading of Afrikaans from being a co-equal language with English, to a minor language, given a greatly reduced allocation of broadcast time, on a par with other African languages. SABC3 was reinvented as an all-English language channel, designed to meet the needs of the urban, educated audiences of all races.

At the beginning of 1996, the SABC broadcast 22 regional and nation radio services. Of these, one in each of the newly official South African languages, 11 were "full-spectrum" stations, by which was meant they offered a full range of programming genres: information (news, actuality, sports programmes, discussion shows); entertainment (music, request programmes, quizzes, novel readings and drama) and education (both formal and non-formal). In addition, these radio stations were specifically charged with the mandate to "build national identity". The radio portfolio also consisted of two national music format stations (Radio Metro and Radio 5) and seven regional music services, including Radio Lotus, aimed specifically at listeners of Indian descent.

The increased competition, the fall in revenue resulting from the loss of significant sections of the well-to-do Afrikaans audience, and the provision of local programming in a plethora of languages way beyond the resource capacity of the Corporation, led to major financial crisis in 1996. The following year the SABC sought to cut costs in a bid to turn its finances around. This it did by undergoing extensive reorganization on the recommendation of international consultants, McKinsey and Associates. As a result of the McKinsey recommendations, approximately one third of the Corporation's staff was retrenched, and the local content component in programming was reduced significantly (Duncan, 2002). Local production is relatively costly, and much of this was replaced with cheaper imported programming, chiefly from America. Although the cutting back on local production this has been regarded as detrimental to the public service mandate of the corporation, it alleviated the cost constraints in two ways: by saving money on acquisition; and, ironically, by attracting more money in the way of advertising revenue through the broadcast of popular sitcoms and dramas aimed at the lowest common denominator audience. The role of local production in the public broadcaster is discussed further at the end of this chapter.

A major change was implemented in the reorganization of the News Division. Previously divided along media lines (radio and television), the News department was re-configured as a "bi-media" operation in order to streamline production and cut costs. While the move succeeded in cutting costs, overall the project was not successful. Different media require significantly different approaches to newsgathering and presentation, with radio coverage particularly suffered from being an after-thought consideration. The staff felt a significant intensification of work pressure to accommodate the needs of producing more "outputs" in more formats than ever before. The bi-media project was scrapped late in 2001, and a return to the logic of separate, but cooperative, radio and television News Divisions is being implemented at present.

Perhaps the most significant change in the re-tooling of the SABC in the wake of the McKinsey Report was the re-definition of the SABC as a publisher-broadcaster rather than a producer-broadcaster. Only the core programming of news and current affairs was produced by SABC personnel, for the rest, programming was commissioned by outside producers. This effected a substantial saving when the South African Television Production (SAFRITEL), the production arm of the Corporation, was closed. Without actually embarking on "privatization" in the usual sense of selling off assets or components of the company, representing privatization through outsourcing by buying in programming content, seen as many to be the "core function" of the broadcaster. The move was not well received in all circles: the then Chairperson of the IBA, Felleng Sekha, commented that "the SABC does as it pleases" without regard to either viewers or the regulator. The IBA itself, however, was under considerable pressure in terms of constraints on financial and personnel resources, and a perception of a lack of legitimacy.

The period of regulated liberalization: 1998–present

The McKinsey Report did have legislative repercussions, since its recommendations fed directly into the Green and White Papers (RSA, 1997a; RSA, 1998) on Broadcasting, and finally the 1999 Broadcasting Act (Number 4 of 1999), repealing the existing legislation of 1976 (RSA, 1976). In terms of the new Act, the SABC was to be governed by a Charter, which spelt out a clear set of objectives for the Corporation, including the development of a series of policies (see below). The Charter contents included detailed prescriptions for the SABC covering, among other issues, national objectives; performance, new services; board appointment procedures; lines of accountability; and enforcement of the Charter. These were to be monitored and compliance enforced by ICASA.

Significantly, the SABC was "incorporated" into a limited liability company, which was to consist of two separate "operational entities": a "public service broadcaster" and a "public service commercial broadcaster" (RSA 2002, Section 22). Cross subsidization of some kind would take place between the two entities. Thus the SABC would now be transformed into a corporate share structure, with the Minister of Communications acting on behalf of the government as the sole shareholder. A number of powers not previously available to the government are associated with this arrangement as well as the traditional obligation to monitor annual and quarterly reports.

Change in licences and the introduction of Channels 4 and 5

From the public's point of view, the most radical change heralded by the Amendment Act was the establishment of two new regional television channels, SABC4 and SABC5. In terms of the Act, the Corporation was required to draw up a business plan and to apply to ICASA to licence the new channels. The process was driven from within the Department of Communications, with strong political backing. The broadcaster was less than convinced, since it was loath to add further responsibilities and costs to their already over-stretched capacity, however, preparations for the applications began in 2003. ICASA too, was not enthusiastic, seeing these demands as politically oriented, and fearing that its autonomy as an independent regulator was being compromised. Nevertheless, after dragging the process out over nearly two years, the licences were finally granted to a reluctant SABC in August 2005.

The thinking behind the new channels was to increase the amount of airtime available to the broadcaster in order to be able to broadcast in more non-English languages, and be able to "reflect regional diversity" (Broadcasting Amendment Act, 2002 Section 22). The licences stipulated that SABC4 was to cover the North West part of the country[6], and cater for the languages five African languages[7]. SABC5 is licensed for the South

---

[6] Limpopo, North West, Northern Cape, Free State and Gauteng.
[7] Setswana, Sesotho, Sepedi, Xitsonga, Tshivenda.

Eastern part of the country[8], and will broadcast in the Nguni group of languages[9]. Both channels are to make up of Afrikaans and English, altogether together these two languages would make up less than 20 per cent of broadcast time on these channels.

A sticking point in the establishment of the new channels remains the uncertainty of the financing model. Unlike the present television offerings, SABC4 and SABC5 are expected to be financed mainly from the public purse. This has caused heated debate within government departments, with the Ministry of Communication advocating full subsidies, and the Ministry of Finance insisting on public-private partnerships. A compromise was reached allowing the channels to carry advertising; however, it is dubious that the lower middle-class audience to whom they are targeted will attract significant commercial revenues. The SABC has made it clear that they expect the majority of the funding will still be required in the form of public grants (SABC statement, 1 August 2005), something the National Treasury has not yet agreed to. It is expected that the construction of a transmitter network will take a further 18 months from the receipt of funding roll out the transmitter network.

Editorial policies

As with any large organization, much of the practice and ways of doing things within the SABC was intuitive, depending more on an unspoken consensus and the "osmosis" of peer pressure than of an articulated position. A pressing priority of the inaugural Board was to develop policy positions over a wide front of issues facing the broadcaster. This task was completed in 1995. In the year 1999, when the same Dr Matsepe-Casaburri who had been the first Chairperson of the SABC was now the Minister of Communication, the newly amended Broadcasting Act (RSA 2002 Section 6) required the broadcaster to develop polices in order to comply with the Corporation's licence conditions. Thus began a major overhaul of promises and procedures, covering news and editorial production, programming, local content, education, universal service, religious programming, language use and more. Drafts of these policies were circulated in printed form and on the Internet, distributed at Post Offices, pension outlets and a variety of other points. Discussion and comment was invited from members of the public, organizations and lobby groups, either in the form of written

---

[8] Mpumalanga, KwaZulu Natal, Eastern Cape, Western Cape, Gauteng, Limpopo and the Northern West Provinces.
[9] isiZulu, isiXhosa, and isiNdebele, SiSwati.

commentary, or oral interventions at one of the many public meetings held in a succession of locations across the country. The final, amended policies were submitted to ICASA in 2003, and explicitly lay out the approach to every facet of programming[10].

Issues and challenges

The challenges facing the SABC in the 21st century are both specific to the Corporation, and general to many public broadcasters. Reading Annual Reports and bi-annual presentations to the Parliamentary Portfolio Committee over the past 10 years, key issues have been reiterated, regardless of the management team and structures in place or the state of legislative play. Primary among these is the contradiction of being a public service broadcaster with predominantly commercial funding, or in the words of the Chief Executive, being able to "comply with legislated public service obligations whilst optimising profitability"[11].

As a public broadcaster, the SABC has a legislated mandate to ensure universal service of both delivery and content to all South Africans in the language of their choice. In practice, this means that the SABC is required, among other things, to expand transmission coverage and to provide appropriate content, and to do both of those in a way that is financially sustainable.

Technology

Technological change has changed exponentially in the past 20 years. As was the case with all broadcasters of the time, the SABC began its radio transmissions on shortwave and medium wave. Today, the SABC services are broadcast to the South African public using various platforms including as terrestrial, satellite and Internet transmission.

Towards the end of the 1950s, the Corporation erected a highly sophisticated network of FM transmitters, one of the first such networks in the world (see Hayman & Tomaselli, 1989). From its establishment in 1975, television was broadcast on the PAL standard, using terrestrial television signals in the VHF and UHF frequency spectrum. In 1995, the transmission division of the SABC was hived off as a separate business entity, setting up Sentech as a wholly owned state enterprise, charged with broadcasting and communication infrastructure in a liberalized market (Marathane,

---

[10] See www.sabc.co.za for a full transcript of the policies.
[11] Presentation to the Parliamentary Portfolio Committee, August 2002.

2005). The terrestrial transmitter network remains the backbone of television and radio broadcasting. The majority of viewers and listeners receive free-to-air radio and television programming from the SABC, e-tv and commercial radio broadcasters through standard radio and television sets and antennas. To support this network, Sentech operates a full range of transmitters, including 220 frequency modulation (FM); five medium wave (used specifically for community and talk-show radio stations); 15 short wave (for continental delivery) and 550 television transmitters country wide (Sentech, 2005).

Despite this extensive coverage, the terrestrial networks do not reach every household in South Africa. To fill in the gaps, the SABC's services utilize a backup satellite transmission as an alternate reception modality. Two platforms are used: Sentech's VIVID satellite platform and Multichoice's DStv satellite platform. Anybody owning a VIVID decoder can access the SABC services for free, while DStv is a subscription bouquet, of which the SABC television channels form only a small part. The SABC's radio services are not available on the DStv platform.

Sentech's terrestrial infrastructure is aging, with most of the radio transmitters now between 50 and 55 years old, while the television transmitters are 20 years of age. Given that refurbishment is an inevitability, and given that international best practice demands that future broadcasting will be on a digital rather than an analogue standard, a comprehensive technology plan was developed in 2002–2003 with a phased implementation process of digitalization over five years (SABC Annual Report, 2003). A one-off grant from government sources will be used to help the financing of the new technology. In terms of programme production, digitalization has already been started. The News Studio is now completely digital and Final Control Centres have been upgraded (SABC Annual Report, 2004). In terms of transmission, the SABC, in consultation with Sentech and the Department of Communication, have opted for digital terrestrial television (DTT) as their new standard, and testing on prototypes of the system have already begun[12].

Not everyone is convinced that DTT is the most efficient route, arguing that a digital satellite platform would be a better long-term investment. This lobby suggests that with the rugged terrain in South Africa, bisected by the Drakensberg and Maluti Mountains, line-of-sight transmission is unnecessarily costly. Further, since satellite transmission is already being used to

---

[12] Personal communication with Sentech.

link terrestrial networks as well as to cover areas where they do not exist and as a "double illumination", it would make more sense to use satellite as the primary means of transmission, with digital terrestrial as the backup, thus inverting the present plan. Champions of the DTT model, including Sentech itself as well as the majority of political players, point to the need for sovereignty as being a paramount concern[13]. At the present time, all South African broadcasting via satellite is carried out via the transponders of the PanAmSat PAS 10, belonging to American interests. The idea that such a strategic installation as the national broadcasting network should be dependent on a satellite owned and controlled by a foreign power is an anathema to the South African political establishment.

Whatever the outcome, and most likely it will be the DTT route; there is mounting pressure for a digital migration. Within the broadcaster, there is a preoccupation with their ability to be utilized by international broadcasters "to host international events to the benefit of the country and the continent" (Annual Report 2005). South Africa has been awarded the 2010 *Fédération Internationale de Football Association* (FIFA) World Cup tournament. Part of the obligation attached to the winning bid was for the broadcaster to be fully digitalized by that date, in fact, the bid plan requires the broadcaster to be able to deliver broadcast in high-definition television (HDTV). With less than five years lead time, the technological modernization of the SABC will prove to be an enormous challenge.

The changes in the technology and delivery of broadcasting are not simply technical: They have regulatory and social implications as well. For the first time in history, as a result of digitalization, there is more spectrum-space and more space for transmission. That is, the available space on the airwaves to broadcast radio and television terrestrially (as opposed to through satellite) is vastly increased, and the public broadcaster can longer claim the right to be the only broadcaster. Taken together, market-led deregulation and technological advancements have led to the proliferation of viewing opportunities with three pertinent results for public service broadcasters.

Firstly, it fragments and segments the audience. The broadcaster shares audiences with a number of other different providers, as viewers and listeners migrate to commercial channels, leaving the rationale of the public service in question. It is no longer possible to have a "public sphere", or a "national experience" in which the whole nation is able to share the same programming and the same perceptions. Actually, given the very heterogeneous nature of the South African public, it is unlikely that such a scenario would ever have taken

---

[13] Based on personal communication.

place; nevertheless, the audience is now more fractured than ever. Secondly, in the case of those broadcasters who are reliant on advertising revenue rather than government grants or licence fees, the additional competition drives down revenue. The reliance on advertising leads to the third consideration: In order to attract audiences, the SABC, and other broadcasters that rely on advertising, provide more and more entertainment programme, much of it very similar to each other. Sitcoms, soap operas, reality programming, quiz shows—these are the formats that "drive" audiences and attract advertisers. The result, paradoxically, is that the more competition a public broadcaster has, the more likely they are to imitate commercial broadcasters in terms of the kind of programming they provide, and the less they are able to function as public broadcasters with a wide diversity of programming and information.

Content

Scholars, broadcast managers and regulators frequently are so concerned with the structure and organization of the broadcasting, they tend to forget that audiences generally are concerned only with what they see and hear—for audiences, programming is everything. In examining the content challenges of the SABC, this paper will concentrate on the provision of local content, the diversification of programming in local African languages, the ideological task of "nurturing" nation-building and democratic ideals, and the vexed question of editorial independence.

The development and nurturing of a national culture, creativity and identity is a major concern for many countries, which have difficulty in maintaining a high level of expensive national television programmes. Globalization has meant that to a great extent, individual countries have experienced a loss of control over programme content. Many countries have chosen to subsidize educational and culturally valuable television in order to support regional, minority or national culture. A second line of attack has been to impose quotas of local production requirements on broadcasters. This has been done in Canada, while similar quotas have also been legislated in the European Union. Indeed, arguing for the principle of "cultural exception" that is a result of the "sensitive" nature and special characteristics of cultural industries, the European Union refused to include audiovisual services, including films, radio, television, the liberalization agreements of the World Trade Organization (WTO). This has allowed countries within the European Union to impose regional (pan-European) and national controls, restrictions and requirements on television programming in the public sector.

The SABC's mission statement includes a call to reflect the reality of South Africa to itself. Through the increased amount of local content—a process not without its financial and logistical contradictions—the SABC has attempted to fulfil this mandate. Despite its cost, local programming is seen to be essential to the project of protecting national identity and national culture, as well as providing for the diverse language needs of the audience.

The first attempt at enforcing local content quotas in South Africa came about as a result of the IBA's Triple Enquiry into broadcasting in 1996. At that time, the SABC was pursuing a vigorous, if idealistic goal of becoming a fully-fledged public service, imitating the likes of the Canadian and Australian Corporations, and proposed an extravagant level of local programming, a proposal that was incorporated into the Triple Enquiry's Report. However, unlike those two august organizations, the SABC was severely cash strapped. Thus, the ambitious targets which seemed so attractive in 1995, created a significant drain on resources, and with the McKinsey process (see above), local programme was cut back very significantly. When the final quotas finally were agreed upon and published, they were far more modest (RSA, 1997b).

The regulations for television quotas were rather complicated. After a two-year phase-in period, the broadcasters were required to meet minimum weekly averages of South African productions, broken down into specific categories such as drama, current affairs and children's programming. Different quotas were set for the commercial channels to that of the SABC, since it was argued, the latter had to carry higher local content obligations to meet its specific mandate as a public broadcaster. The "prime-time" scheduling was higher than the rest of the viewing day, and different obligations were stipulated for specific programme genres. Over the following years, further changes were made to the quota system through a process of consultation, hearings and legislatives processes. Immediately, broadcasters complained that these were too high; concomitantly, producers believed them to be low.

On radio, music was the only genre to be regulated. The quota was very simple: All stations with more than 15 per cent of their format as music, whether they were public service, commercial or community, were required to play 20 per cent local music (RSA, 1997c). Subsequent quotas were more flexible, as the Regulator took note of the many submissions that pointed out the difficulty of finding sufficient local music, especially for adult-contemporary and rock music format stations. The quotas for African-language stations remain high.

Issues arising from local content

Local content is profoundly popular. Weekly audience figures consistently indicate that local content is as popular, if not more popular, than the imported programming[14]. This is despite the complaint that the quality of production is uneven—while there are excellent programmes, at the same time, much of what is produced is below the international best practice standard.

Each of the five terrestrial television channels has a "flagship" soap opera, which accounts for a large percentage of its advertising revenue, and fulfils a significant portion of its "drama" quota. Inevitably, these programmes are among the three most popular slots on the channel, frequently taking top spot. The popularity of the programmes may be attributed not only to the format—soap operas, which enjoy widespread popularity across the world—but also to the ease with which audiences are able to identify with the characters, contexts and situations portrayed. Unlike the stereotypical American soap, South African drama productions, both soaps and sitcoms, avoid an over-reliance on studio settings. Both "Egoli" (18:00, M-Net) and "Isidingo" (18:30, SABC3) shoot a significant proportion on location, a factor which given the subject a flavour of reality. South African soapies tend to be anchored in current reality to a greater extent than their American counterparts. "Rape, HIV/Aids, traffic accidents and racism feature in local shows without any discernable adverse reaction from the majority of viewers" (Addison, 2004: 24).

What differentiates these programmes from the gratuitous violence and sensationalism of their imported counterparts is the strong element of pro-social message embedded into the narrative. "Yizo-Yizo", translated literally as "This is it", the follow-on series, "Gazlam" (SABC1), and to a lesser extent "Backstage" (18:30, e-tv), all deal with gritty, sometimes terrifying circumstances facing the younger generation of viewers, while at the same time providing positive role models and coping strategies for those facing gang violence, substance addiction, domestic abuse, teenage pregnancy and other challenges of a fast-developing society in transition. Positive aspirational messages form the basis of "Generations" (20:00 SABC1), a soap opera in the grand style of Dallas, but depicting the fortunes and tribulations of an upwardly mobile Black family as they make their fortunes in the "new" and multi-racial South Africa.

Most soap operas and sitcoms are multilingual, using English as an anchor language, with generous additions of other South African languages

---

[14] As measured by the South African Audience Research Foundation (SAARF).

interspersed. Despite the popularity, however, more scripts are still written in English, by white writers, and then translated into various languages. The deeply South African nature of the soapies and sitcoms, together with the use of indigenous languages, make them difficult to on-sell into other markets, except in Africa. Among African broadcasters there is an insatiable desire for content that reflects the values and aspirations of the continent, and sales in this area are strong[15].

Despite the preference for local programming, the majority of television and radio fare remains foreign, and South Africans are deeply integrated into the global audience. Mention has already been made of the financial constraints on broadcasters, particularly those who rely on commercial funding (and this includes those nominally "public" broadcasters whose main income is derived from commercial activities, such as the SABC). Since local programming can cost up to 20 times as much as the equivalent genre of imported programming, it is to be expected that a large proportion of programming would be imported, thus exposing the audience to foreign, global programming. Worldwide, most of this is of American origin. In South Africa, this trend was exacerbated during the 1980s. Throughout the period of the cultural boycott, South African television relied on massive amounts of imported American programming, since European nations refused to supply television programming to South Africa. Thus most of the imported programming was American. This created a certain "taste" for American programming, bred on the basis of familiarity. Furthermore, this was intensified by the introduction of subscription television (M-Net), which had, and continues to have, a very low commitment to local content. The introduction of direct to home television (DStv) in 1995 was a further intensification of the process (Mytton, Teer-Tomaselli & Tudesq 2004).

Editorial independence

Perhaps the greatest test of a public broadcaster is their ability to manage the political tightrope between being a "public" player while not becoming a party-political mouthpiece.

In recent times a number of incidents have overshadowed the impartiality of SABC news, leading to fierce public debate. While the structural changes within the SABC have been notable, critics contend that the broadcaster is "a mouthpiece for the government" and that "the bulletins from the Corporation ... have become sterile, reflecting government views more closely and more positively" (*Sunday Independent*, 11 July 2004: 6). In 2005, the Media

---

[15] Personal communication, Naidu, 15 September 2005.

Monitoring Project (MMP) found that 35 per cent of all stories on the SABC news were about the government, compared to 25 per cent on e-tv; and that 44 per cent of stories on SABC3 featured the government in a positive light, as compared to 28 per cent on e-tv[16]. This slant is seen as indicating a less critical and more sycophantic relationship between the government and the broadcaster. The MMP project noted that the difference was explained partly by the SABC's public mandate, "which requires a certain percentage of news to be focused on South Africa", making it "reasonable to expect that SABC news would cover developments within the government to a greater extent than commercial media entities like e-tv"[17], however the notably higher number of affirmative rather than neutral reports throws doubt on its objectivity.

At the heart of the matter have been accusations that the management of the SABC, specifically in the News departments, are far too close to the government's point of view to be able to serve public, rather than political interests. The appointment of an avowedly ANC party member, Snuki Zikalala, who had worked as the government spokesman for the Department of Labour, as the Managing Director of News, has led to the perception that the SABC has reverted to being a government lackey, just as had been the case in the pre-1994 apartheid regime. The premature departure from, or redeployment into other departments of the Corporation by a number of key staff members, including senior journalists, the heads of both radio and television news divisions, and the Chief Executive Officer himself, have all been attributed to acrimonious disagreements between the progressive, professional staffers and more politically dedicated cadres, who are seen as "interfering" with news production in order to "reflect government views more closely and more positively" (Naidu, 2004).

Several well-publicized cases of news bias have been debated within the public arena, and it is perhaps this open debate that is the most reassuring aspect of the current dilemma. In April, Zikalala interviewed Zimbabwe's President Robert Mugabe, whose ruling party had just won an election condemned by Western nations as a farce. Zikalala was lambasted in the media for stepping lightly around controversial questions.

The country's largest labour movement, the Congress of South African Trade Unions (COSATU), has long argued that the SABC has neglected the role of workers and organized labour in its reporting. Matters came to a head in June 2005, when COSATU took umbrage at what they regarded was less than fulsome coverage of a labour issue. However, far worse was to come for the broadcaster. In August 2005, SABC apologized to viewers after

---

[16] Refer www.mediamonitoringproject.org
[17] Refer www.mediamonitoringproject.org

accusations it deliberately failed to report on a public humiliation for Deputy President Phumzile Mlambo-Ngcuka at a Women's Day rally in KwaZulu-Natal, stronghold of her sacked predecessor Jacob Zuma. The Deputy-President was forced to abandon her prepared address to the rally after Zuma supporters repeatedly booed her. SABC reported on the speech, but did not mention the booing[18]. The original incident then turned into a genuine soap opera of its own, leading to an internal board of enquiry, and resulting in the resignation of top members of the Corporation and reprimands for others[19]. The report has exposed several management weaknesses and instances of interference by board members in the running of the SABC[20].

The Corporation clearly was stung by the accusations of partiality. It lodged a complaint with the industry watchdog when rival independent channel e-tv launched a marketing campaign with the slogans: "0 per cent propaganda"; "Warning: No Government Approval" and "No fear. No favour", all of which drew attention to perceived government interference in the SABC. The Broadcasting Complaints Commission dismissed the SABC's application, saying that the slogans were not directly prejudicial as they did not refer to the SABC by name, and the Corporation retaliated by setting up its own billboards with the slogan "We don't write the script. The world does".

Following the COSATU incident, representatives of the SABC and COSATU met to thrash out their differences, and issued a statement to the effect that as a public broadcaster, it "has a duty to tell the South African story in a manner that is accurate, fair and balanced and that SABC News generally succeeds in delivering on this". Furthermore, that "SABC News will continue to work within the framework of the editorial policies of the corporation, that guarantees, among other things, that SABC News contextualizes its reports by disclosing all the essential facts and not suppressing or distorting relevant and available information". (SABC Statement, 2005). Shortly afterwards, the new group chief executive, Dali Mpofu, during an address to the National Press Club, opined that "the biggest disservice the organization can do to itself is to roll it back to be the government's mouthpiece"[21].

The central question here is the relationship between the broadcasting institution and the state, and the ways in which the latter is able to circumscribe the agenda and autonomy of the former. Putting aside the SABC for the moment, we see the success of the claim to political independence depends on the willingness of politicians to abstain from interfering with the

---

[18] Refer www.news24.com, 29 August 2005.
[19] Refer www.iol.co.za, 9 September 2005.
[20] Refer *Sunday Independent*, 11 September 2005.
[21] See www.sabcnews.co.za, 25 August 2005.

day-to-day running of the corporation and the ability of broadcasters to resist such interference by remaining in control of the reporting and analysis of news and current affairs. Only then will there be a measure of public confidence, that is, the acceptance by both pressure groups (reviewers, commentators, political analysts, academics) and the "general public" (in most countries voters, taxpayers) that the broadcasting service is indeed independent.

Conclusion

At the heady outset of South Africa's new democratic period, Dr Ivy Matsepe Casaburri, then Chairperson of the SABC, now the Minister of Communication, opined that: "The old SABC is not yet dead, and ... the new broadcaster we want it to be, is not yet born. The SABC has to "re-invent" itself: It is a vision of the SABC as the national public broadcaster, to deliver services of value to all South Africa's people in more creative and unique ways than ever before" (Republic of South Africa, 1994). The process of "reinvention" has been a long and painful one, and the journey is not yet complete. Nevertheless, the story of South Africa's broadcasting transition from a state broadcaster to a fully-fledged Public service broad-caster-in-the-making remains fascinating, full of hope and disappointment, of inspiration and betrayal, a true modern-day corporate soap opera.

References

Addison, G. (April 2004). Soapies-R-Us. In *The Media: Independent industry intelligence* (pp. 22–26).

Currie, W. (1991). The Control of Broadcasting: Transition Period. In *Jabulani! Freedom of the Airwaves!* African European Institute, Amsterdam.

Currie, W. (1993). The people shall broadcast! The battle of the airwaves. In E. P. Louw (Ed.), *South African Media Policy: Debates of the 1990s*. Chicago: Lake View Press.

Duncan, J. (2002). *Broadcasting the and National Question: South African Broadcast Media in an age of Neo-liberalism*. Johannesburg: Forum for the Freedom of Expression (FXI). Netherlands Institute for Southern Africa, Amsterdam.

Gillwald, A. (2002). Experimenting with Institutional Arrangements for Communication Policy and Regulation: The case of Telecommunications and Broadcasting in South Africa. *The Southern African Journal of Information and Communication*, 2(1), 34–70. University of the Witwatersrand, Johannesburg.

Hayman, G., & Tomaselli, R. E. (1989). Ideology and Technology in the growth of South African broadcasting, 1924–1971. In R. E. Tomaselli, K. Tomaselli & J. Muller (Eds.), *Broadcasting in South Africa*. Chicago: Lake View Press.

Jabulani. (1991). *Jabulani! Freedom of the Airwaves!* African European Institute, Amsterdam.

Louw, E. (1993). *South African Media Policy: Debates of the 1990s*. Chicago: Lake View Press.

Marathane, R. M. (2005). An Investigation of The Implications For The Public Services Of The Restructuring Of Sentech. Masters thesis, Graduate Programme in Culture, Communication and Media Studies, University of KwaZulu-Natal, Durban.

Mytton, G., Tudesq, J-P., & Teer-Tomaselli, R.E. (2004). Transnational television worldwide: Towards a new media order. In J. Chalaby (Ed.), *Transnational Television Worldwide Globalization and transnationality in the media* (Ch. 5). London: IB Tauris.

Naidu, E. (11 July 2004). SABC in war of independence; and Disquiet at Auckland Park over SABC's direction. *Sunday Independent*, 1 & 6.

Naidu, V. (2005). Personal communication with Veena Naidu, Head of programme sales, SABC in September 2005.

Reith, J. (1924). *Broadcasting over Britain*. London: Hodder and Stoughton.

RSA. (1976). Republic of South Africa 1976. *Broadcasting Act* (Repealed) (No. 73 of 1976). Government Printer, Cape Town.

RSA. (1993). Republic of South Africa 1993. *Independent Broadcasting Authority Act* (No 53 of 1993). Government Printer, Pretoria.

RSA. (1995). Republic of South Africa (IBA) 1995. Report on the protection and viability of public broadcasting services; cross media control of broadcasting services; and local television content and South African music (Triple Enquiry). Johannesburg: IBA.

RSA. (1997a). Republic of South Africa 1997. Ministry of Posts, Telecommunications and Broadcasting. *A Green Paper for Public Discussion of Broadcasting Policy*. Government Printer, Pretoria.

RSA. (25 April 1997b). Republic of South Africa 1997b. Independent Broadcasting Authority-South African Music Regulations. Pretoria: *Government Gazette*.

RSA. (2 May 1997c). Republic of South Africa 1997b. Independent Broadcasting Authority-South African Television Regulations. Pretoria: *Government Gazette*.

RSA. (1998). Republic of South Africa (Department of Communications) 1998. *White Paper on Broadcasting Policy*. Government Printer, Pretoria.

RSA. (1999). Republic of South Africa 1999. *Broadcasting Act* (No 4 of 1999). Government Printer, Pretoria.

RSA. (2002). Republic of South Africa 2002. *Broadcasting Amendment Act* (No 64 of 2002).

SAARF. (2002). *South African Advertising Research Foundation Audience Report*. SAARF, Johannesburg.

SABC. (1991). *South African Broadcasting Corporation Annual Report*. SAARF, Johannesburg.

SABC. (2003). *South African Broadcasting Corporation Annual Report*. SAARF, Johannesburg.

SABC. (2004). *South African Broadcasting Corporation Annual Report*. SAARF, Johannesburg.

SABC. (2004). *South African Broadcasting Corporation Annual Report*. SAARF, Johannesburg.

Sentech. (2005). Broadcast Signal Distribution Services. Johnnesburg: Sentech. See also www.sentech.co.za

Teer-Tomaselli, R. E. (2004). Change and Transformation in South African Television. In J. Wasko (Ed.), *Blackwell Companion for Television*. London and New York: Blackwell.

Teer-Tomaselli, R. E., & Tomaselli, K. (2001). Transformation, nation-building and the South African Media, 1939–1999. In K. G. Tomaselli & H. Dunn (Eds.), *Media, Democracy and Renewal in Southern Africa*. Colorado Springs: International Academic Publishers.

Websites

Media Monitoring Project: www.mediamonitoringproject.org

News @ 24 .com portal: www,news24.com

IOL news portal: www.iol.co.za

South African Broadcasting Corporation News: www.sabcnews.com

Germany
Functional Differentiation or Decline? The Impact of Media Liberalization on German PSB

Public Service Broadcasting (PSB) is a vital element of liberal democracy in Germany. Although, like PSB in other European countries, German PSB is currently under pressure from political and economic interests, its necessity and basic functions are not fundamentally disputed among the ruling political class. However, increasing tendencies of media concentration and competition from commercial media, together with a decreasing political willingness to financially support a generally competitive PSB have significantly challenged its capability to adjust to a changing social, political and economic environment. Apart from responding to challenges from national political and media actors, PSB has also to adapt to technological changes, most of all the introduction of new digital communication technologies, and to the ongoing trans-nationalization i.e. Europeanization and Globalization of media systems.

German PSB was introduced after 1945 in order to prevent any totalitarian political control of broadcasting. The National Socialists had used the established centralized broadcasting system as a propaganda tool after 1933. The centralized structure of the former broadcasting system was seen by Western Allies as a major reason for the fact that it was able to be easily streamlined and politically controlled by the National Socialists. Thus, the Allies saw the prime objective of broadcasting regulation as providing independent and pluralistic broadcasting. They pushed for a decentralized PSB system giving the federal states (Länder) autonomous responsibility for developing a legal framework to regulate public and later also private broadcasting within their territory.

In line with the federalist structure of the German political system, under the German constitution (Basic Law) responsibility for the content of broadcasting, including licensing of radio and TV stations, is granted exclusively to the Länder[1] and their parliaments. Apart from the fear of centralized political control, this reflects the general assumption that broadcasting has a fundamental role in collective identity formation and cultural orientation of its audience. Regional state sovereignty in broadcasting regulation was seen as a reflection of the cultural and regional heterogeneity of the Federal Republic of Germany and as an essential precondition to guaranteeing that diverse regional cultural needs were reflected in German radio and TV (Libertus, 2004).

Organized as autonomous public corporations under the jurisdiction of the Länder, German PSB was basically founded on the model of the BBC, which means that it is neither directly controlled by government nor financed by the state. The main financial input comes from user licence fees. The licence fee is proposed by an independent commission (Kommission zur Ermittlung der Rundfunkgebühren) and has to be agreed upon by all regional state parliaments.

Being a pluralist country, German post-war media policies have always aimed at guaranteeing competition in the formation of public opinion: Whereas in the case of private media, i.e. the press, private radio and TV, pluralism and competitiveness of public opinion is thought to result naturally from free market conditions, the basic concept for regulating PSB can be characterized as "administrative coordination" (Kepplinger, 2000). Certain organizational and procedural safeguards ensure that decisions on content and programmes are taken independently of state control, and that respect is given to political and cultural pluralism as well as the general interests of the public. Public channels are supervised by Broadcasting Councils (Rundfunkräte), whose members are supposed to represent a balance of political and social, cultural and economic interests. In order to prevent any partisan control of the Broadcasting Councils, state-related political actors must not form the majority on any Rundfunkrat.

PSB offers a First Federal Programme (ARD) and a Second Federal Programme (ZDF). The First Federal Programme (ARD) is a joint venture based on a network of all regional state (Länder) public broadcasting stations. Like the Second Federal Programme, its operation is regulated by the Interstate Broadcasting Agreement among all Länder (Rundfunk-staatsvertrag). According to this Agreement, the content of the programmes broadcasted by public media networks have to be politically balanced.

---

[1] Germany is a federal republic made up of 16 states, known in German as *Länder* (singular *Land*).

Interstate Broadcasting Agreement

The remit of broadcasting in Germany is laid down in the Interstate Broadcasting Agreement (see Box 1), several treaties on the regional state (Länder) level, regional state laws (Landesgesetze) and the Programming Guidelines of the two federal programmes (Eifert, 2002). With regard to the content of their programmes, ARD and ZDF are committed to a policy of comprehensiveness, balance, mutual respect and quality programming. The role of public service broadcasting is described "as a medium and factor in the process of the formation of free individual and public opinion by producing and broadcasting radio and tv programmes" (Libertus, 2004: 13). It has to provide a comprehensive view on international, European, national and regional events covering all important aspects of life. Apart from that, programmes have to provide information, education, advice and entertainment as well as programmes with a cultural content.

In line with their obligation to offer "integrated", i.e. internally plural-istic, programming, programmes must represent all social and political interests in a balanced manner ("Ausgewogenheit"). However, despite these general guidelines, regional state governments occasionally complain about programmes being either too left wing or too conservative, depend-ing on the party or party coalition governing the respective regional state. Some regional states have even refused to carry specific programmes if they considered them to be biased. Attempts by the federal government to gain stronger control of the decentralized PSB were defeated by the Länder and the Federal Constitutional Court (Bundesverfassungsgericht).

Regional public programmes can be broadcasted on third channels (Dritte Programme). The availability of regional channels in cable networks and their transmission via satellite on ASTRA has meant that the reception of regional channels has become nationwide in the 1990s. Regional states vary significantly in size—some comprise only a large city like the old Hansa cities, others comprise a population of up to 18 million inhabitants. As financial constraints limit the ability of small states to run autonomous stations, several of the 16 *Länder* have chosen to combine their resources and in the 1990s formed multi-state-broadcasting corpora-tions (Mehrländeranstalten). North German Broadcasting (NDR) serves Lower Saxony, Schleswig-Holstein, Hamburg, Mecklenburg-Western Pomerania; Central German Broadcasting Corporation (MDR) repre-sents Saxony, Saxony-Anhalt and Thuringia; Berlin cooperates with Brandenburg to form the RBB; Southwest Broadcasting (SWF) represents Baden-Württemberg and Rhineland-Palatinate. One-state programmes

BOX 1
INTERSTATE BROADCASTING AGREEMENT

Article 41: Programming Principles*

1. Programmes which are broadcasted shall be subject to the requirements of the constitution. They shall respect the dignity of man as well as the moral, religious and political convictions of others. They shall promote solidarity in united Germany as well as international understanding. The provisions of general legislation and those protecting personal honour shall be complied with.
2. Full programmes shall contribute an appropriate share of information, culture and education towards the presentation of cultural diversity in German-speaking regions and in Europe as a whole; the possibility of offering specialized programmes shall remain unaffected.
3. Current affairs and information programmes shall be consistent with recognized journalistic principles. They shall be independent and objective. The accuracy and source of news must be checked with the care demanded by the circumstances prior to its transmission. Commentary must be clearly separated from reporting and be identified as such by naming the author.
4. Paragraphs 1 to 3 shall only apply to nationwide broadcasts.

* Last amendment September 2003

– www.iuscomp.org/gla/statutes/RuStaV.htm –

are: West German Broadcasting (WDR), Bavarian Broadcasting (BR), Hesse Broadcasting (HR), Radio Bremen, Saarland Broadcasting. They all produce a full 24-hours of TV programmes and three to five radio programmes in a variety of formats, popular culture, information, and high culture.

In addition to the two nationwide, full-programme stations and nine regional stations, PSB in Germany currently comprises several specialized channels: Kika, a channel broadcasting specially for children; PHOENIX, a documentary channel focusing on political and other events of general interest; and two transnational cultural channels (3Sat, based on a cooperation between Swiss and Austrian TV, and ARTE, a joint venture with French PSB) and, a total of 61 radio channels, six digital channels and numerous Internet sites.

Introduction of private television in the 1980s

Whereas the Social Democratic Governments of the 1970s were explicitly opposed to the commercialization of radio and television, the conservative Christian Democratic Kohl governments (1982–1998) supported a fundamental shift by introducing private TV channels in the 1980s. Helmut Schmidt, Social Democrat and former Chancellor of the Federal Republic (1974–1982), saw broadcasting primarily as a means of spreading enjoyment of high culture to a wider audience. He was generally rather critical of TV and even proposed a day of abstention from TV each week. Like many other conservatives, Chancellor Helmut Kohl felt unfairly treated and not respected highly enough by PSB and thus encouraged the introduction of private television networks.

Central government provided the new technology, in terms of cable and satellite, and in 1984 the first private broadcasting channels were licensed by the *Länder*, transforming the national media system from a public service broadcasting system into a dual system, in other words a broadcasting order in which public and private broadcasters coexist. The first private television network in German was SAT.1, licensed in 1984 and principally owned by Leo Kirch and the Springer publishing group. The Luxembourg-based RTL was the second private network. Today some 30 TV stations compete for audience ratings, the biggest among the private competitors being the RTL Group, and SAT.1 and PRO7.

In the beginning, majority ownership by one shareholder was not allowed for private television. When the Federal Government lifted this restriction in 1997, Bertelsmann gained majority control of RTL, while Leo Kirch expanded his influence over SAT.1. However, in 2003 Kirch ran into such financial difficulties that his consortium, which also included other private channels, in particular PRO7, was split. Parts of the consortium were bought by Haim Saban in 2003. Eighty-eight per cent of PRO7SAT.1 is currently owned by American venture-capital companies, although a takeover by the Springer group, who also owns the best selling German tabloid BILD, is very likely.

Basic regulations concerning contents and ownership of private broadcasting are laid down in the Interstate Broadcasting Agreement. Whereas PSB is strictly bound to balanced programming, rules for private channels are rather vague and state that "a single programme shall not influence public opinion in a largely imbalanced way" (see Box 2). Whereas PSB has to follow the principle of internal pluralism, it is considered sufficient when private broadcasters achieve pluralism in terms of an outer-pluralism, in other words a pluralism that is created through the competition of different channels on the market. Inherent dangers of opinion-forming monopolies and thus risks of one-sidedness in programmes from private channels are counteracted in Article 26 of the Agreement. Allocating transmission time to independent third parties and political control of licence practices are major strategies in limiting the influence of single competitors.

BOX 2
INTERSTATE BROADCASTING AGREEMENT

Article 25: Plurality of opinion, regional windows

1. The content of private broadcasting must generally indicate a plurality of opinion. Important political, ideological and social groups shall be given adequate opportunity to express themselves in the full programme services; minority views shall be taken into account. It shall remain possible to offer specialized programmes.

2. A single programme shall not influence public opinion in a largely imbalanced way.

Article 26: Ensuring plurality of opinion in television

1. A company (natural or juridical person or association) may itself or through companies attributable to it broadcast nationwide in the Federal Republic of Germany an unlimited number of television programmes, unless it is thereby able to exercise a controlling influence in the manner described in the following provisions.

2. If the programmes attributable to one company achieve an average annual viewer rating of 30 per cent it shall be assumed that it has a controlling influence. The same shall apply if the rating is only slightly less than that proportion where the company holds a dominant position in a related, media-relevant market or an overall assessment of its activities in television and in related, media-relevant markets concludes that the influence obtained as a result of those activities is equivalent to that of a company with a viewer rating of 30 per cent.

3. If a company is able to exercise a controlling influence with the programmes attributable to it no licence may be issued for further programmes attributable to that company, nor may the acquisition of further attributable holdings in broadcasters be declared as acceptable.

4. If a broadcaster achieves with a full programme or an information-oriented specialized programme an annual average viewer rating of 10 per cent he must within six months after the establishment of this fact and after being informed by the state supervisory authority for private broadcasters allocate transmission time to independent third parties pursuant to Article 31.

– www.iuscomp.org/gla/statutes/RuStaV.htm –

The development of the dual broadcasting system by the German Constitutional Court (Bundesverfassungsgericht) has redefined the remit of PSB. Economically-driven private broadcasters tend to seek mass appeal and thus tend to disregard minority interests. This deficit on the part of private broadcasting is only acceptable, the Constitutional Court argues, as long as public broadcasters offer a basic provision (Grundversorgung) for all viewers. This does not mean that PSB is restricted to only offering basic provision, however, it has become its main rationale and justification for its public funding via licence fees (Schäfer, 2004: 49–56; Schulz et al., 2002: 11). The particular definition of "basic provision" is still disputed. While ARD and ZDF would also count specialized programmes like the children's channel Kika, the news channel PHOENIX or the French-German culture channel ARTE, as well as online services as part of its remit, private competitors try to limit the notion of "basic provision" to the two nationwide full programmes and the regional channels.

The dual system—Tendencies of convergence

Although the German Federal Constitutional Court has so far confirmed the necessity of retaining a comprehensive PSB in eight important rulings, public TV channels and radio stations find themselves increasingly under attack. Journalists and conservative politicians criticize the allegedly high level of fees and warrant their criticism by quoting reduced viewer ratings. In their view, PSB should combine its public service obligations with stronger competition with commercial competitors for the highest viewer ratings. However, increasingly restrictive financial constraints have a negative impact on the general competitiveness of PSB. And the resulting need to attract more advertising revenue is criticized by private channels as unfair competition on decreasing resources and rejected by PSB supporters as a step in the wrong direction towards lower standards of programming. While ARD and ZDF received 5.16 and 1.55 billion Euro respectively from licence fees in 2004, advertising revenues contributed only 0.29 billion Euro to their annual budget. Compared to that, private TV channels earned 3.57 billion Euro from their advertising revenues in the same year (Rosenbach, 2005: 143).

A general decline of PSB has not only been stated by those who want to weaken it, but also by those who would like to strengthen an independent broadcasting service. Critics often refer to allegedly lower viewer ratings and a convergence of public and private broadcasting, arguing that PSB has become more and more commercialized and thus lost its high quality programming and "public" character. In the following, I would like to outline some of the aspects of convergence that have been criticized before dealing with the issue of a general decline of PSB and putting forward empirical evidence showing that PSB in Germany has still kept its leading role in many respects of programme evaluation, most of all as a provider of political information.

Private broadcasters and their association VPRT (Verband Privater Rundfunk und Telekommunikation e.V.) as well as representatives from political parties, particularly from Christian Democratic and Liberal Parties, have stressed several changes in the contents of public broadcasting and interpreted them as evidence of a process of adaptation to private broadcasting, and part of a planned strategy to regain viewers lost to private channels and to prevent any future losses (Brenner, 2002: 130–187). These are the main changes criticized:

- *The decline in programming quality*
  Although it would be difficult to establish any empirical proof of an overall drop in quality within channels offering the full range of programmes, there is some evidence confirming changes in the modes of presentation. For instance, a linguistic analysis of the language used in news bulletins in private and public broadcasting, carried out at the University of Bochum, shows that in terms of length of sentences as well as in terms of use of main clauses, ARD and ZDF have adjusted to the private channel RTL in the last 20 years. Whereas in 1983 the average sentence in ARD news comprised 20 words, it currently comprises only 13 words. During the same period RTL increased the length of its sentences from 13 to 14 words (DIE WELT, 11 February 2000: 39).

- *The targeting of high viewer ratings*
  Due to growing competition from private broadcasters, public channels are trying to improve their share of the television market. The First Federal Programme (ARD), for example, has set specific targets for viewer rates for its prime time programmes in its internal proceedings. Furthermore, they are trying to win back younger viewers in particular. Critics argue that this kind of general targeting runs counter to the function of PSB as defined in the Constitutional Court decisions and the Interstate Broadcasting Treaty. Programming diversity could not be achieved by addressing all programmes to a younger audience but only by creating a diversity of programmes that addresses diverse groups of viewers (Brenner, 2002: 155; Stock, 2005: 58). Critics even talk of a process of self-commercialization that will lead to substantial "dump-

ing down" within channels that offer the full range of programmes. Elite-oriented, high quality programmes would be increasingly left to specialized channels like the French-German culture channel ARTE or the public news and public events channel PHOENIX (Jessen, 2002; Scheidt, 2004; Weischenberg, 2004).

- *The disregarding of minority interests*
  Striving for higher viewer ratings and a younger audience has had a particularly negative impact on programmes addressing minorities that so far had contributed to securing a diversity of opinions and lifestyles in the PSB programmes. Minority programmes, it is argued, have either been shifted to late-night transmission or specialized channels, or they have been cut completely, leaving prime time to superficial, low quality, mass-oriented programmes.

- *The trend towards mass appeal programmes*
  In the competition for higher viewer ratings, early evening programmes broadcasted on public television channels are increasingly characterized by daily soaps, talk shows, VIP and human interest magazines.

- *The copying of programme formats*
  The scramble for the highest viewer ratings means public broadcasters have copied several successful entertainment formats from private channels or bought popular entertainment stars from private channels. Private broadcasters have been more successful in the area of entertainment in the past. Instead of competing with them by developing new attractive entertainment formats, ARD and ZDF have preferred to simply imitate them. Thus they give the impression of not being able to fulfil the self-defined task of innovative programming.

PSB—Still leading in information and education

Despite these tendencies of convergence, empirical content analysis also gives strong evidence that the distinction between public and private broadcasting in Germany has not changed. The public broadcasting system is required by law to provide news, political discussion and current affairs reports as well as sports and entertainment as a public service. On 14 September 2004, the Assembly of the First Federal Programme announced its most recent Programming Guidelines. The guidelines sum up the fundamental principle of public broadcasting of the ARD (see Box 3) and in particular emphasize that the main function of broadcasting by the First Federal Programme is provision of information.

BOX 3
PROGRAMMING GUIDELINES OF THE
FIRST FEDERAL PROGRAMME (ARD)

Information plays an extraordinary role within the programmes that are broadcasted as part of the responsibility of the First Federal Programme (ARD). Information programmes represent the largest part of the overall programming, they shape the public broadcasting profile of the ARD, including during prime time evening viewing. ARD informs in all journalistic formats on all important political, social, economic, cultural, ecological, sports-related and everyday-life-related issues. The principles of journalistic fairness as well as objectivity, balance and plurality of opinion are always respected by the ARD. Thus ARD encourages societal dialogue, serves freedom of information and opinion, and contributes significantly to public opinion and will formation.

All national and regional programmes of the ARD are to ensure that information represents at least 40 per cent of their overall content. This does not include 10 per cent information on sport events.

– ARD Jahrbuch 2004/05, 388 (translated by the author) –

An analysis, of the percentage of information programmes as part of overall TV programming in Germany, shows clearly that the commitment to information by PSB is not just lip service to legitimize public funding. Since the introduction of private broadcasting, the percentage of information programmes to overall transmission time has varied significantly and steadily: Whereas it was 36 per cent in PSB versus 15 per cent in private channels in 1985, in 1995 it stood at 42 per cent versus 12 per cent, and 46 per cent to 22 per cent in 2003 (Institut für empirische Medienforschung, Köln, cit. in Krüger, 2005: 258). In 2003, the two national PSB channels ARD and ZDF devoted much more time to broadcasting information as part of their overall programming than the three most important private channels. Taking the time slot between 5 p.m. and 1 a.m., 86 per cent of all information programmes are broadcasted by ARD and ZDF whereas only 14 per cent of all information in that period of time is broadcasted by the private channels RTL, SAT.1 and PRO 7 (Krüger, 2004). There is a particularly marked difference in the development of news as part of overall transmission time: In 1991, the percentage of news to overall transmission time of public broadcasting television was 7.7 per cent, as opposed to 4.1 per cent in private channels. Whereas PSB shows an upward trend for news to 10.1 per cent of overall programming in 2003, private channels only devoted

2.6 per cent of their time of broadcasting to news programmes in the same year (Institut für empirische Medienforschung, cit. in Kröger, 2005: 262).

PSB not only delivers more information and education programmes, these programmes are also well ahead in viewer ratings. This is particularly true for news programmes, which are not only the chief source of information for citizens but the major source for image formation of TV channels. Although in the 1990s private channels significantly broadened and professionalized their news programme, the eight o'clock "Tagesschau" evening news broadcasted by the First Federal Programme (ARD) still attracts the greatest resonance among German viewers, followed by "heute", the 7 p.m. news put out by the Second Federal Programme (ZDF). The "Tagesschau" attracts an average of 9.62 million and ZDF "heute" 5.17 million viewers, whereas the figures for the main evening news of the three most successful private channels are: RTL aktuell (6.45 p.m.), 3.89 million; SAT.1 18:30 (6.30 p.m.), 1.73 million; and PRO 7 Nachrichten (7.30 p.m./7.55 p.m.), 1.3 million. The percentage of all viewers watching the main evening news is as follows: ARD Tagesschau, 34.8 per cent; ZDF heute, 23.6 per cent; RTL aktuell, 18.8 per cent; SAT 1 19:30, 9.4 per cent; and PRO7 Nachrichten, 4.8 per cent (Darschin/Heinz, 2003: 164).

This positive market position held by German PSB news programmes can also be illustrated by the late news and political magazines: Of the 23 most viewed political magazines there are only three that are broadcasted by private channels and those three occupy the 15th, 19th and 20th positions in viewer ranking. Whereas the highest ranked programme "Brennpunkt" from ARD regularly attracts 5.08 million viewers or 18.2 per cent of all viewers, the highest ranked political magazine from a private station, Stern TV from RTL, only attracts 2.69 million viewers or 15 per cent of all viewers at transmission time (ibid.).

Contrary to the assumption of a generally declining interest in politics, the data on TV viewing in Germany show a stable and even slight increase in consumption of most political information and discussion programmes. While in 2001 the average German viewer spent 56 minutes watching political information programmes, in 2002 this figure had risen to 59 minutes. Of these 59 minutes, viewers devoted 41 minutes daily to information programmes from PSB (ARD, ZDF and Regional Channels) and only 18 minutes to equivalent information programmes from private TV channels.

These viewing habits are reflected in opinion surveys asking viewers about their evaluation of German TV channels and programmes. Although since liberalization of the TV media market in the mid 1980s, TV consumption has significantly shifted in favour of private channels, in representative surveys German citizens still consider PSB to be indispensable.

Chart 1
Indispensability of German TV Channels (in %)

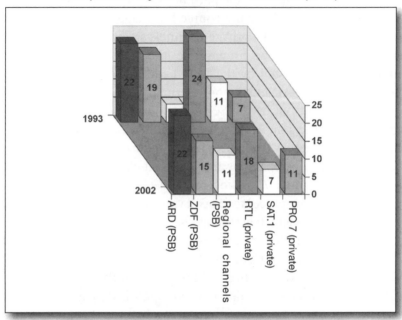

	1993	2002
ARD (PSB)	22	22
ZDF (PSB)	19	15
Regional channels (PSB)	5	11
RTL (private)	23	18
SAT.1 (private)	11	7
PRO 7 (private)	7	11

*Interviewees were asked: If you could only keep one TV channel, which one would you choose?
(Sources: 1991–1994: ARD/ZDF Marketingstudie; 2002: ARD-Trend)

If Germans (all interviewees were over 14) had to decide to keep only one out of all TV channels, the First Federal Programme (ARD) has kept its leading position in viewers' preference. Compared to figures from 1993 it was even able to improve its position in terms of perceived indispensability. This high regard for PSB is also expressed in judgements on the quality of TV programmes. Asked about the best channel in terms of quality, in winter 2002 Germans made the following ranking.

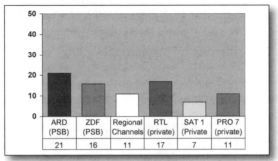

Chart 2
Judgement on Quality of TV Channels in 2002 (in %)

ARD (PSB)	ZDF (PSB)	Regional Channels	RTL (private)	SAT 1 (Private)	PRO 7 (private)
21	16	11	17	7	11

*Interviewees were asked, which channel they thought would be the most qualified.
They could name only one channel.
(Source: ARD Trend 2002)

The difference between channel perception is even more marked when people were asked about the credibility of programmes. Over the years, PSB has even increased its lead over private TV.

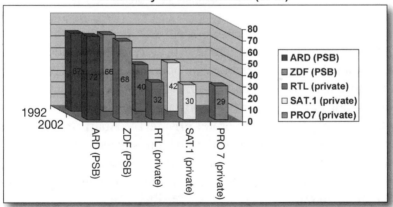

Chart 3
Credibility of TV Channels (in %)

■ ARD (PSB)
▨ ZDF (PSB)
■ RTL (private)
□ SAT.1 (private)
■ PRO7 (private)

	1992	2002
ARD (PSB)	22	22
ZDF (PSB)	19	15
RTL (private)	23	18
SAT.1 (private)	11	7
PRO 7 (private)	7	11

*Percentage of those who attribute channels high and very high credibility on a six-step scale
(Sources: 1991–1994: ARD/ZDF Marketingstudie; 2002: ARD-Trend)

However, there seems to be a significant difference between perceptions of quality and likeability. Even in likeability, PSB scored overall better than private TV. Figures for PSB have even improved compared to 1993. However, there is no gap between the highest scoring PSB channel (ARD) and the highest scoring private channel (RTL):

Chart 4
Likeability of German TV Channels

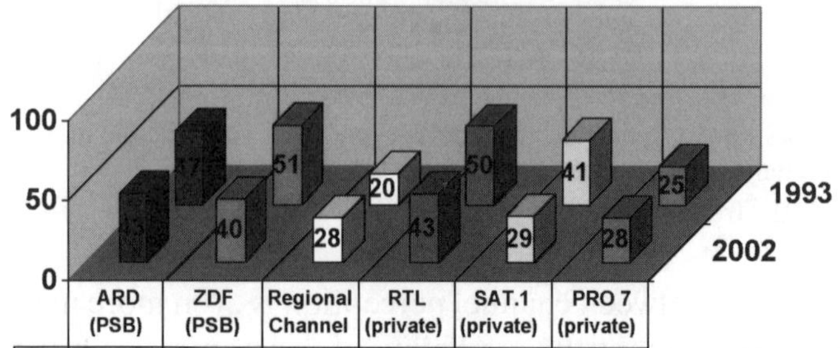

	ARD (PSB)	ZDF (PSB)	Regional Channel	RTL (private)	SAT.1 (private)	PRO 7 (private)
1993	47	51	20	50	41	25
2002	43	40	28	43	29	28

*Three choices were possible
(Sources: 1991–1994: ARD/ZDF Marketingstudie; 2002: ARD-Trend)

Differences in individual channel preferences is explained by data suggesting a significant correlation with opinions on political efficacy: 66 per cent of those who favour PSB over private TV state that they have a good understanding and judgement of important political issues. This is true for only 43 per cent of those who prefer private TV. Apart from that, viewers of private TV appear to have a more pessimistic view on the morality of politicians and they are less content (31 per cent) with the current state of democracy in Germany than those who prefer watching PSB (44 per cent) (ARD Trend 2002).

Functional differentiation or decline?

Trying to draw conclusions on the future of PSB, data on viewing habits and the perception of channels does not confirm the pessimistic premise of a general convergence and decline of PSB, at least not in Germany.

Today there are a lot of more PSB channels than before the introduction of private TV. And although viewing habits have subsequently changed, PSB still gets the highest marks from viewers in terms of perceived indispensability, credibility and programming quality.

A functional differentiation between public and private channels drawn along the line of information versus entertainment seems to describe current trends in Germany much more adequately than the assumption of a general decline of PSB. While PSB programmes are clearly perceived as doing best in comprehensive information, private channels are mainly defined by their function of entertainment and relaxation (see results of NFD Infratest, cit. in Darschin/Zubayr, 2003: 206). This favourable evaluation of the entertainment function of private TV is also mirrored in actual viewing habits. If we take viewer ratings for all entertainment and fiction programmes, viewers prefer private channels: 59 per cent of all TV entertainment consumption is made up of programmes from private channels and only 41 per cent from PSB. In viewing time this equates to a proportion of 54 to 38 minutes daily of average viewing time, Monday to Sunday among viewers over 14 (Darschin/Heinz, 2003: 162).

As mentioned earlier, often the argument that the contents of private and public TV programmes are converging is asserted in order to sustain the notion of decline. Comparative content analysis of news programmes on German TV has given ample evidence for trends towards convergence in terms of news selection and presentation (Bruns/Marcinkowski, 1996). On the one hand, private channels like RTL and SAT.1 have made efforts to improve the standard of their news making and shifted their contents away from human interest stories towards national and foreign political news. Apart from that, they have focussed more on state and party political actors and less on crime and violence. On the other hand, news production in PSB has laid stronger emphasis on visualization, so-called soft political issues and reporting of crime and violence. Changes in news presentation by PSB also led to shorter contributions, more rapid cuts or shorter sentences, as stated earlier. Whether these changes in the mode of presentation are due to deliberate processes of adaptation to styles of communication on private channels or whether they are simply part of a general process of modernization of news presentation is still open to debate (Pfetsch 1996). Despite these changes, there are also clearly defined limits to the ongoing adaptation or modernization of news presentation: News presenters on the "Tagesschau", the 8 o'clock news from the First Federal Programme (ARD) and the most successful TV news in Germany, for instance, still do not use a teleprompter. Apart from still reading the news from sheets of paper, they defy the general trend to present news less seriously and to expose the personality of the news presenter/reader.

Whether functional differentiation between information and entertainment will be a permanent feature that distinguishes between public and private TV in Germany and whether PSB will be able to keep the lead in information and education, as well as in the perception of general indispensability, quality of programming and credibility of information remains an open question. Viewing habits as well as TV perceptions are not only dependent on political opinions but also on social structural factors, most of all on age. And regarding the age of viewers, the future seems to favour private TV channels: In the 14–19 age group, only six per cent prefer public TV, while 35 per cent prefer private TV programmes; in the 30–49 age group, the percentages are 29 versus 41 and only among those over 50, PSB is the leading channel, with 65 per cent preferring PSB against 24 per cent preferring private TV (ARD Trend, 2002).

Youth is usually identified with the future. However, when interpreting these figures with regard to the future of PSB in Germany, we have to bear in mind that Germany has a particularly ageing population, therefore those over 50 will have increasing representation in viewer ratings in the near future.

References

ARD-Trend. (2002). Retrieved from www.daserste.de/forschungsergebnisse

ARD. (Ed.) (2005). *ARD-Jahrbuch 04/05*.

Baringhorst, S. (2002). Medienpolitik. In H. Schanze (Ed.), *Metzler Lexikon Medientheorie/ Medienwissenschaft. Ansätze—Personen—Grundbegriffe* (pp. 236–239). Stuttgart: Metzler.

Brenner, C. (2002). *Zur Gewährleistung des Funktionsauftrages durch den öffentlich-rechtlichen Rundfunk. Eine Konkretisierung der Aufgaben des öffentlich-rechtlichen Rundfunks im Fernseh-, Hörfunk- und Online-Bereich*, Tübingen.

Bruns, T., & Marcinkowski, F. (1997). *Politische Information im Fernsehen. Eine Längsschnittstudie*, Opladen.

Darschin, W., & Heinz, G. (2003). Tendenzen im Zuschauerverhalten. *Medien Perspektiven, 4/2003*, 158–166.

Darschin, W., & Zubayr, C. (2003). Was leisten die Fernsehsender? *Media Perspektiven, 5/2003*, 206–215.

Eifert, M. (2002). *Konkretisierung des Programmauftrags des öffentlich-rechtlichen Rundfunks. Verfassungsrechtliche Verankerung, rechtliche Ausgestaltung und neue Herausforderungen der Selbstregulierung des öffentlich-rechtlichen Rundfunks*, Baden-Baden.

Jessen, J. (2002). 50 Jahre Fernsehen. *DIE ZEIT*, No. 1, 33.

Kepplinger, H. M. (2000). Kommunikationspolitik. In Noelle-Neumann et al (Ed.), *Fischer-Lexikon Publizistik-Massenkommunikation*. Frankfurt/M.

Krüger, U. M. (2002). Entwicklung des Politikangebots im Fernsehprogramm. In C.-M. Ridder, et al. (Eds.), *Bausteine einer Theorie des öffentlich-rechtlichen Rundfunks*, Wiesbaden (pp. 252–271).

Krüger, U. M. (2004). Spartenstruktur und Informationsprofile im deutschen Fernsehangebot. Programmanalyse von ARD/DasErste, ZDF, RTL, SAT.1 und ProSieben. *Media Perspektiven*, 5/2004, 194–207.

Libertus, M. (2004). *Essential Aspects Concerning the Regulation of the German Broadcasting System. Historical, Constitutional and Legal Outlines*. Arbeitspapiere des Instituts für Rundfunkökonomie an der Universität zu Köln. Working Paper No 193, Cologne.

Marcinskowski, F., & Bruns, T. (1996). Politische Magazine im dualen Fernsehen. In H. Schatz (Ed.), *Fernsehen als Objekt und Moment des sozialen Wandels* (pp. 255–286). Opladen.

Pfetsch, B. (1996). Konvergente Fernsehformate in der Politikberichterstattung? Eine vergleichende Analyse öffentlich-rechtlicher und privater Programme 1985/86 und 1993. *Rundfunk und Fernsehen*, 44, 479–498.

Rosenbach, M. (2005). Zwischen Heuchelei und Hybris. *DER SPIEGEL*, No 30, 142–144.

Schatz, H. (1994). Rundfunkentwicklung im ‚dualen System': die Konvergenzhypothese. In O. Jarren (Ed.), *Politische Kommunikation in Hörfunk und Fernsehen* (pp. 67–80). Opladen.

Schäfer, H. F. (2004). *Neue Betätigungsfelder des öffentlich-rechtlichen Rundfunks. Entwicklung und rechtliche Bewertung*. München.

Scheidt, W. (200). Quoten-Dienst. *Journalist*, No. 4, 10–18.

Schulz, W., et al. (2002). "Regulation of Broadcasting and Internet Services in Germany. A Brief Overview". Working Papers of the Hans Bredow Institute, No. 13, Hamburg.

Stock, M. (2005). Duales System: funktionsgerecht ausgestaltet? In C.-M. Ridder, et al. (Eds.), *Bausteine einer Theorie des öffentlich-rechtlichen Rundfunks* (pp. 54–77). Wiesbaden.

Wagner, A. M. (1999). Competition Regulation, State Aid and the Impact of Liberalization. Paper given at the Seminar on Liberalization and Public Service Broadcasting held in the British Film Institute on 15 October 1999.

Weischenberg, S. (2004). Goethe im Sinkflug? Eine Diagnose zur Wirklichkeit des öffentlich-rechtlichen Rundfunks in Deutschlands. *epd medien*.

Malta
Countering the Challenges of Media Liberalization in a Small Island State

The 20s and the 30s brought with them a great expansion of radio broadcasting services in the United States and Europe. The broadcasting system in the former reflecting the liberal and capitalist mentality developed mainly as a commercial system, while the strong social conscience present in the latter gave rise to the public broadcasting system. The actual independence of these media organizations from the respective governments, the level of the regulatory regime and the method of financing varied from one European country to another.

A hybrid of these two models was adopted when radio broadcasting was introduced in Malta[1] in 1935 through the British owned company, Rediffusion Ltd (Borg, 2004). The model adopted was that of a station owned and run by a commercial company but whose content reflected

> The development of the Maltese mediascape is marked by five characteristics: the importance of the institutions (state, political parties, Catholic Church); the fall and rise of public service media especially radio; the bilingual colonial heritage of the country; the David and Goliath syndrome; and the giving of a new dimension to Malta's oral culture.
>
> – Borg, J. *Maltese Media Landscape* –
> *European Journalism Centre, Netherlands, 2003*

[1] The Mediterranean Islands of Malta with a surface area of 316 km sq. and a population of almost 400,000 consitute one of the smallest but most densely populated countries. The country is made of the main island, Malta and a secondary island, Gozo. It is a member of the European Union. There are two political parties represented in Parliament. The Partit Nazzjonalista, a member of the European Popular Party, is in government. The Malta Labour Party, a member of the European Socialist Party, is in opposition. The main religion of Malta is Catholicism with more than 95 per cent of its inhabitants baptized in that religion.

that usually associated with public service radio. The service introduced in the form of cable radio was given against a stipulated subscription fee. After the War advertising was introduced as a way of supplementing income.

The Maltese could receive television transmissions from Italy (see box below) since early 1957 when RAI set up a booster in Sicily on Mount Camarata to strengthen its signal. Five years later Malta Television, also run by Rediffusion Ltd, was inaugurated in September 1962. An important milestone in the history of broadcasting was the setting up in 1961 of the Broadcasting Authority as the regulator of the sector. It is expected to ensure balance and impartiality in matters of political and industrial controversy and in matters of current public policy.

In 1975 broadcasting was nationalized by the Labour Government, following an engineered take over by the workers of the Rediffusion run

THE DAVID AND GOLIATH SYNDROME

Malta is a very small country lying at the southern tip (just 96 km away) of a large country, Italy. This has influenced, and is still influencing the development of Maltese media. Italian refugees who sought haven in Malta in the middle of the 19th century, when the struggle for the unification of Italy was on, practically dominated Maltese print journalism. Their presence also aided the pro-Italian movement that, at that time, many looked at as a counterbalance to the influence of the British colonizers.

Radio broadcasting was introduced in the middle of the 30s partly to counter the Fascist propaganda that was reaching Malta through Italian radio stations. Radio broadcasting was introduced in the form of cable radio and during the war was an important instrument used to alert people of enemy's attacks. Malta Television was inaugurated in September 1962; five years after the Maltese started receiving television signals from Italy. This happened in early 1957 when RAI set up a booster in Sicily on Mount Camarata to strengthen its signal there. Italian television was always very popular in Malta. The Maltese national station started transmitting in colour in 1981 when the Maltese were already accustomed to tune in to colour programmes on Sicilian and TV stations from mainland Italy thanks to illegally imported sets. In 1995—the first year of pluralism—the Maltese spent 51 per cent of their TV viewing time following Italian channels, mainly the Berlusconi ones (Broadcasting Authority, 1995). A good part of their viewing on Maltese stations consisted of foreign programmes. Goliath had the upper hand over David. The situation changed as little by little Maltese stations made inroads in that high figure. Today the Maltese spend most of their TV time watching Maltese programmes on Maltese stations but the Italian stations are still very popular. David is now definitively the winner.

– Borg, Joseph. Maltese Media Landscape –
European Journalism Centre, Netherlands, 2003

stations. The commercial company running broadcasting on public service criteria was now replaced by an organization owned and controlled by the government. This was a paradigm shift from the model adopted since the 30s and can be considered as the formal beginning of broadcasting totally owned and controlled by the state.

The paradigm was changed once more following the White Paper by which a Nationalist government committed itself to broadcasting pluralism and to an editorially independent public broadcasting service[2]. State broadcasting was turned into a limited liability company, called Public Broadcasting Services Ltd (PBS Ltd), in preparation for the introduction of pluralism through the Broadcasting Act of 1991.

The first private radio stations were those owned by the political party—Super One Radio and Radio 101—which went on the air in 1991. The number of stations eventually increased to 13 broadcasting nationally and to 25 community stations (Broadcasting Authority, 2005). There is now a national or community radio station for every 10,000 persons and one for every 8 square km! The Broadcasting Act was amended in 1993 to fully liberalize the television sector. There are currently five Maltese television stations or a Maltese station for every 51,000 persons aged 16 years and over (Borg, 2003).

The challenges of liberalization

The advent of pluralism in 1991 threw public service broadcasting into a crisis, which affected its audiences, increased its financial losses and challenged its identity and existence. The same pattern occurred in the major industrialized democracies, which also witnessed a widespread assault on the importance and legitimacy of public service broadcasting (Tracey, 1998). What was considered to be the "natural monopoly" of broadcasting was now challenged. This liberalization of the airwaves, the prime mover of the assault, was brought about by a political, economical, technological and cultural infrastructure. The 70s and 80s, in fact, brought with them a new communication environment and a new ideological environment (Tracey, 1998).

The new communication environment is characterized by the sheer growth of the commercial communication industrial sector and by the technological developments, which eventually led to the revolution of digitalization. This new environment helped critics of Public Service Broadcasting (PSB) organizations claim that their original rationale i.e. spectrum scarcity

---

[2] See Broadcasting: A Commitment to Pluralism, 1990.

and difficulty in financing broadcasting organizations, had disappeared (Scannel, cited in Raboy, 1995).

Thatcher and Reagan ushered in the new ideological environment. Their neo-conservative ideology brought with it the belief that the market is supreme also in the area of broadcasting. This undermined the idea that broadcasting is a public good and pushed the transition from the concept of audience-as-public to audience-as-market (Raboy, 1995; Tracey, McQuail, 1992; Ang, 1991). Media organizations were considered to be exactly like all other commercial organizations. "What is the difference between a television programme and this lighter?" Michael Green, the Chairman of Carlton Communications was quoted as saying by *The Independent* in May 1988.

These developments brought what Tracey describes as a "collision between a "cultural" or civic model for the development of broadcasting and the economic or circus model for the larger construction of a culture of communication" (Tracey, 1998: 11).

Even in Malta the change in the political environment was the motor of media liberalization but its basis was different from Thatcher's right wing philosophies. The nationalization of broadcasting by the Labour Party had brought with it the negative experience of broadcasting overtly used for political propaganda and replete with examples of extensive manipulation. The Nationalist Party reacted by promising liberalization, which it did when it was returned to government.

This liberalization was different from that of other Western industrialized democracies as it included extensive media ownership by the political parties and the church. As a result, while the PSBs in other countries faced stiff competition from commercial stations, PBS Ltd faced a different kind of challenge from these organizations. While commercial media organization emphasizes entertainment and trivializes news, the political party stations manipulate news but, on the other hand, they also produce many other programmes that could very easily be part of the schedule of a public service station. This highlighted the challenge liberalization presented to the identity of PBS Ltd.

Faced with competition from the new radio stations, those run by PBS Ltd started losing audiences. In 1992, Radju Malta, the main radio station of PBS Ltd, was in the first position with 36 per cent of the audience share (Broadcasting Authority, 1992). By early 2001 the same station slipped to the fifth position with an audience share of 7.8 per cent (Vassallo, 2001a). The restructuring process of the radio sector gradually changed the situation. Radju Malta is now the second largest radio station (Broadcasting Authority, 2005).

TVM, the TV station of PBS Ltd, did not go through the same audience crises, however there were times when it lost the first place to Super One TV which is run by the Labour Party (Vassallo, 2001b). Since then TVM has consistently been the station with an audience that is larger than that of the other Maltese TV stations put together (Vassallo, 2003a; Media Warehouse, 2004; Broadcasting Authority, 2005).

ROLE OF THE CHURCH IN BROADCASTING

The Catholic Church has a strong presence in the radio broadcasting sector through two national stations and a number of community stations.

RTK, which started transmitting in 1992, is the radio station officially owned by the Catholic Church. It is one of the group of three stations which hold the second position vis-à-vis their audiences. RTK's policy is based on the theology of Vatican II's Pastoral Constitution The Church in the Modern World (1965). As a consequence it aims to evaluate and reflect on all human experience from a Christian perspective. This is structurally translated into a generalist radio station featuring a full format schedule but for many years with a sane, low definition, presence of a Christian perspective. The purely religious content of the station amounts to 14 per cent of its output.

In 2004, Radju Maria, started transmitting on a national frequency. The station is very close to the Dominican Order. Its contents are radically different from those of RTK since almost all of Radju Maria's programmes are religious ones.

The Church is also strongly present in the broadcasting field through a number of community radio stations. The majority of community stations are owned by Church groups, mainly parishes and the vast majority are located in the small island of Gozo. The community stations are religious stations in the strict sense of the word. These stations look at radio broadcasting as an extension of the pulpit. They are almost a literal extension of the parish as several are physically wired to a church. Most can be considered as the *lunga manus* of the parish priest.

This presence of the Church should not be looked at as a monolithic one. In fact it is evidence of competing theological models and methods of evangelization through the media.

The Church does not own a TV station. Though the bishops have on more than one occasion positively expressed themselves about the principle behind this proposal the Archdiocese of Malta has opted—at least for the time being—in favour of having a production house that supplies different TV stations with religious programmes. There are two other Church oriented production houses which produce for Maltese television stations.

– Borg, Joseph. Maltese Media Landscape –
European Journalism Centre, Netherlands, 2003

Unfortunately, the increase in the audiences of the stations of PBS Ltd was not accompanied by an improvement of its financial situation. Despite the fact that since 1997 PBS Ltd received all monies accruing from licences and could also sell advertising time the company has regularly registered substantial losses. These were mainly due to inefficient work practices, a bloated workforce, a weak management system and an almost inexistent advertising department. This bad financial situation together with the identity crisis could not be tolerated indefinitely.

The National Broadcasting Policy

Between 1996 and 2001 several reports were commissioned and each proposed radical reforms which were commonly described as "major surgery" (Restructuring the Company, 2001). There recommendations were hardly ever put into practice.

Following the 2003 election, the government, for the first time, took the political decision to make PBS Ltd accountable to two ministries. The Ministry for Tourism and Culture remained responsible for broadcasting policy. The Ministry for Industry, Investment and Information Technology was made responsible for PBS Ltd because of government's investment in it.

The Minister for Industry, Investments and Information Technology, Dr Austin Gatt, took the bull by the horns and earnestly embarked both on the task of restructuring the company and on the preparation of the necessary policy documents. The structural and editorial aspects were to be treated almost simultaneously, though through separate documents.

In October 2003, Cabinet approved Minister Gatt's memorandum charting the way forward for organizational restructuring and the financial viability of PBS Ltd[3]. Then in May 2004, the government published the National Broadcasting Policy[4]. This paper is mainly concerned with the different policies outlined in the National Broadcasting Policy (NBP).

---

[3] In the Memo approved by Cabinet in October 2003, the government reaffirmed its commitment to maintain PBS as Malta's leading broadcaster and voted to fund its public service obligation (PSO) through a subvention of Lm 500,000 for 2004. It established that within the context of its PSO PBS also needed to become commercially viable. The Memo mooted the idea of the PSO Contract and confirmed that it would not subsidize the company beyond the public service output of the broadcaster. It also made a distinction between the Core and Extended PSO and underlined that PBS was to serve as a motor to stimulate the growth of local independent producers. This package included a downsizing of the work force from 190 to just less than 70, a radical change in work practices, the adoption of a new method of financing the company and the outlining of new structures that would guarantee the fulfilling of the company's public service obligation.

[4] The National Broadcasting Policy can be retrieved from www.miti.gov.mt/docs/broadcasting%20policy.pdf.

Three principles are the basis of the policy's vision: a strong public service broadcaster is essential to a democracy; media organizations are multifaceted; and media organizations are also consciousness industries (NBP, 2004). In the light of this, the NBP looks at media organizations "as partly similar and partly different from other business organizations" (NBP, 2004: 4). It states that "the business aspects have to be run along strict commercial lines" but also that "media organizations of the public service kind cannot be run as if they are **only** a business" because media organizations are also consciousness industries that are among the prime movers of the symbolic universe integrating a particular culture (NBP, 2004:4).

This attitude towards media organizations in general, and public service media organizations in particular, differs from the Thatcherite mentality mentioned earlier. McQuail (2005) and Potter (2001), among many others, discuss the economic principles of media markets and how media organizations are businesses of a different kind from others, say, manufacturing. But the point brought forward in the NBP refers to another and more dynamic difference. As McQuail (2005) explains, a media institution is not just any other business because "its activities are inextricably both economic and political" and also because "information, culture and ideas are considered as the collective property of all" (McQuail, 2005: 218). Masterman (1985: 4) describes the media as consciousness industries which "provide not simply information about the world, but ways of seeing and understanding it". He quoted Smythe suggestion that "the prime item on the agenda of Consciousness Industries is producing people ... who are ready to support a particular policy, rather than some other policy".

These two aspects are tackled by the NBP which tries to give institutional and structural remedies to harness and balance them. On one hand it emphasizes financial sustainability. The two page introduction signed by both ministers responsible for the sector refers five times to the financial aspect and states that "financial sustainability is paramount" (NBP, 2004: 2). On the other hand the NBP sets high targets regarding content. It opts for the model where the organization tries to achieve both a good share of the market and distinctiveness of programmes.

> A public service broadcasting organization also serves society when its programming strategy makes it the market leader and the trendsetter in the area. Besides being characterized by distinction in programme quality, PBS Ltd should also have a leading share of audiences by its service to generalist and niche audiences. One cannot serve the public if there is no public that follows.
>
> (NBP, 2004: 4)

This dual role is given so much importance that it is now part of the PSO Contract and the Mission statement of PBS Ltd (NBP, 2004). According to the Mission statement:

> Public Broadcasting Services Ltd serves the general public as well as particular segments of the population by striving to be the most creative, inclusive, professional and trusted broadcaster in Malta.
>
> (NBP, 2004: 1)

This strategy is in line with the conclusion of the McKinsey Report (1999) that the most effective PSBs are those that combine both distinctiveness of programmes and market share as this creates a "virtuous circle," whereby commercial broadcasters follow successful programming examples set by public broadcasters.

The NBP adopts the following innovative structures to put into practice the above stated vision.

- A new relationship between the government and PBS Ltd in the form of a Public Service Obligation (PSO) contract. This outlines the Public Service Obligation (PSO) Programming the company is obliged to carry and the government's financial contribution towards the cost of these programmes.
- An attempt at creatively harnessing the financial versus symbolic/ cultural tension by setting up an editorial board alongside the board of directors.
- A new programme acquisition policy whereby most programmes are outsourced after a process initiated by the publication of a Programme Statement of Intent (PSI).

The Public Service Obligation Contract
The relationship between PBS Ltd and the government is now covered by a five year long PSO contract detailing programming content the government would like PBS Ltd to air and for which it is paid a sum of money (NBP, 2004). The contract (see box) outlines four principles which form the basis of the government's policy.

A public service broadcaster is essential to democracy
The NBP states that a public service broadcaster is essential to democracy. This position reflects that taken by different international bodies (Treaty of Amsterdam, 1997; Council of Europe, 2004). To fulfil this role such a broadcaster has to be both independent and very strong (NBP, 2004). The

---

PUBLIC SERVICE OBLIGATION CONTRACT

1. An independent public broadcasting service is essential to a democracy.
2. The government recognizes PBS Ltd as the sole company catering for public broadcasting.
3. PBS Ltd should also carry programmes that fulfil the public service obligation.
4. The government shall financially support PBS Ltd in this regard.

– NBP, 2004: 38 –

---

policy states that media organizations "are anchored in the public domain and public interest" (NBP, 2004: 4). All this shows that government considers PBS Ltd as important for the proper functioning of the public sphere.

Recommendation 1641 of the Assembly of the Council of Europe points to how important it is for a PSB to be independent from those holding economic and political power (Council of Europe, 2004). The NBP makes reference only to independence from political powers. A reference to independence form economic powers is more important today since PBS Ltd is becoming more dependent on those holding economic power because its new model of financing is making it more dependent on advertising and selling of programme air time.

The government recognizes PBS Ltd as the national public service broadcaster

After outlining this general principle about public service broadcasting, the NBP, next moves on to its application to PBS Ltd by opting for the organizational concept over the genre concept of public service broadcasting.

The public broadcaster's remit can be linked to a specific organization. The European Parliament if not the Council and the DG for Culture also adopt this organizational concept of a PSB (Harrison & Woods, 2001). The organizational model is the one generally accepted.

Through the NBP and the PSO contract, the government has for the second time in five years opted in favour of the organizational over the genre concept of public service broadcasting. The government had already taken on this kind of commitment in 2000 (Galea, 2000). The policy, thus, places PBS Ltd with the mainstream public service broadcasters.

Programmes that fulfill the public service obligation

Some think that the scope of a PSB should be defined by reference to types of programmes while others hold that a PSB should be defined by qualitative criteria rather than by genre (Harrison & Woods, 2001). The European Parliament, for example, takes the "quality" position and, in one of its resolutions, makes an appeal in favour of this position (Harrison & Woods, 2001).

McKinsey (1999, 2004), on the other hand, follows the genre approach and assesses different PSBs according to the type, not quality, of programmes broadcast. A similar approach though coupled with a financial consideration is adopted in Malta. Public service obligation programmes are those whose "content is normally such that it would not attract advertising revenue as its primary scope and it is not commercial but cultural, educational or social oriented" (NBP, 2004: 14).

The advantage of such an approach is that it can be more easily verified empirically. The other approach would expose the policy maker to the ongoing multifarious and controversial debate about what constitutes quality (Biernatzki, 1995).

Programmes considered to fulfil the public service obligation are divided into core and extended. The core PSO programming is news, one sports programme and programmes emanating from legal obligations. The extended PSO programming is made up of, among others, drama in Maltese, children's, religious, cultural, general information and educational programmes, discussions and current affairs (NBP, 2004). The amount of such programming can be slightly less than 55 per cent for TV and slightly more for radio (NBP, 2004). This relatively high amount of PSO programming should be seen in the light of the fact that 16 different genres of programmes are included.

Financial support by the government

Volumes literally have been written about the financing of a PSB as this has a direct bearing on the kind of PSB envisaged and how it fulfils its mission.

McKinsey (1999) outlines four different models of financing PSBs.

- Model A: No advertising but government grant
- Model B: Some advertising and government grant
- Model C: Some advertising and licence fees.
- Model D: No advertising but licence fees

PBS Ltd has been traditionally financed like the majority, i.e. Model C. Sixty five per cent of its income accrued from licence fees while the rest was netted from advertising and other income. The NBP theoretically changed the method of financing to one similar to Model B but in actual fact created a new model consisting of some government grant and a majority of commercial monies. The government grant for the first year is expected to be approximately 20 per cent of income instead of the previous 65 per cent. The rest of the income is expected to be earned through advertising, sale of airtime to independent producers and income from new services that the company is expected to initiate. Indications show that the sale of programming airtime (i.e. a producer pays to have a programme broadcast but is allowed to sell the advertising time allotted to that programme) is becoming a substantial source of income.

It is useful to compare this model of financing with comments about the financing of other PSBs. It is hotly debated whether the size of the percentage (if any at all) of advertising monies out of the whole income of a PSB helps or hinders them to better fulfil their mission. The Canadian Mandate Review Committee, 1996 (cited in Price and Raboy, 2001: 16–17) believe that income should be largely independent of advertising revenue. Mendel's survey of the UK, New Zealand, France, Canada and Australia concludes that a limited amount of commercial advertising helps to produce more and better shows but opines that that adequate public funding should remain the rule for public broadcasting (Mendel, 1999). An analysis of the income of European PSBs shows that in approximately 80 per cent of the organizations analysed public funds are larger (generally considerably larger) than advertising income (European Audiovisual Observatory, 1998).

The Maltese model of financing is therefore out of synch with the vast majority of PSBs analysed. Will this model enable PBS Ltd to achieve its stated objective of distinctiveness in programme quality? McKinsey (1999: 4–5) would answer in the negative. It claims to "have found evidence that the higher the advertising figure as a proportion of total revenues, the less distinctive a public service broadcaster is likely to be". The Maltese model complicates the situation by adding the sale of programming airtime to advertising.

The editorial board

The setting up of an editorial board totally independent from the government and, in news matters, also totally independent from the board of directors of PBS Ltd is an innovative structural attempt to address two different tensions:

- The business vs. the cultural/symbolic (i.e. programming) tension.
- The tension between government ownership (implying control) and editorial independence.

Business vs. programming tension

The first tension is specifically stated in the NBP which describes the setting up of the board as a creative attempt to "harness the institutional tension between the business and the programming dimensions" (NBP, 2004: 33). The board of directors is mainly responsible for the business aspects of the company and strives to achieve a black bottom line as strongly directed by the government in its role of shareholder. The editorial board, on the other hand, has the brief to strive to give the best programming deal to audiences emphasizing qualitative social obligation programming.

The de facto dialectic relationship existing between the business and the programming dimension is embodied in structures on two different levels. On the political level there is the dialectic between the Minister for Culture responsible for policy and the government's financial contribution for extended public service obligation programmes and the Minister for Industry, Investments and Information Technology responsible for government's investment in PBS Ltd as an organization. On the corporate level this dialectic is reflected in the existence of the board of directors and editorial board, each being the guardian of an important dimension.

The editorial board grades programme proposals, takes responsibility for the quality and the content of programmes broadcast as well as for the drawing up of the schedules of programmes (NBP, 2004). On the other hand the board of directors can issue policy guidelines covering programming which the editorial board has to follow and it holds the final decision depending on the financial aspects (NBP, 2004).

During the first year in which the NBP has been in operation it seems that the constraints resulting from the new mode of financing PBS Ltd are creating a strain on the public service ethos and consequently on the editorial aspect of the company. There is the temptation to consider the commercial aspect as of greater relevance than the editorial one.

Government ownership vs. editorial independence

The second tension had been addressed in the National Broadcasting Plan, which stated that "the public broadcasting services should remain independent of the government editorially" (*Broadcasting: A Commitment to Pluralism*, 1990). In the NBP, the government confirmed "its conviction that it is not the role of the government to interfere in editorial policy and decisions" (NBP, 2004: 2). The Minister for Industry, Investments and Information Technology more than once told this author that the editorial board was set up as a clear sign that the government wanted to be, and be seen to be, at an arms length from the news department of PBS Ltd.

It was important for the government to couple its declared policy of non-intervention in the newsroom with a concrete structure to achieve it. This was also important since past performances gave rise to the perception that the PBS newsroom cultivated a culture of subservience to those in power. The answer was the setting up of the editorial board totally responsible for the news content of the company and accountable only to the constitutionally set up regulator, the Broadcasting Authority. The editorial board has the task of ensuring that news programmes are to be presented in a balanced and impartial manner as provided for by the constitution of Malta (NBP, 2004). It is also expected to see to it that "the news and current affairs programming of PBS Ltd should be characterized by the highest journalistic and ethical standards. Their core values should be accuracy, truthfulness, due impartiality and editorial integrity" (NBP, 2004: 74).

The position of the editorial board in the company's organizational structure, the method of appointment and the people actually appointed clearly indicate the will to achieve the declared policy objectives. The editorial board's organizational placing "alongside" the board of directors indicates that it is being given the status and responsibility needed to fulfil its duties (NBP, 2004). The voting members of the editorial board[5], like the members of the board of directors, are also appointed by the government specifically to immediately highlight "that the government is giving as much importance to the content aspect of PBS Ltd as it gives to the business aspect" (NBP, 2004: 34). But unlike the board of directors, the members of the editorial board are not appointed for a specific period of time and the minister bound himself publicly not to remove its members during his tenure of office (DOI PR783, 13 May 2004).

The minister is also bound to "appoint persons who are capable of taking fair, balanced and impartial decisions dictated only by the public service mission of the organization" (NBP, 2004: 34). The members appointed on the board reflect different political leanings, backgrounds and experiences in the field of broadcasting. Their collective CV includes the setting up and running of a radio station, production and presenting of TV and radio programmes, a former board member of the Broadcasting Authority, a former editor of a newspaper, experience in media education and media research as well as academic work in the area.

---

[5] Besides these three voting members (one of them is the chairman) appointed by the government there are three ex-officio members. These are the chief executive, the manager programming and the manager news.

The structure set up in Malta seems to be quite unique. It is different from the "model statute" drafted for the European Broadcasting Union by Dr Werner Pumphorst (Public Service Broadcasting in Transition, 2001). This author also analysed the structures of 13 PSBs in 10 different countries in five continents to try and make a comparison with the new structures operative in Malta. The countries analysed are Australia, New Zealand, Japan, South Africa, Canada, United Kingdom, France, Italy, the Netherlands and Sweden. While all these PSBs have different structures to regulate their content none have a similar structured dialectical balance between the commercial and content aspect as the NBP set up in Malta. None have a structure similar to that of the editorial board which has ultimate responsibility for the news content. In the PSBs analysed the ultimate responsibility for all aspects of programming lies with the board of governors or board of directors.

Outsourcing policy and programme statement of intent

The NBP adopts a policy strongly in favour of outsourcing of programmes and adopts a public instrument—the Programme Statement of Intent—to actualize that policy.

Outsourcing of programmes

The NBP states that "whilst news bulletins should be produced in-house, all other programmes should, as much as possible, be outsourced to independent producers" (NBP, 2004: 52). This marks a radical development on the National Broadcasting Plan which had stated that PBS Ltd can consider the farming out of any of its programmes on an *ad hoc* or contractual basis (*Broadcasting: A Commitment to Pluralism*, 1990). The "consideration" of the early 90s has now become the rule.

The NBP gives three reasons of a financial nature and one of creativity to justify this "aggressive outsourcing policy" (NBP, 2004: 28). The policy should make PBS Ltd more financially stable, help it better manage its financial resources and encourage the development of the audio visual market. On the other hand, it encourages and maximizes creativity as it helps PBS Ltd to pick and choose the most creative programmes that exist at a point in time.

Outsourcing of programmes is commonly found in media organizations; in fact in Europe it is compulsory. The Television without Frontiers Directive (1989) says that European independent production should make up 10 per cent of transmitted hours. However the high amount of outsourced programmes asked for by the NBP is quite uncommon when compared to what happens in many other PSBs.

The McKinsey Report does not give the percentage of programmes produced by PSBs or outsourced. A strong indication that the latter is, on average, in a minority is given when the report states that European PSBs spend only seven per cent of their programming budgets on acquired programmes (McKinsey, 1999).

The 1986 Peacock Committee on financing the BBC recommended the introduction of a 40 per cent independent quota on the BBC and ITV while the ITC Programme Supply Review recommended that the 25 per cent quota set up by the Broadcasting Act remain in force and continue to be measured in hours (Ofcom, 2005).

There are indications that some medium and small sized PSBs in Europe do have a high percentage of acquired programmes. RTE 2 of Ireland is an example as 54 per cent of its peak time programmes are acquired programmes (RTE: Reaching Our Audiences, 2004). But the level of such programming on TVM, the station run by PBS Ltd, is much higher.

Programme producing is at the heart and pride of any media organization. Consequently this extraordinary high level of outsourcing is not healthy. One notes that this is not a consequence of the requisites laid down in the NBP but rather of its mismanagement. In fact the NBP clearly states that "the scope of the policy is not meant to kill in-house creativity" (NBP, 2004: 28). The policy also considers co-productions as one of the outsourcing models. If these two aspects of the policy are put into effect then the status of PBS Ltd as a national station can be enhanced.

Programme statement of intent

Besides promoting outsourcing, the NBP adopts the instrument and procedures for the actualization of this policy.

For the first time PBS Ltd is publishing a Programmes Statement of Intent a number of months before every schedule. This is a public statement outlining its programmes policy, programmes needs, outsourcing models and evaluation criteria (Programme Statement of Intent, October 2005–June 2006). The proposals submitted are first analysed by the editorial board from the perspective of content. It then submits its recommendations to the board of directors. The latter are expected to normally follow the "content" recommendations of the editorial board but they have to ensure that the budgets allocated are not exceeded (NBP, 2004).

During its process of evaluation the editorial board gives importance, among other things, to creativity, guarantee of aesthetic and technical quality; guarantee that content will be free of stereotypes especially gender, racial and age stereotypes and the skilful use of the Maltese language in the scripts.

It is expected that the process is finalized four months before the beginning of the schedule and that each proponent receives a short report about the proposal submitted.

The process has brought a level of transparency to the process of choosing programmes for PBS Ltd and gave new possibilities to several independent production houses. Experience is showing that these new programmes' procurement procedures adopted by PBS Ltd are putting pressure on the independent producers to organize themselves in a better way and adopt new strategies to be able to meet the requirements asked for in the Programme Statement of Intent.

Conclusion

This new strategy to take the company out of the crisis it went through after the liberalization of the airwaves is in its initial stages and the learning curve is still not over. Success or otherwise will depend on how the new policies set up by the NBP and will be adopted by the newly restructured company.

Last year's results have shown that the company's objective of achieving market share has been consolidated. Its other objective, i.e. distinction in programming, is still in the balance. Many questions are still unanswered. Will the editorial board succeed in changing people's perception that PBS Ltd is at the service of the public and not of the political powers that be? Is the new workforce big enough to run the place efficiently? Will the outsourcing policy provide quality programming? Will the restructuring of PBS Ltd lead to the restructuring of the organizations run by independent producers? Is the sum annually given by the government sufficient to produce good public service obligation programming? Will PBS Ltd manage to exploit the advertising market to the extent needed to make it a going concern? Will the dual accountability structure at the ministerial level and the duopoly of boards at the corporate level provide a healthy and creative synergy or will it lead to conflict?

The answers to these questions will indicate the success or otherwise of the new policies trying to counter the effect of media pluralism. The future will depend on whether management and the members of both boards will be able to serve the public service obligation of the company while balancing its books.

References

Ang, I. (1991). *Desperately Seeking the Audience*. London: Routledge.

Biernatzki, W. E., & Crowley, J. (1995). Quality in Television Programming. *Communication Research Trends*, 15(1), 1–40.

Borg, J. (2004). Die Medien in Malta. *Internationales Handbuch Medien 2004/2005*. Hans Bredow Institut, Baden-Baden.

Borg, J. (2003). Standard Bearers, Oasis seekers and wily contestants. Socio-cultural aspects of the Right for information in Malta. Paper submitted to the Commonwealth Human Rights Initiative for CHOGM 2003 Report on Right to Information in the Commonwealth. Retrieved on 25 March 2004 from www.humanrightsinitiative.org/programs/ai/rti/international/laws_papers/malta/joeborg_malta.pdf on

Broadcasting: A Commitment to Pluralism. (1990). A White Paper. Malta: Department of Information.

Broadcasting Act chapter 350. (2005). Retrieved on 1 August 2005 from www.ba-malta.org

Broadcasting Authority. (1992). Annual Report. Malta: Broadcasting Authority.

Broadcasting Authority. (2005). Radio and Television Audiences in Malta. April–June 2005.

Brown, A. (2001). Australian Public Broadcasting Under Review: The Mansfield Report on the ABA. *Canadian Journal of Communication*, 26(1), 107–118.

Council of Europe. (2004). Recommendation 1641. Assembly Debate on 27 January 2004. Retrieved on 1 August 2005 from assembly.coe.int/Mainf.asp?link=http://assembly.coe.int/Documents/AdoptedText/ta04/EREC1641.htm

European Audiovisual Observatory. (1998). *Film, television, video and new media in Europe. Statistical Yearbook 1998.* Council of Europe, Strasbourg.

Harrison, J., & Woods, L. M. (2001). Defining European Public Service Broadcasting. *European Journal of Communication*, 16(4), 477–504.

Galea, L. (2000). *Recommendations for the Restructuring of Public Broadcasting.* Press Handout MOEDPR08600.

Masterman, L. (1985). *Teaching the Media*. London: Comedia.

McKinsey & Co. (January 1999). *Public Service Broadcasters Around the World.* A McKinsey Report for the BBC.

McKinsey & Co. (1 May 2002). *Comparative Review of Content Regulation.* A McKinsey Report for the Indepenedent Television Commission.

McKinsey & Co. (September 2004). *Review of Public Service Broadcasting around the world.*

McQuail, D. (1992). *Media Performance. Mass Communication and the Public Interest.* London: Sage.

McQuail, D. (2005). *McQuail's Mass Communication Theory (5ᵗʰ Edit.).* London: Sage Publications.

Media Warehouse. (October 2004). *Audience Survey. Television.* Malta: Informa Consultants.

Mendel, T. (1999). The Organization and Funding of Public Broadcasting. Retrieved on 6 January 2001 from www.article19.org/docimages/636.htm

National Broadcasting Policy. (2004). Ministry for Information Technology and Investment and Ministry for Tourism and Culture, Malta.

Ofcom Review of television production sector: Project terms of reference. (2005). Issued on 11 May 2005.

Potter, W. J. (2001). *Media Literacy (2nd Edit.)*. London: Sage Publications.

Price, M. E., & Raboy, M. (2001). *Public Service Transition: A Documentary Reader.* September 2001. Report commissioned by The European Institute for the Media.

Programme Statement of Intent. (October 2005 - June 2006). Public Broadcasting Services Ltd., Malta. Retrieved on 10 June 2005 from www.pbs.com.mt

Public Service Broadcasting in Transition: A Documentary Reader. Compiled by Programme in Comparative Media Law and Policy 2001.

Raboy, M. (Ed.) (1995). *Public Broadcasting for the 21st Century*. Luton: John Libbey Media.

Restructuring the Company. (16 July 2001). Report by the Task Force.

RTE: Reaching Our Audiences. (2004). Annual Report and Consolidated Financial Statements 2004.

Tracey, M. (1998). *The Decline and Fall of Public Service Broadcasting.* Oxford: Oxford University Press.

Treaty of Amsterdam. (1997). Retrieved on 18 August 2005 from www.eurotreaties. com/amsterdamtext.html

Television without Frontiers Directive. (89/552/EEC). Retrieved on 18 August 2005 from europa.eu.int/comm/avpolicy/regul/regul_en.htm#2

Vassallo, M. (2001a). *A Report and A Study of TV and Radio Audiences in Malta.* April 2001. Broadcasting Authority, Malta.

Vassallo, M. (2001b). *A Report and A Study of TV and Radio Audiences in Malta.* November 2001. Broadcasting Authority, Malta.

Vassallo, M. (2003a). *A Report and A Study of TV and Radio Audiences in Malta.* April 2001. Broadcasting Authority, Malta.

Sri Lanka
Commercialization and Political Interference on Public Service Broadcasting and the Role of Private Media Networks

As the 21st century world gropes towards democratic models that empower people, public broadcasting is rightly seen as central to a functioning society. The core value that underpins public broadcasting is that all communities are entitled to independent news, information and knowledge. It should be a vehicle that enables each society, each community to tell its own stories the way it wants to.

One of the most striking developments in the past decade has been the decline of a public service broadcasting system everywhere in the world. These are services, which are non-profit making and non-commercial, and are supported by public funds and ultimately accountable in some legally defined way to the citizenship. These aim at providing a service to the entire population. PSB is one which does not apply commercial principles as primary means to determine its programming.

This chapter explores some of the questions related to the commercialization and political interference of public service broadcasting (Sri Lanka Rupavahini Corporation and Sri Lanka Broadcasting Corporation) and the role of private media network in Sri Lanka.

Overview of the media dynasties in Sri Lanka

At the beginning of the post-independence era, broadcasting was a state monopoly and the press was a private duopoly. Over the last half a century, the country's media scene has changed rapidly and considerably with the government asserting a dominant role in press operations while conceding to a role for the private sector in broadcasting operations.

In 1924 the colonial government of Ceylon recommended that the Radio broadcasting should be set up to cover the whole country. Television broadcasting was introduced in Sri Lanka in 1979 by a private organization named Independent Television Network (ITN). But discussions were soon under way for the establishment of a state television network. This culminated in the formation of Sri Lanka Rupavahini Corporation (SLRC) in 1982 under Act No. 68 of parliament.

Radio and television were a government monopoly until the mid-1980s. Since then, several privately-owned television and radio stations have been established. In the North and East, the areas under the control of the Liberation Tiger Tamil Elam (LTTE), the Voice of Tigers, the radio broadcast of the LTTE, could be heard within a limited radius.

The media in Sri Lanka can be broadly placed into two categories—those owned and controlled by the state and those owned and controlled privately. There are three electronic media institutions that are directly under the control of the government of Sri Lanka.

* Sri Lanka Rupavahini Corporation (SLRC)
* Sri Lanka Broadcasting Corporation (SLBC)
* Independent Television Network (ITN)

THE PUBLIC SERVICE BROADCASTING MAP OF SRI LANKA

* Government TV Services
  Sri Lanka Rupavahini Corporation (SLRC)
  Channel EYE (SLRC)
  Independent Television Network (ITN)

* Government radio services
  Sri Lanka Broadcasting Corporation (SLBC)
  Lakhanda Radio (ITN)
  Commercial Service (Sinhala) (SLBC)
  Commercial Services (Tamil)
  City FM

* Regional broadcasting services
  Ruhunu Service (SLBC)
  Rajarata Service (SLBC)
  Mahanuvara Service (SLBC)
  Pulathisirawaja Service (SLBC)

* Community radio services
  Giradurukotte Community Radio (SLBC)
  Mahaweli Community Radio (SLBC)
  Kotmale Community Radio (SLBC)

Sri Lanka Broadcasting Corporation (SLBC)

This is the pioneer broadcasting service in Sri Lanka that was started in 1924. At the outset this service was launched as a government broadcasting service. Later it was transformed as Government Department of Broadcasting Services and then as Sri Lanka Broadcasting Corporation.

Sri Lanka Rupavahini Corporation (SLRC)

The Sri Lanka Rupavahini Corporation (SLRC) was inaugurated through an outright grant from the government of Japan in 1982, which helped to build the original infrastructure. SLRC recently launched another channel called Channel EYE. The Sri Lanka Rupavahini Corporation (SLRC) caters to a wider audience with programmes in all three languages, Sinhala, Tamil and English.

Independent Television Network (ITN)

The Independent Television Network (ITN) was launched in 1979 as a private venture but was taken over by the government in 1981. Today it is functioning as a government company and comes under the control of the Secretary to the Treasury. In 1996 "Lakhanda" Radio, which was an affiliate to ITN was also taken over by the government.

Free Media Movements

There are several journalists' organizations that are working for the promotion of their profession. Among them are the Free Media Movement, Working Journalists' Association and the Photo-Journalists Association are the most outstanding. There is also the Editors' Guild of Sri Lanka, and a Foreign Correspondents' Association. There are other trade unions of media workers and the Federation of Media Employees Trade Union (FMETU), which unites all of them. The Free Media Movement (FMM) which is a grouping of independent journalists and persons working in different fields of media is the most active organization in Sri Lanka that advocates and lobbies for the freedom of expression and information.

Commercialization and political interference on PSB

How do the media maintain the balance between transparency of politics, and that of commercialization? Can the media meet the imperatives of market forces, sensationalism and commercialization, and at the same time create a forum for serious and responsible public debate? The problem of PSB in Sri Lanka is how to protect their "independence" when the world around them asks them to follow strategies and ethics which bind them to a certain ideology and path.

The policies, activities and achievements of political parties need publicity, especially through electronic media if it is to attain the helm of political power. Through repeated publicity, people with diversified ideologies may be influenced to change their views. When they become aware of the benefits they get by way of a crime free society, employment, taxation, cost of living, housing etc.; they tend to change their negative attitudes towards a political party, and vote them to power.

The media has projected several political images that will bring peace and prosperity to the country. The image built by media has cleared the way to achieve political power. Different religions, languages and cultures play an important role in supporting or not supporting the actions and policies of the government and other Political parties. This is one of the main reasons why different media institutions are linked to different political parties, ethnic communities and regions and issues directly affecting them are raised.

During the last few decades, the change of culture in electronic media has made an impact on communal harmony, morality, and social and economic factors of the country. These changes were directly or indirectly associated with the growth of the media commercialization and political interference dynasties.

In a government-ran media, it can be too easy to abandon ethical values or sway with the prevalent political breeze. The independent and creative values of public broadcasting will depend on genuine independence of spirit enjoyed by those who work in it. It will mean an end to the political partisanship of the past.

The victory of the People's Alliance (PA) in 1994, with a pledge to restore the press freedom, had given greater hopes to the people. Their election campaign was strongly supported by the Free Media Movement. The PA government appointed an official committee—the R. K. W. Goonesekara committee (1996)—to report on the laws affecting the media freedom and freedom of expression. The committee recommended, inter alia, the enactment of a Freedom of Information Act, the setting up of an independent broadcasting authority, and the replacement of the Press Council Law with a Media Council Act. It also called for the repeal of the Official Secrets Act, the outdated criminal defamation law, and the Parliament (Powers and Privileges) Act of 1953 as amended in 1978, 1980, 1984 and 1987.

The government had strictly limited the access of domestic and foreign media to information and censored news relating to military and police matters.

Public space for Sri Lankan audience to express themselves was still lacking. Whilst the growing media had brought TV and FM Radio, it has hindered access of new entrants to station ownership, and the structure was unable to cope up with rising demands from both advertisers and audiences. It was neither a free market concept nor was there freedom of expression.

There is no set legal definition for media freedom and no editorial freedom in the government or private media institutions. Journalists who do not satisfy either the government or private owners' agendas are left in the wilderness by preventing their news gathering rights and blocking their promotions. Journalists are not given proper training in their profession. There is no gender equity in the Sri Lankan media.

During every election, one of the key issues was freedom of expression and the public's right to know. The state media, radio and television, were used to legitimize the government discourse. Hence, all oppositional discourses were censored.

The Centre for Policy Alternatives (CPA) and INFORM (a local NGO), monitored the electronic media coverage of the General Election in September 2000 with the assistance of Article 19 with an international organization working to combat censorship by promoting freedom of expression and access to official information. This was the first ever such monitoring exercise organized in covering all electronic media (radio and television, private and state) during a general election in Sri Lanka.

Table 1 shows the electronic media coverage of this issue.

Table 1

Category	Total time (min)	For EC %*	Against EC %*
All government channels	170.6	23.64	70.49
All private channels	68.46	64.4	17.25

*Neutral news reports are not included in the percentages. Rupavahini, ITN, MTV and TNL channels were monitored as part of this exercise.

Two factors stood up in the coverage of this incident by electronic media owned by the state:

The views of the governing politicians of Peoples Alliance (PA) dominated the programmes and there was no significant time allocated to present cover the views of the Opposition. In particular, the participants in discussions and special programmes were limited to PA politicians and campaigners for the PA.

The views of the Election Commissioner (EC) were given limited coverage in terms of time allocated and by prominence.

The private media was no better. As the report states:

> There was a clear difference in the way in which the Election Commissioner's issue was reported in the channels owned by the two groups monitored (MTV and TNL). While the MTV channels attempted to be "balanced" by presenting both government and opposition party perspectives, TNL (Sinhala and English news) had little representation of government views. Although Sirasa (MTV) Sinhala news did spend 60.6 per cent of the time spent on reporting the issue in favour of the Commissioner, it also spent 33.75 per cent of the time in items reflecting negatively on the Commissioner. On the other hand, TNL Sinhala news spent 73 per cent of the time spent on the issue in favour of the Commissioner, and the government perspective was not represented at all. In addition, where the TNL news defended the Election Commissioner's actions, it did so mostly by attacking the ruling party rather than by promoting the ideals of democracy and the independence of the Election Commissioner.

Sri Lankan has been a practicing democracy for over 50 years and thus the people are highly politicized with a very high level of literacy and education right across the country. This leads to intensive coverage of elections in the media. Voters received a great deal of information on the campaign of individual candidates, as well as political parties together with the activities of the election administration. The national broadcasters and the press present contrasting editorial policies, thereby offering the people of electorates a plurality of views.

State television and state radio had also allocated free broadcasting time for political parties allowing them to present their electoral platforms to the electorate.

In the 2004 general elections, media attention was focused on the two main coalitions, with smaller parties regrettably receiving limited or no coverage, particularly in the electronic media. Election coverage was polarized along party lines, supportive either of the United National Front or the United People Freedom Alliance.

The 2004 elections was a unique exercise by itself, a first in Sri Lanka, where the executive president Chandrika Kumaratunga came from the UPFA, while the Prime Minister Ranil Wickremasinghe and his Cabinet came from the UNF. Just before dissolving parliament and calling a general election, President Kumaratunga has taken over the media ministry under her authority, thus the state media coming under the control of the opposition UPFA[1].

The state media displayed an evident bias in favour of the UPFA with regards to news and informative programmes in breech of its duties to provide equitable and fair coverage of the election contestants. However, it has to be said that the decision taken by the main constituent party of the UNF, the United National Party, to boycott debates and electoral programmes carried by state broadcasters, although not the main factor, contributed to unbalanced coverage on the part of the state media.

With regards to private electronic media, the law does not provide an effective remedy to ensure equal access and fair treatment. As a result, on many occasions the private media was able to disregard its responsibility to provide balanced and unbiased coverage. In fact, the private media, although less partisan, was generally supportive of the UNP.

The Commissioner of Elections adopted a consensual approach with regards to decisions relating to the regulation of media and attempted, throughout the electoral process, not to interfere unduly in their editorial choices and their right to report on the electoral process freely. The decision to appoint a Competent Authority to oversee Sri Lanka Rupavahini Corporation and Sri Lanka Broadcasting Corporation, although representing a positive step to guarantee fair coverage, was taken too late in the election campaign to have a substantial effect on the overall conduct of the state media.

According to data from the European Union Election Observation Mission (EU EOM) media monitoring, the state television (Rupavahini and ITN) dedicated 72 per cent of their Sri Lanka Parliamentary Elections 2004 coverage to UPFA while only 23 per cent to UNF. In addition UPFA was generally covered in a very positive manner while a large part of the time devoted to UNF was negative. State print media displayed a similar tendency by devoting to the UPFA 57 per cent of the total space compared to 38 per cent allotted to UNF.

The private dailies monitored by the EU EOM provided the UNF with greater coverage than UPFA, receiving respectively 54 per cent and 34 per cent of the total space devoted to election and political coverage.

---

[1] Under Sri Lanka's 1978 constitution, the president and the parliament is elected by the people in separate elections. The president is elected for a six-year term while the parliament is elected for a five-year term. The president holds the right to dissolve parliament at any time, a year after a general election. In this case, the president was elected in 1999 and the parliament was elected in 2000.

PAFFREL EXPOSES STATE AND PRIVATE MEDIA BIAS

The PAFFREL interim report on media behaviour on the Presidential election has stated that the state media, both print and electronic, have been heavily biased in favour of the UPFA candidate Mahinda Rajapakse.

The report also stated that the state media had allocated more time to the ruling party candidate Mahinda Rajapakse.

However the report also said that a few private sector media institutions had given more time to UNP candidate Ranil Wickremesinghe in both print and electronic categories.

In the print media, state-controlled daily newspapers have given more coverage to the Prime Minister. Accordingly, Dinamina had given 78 per cent of its space to Mr Rajapakse against 13 per cent to Mr Wickremesinghe. The Daily News had given 50 per cent to Mr Rajapakse compared to 11 per cent to Mr Wickremesinghe.

Of the print media in the private sector Irudina had been found to be the most biased as it had not allocated any space to the UPFA candidate while it had allocated 100 per cent of its space to the UNP candidate. Out of the English daily newspapers in the private sector the Daily Mirror has emerged as the most impartial newspaper by allocating 34 per cent of its space to Mahinda Rajapakse and 47 per cent to Ranil Wickremesinghe. This is against 50 per cent to Mahinda Rajapakse and 11 per cent to Ranil Wickremesinghe in the Daily News and 44 per cent to Mahinda Rajapakse and 24 per cent to Ranil Wickremesinghe in The Island.

In the electronic media category, the state media had given more time to the ruling party candidate. Accordingly, SLBC has allocated 404 minutes of its news time to Mahinda Rajapakse while it has given only 297 minutes to Ranil Wickremesinghe. A similar situation prevailed at the SLRC, ITN and Lakhanda.

However, when it comes to private TV stations, most of them have given more time to Mr Wickremesinghe. TNL has been most biased as it had given eight minutes of its news telecast to Mr Wickremesinghe while giving only one minute to Mr Rajapakse in its night news telecasts. Sirasa and MTV too have given more time to Mr Wickremesinghe. The figures are eight minutes to Mr Wickremesinghe and five minutes to Mr Rajapakse. Out of the private radio channels only Surian FM had given more time to Mr Rajapakse while all the others channels had given the Opposition Leader two to three minutes extra.

According to the report, the Kinihira programme of Swarnavahini had been biased as it did not interview the prime minister although the opposition leader and his wife Maithree were interviewed.

The report also said the "Road to Presidency" feature of Sirasa had been more favourable towards Mr Wickremesinghe.

– Source: Daily Mirror, 17 November 2005 –

Swarnavahini, the private channel monitored by the EU EOM, allotted 54 per cent to UNF and 37 per cent to UPFA.

However, both coalitions were generally covered in a neutral or positive way.

During the November 2005 presidential elections, the perceived bias of the media towards one or the other of the two main candidates, Prime Minister Mahinda Rajapakse of the UPFA and opposition leader Ranil Wickremasinghe of the UNF, became part of the election campaign itself (see box). The UNF camp accused the government media of bias towards Rajapakse's campaign while the UPFA campaign coordinator described the private media, especially television stations MTV and Swarnawahini as part of the UPFA campaign team.

In a unique twist of events, on the same day the election monitoring body, Peoples Action for Free and Fair Elections (PAFFREL) said that, the private media institutions were biased towards the opposition candidate Wickremasinghe, he wrote to President Kumaratunga complaining that the state owned television networks (SLRC and ITN) were refusing to give him airtime to broadcast campaign "inforcommercials", are a series of debates on election issues. The two networks responded saying that their advertising slots were all sold out until 18 November (the day after the elections).

Commercialization of the state media

Commercialization of the public service media, Sri Lanka Rupavahini Corporation and Sri Lanka Broadcasting Corporation, has increasingly attracted peoples' attention in recent years. SLRC and SLBC have suffered difficulties in finding financial backing for their operational needs, as well as the huge investments required to keep up with fierce media competition. Since a public organization does not have profit incentives, it finds it hard to compete with private sector media organizations.

Normally the public service must rely on advertising revenue as its major source of income. A policy on production and programming are focused towards advertisers targeting the consumer market and does not reward the need of the audience. At present, the majority of the programmes are aimed at teenagers, and women—both housewives and working women—men and children from upper middle class to upper lower economic groups. There are no programmes for minorities or underprivileged people, the homeless or single parents. Advertisers want to reach the largest audience in a cost-effective manner and television programmes are seen as the means to capture audiences for advertisers. Hence, they search for the lowest common denominator in order to achieve their prime objective.

On public service broadcasters, entertainment programmes are narrowed down to three or four main types to serve market objectives and the quality of the programmes are made low in order to save costs. These are teledramas, talk shows, and variety musical shows that help to promote consumerism. Talk shows, for example, are devised to sell products and to promote actors, actresses and celebrities. The format, which in theory is open to audience participation, is turned into real show biz since participants in the programmes are usually drawn from the village level and are not outside applicants or volunteers from the audiences.

Recently, more light entertainment programmes, such as situation comedies and talk shows, have been devised to appeal to the younger audiences. New production techniques and a variety of advertising tactics are also used to capture larger audiences as well as to promote consumerism. For example, songs with the glamorous dances, open stage live musical programmes appear in a large number of programmes, as part of the advertising package. These kinds of tactics may produce subliminal effects on audiences, particularly on young children. This means that advertising could control the structure of television programmes. It is quite obvious that market discourse now cuts deeper into the public arena as presented on the television.

PSBs are problematic, in part, because of their narrow focus. Examining PSB prime time programming in its entirety reveals that programmes which primarily have focused on public affairs documentaries—in fact involves only a small percentage of the schedule on PSB stations.

Consequently, 7.00 p.m. to 10.00 p.m. television viewing comprises of news as a starter followed by hit serial dramas, music programmes and talk shows, and late night movies and recorded or live musical shows.

As advertising expenditure becomes the main source of financial support for government media, its hegemony increases. It dictates what kinds of programmes should be produced as well as the broadcast time—of these programmes.

Three major crisis factors placed the public broadcasting services under pressure.

- The expansion of the television and radio production institutes and advertising agencies which brought about challenges from private media services and viewers.
- The diversification of viewers demand which overtaxed the capability of the public media services.
- The once dominant political powers having lost control over broadcast information initiatives.

On the other hand it is much better to consider some of the other relevance problems too.

- What programming does PBS offer to viewers?
- Whose viewers are included in public service media public affairs programmes?
- How does PBS address some major contemporary issues?

Role of private electronic media networks as a provider of independent news and information

The Sri Lanka government was the first in South Asia to create private electronic media. The government gave a green light to establish private television stations under the open economy policy. The government announced this policy in early 1978. Mr Shan Wikramasinghe, the pioneer of the television in Sri Lanka, started his television company, the Independent Television Network (ITN) in 1979. It was taken over by the government within a few months. In 1994 several private television stations commenced broadcasting local programmes as well as programmes in association with

---

PRIVATE BROADCASTING MAP OF SRI LANKA

- Non-governmental TV services
  Sirasa TV (Maharaja Group) (Sinhala)
  Shakthi TV (Maharaja Group) (Tamil)
  MTV (Maharaja Group) (English)
  Swarnavahini (EAP Group)
  TNL TV (Teleshan)
  ART TV (ART Broadcasting Pte. Ltd.)
  ETV (EAP Group)
  TV Lanka (TV Lanka Pte. Ltd.)

- Non-government radio services
  Maharaja Organization: Sirasa , Yes FM , Shakthi, Classsic FM
  EAP Group: Raja FM, Swarnaoli (Tamil), E FM
  Sri FM
  ABC
  Hiru
  Shar FM
  Teleshan
  Esira FM
  Asura FM
  TNL Radio

foreign television institutions. Today, there are seven privately-owned establishments of electronic media on radio and television in three languages. Some of those channels are carrying local news bulletins.

Sirasa Radio and TV

Sirasa Radio was established in 1993 and is a much younger private channel. Sirasa came into existence in 1998. They specialize in entertainment programmes and there is daily news coverage for one hour.

Swarnavahini (1997) and TNL (1993), another colourful private TV channel that features programmes focusing very much on entertainment and news programmes, are also broadcast. Some political coverage is represented in the current affairs category.

Sirasa Radio and TV news are more reliable than the government controlled electronic media. In the government media, important news items are camouflaged. However, many people appreciate when the government-owned TV channels present news with special emphasis to prevent social upheaval or aggression.

The private media giants always demand and work for a broadcasting system where the commercial logic is central and public service remains on the margin. Many private TV media stations have re-broadcast arrangements with international TV services: Sirasa TV relays Sun TV India in addition to local programmes, which is simulcast on Sirasa FM radio; MTV relays BBC World; TNL relays Music Television in addition to local programmes, which is simulcast on FM 89 MHz; Swarnavahini relays Raj TV in addition to local programmes; ETV relays CNBC Asia, CBS News and ABC News; ART TV relays CNN and Cartoon Network.

At the same time the private broadcasting media, direct a never-ending publicity and political lobbying campaign to promote the merits and genius of a commercial media system and, correspondingly, deny and denigrate the supposed merits of public service broadcasting.

The argument of the private broadcasters states that "any government intervention in the affairs of the media is prohibited, regardless of the social or political implications". Any government intervention will invariably produce anti-democratic outcomes, regardless of the intent, even if the market does not produce especially desirable outcomes.

Although it goes unstated, the implicit belief among the private broadcast media is that it is OK for government to turn a scarce spectrum over to certain private broadcasters and effectively subsidize them.

The commercialization of the media was the critical factor that accentuated the problem of maintaining a strict line between political and

Chart 1
**News percentage
Two weeks, July 2004
(Sirasa, Swarnavahini, TNL)**

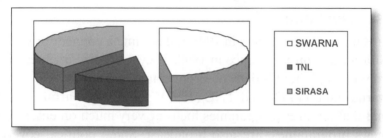

Channels	News	Other programmes
Sirasa	9%	81%
Swarnavahini	11.3%	88.7"%
TNL	3.4%	96.6%

Chart 2
**News percentage
Two weeks, July 2004
(Sirasa, Swarnavahini, TNL)**

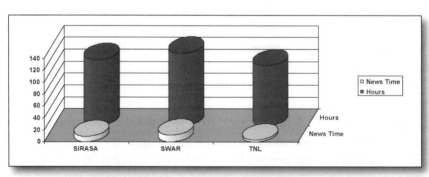

TV channels	Hours	News hours
TNL	100	3.4
Swarnavahini	121	11.3
Sirasa	110	9

commercial speech. Although discussions of the "free media" often simply take individual speech and apply them to the media without qualification, there are important differences. It is one thing to assure individuals have the right to say whatever they please without fear of government regulation. This is a right that can be enjoyed by every individual on a relatively equal basis, since everyone has a right to say what he likes on the proverbial street corner soapbox. It is quite another thing to say that every individual has the right to establish broadcast network with which to disseminate his or her free speech to a broader audience.

Conclusion

Free economy has facilitated the diversification of the media in Sri Lanka. Electronic media is considered as one of the most effective mediums that transmit news, information, entertainment programmes and views to society. The rapid expansion of TV audience and Radio listeners has persuaded business establishments to invest in commercial broadcasting and content production.

The politics of PSB programmes are far more complex. Our analysis of PSB programming suggests that the conservatives have little empirical ground on which to stand, beyond their own criticisms of particular programmes.

This conflict first emerged in the Progressive Era, when chain media ownership and commercial advertising had converted much of the Sri Lankan private media into blatant advocates for the status quo, while the nominal right to launch electronic media meant little to dissidents who could not survive commercially in a semi-monopolistic market. By the logic of "professionalism", journalists would produce a neutral product that did not reflect the biases of the owners, the advertisers or themselves. How successful or viable professionalism has been as a counterbalance to corporate private media control has been the subject of considerable debate over the years.

References

Hettige, S. T. (Ed.) (2001). Globalization, Electronic Media and Cultural Change: The Case of Sri Lanka, Colombo.

Behrens, S. (2002). Premiere Sponsorship plan PBS considers stretching some underwriting credits to 30 seconds. *Current.*

Eashwar, S. (2000). Public Service Broadcasting: Challenges and New Initiatives. Asia Pacific Institute for Broadcasting Development, Kuala Lumpur.

Freedom House. (1997). Freedom in the world: The annual survey of political rights and civil liberties, 1996–1997. Freedom House, Washington, DC.

French, D., et al. (2000). *Television in Contemporary Asia*. London: Sage.

Garnharm, N. (1990). *Capitalism and Communication, Global Culture and the Economics of Information*. London: Sage.

Golding, P. (1999). *Media and Social Policy*. London: Sage.

Goonasekare, A., et al. (2001). *Asian Communication Handbook*. Singapore: AMIC.

Hattotuwa, S. (2003). Media and Conflict in Sri Lanka, Consultative Workshop on Managing Ethnic and Religious Conflict. In *Southern Asia: Role of Education and the Media*. Centre for Policy Alternatives, Colombo.

Kesh, D. (1998). *Electronic Empires – Global Media/Local Resistance*. London: Arnold.

Mahmood, W. (2001). Policy Analysis of Electronic Media Practices. In *South Asia, A Comparative Study*.

McChesney, R. (1997). The Mythology of Commercial Broadcasting and the Contemporary Crisis of Public Broadcasting. University of Wisconsin-Madison, USA.

McQuailL, D. (2000). *McQuail's Mass Communication Theory (4ᵗʰ Ed)*. London: Sage.

Radenko, U. (2001). Public Broadcasting Service Between News Media and Institution, An Analysis of Radio Bh1's News Programming.

India
Public Broadcasting vs. Commercial Broadcasting in Remote Indigenous Communities

> The public service broadcaster also needs to take into account the media needs of the minority audience, whether they be ethnic, religious or linguistic. Such a broadcaster needs to concern itself with developing taste, promoting understanding, spreading literacy and development, creating informed debate and empowering the disadvantaged—major issues that a commercial broadcaster rarely addresses.
>
> *– Report of the Review Committee on the Working of Prasar Bharati, 2000 –*

The rapidly increasing number of foreign satellite television channels, with mainly western programmes as well as the subsequent mushrooming of cable television networks, have led to the demands to allow private broadcasting from within India. The Indian Telegraph Act (1885) did not prohibit cable television networks from operating in India, hence CNN began broadcasting in 1990 with coverage of the Gulf War. Cable television networks gradually expanded, challenging the dominance of Doordarshan, the Indian national television broadcaster. The Government of India (GOI) decided to end the broadcasting monopoly of All India Radio and Doordarshan on 9 February 1995. This historic decision was made after the Supreme Court of India, in a landmark decision, said that there was no right to broadcast implied in Article 19 (1) (a), Freedom of Speech and Expression of the Indian Constitution. In order to safeguard national security, the Supreme Court suggested regulation and licensing as a remedy. The Supreme Court also recommended an autonomous broadcasting authority, independent of the government, to control all aspects of the electronic media.

Realizing this, the government of India sought to regulate satellite television by enacting a new Broadcasting Bill (1997). According to this Act, all the private televisions stations are required to uplink from India and not from overseas. Furthermore, they need to apply for a license from the Broadcasting Council based in New Delhi. However, public service broadcasters (PSBs) and news channels like BBC and CNN are exempted from this procedure, so long as they remain a free service to the audience (Cherian, 1996a, 1996b). These legislative changes created a very competitive mediascape, forcing Doordarshan to broadcast mainly film-based entertainment programmes in order to attract viewers and maintain the highest possible audience share.

Monteiro argues that:

> With the growth of cable television and multinational satellite networks in the recent period, Doordarshan has intensified its strategy of going commercial. The change in programming, with more time for future films and entertainment serials ... all these are being seen as inevitable if Doordarshan is to survive the competition from its new challengers.
>
> (1998: 162)

Until 1997, the electronic media in India was under the direct control of the government. After a lengthy historic and political struggle for media autonomy (Reeves, 1994; Thomas, 1990), the Prasar Bharati Act, which provides autonomous status to the government-owned radio and television services, was enacted in 1990. Some amendments were made in July 1997 and implemented on 15 September 1997[1]. This act aims to support the remote and tribal audiences, who could be better served by radio. The recent "Report of the Review Committee on the working of Prasar Bharati" (MIB, 2000), instituted by the Ministry of Information and Broadcasting (MIB), discussed the implications of the Prasar Bharati as a public service broadcaster, stating:

> The problem is (that) commercial broadcasting always compete(s) for the audiences of such programmes. On the other hand, PSB intends to account for the needs of audiences and their requirements. The programmes on PSB should be appealing to the audiences, need-oriented and also achieve audience share.
>
> (MIB, 2000: 8)

The review committee of the Prasar Bharati Act, also emphasizes the importance of bringing changes to people's lives through the use of programmes. The report said, "The objective of (the) Prasar Bharati is to broadcast meaningful high quality programmes, spreading knowledge and education, fostering social change and in catalysing development" (MIB,

---

[1] Prasar Bharati Act Effective from 15 September 1997).

2000: 12). The report also suggested that radio and television in India, should have an autonomous status, functioning without any interference from the government. But how can the Prasar Bharati be an autonomous corporation when it has to depend on government funding?

When radio and television were under the control of the Ministry of Information and Broadcasting (MIB), their expenses were met by the government. Now, under the Prasar Bharati, it should be made to generate its own revenue to meet all its expenses. "In the early 1980s although radio and television enjoyed a monopoly, a reduction in the budgetary support and pressure to raise more revenues to fund rapid expansion forced the pace of commercialization in India" (MIB, 2000: 11). The committee also suggests that to increase the revenue the Prasar Bharati need not produce "mindless" programming but should produce programmes that inform, educate and entertain its audiences. As it was difficult to administer and implement, the license fee was abolished in 1985. This option was not acceptable politically. The review committee also recommend against funding through advertisements and sponsorships "as this model may not correct market deficiencies" (MIB, 2000: 24). Until the Prasar Bharati can generate its own revenue, it is going to be dependent on the government of the day for its funding, which may force radio and television services to function like a government mouthpiece, for which it has been subjected to previous criticisms for many years. In terms of programming, public service broadcasters (PSBs) have had to compete with private broadcasters. Kiran Karnik, CEO of Discovery channel India, said, "PSBs must compete with private broadcasters in producing quality programmes and addressing audiences that have not been reached" (AMIC, 1999: 1).

Leonard, defining public service broadcasting, said:

> Public Service Broadcasting is programming transmitted in the interests of the public. It might be educational, or cultural or informational programming. It is programming that provides some sort of service to the public to help people in their daily lives.
>
> (1993: 31)

Raboy (1999: 19) argues that public service broadcasting thrives to empower individuals, social groups and reach audiences most effectively. However, PSBs are facing increasing competition from commercial broadcasting in India. Addressing the issue of challenges to public service broadcasting in the Asia Pacific region, the seminar titled "Media Proliferation: How can Broadcasters Best Serve Public Interest", held in New Delhi, articulated that public service broadcasters need to create "new audiences" and produce "quality programming". This will help PSBs to be more responsible and competitive so that they can manage the issue of competition from other commercial channels (AMIC, 1999). This is important because commercial broadcasting in India has made a dramatic impression on audiences, bringing a great variety of programmes into rural and urban homes, which have entertainment value and commercial interest (Rahim, 1994; Rajagopal, 1993).

The proliferation of satellite and cable television channels in India fulfilled the entertainment needs of the audiences, but left a huge gap in development programming (MIB, 2000). In order to sustain audiences and gain commercial revenue, Doordarshan, the national public television service, broadcast film-based entertainment programmes, and remains largely an urban phenomenon rather than rural (Jayaprakash & Shoesmith, 1999; Joseph, 1996; Karnard, 1989). Rowland and Tracey (1990: 21), while reviewing PSBs worldwide argue that "in their efforts to survive, many public broadcasters seem all willing to abandon their public service commitments". Many authors, researchers, and activists in India and overseas believe that radio, with its cheap cost, easy access, reach and portability, can be more effective than other forms of media communication (Joseph, 1996; Powell III, 1999). Joseph argues that:

> With growing commercialization, privatization and globalization, television has increasingly become identified with entertainment, with programmes designed primarily to cater to the tastes of the urban middle and upper classes. The dilution of educational content of television naturally reinforces the existing disparities in conventional educational facilities, which, in turn, hinder human development by accentuating inequalities in information levels and thereby help perpetuate exploitative processes.
>
> (1996: 64)

In order to attract audiences, the Indian television service, Doordarshan, recently decided to broadcast mainly film-based entertainment programmes. The television audiences, however, choose these programmes to watch and the medium is mostly preferred for its entertainment value. The studio-based developmental programmes, including agricultural programmes on DD are unpopular and often ignored. Hence, scholars and media experts believe radio can better serve as a developmental tool than television. Moreover, its low-cost and accessibility enhances audience participation (Hassan & Zakariah, 1993; Varghese, 1995). These characteristics help radio to be more intimate than any other medium of mass communication. However, it is also important to consider that rural audiences need entertainment and that film songs, drama and short stories, along with "service" programmes. When it comes to audience preference of programmes, Mody

(1991) argues that even though audiences have asked for programmes to solve their problems in agriculture and health, entertainment is still their primary interest area.

Meanwhile, rural and indigenous audiences in South India, also consider the cultural programmes, village profile, folk songs, tribal songs and devotional songs as useful and interesting programmes. In the recent past, AIR realized the importance of field-based programmes and radio personnel began respect the rural audience views, irrespective of their socio-economic, political and educational background. In other words, radio, thanks to the decentralization policy, is becoming more accessible for audience participation than television:

> The fact that there has been no attempt to promote local or community television through the provision of simple programme generating and playback facilities on a local transmitter—which could be done at a reasonable cost—suggests that there is little remaining interest in using television as a catalyst for education, social progress, or participatory democracy, or even in increasing access to it among the poor, especially in rural areas.
>
> (Joseph, 1996: 65)

Use of radio for entertainment and information by indigenous communities

Considering these factors, this paper critically analyses how indigenous audiences of Nilgiri hill areas in South India use Ooty Radio Station (ORS), a low power regional radio station of AIR, for public service and commercial programmes. AIR is the only national public service broadcaster in India. In this context, a public service broadcaster like ORS, located near the tribal settlements to empower tribal audiences, can produce programmes, which are locally relevant, and also encouraging audience participation in both field-based and studio-based programmes. Scannell (1989: 142) argues that "it is important to acknowledge the ways in which radio and television have given voice to the voiceless and faces to the faceless, creating new communicative entitlements for excluded social groups". In contrast commercial channels, such as regional satellite television telecast programmes, which are largely irrelevant to the tribal audience life styles and their everyday problems. However, PSB increasingly encounter competition from the commercial channels through its purely entertainment programmes.

India planned the introduction of state sponsored local radio in the 1980s. The first ever local community radio service was introduced in Nagercoil, Tamil Nadu, South India in 1993. Although Nagercoil is well documented as a success story (Anjaneyalu, 1989; Jayaprakash, 1993), the programming policy was changed in the 1990s, the station then operated largely as a relay mechanism for programmes originating from the major regional radio stations of AIR. It has been argued elsewhere (Jayaprakash, 2000), that the concept of local or community radio in India has been defeated. However, by contrast, ORS, although in policy term remains a regional radio service, actually serves its tribal audiences distinctively like a community radio. Considering its location and the people it serves, ORS is probably one of the most effective community based radio stations in Tamil Nadu, South India. It serves a very specific and in some senses, limited minority audiences. The tribal audiences are very obviously secluded from the mainstream population, the majority of them being illiterate, or below high school education standard. Agriculture is the main profession of many of the audience, very few are employed as public servants.

Recent shifts in the indigenous mediascape

Critically reviewing the growing popularity of television and cable TV images in the Nilgiris, a journalist from this region, wrote:

> I believe that television demeans and trivializes everything and everyone connected with it. I feel that the TV is going to be the cause for the downfall of civilization—in short, it is the advent of the Dark Ages. This Dark Age has been brought about, not by suppression of knowledge and information, but its dazzling assault on our senses. The result is nothing short of a catastrophe. For all practical purposes, everything in Indian society has become a branch of entertainment-business, news, politics, religion, sports, culture, you name it. Why? Because people can no longer make sense of their own world; they are fed with an overwhelming volume of "information". This mysterious "information" and the sheer complexity of it, it is bombarded every day into the minds of eager and yielding recipients. The "information" encourages all those along their pursuit in front of their idiot boxes. But do they find a coherent image? The answer is a resounding "No".

(Ullash Kumar, 1998: 7)

Toda settlements are located in the highest altitude areas in the hills of Nilgiris, their settlements are scattered and often located in the most remote regions where cable television operators cannot reach. Cable service providers do not think of the Toda settlement audiences as viable business propositions. On the other hand, the Kotas live as communities, in regions of comparatively lower altitude, compared to the Todas. In the Kota settlements, there can be more than 50 houses with power, giving them access to cable television.

Although the tribal audiences have access to cable television, radio is still considered an important medium for information, entertainment and development. When the Kotas first obtained a satellite television dish for 20,000 rupees for their settlement in Tiruchikadi (a Kota settlement), there was a temptation to ignore radio.

However, audiences realized that they could not simply sit in front of the television set for long periods. Tribal audiences felt that exposure to television would affect their children's education and their everyday work. Considering this, elders from one of the Kota villages (Kundha Kothagiri), did not permit cable television in their village. This scenario is clearly understood from the critique of Ullashkumar (1998: 7), "I hold television responsible for the current deplorable state of affairs in society. The lack of thinking, the lack of will to act, the death of civilization; all because of television—it has become a role model for all".

Increasingly, tribal audiences hesitate to visit their neighbours' houses to watch television because they do not want to disturb them. In short, the introduction of television has disrupted the rhythm of normal tribal life. On the other hand, non-television households, as well as those who own a radio at home, listen to radio programmes regularly. Audiences who listened to radio regularly, before subscribing to cable television, tended to ignore radio programmes after the arrival of cable television at home.

Jegannathan (field interview, 2004), a 30-year-old Kota man from Tiruchikadi village, notes:

> When we had a cable connection at home, we placed our radio set in the corner of the house and the radio set gathered dust. Now after few months, we have started listening to radio again.

The locally relevant cultural programmes, however, brought the audiences back to radio listening. Tribal audiences attach considerable importance to locally produced cultural programmes which are relevant to their lifestyles, because their culture has never been presented in mass media like this before. As a social worker, from the Toda community, Pothali Kuttan (field interview, 2004), points out:

> If there are radio programmes relevant to the hill audiences, people are ready to switch off their televisions and tune into radio programmes.

He had observed this trend when he visited a number of the Toda settlements. My observation of radio-listening behaviour also confirmed this pattern of media use. Later in my fieldwork, a 30-year-old man compared agricultural programmes on radio and television saying:

> Agricultural programmes shown on TV are irrelevant to this place and climate. They don't give information about carrot and potato, which we are largely cultivating here.

It is also interesting to observe that in the context of media use in developing countries, villagers generally do not hesitate to visit their neighbours to watch television. This pattern of television viewing is prevalent in the tribal settlements of the Nilgiris, where the trend is transforming the patterns of media use. A 15-year-old male high school student from Sholur Kokkal, Subramanyam (field interview, 2004), said:

> I don't use television much because when I go to my neighbour's house to watch television sometimes they have guests. If I go there it will be disturbing to them. So I hesitate to visit my neighbour's house to watch television.

Parents are also cautious about their children's everyday media use because they feel strongly that exposure to television could affect their children's education, as well as their everyday work. Particularly agricultural-related work, hence their economical development. Tirumurugan (field interview, 2004), a 35-year-old Kota man, suggests:

> Television viewing would affect our children's education and our everyday work.

He felt that the entertainment value of cable television would tempt them to watch television for many hours, as many of them would get completely carried away by its film-based entertainment programmes. However, we cannot deny the impact that the arrival of television in the home has had on radio. After the arrival of a television set in the home, listening to radio drama is reduced. Also, listening to the radio has decreased in the evening and at night.

Jegennathan (field interview, 2004) said:

> We used to listen to radio news in the evening especially BBC Tamil news. However, for the past eight months (since they got cable television) we have stopped listening to radio at night. Nowadays we watch Sun TV (regional private satellite television) news at 8 p.m.

Audiences of this region are entertained with many other regional satellite television channels, such as Raj TV, Vijay TV, Udaya TV, Gemini TV and Asianet. Apart from satellite television, the Nilgiris town has access to two CCTV networks, Nilgiri television network and Ooty Television network (Ullash Kumar, 1998). Elderly people listen to the radio regularly, whereas children and teenagers are looking for entertainment through cable television, visiting their neighbour's houses to watch television. Furthermore, some economically well-off families feel that television provides them with informative and entertaining programmes, so feel they do not need the radio for news. It is also useful to mention here that AIR newscasts often ignore development news or rural news. Shah (1988: 428) argues that "AIR newscasts contain relatively little content that can be called development news". Shah further insists that "more thorough and more frequent reporting of a wider range of development issues is likely to improve the quality of AIR development news" (1988: 429).

My interaction with the literate tribal audiences reveals that they rely more on regional Tamil language newspapers, such as the *Daily Thanthi, Dinamalar, Dinakaran* and so on for local news. Newspaper reach is almost negligible in remote settlements but a few settlements, located near the main road arranged through bus drivers, hand over the newspapers to a person who is waiting alongside the road. Since the Toda live in a higher altitude of the Nilgiri hills, it is very hard for them to get newspapers. When the Toda men visit Ooty once a week, they get newspapers, take them back to their settlements, and pass the papers onto other members of their family and friends. However, due to the high illiteracy rate among tribal audiences, newspaper readership is negligible. When comparing radio to other mass media like newspapers and magazines, Pothalikuttan said, "Radio is like headlines" because it provides news and information briefly whereas print medium investigates and informs through detailed information. He also mentioned that for remote audiences, newspapers are not easily accessed. He feels that radio is the only source of information and that Todas really love radio listening.

This observation was confirmed by a 30-year-old Toda man (field interview, 2004), who said:

> TV means mainly drama and cinema and we can watch games such as football, cricket … Radio we can listen through our ears. The news bulletins are same in radio and TV. News, it is sufficient if we could hear from our ears. Not necessary to see (on TV). When we are busy with our activities, we will not be having free time until the evening, radio means we can keep it next to us and listen to news and we can go …

The audiences mostly prefer radio-listening, because they feel it is easier to listen to radio than to watch television. The basic characteristics of radio, such as intimacy and portability, encourage them to use radio as a "family medium".

Since many television serials and dramas are scheduled after 7 p.m., it is generally considered the television viewing time, especially for audiences in the Kota settlements who have cable television. In order to attract audiences, ORS could concentrate programmes between 4 p.m. and 7 p.m. in the evening and also introduce morning broadcasts as well. However, we should not forget the fact that if there is no television set in a household all the members of the family listen to radio. In rural areas, very few people can afford to buy television sets so radio still plays a major role by informing about current affairs and entertaining its listeners through film songs, dramas and various other programmes. Some audiences say that they know at what time AIR broadcasts certain radio programmes and listen to them. Women audiences also select their favourite programmes and film songs at appropriate listening times. Tribal audiences also listen to overseas radio, such as Singapore, Malaysia etc. in the morning hours. These stations broadcast new Tamil songs in their Tamil language broadcast. Sri Lanka radio is very popular among the audiences. Unlike AIR, Sri Lanka broadcasts Tamil film songs throughout the day, and some housewives tune into Sri Lanka radio all the time.

On ORS, apart from news, local cultural programmes are very popular among the hill radio audiences. Since the hill audiences like to listen to locally relevant cultural programmes, ORS broadcasts many local programmes. Thus local audiences feel Ooty radio station is useful and important to them. Local programmes are popular, one young educated youth said, "We don't miss local programmes from radio". During my fieldwork, I could see that radio listeners have an awareness of local issues and political news.

Ooty radio personnel give importance to audience participation and are not very particular about "elite" participation. Men and women, rich and poor, literate and illiterate are all given the opportunity to participate in various cultural and folk programmes. Meanwhile, after listening to a certain number of good programmes, audiences themselves approach AIR Ooty and express their intention to be involved and present locally relevant cultural programmes. In this category, "Malai Aruvi" is one of the most popular programmes among the audiences. Agricultural families still expect a lot of information from radio, listening and participating in the agricultural programme, "Thottamum Thozhilum".

I observed the Kotas who have recently gained access to satellite television and saw how this recent exposure has altered the ways in which they use radio. I explore how, in this new media environment for tribal audiences, ORS can serve as a channel for public service broadcasting. In this chapter, I have mainly considered agricultural programmes, news, current affairs, cultural and locally produced programmes that deal with the tribal audiences' lives as public service programmes. ORS is mainly concerned with local issues and the everyday lives of tribal audiences of this region, apart from a few sponsored commercials and relay programmes from the regional and national radio stations. It is important to have PSB because the informational and educational needs of the audiences may not be met by commercial broadcasting. This paper also traces the programmes people listen to in "service" and commercial programmes. Another important issue arising from the shift in the indigenous mediascape is that in India "the proliferation of channels has fuelled many wants and fulfilled some needs, but has left gaps. A PSB should fill these gaps" (MIB, 2000: 8).

Satellite television and PSB radio

The Audience Research Unit (ARU) of AIR and media researchers in India, have not looked at the recent introduction of satellite television channels among tribal audiences, or their impact on radio listening. It is important to see how radio could be used as a Public Service Broadcaster, as the newly set up autonomous corporation, Prasar Bharati, strongly believes radio has enormous potential to serve the rural and remote audiences.

Considering this strong hope for radio, my research found that ORS has many limitations as a public service broadcaster, serving the remote tribal audiences of the Toda and Kota. I argue that the recent introduction of cable and satellite television in Kota, as well as few other tribal settlements, has altered the way the Kotas use radio in their everyday life. I will also show that ORS is unpopular among the Kotas in spite of its programming that largely concentrates on tribal people, their culture and lifestyle. On the other hand, many regional radio stations and their public service programmes, particularly agricultural programmes, although they are irrelevant, are tuned into by the tribal audiences of this region because of the various reasons that are dealt with here. It is highly important for this low power radio (ORS) to know the pulse of these tribal audiences because none of the other radio stations have access to these people who are located in the remote areas and are often secluded from the mainstream media and population.

The Todas live in the regions of highest altitude in the hills of Nilgiris, their settlements scattered, often located in remote regions. There are only three to five houses in a settlement, most of them do not have a power supply. Hence, cable television operators cannot reach these Toda settlements and do not think it is viable for them to extend their business to these areas. On the other hand, the Kotas live as communities, in regions of comparatively lower altitude than the Todas. In the Kota settlements there can be more than 50 houses with a power supply, and so they have access to cable television. A Kota man from the Tiruchikadi village very happily said, "We get 18 channels including Star Movies, Star Plus, Star Sports and so on". However, in Kota settlements, audiences still feel that radio is important, as the majority of households do not have television sets. For example, Sivan (field interview, 2004), a 20-year-old man from the Kollimalai village argues:

> Even if television is here, radio is still important. For those who do not have television at home, radio is the "main use".

During my fieldwork, I found only two rich families who had access to cable television. There were houses located far away from the other Toda *munds* (villages). There were no signs of the Todas visiting these houses to watch satellite television programmes. In town settlements audiences have access to Doordarshan (DD), and the mythological serials such as "Jai Anuman", and "Sri Krishna" are very popular. Ratheesh Singh, a 12-year-old Toda boy listens to ORS for *malai aruvi* and film songs. Though they listen to radio every day in his house he said "they mainly watch television", rather than listening to radio. During this interview, Ratheesh Singh was listening to Tamil film songs on ORS. I asked him, "But now you are listening to radio?" He replied, "We listen to ORS in the evening between 5.30 p.m. and 6 p.m. for Tamil film songs".

Traditionally, AIR broadcasts devotional songs when they start their broadcasts each day. It was a very bold move on the part of the then Assistant Station Director (ASD) of ORS to schedule Tamil film songs right at the start of the broadcasts. This innovative step made the listeners tune into ORS in the evening because Tamil film songs are largely used as background music by radio listeners. Generally, settlements, which have access to DD, still listen to radio for two reasons. Firstly, they listen to ORS for its locally produced tribal programmes, such as *malai aruvi* and *yengal giramam*. Secondly, they listen to film songs as background music.

It is not possible for the Toda children and other age groups to visit other settlements which have television because the distance between one settlement and another is not easily covered due to the poor roads and long distances. They need to walk two or three miles to reach another settlement that has a television. While access to DD programmes was somehow possible for the remote settlements, cable television access is very difficult.

Many tribal children I spoke to through interviews and focus group discussions told me that they watch films, dramas, mythological serials and occasionally news. It is also important to remember that there are 80 houses in Tiruchikadi, a Kota settlement, where only 15 houses have television sets able to receive cable television. Sun TV[2] is the most popular cable channel,

---

[2] Sun TV is a regional Tamil language Indian cable television station. It is the premier flagship channel of the Chennai-based Rs 600-crore Sun Network. Sun TV is the most viewed channel in Tamil Nadu. It was the first fully privately owned Tamil channel in India when it emerged in 1992.

people like it for its wide coverage of world news and interesting talk shows during the weekend. Sun TV also telecasts regional news with colourful graphics and staff correspondents throughout the country. However, most cable TV households watch news on Sun TV in the evening and usually listen to morning news on radio. Few cable television households also listen to radio. So we cannot rule out that cable television households completely ignore radio. Cable television households who continuously watch Sun TV news ignore Doordarshan's news. Some women also said they still listen to film songs from radio. However, a cable television subscriber said:

> Cable TV frequently broadcast films which contain sexual themes and obscene scenes. We cannot sit and watch those films as a family. Meanwhile, Doordarshan chooses good films and we won't be embarrassed when we sit and watch.

Some audiences say that they know what time AIR broadcasts certain radio programmes, so can listen to news on time. Women audiences also select their favourite programmes and film songs at appropriate times. However, in rural areas very few people can afford to buy television sets, hence radio still plays a major role by informing them current affairs and entertaining the listeners with film songs, dramas and various other programmes. However, after 7 p.m. it is generally considered a television viewing time and audiences sit down to watch television programmes.

We cannot say that in rural areas those who do not have television set, always watch television in their neighbours' houses. Audiences still hesitate to go to neighbouring houses to watch television.

Maintenance of radio

While radio is actively used, one thing that I had not anticipated as a significant factor in media use was the maintenance of a radio set, which according to the hill audiences is very important. During my visits to many households in the remote settlements, I observed radio sets that were not in use. They struggle to maintain a radio for a long time. Revethi (field interview, 2004), a 21-year-old married Kannikaran woman from Piravilai settlement said:

> I had a radio earlier but it is under repair for five months so I go to my neighbour's house to listen to radio.

In contrast, the scenario in Kota settlements in the Nilgiris is different. A 22-year-old Kota woman Devi (field interview, 2004), who is a housewife from Tiruchikadi, gets to watch television in the absence of radio. She said:

> We had radio set before, now it is under repair. I go to my neighbour's house at 12 noon to watch Sun TV. Before that I'll make sure that I finish my entire household work and cooking. My husband comes at 1 p.m. from work for lunch When Sun TV shows news, at that time I come home, serve him food (lunch) and go back again to watch Sun TV. Then again in the evening I cook at 4.30. My husband comes back at 5 p.m. Again he will go to work, I go again to watch Sun TV. My husband does not watch television.

However, there are instances where people replace their old radio sets with new ones. A 34-year-old agricultural labourer who lives in Thalapatheri *mund*, a Toda settlement which is located 17 kilometres from Ooty town, had a brand new transistor radio. He paid 480 Rupees (approximately 20 US dollars) to replace his "very old" radio, which he had used for more than 25 years. Another illiterate Toda man expressing the same view said:

> We've been listening to radio for the past 20 years or so, when it is old we buy a new radio set.

Muthulakshmi (field interview, 2004), a 35-year-old Kota woman, said radio is still in use among cable television households. She herself having a cable television at home still tunes in on Wednesday nights and Saturday mornings for radio drama. Audiences also appreciate the programme format and programming of AIR. Sivan, aged 28, argued that technologies such as cable television and tape recorders cannot replace radio because radio always comes up with new programme formats and sometimes the visual media adopt these formats in their programmes. While explaining about tape recorders and radio, he said, "With the tape recorder we always know what the songs are going to be, but on radio it will be always be unexpected songs". Sankaran (field interview, 2004), aged 30, said that though radio listening had been reduced, it was still important to have radio to listen to news and devotional songs in the morning.

Although Kota audiences from Tiruchikadi settlement are talking about the low popularity of radio after the arrival of cable television, Kollimalai (field interview, 2004), in another Kota village which does not have cable television, in spite of the availability of a power supply in this village, says radio is still popular. Audiences from Kollimalai watch DD (national television), but radio remains very much in use. When I looked into the data of these two villages separately the difference was very obvious on radio use. At Tiruchikadi, radio is mostly used in the morning, mainly for news and devotional songs, but at Kollimalai, Kota audiences listen to all kind of programmes, such as agricultural programmes, women's programme news, local programmes and so on in the morning, afternoon and at night by tuning various radio stations.

The Kannikaran tribal community is one of the most remote communities in the Kanyakumari district where many have not seen cable television programmes. They rely on radio for both entertainment and information. However, Kannikaran men complained that agricultural programmes from the local radio station at Nagercoil are irrelevant to the hill locations where they cultivate tapioca, pepper, bananas and so on. While Sun TV is popular in the Kota settlements, it is not widely known in Kannikaran hamlets. A 35-year-old Kannikaran woman, Sri Devi from Koovaikadu Malai, has not heard about Sun TV at all. Moreover, the community television provided in this village for public service broadcasts has been used for watching entertainment programmes. At the time of this research, the television set was under repair due to the poor maintenance by *panchayat*[3] officials. This does not allow the audiences of this settlement to watch DD programmes as well.

Conclusion

Media consumption has undergone a major change, which necessitates some important changes in the programming level as well as the manner in which we think about the modern mass media among communities in remote locations. Although remote audiences in this study are aware and exposed to all levels of radio broadcasting such as local, regional, national and international, they still rely on low power radio stations for service programmes especially agricultural programmes and local news. The findings of this research reinforce the view that radio can be a very useful medium for social, economic and cultural development among rural and remote hill audiences.

There has been a shift in the indigenous mediascape of India recently with the arrival of satellite and cable television. Tribal communities have dramatically changed the way radio is used for development, information, and entertainment. Tribal audiences spend their time moving between radio and television, with radio being used largely in the morning and television in the evening. The regional satellite and cable television services target audiences in the evening with film-based entertainment programmes, and these audiences tend to now watch television programmes, rather than listen to radio programmes at these times.

---

[3] *Panchayat* is a council of elected members taking decisions on issues key to a village's social, cultural and economic life: thus, a *panchayat* is a village's body of elected representatives.

For many years (until 1997), AIR has functioned as a propaganda arm of the ruling party's political movements, as far as news is concerned. Developmental news reporting is comparatively scarce and generally rural people's views have been ignored. On the contrary, AIR news formats predominantly use the official version of the facts rather than ordinary people's views. For the past 50 years, AIR's news and current affairs programming have been viewed in many quarters as propaganda for the ruling political party's interests. This has included development news and communication in many respects. According to the Director-General of AIR news services division:

> Development news has to concern itself with all that happens to the whole people and their welfare in the broadest sense of the word. It cannot be only about government plans and official speeches or statistics about projects. A particular person, a family, a village or a particular community should be the stuff of development news.

> (Bhaumik, 1996: 9)

This system of programming "alienates instructions from the target groups", and the purpose of development communication has failed miserably in India. Apart from the failure of development programming at the production stage, there were some serious problems at the reception stage. Community radio sets provided in the villages by the governments were mostly guarded by the rich elites in the villages thereby preventing common peoples from accessing this media (Singh, 1996; Yadava, 1996).

The recent autonomous status has helped AIR radio to be more flexible in terms of programme format, presentation, audience participation and production of programmes. ORS serves its tribal audiences distinctively like a community radio in India. The findings revealed that the locally relevant cultural programmes brought tribal audiences back to radio listening. Although cable television households ignore radio, it is still popular among the remote audiences.

The introduction of commercial media and its increasing availability among tribal audiences raises major questions about cultural preservation and continuity. The availability of western programmes essentially urban in its orientation may be viewed as potentially problematic. To date tribal audiences appear to have adopted a cautious attitude, although the young, especially male interest towards sports such as cricket seems to be rapidly changing. Further change is inevitable as the reach of different media continues to penetrate the more remote communities in South India.

References

AMIC. (1999). New Strategies Needed for Public Service Broadcasters in the Asia-Pacific. *Asian Mass communication Bulletin*, 29, 1–20.

Anjaneyalu, K. (1989). Local Radio: Making an Impact. *Agricultural Information Development Bulletin*, 11(4), 2–3.

Bhaumik, D. C. (1996). Development News and Electronic Media-Some Questions. *Kurukshetra*.

Cherian, V. K. (1996a). Comprehensive Bill on Broadcast Sector Soon. Retrieved on 14 May 2000 from www.indiaserver.com/news/bline/1996/09/06BLFP03.html

Cherian, V. K. (1996b). Do Private TV Channels Stand to Lose? Retrieved on 14 May 2000 from http://www.indiaserver.com/news/bline/1996/04/03/BLFP04.html

Hassan, M. S. H. & Zakariah, A. T. (1993). Audience Participation in Radio Development Programmes: A Study of Radio Seremban, A Malaysian Local Radio Station. *Asian Journal of Communication*, 3(2), 128–140.

Jayaprakash, Y. T. (1993). Decentralization and Communication: A Study of the Local Radio Station in Nagercoil (Tamil Nadu). Unpublished M.Phil Thesis, University of Madras, Madras.

Jayaprakash, Y. T. (2000). Remote Audiences Beyond 2000: Radio, Everyday Life and Development in South India. *International Journal of Cultural Studies*, 3(2), 227–239.

Jayaprakash, Y. T. & Shoesmith, B. (1999). Feeling the Pulse: Radio, Audiences and Changes in the Nilgiris. Paper presented at the Asian Media Information Centre's (AMIC) 8th Annual Conference held in Chennai, India.

Joseph, A. (1996). Electronic Democracy: An Indian Perspective. *Media Asia*, 23(2), 63–67.

Karnard, G. (1989). Theatre in India. *Daedalus*, 118(4), 331–352.

Leonard, H. (1993). Asian Broadcasting: The Changing Scene. *Media Asia*, 20(3), 123–126.

MIB. (2000). Report of the Review Committee on the Working of Prasar Bharati. (Unpublished Report). Government of India, New Delhi.

MIB. (2000). Report of the Review Committee on the Working of Prasar Bharati. (Unpublished Report). Government of India, New Delhi.

Mody, B. (1991). *Designing Messages for Development Communication: An Audience Participation based Approach*. New Delhi: Sage.

Monteiro, A. (1998). Official Television and Unofficial Fabrications of the Self: The Spectator as Subject. In A. Nandy (Ed.), *The Secret Politics of our Desires: Innocence, Culpability and Indian Popular Cinema* (pp. 157–207). London: Zed Books.

Powell III, A. C. (1999). You Are What You Hear. *Media Studies Journal*, 7(3), 71–76.

Prasar Bharati Act Effective from 15 September. (8 September 1997). *The Hindu*, 13.

Raboy. (1999). The World Situation of Public Service Broadcasting. In AMIC (Ed.), *Public Service Broadcasting in Asia: Surviving in the New Information Age*. Singapore: AMIC.

Rahim, A. (1994). Impact of Cable TV on television and Video Viewing in Hyderabad: A Survey. *Media Asia*, 21(1), 15–20.

Rajagopal, A. (1993). The rise of national programming: The case of Indian Television. *Media, Culture and Society*, 15(1), 91–111.

Reeves, G. (1994). Indian Television: The State Privatization and the Struggle for Media Autonomy. Paper presented at the Media and Cultural Studies, Centre for Asian Communication, Edith Cowan University, Perth, Australia.

Rowland, W. D. & Tracey, M. (1990). Worldwide Challenges to Public Service Broadcasting. *Journal of Communication*, 40(2), 8–27.

Scannell, P. (1989). Public Service Broadcasting and Modern Public Life. *Media, Culture and Society*, 11(12), 135–166.

Singh, A. (1996). Mass Media and Rural Development in India. *Kurukshetra* (January–February), 37–40.

Thomas, T. K. (Ed.) (1990). *Autonomy For the Electronic Media: A National Debate on the Prasar Bharati Bill, 1989.* Konark PVT LTD, Delhi, India.

Ullash Kumar, R. K. (1998). Television and the Dark Ages. *The Downstown Chronicle*, 3(20), 7.

Varghese, K. (1995). Rethinking Mass Media's Potential in Participative Development: The Relevance of Access. *Media Asia*, 22(3), 144–153.

Yadava, J. S. (1996). Media and Participatory Development. *Kurukshetra* (January–February), 16–20.

Japan
Public Broadcasting and the Community

Contemporary Japan is involved in a heated debate on the public nature of the nation's public service broadcaster, NHK[1] (Nippon Hoso Kyokai). The debate follows a series of scandals involving NHK, including a programme alteration, fraud committed by a producer, and some "staged" documentary programmes. During the controversy over the programme alteration in 2001, NHK's close relationship with the government was discussed. Ever since, the people's distrust of NHK has been exacerbated. This is evident from the fact that the non-payment movement with regard to the receiving fee has persisted across Japan[2] despite the resignations in January 2005 of the President, Vice President, and Executive Director-General of Broadcasting, who assumed responsibility for the scandals. Against this backdrop, the public nature of NHK has become a subject of public debate. In other words, the role of NHK as a national public service broadcaster in the society is being questioned. In order to recover the people's trust and retrieve its status as a public service broadcaster in Japan, NHK is required to reconsider its relationship with not only politics and the corporate world but also with the public.

On the other hand, some successful examples of a broadcaster enjoying a good relationship with the public can be found across the country. These broadcasters are mainly local community channels,

---

[1] NHK is Japan's public broadcaster and operates two terrestrial television services, three satellite services and three radios. For audiences overseas it also broadcasts NHK World TV, NHK World Premium and NHK World Radio.
[2] Residents of Japan who own a TV are obliged to pay a fee of about USD 12 per month under the "Hÿsÿ Hÿ" (Broadcasting Act). However, the act does not stipulate any punishment for failure of payment (wikipedia.org). The number of households that have stopped paying the receiving fee had increased to 1,300,000 by the end of September 2005.

such as CATVs or Internet channels, in which the locals actually participate in the production of programmes and the management of the channel. This small-scale broadcasting might appear to be entirely different from the case of NHK, which is a national broadcaster. However, this type of close and successful relationship between these broadcasters and the people in a community might provide hint for the regeneration of NHK. These cases actually demonstrate some of the primary roles of broadcasting in a community, or, more broadly, in civil society.

In this chapter, "public broadcasting" in Japan will be re-examined in both the national and local contexts. For this purpose, I will first introduce current arguments on the public nature of broadcasting and the criticisms of Japan's national public service broadcaster, NHK. Subsequently, I will discuss examples of local community media, namely, Chukai Cable Television and Tottori Kenmin Channel. The former has the first public access channel in Japan and the latter is a brand-new community-based channel that uses technologies such as the satellite, the Internet and CATV in a complex manner. Both these are based in Tottori prefecture, which is in West Japan and has the lowest population in the country. Based on these discussions and a comparison between the above mentioned big and small stories of success and failure, the relationship between broadcasting and the public will be re-examined in the context of Japan. Finally, after these discussions, suggestions for reconsidering the concepts of public broadcasting and "public sphere" in contemporary civil society will be provided.

Public service broadcasting in Japan

Nippon Hoso Kyokai (NHK) and changing public nature

Along with the BBC in the UK, NHK is often referred to as one of the best models of public service broadcasting. It organized not as a government affiliate or a commercial corporation but is endowed with a special status. Its role as a public service broadcaster is outlined in Article 1 of the Broadcast Law (see Box 1).

This law considers NHK to be a successful public service broadcaster that satisfies public interests through its extensive funds, which are sourced from the receiving fee. It is also believed that the receiving fee system enables NHK to produce programmes that are independent of government and private organizations and thus hold the opinions of their audience in high regard.

However, these days, this type of discourse is gradually becoming obsolete and NHK's public nature, as mentioned above, is being ques-

---

BOX 1
JAPAN'S BROADCASTING LAW

Article 1

The purpose of NHK is to conduct its domestic broadcasting or to entrust its broadcast programmes to be broadcasted with abundant and high quality broadcast programmes for the public welfare and in such a manner that these broadcasting may be received all over Japan, also to conduct business necessary for the development of broadcasts and reception and at the same time to conduct international broadcasting and NHK's international broadcast programming operations.

Article 44

(1) NHK shall, in compiling and broadcasting broadcast programmes of the domestic broadcasting, or compiling broadcasting programmes for entrusted domestic broadcasting and entrusting them to be broadcasted, follow, in addition to the provisions of Article 3-2 paragraph (1), what is stipulated in the following items:

   (i) Shall exert all possible efforts to satisfy the wishes of the people as well as to contribute to the elevation of the level of civilization by broadcasting or by entrusting for broadcasting abundant broadcast programmes.

  (ii) Shall keep local programmes in addition to national programmes.

 (iii) Shall strive to be conductive to the upbringing and popularization of a new civilization as well as to the preservation of past excellent civilization of our country.

– Source: Extracts from Japan's Broadcast Law –

---

tioned. The major reasons, needless to say, are the scandals, which will be discussed in detail later. However, there is yet another reason. This is, in fact, more a general background of every current issue related to public service broadcasting and the current trend in the media environment. As witnessed in other countries, in the light of the digitization and globalization of the media, the people's expectations for NHK as a public service broadcaster have been changing gradually. For example, broadcasting and the Internet have been converging at a rapid pace and the trend to broadcast programmes that have previously been aired on TV via the Internet has been gaining in popularity.

In order to meet the needs of the audiences and satisfy public interest under the name of public service broadcasting, NHK has also been exploring the possibility of the secondary use of programmes through the Internet. However, its progress in this direction is a cause for concern for commercial broadcasters and the management because this may increase NHK's profits excessively, hypertrophying the organization and thus putting it under pressure. This gives rise to arguments regarding NHK's role as a public service broadcaster and its commercial or market purposes.

On the other hand, audiences across the country had begun to criticize NHK's programmes even before the recent scandals were detected. Audiences expressed their discontent about NHK, stating that it lacked the critical attitude required for journalism, that it displayed a weak attitude with regard to the authorities, its recent programmes tended to be lowbrow, etc. (Matsuda, 2005). The current non-payment movement with regard to the receiving fee might not be only because of the scandals, which were perhaps simply a trigger; the roots of the movement perhaps lie deeper in the dissatisfaction with NHK accumulated over the years. In Japan these days, the digitization of broadcasting has almost been established and interactive communication has just begun. In such a situation, audience demands are becoming diverse. How NHK will meet these demands while dealing with the pressures of commercial broadcasting is also under scrutiny.

In this way, a number of debates centred around NHK's public nature have been simultaneously thrown up from different perspectives. The scandals have accelerated these debates. These scandals and their influence on the public will now be discussed in order to re-examine what the public nature of NHK should be and what is expected of public service broadcasting in contemporary Japan.

The NHK problem

As mentioned earlier, NHK's scandals enlivened the Japanese media in the last couple of years. These series of scandals, generally referred to as the "NHK problem", have given rise to various debates on public service broadcasting. Among them, the scandal that had the biggest and the most serious impact on Japanese civil society was the alteration of a documentary about a mock trial concerning sex slaves in World War II, which was aired in January 2001[3]. The documentary featured a mock trial held by a Tokyo-based women's group, "The Women's International War Crimes Tribunal on Japan's Military Sexual Slavery", in December 2000, in which the then emperor was found responsible for the Japanese military's sex slave system. The original 44-minute documentary was completed two

---

[3] The programme was titled "The Question of Wartime Sexual Violence," the second programme on the educational television ETV 2001 series "How is War to be Judged," aired on 30 January 2001. The edited version has led to a lawsuit.

days before broadcast and had been approved by the head of educational programming. However, four minutes of the film, which included the testimony of a former "comfort woman", were cut from the final documentary; it was finally broadcast as a 40-minute programme.

There is a suspicion that some LDP[4] members applied political pressure on NHK to alter the documentary, which, according to them, lacked balance and fairness. Common perception is that NHK buckled under this pressure and drastically revised the programme. The biggest concern of the people was whether NHK had been in fact imposed this type of "censorship" on the documentary, and whether this had been done routinely with other programmes. NHK has never provided the public with a reasonable explanation about this and neither has the incident been clarified thus far. The most serious implication is that people have come to distrust NHK's broadcasts and doubt its ability to satisfy public interests. This is demonstrated, for example, by the fact that an increasing number of households are refusing to pay their receiving fees. A recent article in a newspaper stated that the "non-payment movement with regard to NHK's receiving fee has already come to be more than the audiences' indication of protest and has become a movement that questions the organization of NHK as a public service broadcaster"[5]. This movement may not stop until NHK gives the audience a reasonable explanation and proves that its attitude towards reconstructing its inner and rigid organization is sincere[6].

The increase of the number of subscribers who refuse to pay their receiving fee reveals the corruption of the relationship between NHK and its audiences. The above-mentioned case of programme alteration and its suspicious connection with the government became a definite opportunity to reconsider the relationship between NHK and the government. In fact, these days in Japan, debates on NHK's public nature are concentrated on the issue of its independence from the government. However, this fact demonstrates that the relationship between NHK and the public, rather than the political influence on NHK, should be emphasized. While it is naturally important for a public service broadcaster to break away from an unsound relationship with the government, it is more important that it construct a good relationship with its audiences. In this context, in order to retrieve its position as a public service broadcaster in Japanese society,

---

[4] The Liberal Democratic Party is Japan's conservative party.
[5] Source: *Mainichi Shimbun*, 5 February 2005.
[6] At this point, NHK has taken a "legal solution" path with the unveiling of a revival plan that was announced on 20 September 2005.

TV MOCK TRIAL OF WARTIME EMPEROR CENSORED

Senior Japanese Liberal Democratic Party lawmaker Shinzo Abe has admitted that he told the country's national broadcaster NHK TV to censor coverage of a mock trial that found the wartime Emperor Hirohito guilty of war crimes.

The government has denied that Abe's conduct constituted state interference in public media, even though he was deputy chief Cabinet secretary at the time. The programme, part of a series on how Japan's responsibility for the war was judged, covered a mock tribunal organized by civic groups. In the trial, the government was held responsible for forcing thousands of women into sexual slavery for its troops at frontline brothels during the war. The verdict found the late Emperor Hirohito guilty of approving a policy that allowed the institutionalization of sexual slavery. The verdict was issued in December 2000. After Abe and LDP colleague Shoichi Nakagawa asked NHK to edit out the contentious parts of the programme it was finally aired in January 2001. Nakagawa is now Japan's minister of economy, trade and industry.

– Source: Index on Censorship (www.indexonline.org) –

NHK is expected to reconstruct its relationship with its audiences; in turn, this will enable it to solve its organizational problems.

Reconstructing the relationship: From "audience" to "citizen"

As already discussed, the distance between NHK and the public is growing, despite the fact that NHK is a public service broadcaster. Although this situation was triggered by the scandals, it appears to be deeply connected to problems with NHK's organization. There is criticism that NHK has tended, in the past, to neglect public opinion while pursuing technological development and profit as well as attached great importance to political concerns. In fact, as a result, NHK's scandals were brought to light and the non-payment movement has been growing ever since.

With regard to this, Okamura insists on the importance of the relationship between television and audiences by asking the question, "What are the keywords for the expansion of television?" According to him, the keywords are not technologies such as "broadcasting", "digitization" or "broadband," they should be "audiences", "citizens" and "human" (Okamura, 2003: 200). Matsuda also indicates three essential points for the revival of a public service broadcaster:

- Independence from authority.
- Openness to the public and public participation in the growth of the relationship between the public service broadcaster and its audiences.

- Importance of national debate and initiative by the audiences/citizens in public service broadcasting.

(Matsuda, 2005: 20)

According to Matsuda (2005), NHK should be reconstructed as a public service broadcaster "for the public" and not "for the nation", a broadcaster that supplies audiences with all the information on public service broadcasting and which they, as citizens, can support and actively participate in. Therefore, both Okamura and Matsuda suggest "participatory broadcasting" as the ideal future for broadcasting. However, it should be noted at this point that we, the audiences, have in the past considered ourselves merely as audiences. In order to build a new relationship between a public service broadcaster and citizens, it is crucial for audiences to be conscious that, in a broad sense, they are also members of public broadcasting and be strongly motivated to participate in broadcasting.

Moving on to another issue, the simplification and affordability of digital equipment have provided the backdrop for an autonomous movement in Japan, in which people who previously constituted the audience have begun using their digital cameras and editing machines to communicate their messages to society. In this situation, as some researchers have indicated, there is a need for the hitherto closed world of TV stations and programming to open its doors to "citizens" instead of "audiences". Moreover, an attempt should be made to build a new relationship between broadcasting and the citizens. We were "an audience" that previously lay about in the living room, watching TV. However, now as "citizens," we must begin to think about the broadcasting that in our society.

In this way, the role of public service broadcasting is being questioned against the backdrop of a change in media technology and the diversity of people's demands from public service broadcasting. In a contemporary society, the public nature and role of not only NHK but also other public service broadcasters are being questioned. In Japan, although the relationship between broadcasters and audiences has been discussed, the argument about the relationship between broadcasting and "citizens" has hardly been raised. In order to reconsider the public nature and role of public service broadcasting in a contemporary society, a new structure and relationship between broadcasting and the public needs to be sought. Through the process of attempting to reconstruct the relationship with the public, NHK might be able to gain a new, contemporary public nature. This discussion has just begun and it is expected that NHK will give the audience a new style of public service broadcasting.

Community broadcasting: Challenges of the smallest prefecture, Tottori

While the NHK story is set in a national and rather broad context, the relationship between broadcasting and the public is more evident in local examples. In Japan, unfortunately, it is true that community media activity is seldom outstanding. However, in recent times, some examples of innovative media as well as a new relationship created by these local media between broadcasting and the citizens can be found. The oldest example, for instance, is of the public access channel of Chukai Cable Television in Tottori prefecture[7]. This public access channel was established in the beginning of the 1990s and has broadcast programmes produced by ordinary people for more than 10 years. In Kumamoto, there exists a system called "resident directors". Through this system, ordinary people, including housewives, regularly produce programmes and broadcast them on local TV.

There are some other examples of ordinary people producing and broadcasting TV programmes around Japan. However, most of these cases are dependent on the contribution of small media such as CATV or the Internet channels. This section will introduce one of the most epoch-making community media that reciprocally related two community media—Chukai Cable Television and Tottori Kenmin Channel—in the smallest prefecture in Japan, Tottori.

Chukai Cable Television

Chukai Cable Television System Operator (CCO) started broadcasting in 1989 in a small city, Yonago, in Tottori, which has a population of only 130,000. CCO now covers approximately 32,000 subscribers around Yonago. CCO originally started with the principle "CATV will be the media for people in the community" and now has four self-producing channels: News Channel, Event Channel, Message Board and Disaster Information (text information), and Public Access Channel.

The most notable among these is the Public Access Channel, which was established in 1992 as the first and only public access channel in Japan under the above principle; this channel is still and frequently considered

---

[7] Japan is divided into 47 prefectures and each prefecture is further divided into municipalities. These prefectures and municipalities have no overlapping districts or uncovered areas. Prefectures and municipalities are not merely set up as the nation's administrative section, but also as corporate bodies—independent from the country—that possess their own basic governing areas and local residents as their constituents. They hold administrative power within the districts in question.

a model for public access channels in Japan. For over 10 years, the public access channel has broadcast a number of programmes produced by civic organizations, high school students, or other skilled individuals. The topics of these programmes are varied, including local events, group activities, festivals, ceremonies, and nature—even private travel can be a topic. One of the features of this channel is that it has few programmes that raise social or political issues or initiate debates, unlike in the case of America, where the public access channel is very popular. However, the nature of the programmes is both private and public, local and international, and amateur and professional.

CCO never revises or edits a contribution, unless the Broadcast Law is infringed upon. It broadcasts the entire programme. Broadly speaking, this channel is completely open to every citizen. However, the channel is concerned that the number of contributions is small and that audience rating remains low. One problem may be finding ways in which ordinary people can be motivated to use this channel for their benefit.

CCO's unique news channel deserves a mention. The news programme "Com Com Studio Chukai TV News" is broadcast every evening for 30 minutes. Its community-based coverage is held in high esteem and has a high audience rating. In addition to the community-based news coverage, the channel frequently attempts to apply national news to the local context. For instance, it airs stories about the implications of new regulations on life in Yonago. In other words, the channel attempts to replace the national context, which is not necessarily familiar to the locals, with the local context. In addition, its news stories do not end with one report. If the story could have a harmful influence on people's lives, the channel pursues the issue until it is resolved.

For example, after airing a news story about a site where traffic accidents occurred frequently, they attempted to understand the cause behind this and finally succeeded in decreasing the number of accidents. The channel's "Nakaumi Project" is another interesting story. This project was started in order to regenerate the fifth biggest lake in Japan, the Nakaumi, which is located to the west of Yonago. The issue of water pollution in this lake has been debated for decades. The Nakaumi Project aims to purify the water of Nakaumi, that is, to make it pure enough to swim in by 2010, through the use of a documentary programme "Nakaumi Story". In the programme, the various purification activities undertaken by citizen groups, companies, and the government are taken up and public opinion on their use is sought. This programme is also accompanied by actual activities such as a cruise for hands-on learning, cleaning campaigns, and study meetings. These days, the citizens, and not CCO, have become the core members of the project. The public took over the agenda that the CCO programme had set and developed it further, working towards a better community and environment. In this way, CCO's news and documentaries are often connected to community development.

CCO also takes certain measures to preserve its good relationship with the locals. In order to reflect public opinion in the programmes that it produces, CCO has a "programme council system", a "conference system", a "programme monitor system" and a "local gathering system", the members of which are all local people. Members of the programme council system comprise knowledgeable people who can also be termed as the "complaining" sort. In order to improve the programmes, this group assesses CCO's whole programmes. The conference system, whose members also comprise knowledgeable citizens, it mainly assesses if CCO's coverage is fair and sufficient. The monitor system is more open to the public. Any local person can volunteer to be a monitor. The local gathering system is unique to CCO, for which it holds a dinner meeting in each town. During the meeting, producers and directors of the programmes listen directly to the views and demands of the local people; they even obtain some local news, which is often difficult to find in ordinary fact gatherings. These devices work towards reflecting public opinion in the production of programmes.

In this way, CCO has always attempted to create and maintain a good relationship with the local people. Furthermore, it is noteworthy that CCO's endeavours are always based on community development and community activation. The key person concerned with the public access channel of CCO and the mastermind behind the Tottori Kenmin Channel, Takahashi[8], says, "Citizens lead the CATV". According to him, the role of CATV as community media should be:

- to encourage the local community;
- to interest local people in politics, administration and their town;
- to assist the local people's autonomous attempts at problem solving;
- to give local children dreams and hopes; and
- to enhance local people's motivation to inform the public of their activities.

In Takahashi's words, we can re-discover the role of broadcasting and media, which we tend to forget in Japanese society. His concept was further developed to the Tottori Kenmin Channel, which is discussed below.

---

[8] These comments are based on a personal interview done in 2005.

Tottori Kenmin Channel

The most innovative of community media initiatives, "Tottori Kenmin (people in Tottori prefecture) Channel (TKC)[9] was recently established on the basis of CCO's experience and know-how. TKC is a type of network medium that utilizes the Internet, CATV and CS[10] through which every region within Tottori prefecture can be connected. Its most unique aspect is that it was established through the collaboration of industry, academics, the government and the public. Through this channel, various pieces of information from within Tottori prefecture, such as information regarding prefectural assembly, industry, welfare and medical information, are to be transmitted to each home in Tottori. The channel can also transmit disaster information in case of an emergency. Furthermore, using CS, it can disseminate information regarding tourist attractions or other local events across the nation and to other countries around the Japan Sea.

The programmes produced are to be transmitted and broadcast through the information highway, CS and CATV. This channel also enables hitherto unexplored communication networks or paths, such as those from a university, bank or hospital, to each home and those from a prefecture to the entire country, since the current communication flow inevitably follows a top-down order in Japan. Thus, this can be thought of as a fairly original but extremely applicable information medium for the public.

The contents and production system of the TKC are also unique. The "Contents Council" was established in order to discuss and produce contents in 2003, earlier than the launch of the channel. The main aims of the Contents Council are as follows:

- It discusses and assesses the contents of programmes and the directions of TKC in order to provide abundant living information services for people in the prefecture.
- It reflects the demands and opinions of the industry, academics, the government, and the public on the channel.
- It supports to build a channel by and for the people in the community by means of listening to the views of the people and promoting their participation in the community.

(Extract from the prospectus of *The Contents Council of TKC*)

---

[9] Although the "Tottori Kenmin Channel" originally aimed to start in 2004, broadcast was suspended for a while due to technical difficulties. However, programmes are already being produced and currently broadcast in each media (CATV and the Internet) as spot programmes.

[10] Communication satellite managed by Sky Perfect TV.

It aims to develop the channel as the first prefectural community media established in Japan, which can provide meticulous and quick information to the people in the prefecture by means of collaboration with the industry, academics, the government, and the public.

The Contents Council has three categories: "administration and industry", "education, culture, and sports" and "medical treatment, welfare, and environment". Each of these categories comprises programme producers and experts from various fields, including government corporations and universities. They plan and produce programmes in each category based on the insights gained from various points of view and through their interaction with ordinary people. The council also aims to produce programmes that inform people about contemporary local situations and topics, reflect the voices of the local people, contribute to the interaction between people and activate community participation, raise people's consciousness of local politics and economics, culture, and sports, motivate people to share and transmit local information, etc. In other words, TKC attempts, through the programmes and programme production, to awaken the consciousness of the people in the prefecture and to encourage them to participate in community and local activities, in addition to intelligibly and readily conveying necessary local information.

TKC also plays a role in nurturing talented persons for programme production and broadcasting. It organizes training seminars in order to encourage people within the prefecture to try their hand at programme production. These seminars are held in two different venues in West and East Tottori, where, for a couple of months, professional producers and directors teach 10 to 20 ordinary people to produce a TV programme. During these seminars, the trainees are expected to cultivate their ability to gather information, shoot and compile a programme on various topics (for example, the cultural features of or local activities in the region) by using digital cameras and other digital equipment, and then broadcast the programmes by themselves via CATV and other such mediums. Consequently, their activities encourage ordinary people to send local information to people both inside and outside the prefecture, as well as to record and preserve local culture and activities.

TKC's most interesting attempt is to get ordinary people to produce TV dramas. The theme of the drama is "Tottori" and the actors and production staff are selected by the audition. Even a scenario and an original story are selected by means of a contest. This is in fact and completely a citizen's participatory drama production. People can participate in the project in any capacity that they wish—as actors, production staff or sponsors. Participating in the production of a programme that is actually broadcast in the community could raise people's consciousness of their own community. It could also motivate people further to seek another local story or more information and dispatch it. Their involvement should not end here; this should not be a temporary interest. Local media and information have the power to make people aware of issues related to their daily lives and propel them to participate in the community. It should be noted that community media can enable local people to rediscover their local culture and identity; in other words, it can re-create a link between ordinary people and their communities.

The most notable feature of TKC, therefore, is that the production of the programme and its contents are connected to the local identity and the daily lives of the people in that community. This, in turn, leads to their participation in community development. In this sense, TKC can be considered to be a medium for connecting not only people and information but also people and the local community.

Media of the people, by the people, for the people

Community media and its broadcasting of local content tend to fail, as is often the case in Japan; however, the reasons for this have not yet been clarified. Such local media activity is sometimes quite a closed activity and its influence does not extend beyond the community. The Tottori examples are some of the few successful cases. As Takahashi says that the potential for success of community media lies in the people's consciousness and their concerns about the place in which they live. In this sense, community media should work to stimulate the people's consciousness of and encourage their participation in community activities, just as TKC and CCO do. He adds that the community media should be connected to community development or "town making" in the local context.

TKC was designed as the "base" for programme production by ordinary people for the delivery of local information as a part of community development extending beyond the boundaries of government and private, senders and receivers, and specialists and amateurs. In contemporary society, information no more belongs to only the senders and the specialists. Abundant and diverse information can be produced by the dialogue and collaboration of hitherto unconnected relationships. A sender can no more be privileged as a "sender". The cooperation of the public is indispensable in order to collect varied and as much local information as possible. In this context, co-production between the senders and receivers as well as the experts and laypersons is quite effective. During the process of production, the participants can think about their community from different perspectives and arrive at new conclusions and provide new suggestions for community development. This consequently encourages other local people, thus activating the community.

Takahashi also speaks of the role of media. It should work, he says, to make the lives of the people in the community more secure. In order to promote their autonomy, community media should let people on the community "stage" and encourage their participation in local activities. TKC therefore attempts to encourage people to participate in the community through programme production. Following Takahashi's idea, community broadcasting should not only be a medium for information delivery but also a medium for connecting government and citizen, region and region, person and person, and power and power for community development and the autonomy of the locals. Subsequently, it should develop the ability to produce local culture and activities.

In a discussion of the local media, Okamura (2003: 184) stated that "local autonomy is the beginning of democracy and the democratic school of thought. Democratic broadcasting should exist for the sake of autonomy and its starting point is the community". CCO and TKC can thus be thought of as agents for the realization of democratic broadcasting in the local context. Public broadcasting is also expected to play a similar role.

Towards a new public sphere

TKC and CCO are merely examples. TKC, in particular, was launched recently; therefore, its effectiveness and implications cannot be discussed in detail yet, although CCO's success is evident in its high audience ratings and the success of certain civic activities, CCO such as the Nakaumi project. However, it is certainly an impressive scheme that enables us to consider the relationship between broadcasting and the public. It is also true that we, as citizens, should realize the importance of community media and local information delivery through an awareness of the social problems faced by the community in order to utilize this kind of media as a "base" for community development, and enable this public media to take root in Japanese society. As mentioned earlier, community media and local content tends to fail in Japan. This is probably because our social consciousness is lower than that of people in other countries. Compared to people in other Asian countries, there appears to be a lack of concern in Japan with regard to development. If each person supports community media, instead of just a handful of people running it, a new public relationship and a new public sphere might be possible.

Cooperation among existing media is also essential for this purpose. If broadcasting restricts itself to viewing citizens merely as audience, it would prevent the creation of this new relationship. Community broadcasting, including TKC and CCO, aims to establish some "interaction" with the citizens. This is evidently not the same interaction as that realized by the digitization of broadcasting. In the age of the digitization of the media, broadcasting firms are eager to establish new relationships between their services and the audiences through interactive digital communication channels. However, it is more important to build a relationship between broadcasting and the citizens.

Turning the discussion back to the national context, NHK, as a Japanese national public broadcaster, appears unprepared for the construction of this type of relationship with Japanese citizens. NHK, like CCO, formerly had a public access programme, CCO "Anatano Studio (Your Studio)". It started in April 1975 but did not last even six months. Matsuda (2005: 181) indicated that the reason for the programme's failure was that NHK lacked the foresight to nurture culture and journalism among the audiences; civic programmes, he stated, can grow technically and qualitatively only if they spend time nurturing their audiences. However, much time has gone by since then and the circumstances of public service broadcasting have changed considerably. This may be the right time for NHK to reconsider its relationship with the public, even if this is not the way to public access.

Even though NHK's case is very different from that of Tottori's local channels, NHK could learn some lessons in public broadcasting from these small success stories. Further cooperation between NHK and other broadcasters, including local CATV, might be desirable. However, as Okamura (2003: 112) insists, NHK and other national commercial broadcasters place CATV in the "margins" of the broadcasting industry and "may not understand the idea that they can learn from the novel trials of local broadcasters despite the fact that these might be very small and their programmes artless, and that the entire broadcasting industry can be developed through the cooperation of the broadcasters". With regard to this predicament of public service broadcasting, the manner in which NHK faces citizens and cooperates with other broadcasters will decide the future of public broadcasting in Japan.

On 20 September 2005, NHK announced a revival plan, which comprises three points:

- To respect the "viewers first" principle and seek programming that only NHK is capable of offering.
- To streamline the organization.
- To spread the burden of viewer fees more fairly among the public.

However, there is a criticism that "the revival plan lacks originality, and it is unclear if it will help NHK regain the trust of its viewers" (Asahi.com, 2005).

NHK'S REVIVAL PLANS

Japan Broadcasting Corp. (NHK) has announced its revival plan amid a sense of crisis. With more than one million households refusing to pay mandatory viewer fees after a series of scandals came to light, the public broadcaster's operating revenues for the current fiscal year may fall short of the budget by as much as 50 billion yen.

The revival plan, however, lacks originality, and it is unclear if it will help NHK regain the trust of viewers.

NHK's plan consists of three main concepts:

- The first is to respect the "viewers first" principle and seek programming that only NHK is capable of offering. NHK should indeed go back to the basics, but the plan does not explain what should change and how such changes can be accomplished.
- The second concept is to streamline the organization. The plan calls for eliminating 1,200 employees, or 10 percent of the work force, within three years from next fiscal year. This is an unavoidable measure to balance the NHK budget.
- The third concept is to spread the burden of viewer fees more fairly among the public. NHK will introduce a student discount, while it will also consider legal action through summary courts against non-paying viewers. The latter move is bound to be bitterly opposed, even though we can appreciate why NHK feels it has to go this far.

Not all non-paying viewers are those who have boycotted their fee payments after signing contracts with NHK. There are actually 9.5 million households that have never signed a contract with NHK. It would be simply impossible to completely eliminate unfairness in the fee-collecting system.

Even if these measures enable NHK to staunch the "bleeding" caused by the boycott, there remains a fundamental problem: The revival plan was conceived within the current system and does not present any clear picture of how NHK will change in a new era.

– Source: Editorial, The Asahi Shimbun, 21 September 2005 –

Another irony is that NHK's catch copy of "all for the audiences" was mistaken for "all for NHK's existence" (Kahoku, 2005). Now in Japan there even appears a debate on the necessity of NHK as a public service broadcaster. Although this endeavourer of NHK may be evaluated, it is important to consider whether the revival plan will actually work. We hope the plan was not furnished as a mere excuse to draw attention away from the scandals or as a performance to rebuild audiences trust, but that NHK actually embodies its role as a public service broadcaster again. On this basis, NHK should seek a new relationship with the citizens of Japan, as repeated above.

Finally, this is also a time for us to reconsider the nature of public broadcasting—what it is and what it should be—and the public sphere created by it. When discussing public service broadcasting in the new era, a public sphere that can be realized by the relationship between broadcasting and citizens must be envisioned.

References

Asahi.com (2005). Retrieved from www.asahi.com/english/Herald-asahi/ TKY200509220111.html

Captain Japan. (2005). NHK's revenue getting slammed, Sake-Drencg Postcards. Retrieved from www.bigempire.com/sake/nhk_revenue.html

NHK censored TV show due to "political pressure". (14 January 2005) *Japan Times*. Retrieved from www.japantimes.co.jp/cgi-bin/getarticle.pl5?nn20050114a1.htm

Kahoku Shimpo. (2005). Retrieved from www.kahoku.co.jp/shasetsu/2005/09/ 20050922s01.htm

Matsuda. (2005). *NHK: Towareru Kokyo Hoso* (NHK: Questioning Public Service Broadcasting).

Okamura, R. (2003). *Terebi no 21 seiki*. Japan.

Websites

NHK: www.nhk.or.jp/english
Sky Perfect TV: www.skyperfectv.co.jp/en/

USA
The State of Public Broadcasting—Promoting Democratic Access?

In the introduction to their book, *Public Broadcasting and the Public Interest*, McCauley, Peterson, Artz and Halleck (2003), argue that there are three ways to conceptualize broadcasting in Northern democratic societies in general, and in the United States in particular. The first is "the public service approach" in which the government provides funding for public broadcasting. In the United States, the Corporation for Public Broadcasting (CPB) provides funding for the Public Broadcasting Service (PBS), National Public Radio (NPR) and Public Radio International (PRI) to provide niche television and radio broadcasting services. The second is "the commercial approach", which utilizes advertising to garner funding and, ultimately, profits. This approach is used by the majority of television and radio broadcasters in the United States. The third is "the public sphere approach" in which listeners and volunteers provide the bulk of the funding. The Pacifica Radio Foundation is the primary example of this type of public broadcasting in the United States.

This chapter will discuss the state of public broadcasting in the United States. It will begin with a brief history and description of PBS, NPR, PRI and the Pacifica Radio Foundation. It will then examine the challenges and successes currently facing "the public service approach" and "the public sphere approach" to public broadcasting in the United States.

Public Broadcasting Service (PBS)

PBS was incorporated in 1969 in Washington, D.C. It was designed to connect all of the public television stations in the United States into a new national network, much like the commercial networks. Local stations, however, wanted to remain autonomous. As a result, the structure of PBS became decentralized and diverse. It became less of a network, and more of a membership organization. Today, 349 stations are members of PBS. Many are community television stations or university television stations.

PBS' mission is "to inform, inspire and educate". Three key principles guide its programming decisions:

- **Building trust:** Projects should be definitive, offer diverse perspectives, and be informed by integrity and journalistic strengths.

- **Developing opportunities to connect:** We want programming that is differentiated and distinctive, compelling and engaging, relevant to our audience and encourages participation.

- **Providing opportunities for audience participation:** Proposals or programmes should be innovative in format, structure and approach, educational, with public service at their core, provide added value for interactive platforms, and foster impactful outreach. We honour the intelligence of the viewing audience. Our programmes are smart, relevant and definitive. PBS has defined certain genres for television in our past and popularized others. We are eager to continue to lead by being innovative, risk-taking and open to new thinking, new concepts, new talent and new ways of telling stories. We welcome individual expression and are committed to presenting diverse points of view.

(PBS, 1995–2005: 4)

While PBS receives government funding from the CPB, most of its operating budget comes from private sources. The television audience is the largest source of funding. Funds are raised during pledge drives in which staff, local supporters and celebrities ask for money on the air. Special programmes or reruns are also aired to inspire the audience to contribute funds. Additional funding comes from corporate underwriters who provide grants for programmes or products/services for fund-raising auctions. Major corporations that contribute to PBS include Ford, General Motors, Kellogg's, Mobil Oil Company and Pfizer Pharmaceuticals.

PBS was designed to provide niche programming that the commercial television networks did not provide because it was not profitable. These have included adult's instructional programmes, children's educational programmes, community affairs programmes and public affairs programmes. PBS also airs avant-garde art, documentaries and dramas. PBS does not produce the programmes it distributes. PBS has aired some very popular programmes, including "American Experience", "Julia Child: Lessons with

Master Chefs", "Nova", "NOW" and "Sesame Street". It has also imported popular programmes from the British Broadcasting Corporation (BBC), including "BBC World News", "EastEnders", "Keeping Up Appearances" and "Teletubbies".

National Public Radio (NPR)

NPR was incorporated in 1970 in Washington, D. C. Like PBS, it was designed to connect public radio stations throughout America. It has done this by producing and distributing programmes to public radio stations throughout the United States. Today, there are 780 stations affiliated with NPR. The majority of NPR radio stations are based at colleges and universities. Others are affiliated with community organizations.

NPR's mission statement indicates that it is committed to serving the individual. It lists seven main goals to achieve this:

1. To provide an identifiable daily product which is consistent and reflects the highest standards of broadcast journalism.

2. To provide extended coverage of public events, issues and ideas, and acquire and produce special public affairs programmes.

3. To acquire and produce cultural programmes which can be scheduled individually by stations.

4. To provide access to the intellectual and cultural resources of cities, universities and rural districts through a system of cooperative programme development with member public radio stations.

5. To develop and distribute programmes to specific groups (adult education, instructional, modular units for local productions) which meet needs of individual regions or groups.

6. To establish liaison with foreign broadcasters for a programme exchange service.

7. To produce materials specifically intended to develop the art and technical potential of radio.

(Siemering, 1970/1999: 7)

While NPR receives government funding from the CPB, most of its operating budget comes from private sources. The radio audience is the largest source of funding. Funds are raised during local station pledge drives in which staff, local supporters, and celebrities ask for money on the air. Additional funding comes from corporations and foundations that provide grants for programmes or products/services for pledge drives. The largest contributors to NPR include the John D. and Catherine T. MacArthur Foundation, the Doris Duke Charitable Foundation, the Ford Foundation and the Kresge Foundation.

Like PBS, NPR was designed to provide niche programming that the commercial radio stations did not provide because it was not profitable. These have included arts and performance programmes, event programmes and many kinds of news programmes. NPR has produced some very popular programmes, including "All Things Considered", "Fresh Air", "Morning Edition", "Performance Today" and "World Café".

Public Radio International (PRI)

PRI was originally set up as American Public Radio (APR), which was founded in 1983 in Minneapolis, Minnesota. APR was established by Minnesota Public Radio when NPR did not choose to nationally distribute its popular programme "A Prairie Home Companion". APR was originally founded to develop distinctive and diverse radio programmes for the American public. In 1994, the name was changed to PRI. This is because the programming took on a global perspective and was distributed internationally. PRI has 734 affiliates throughout the United States and its programmes are distributed throughout the world.

PRI's mission is to produce programmes that provide diverse cultural experiences, information and insights to help listeners live in a diverse, interdependent world. It has four core principles that recognize the following:

- The central role played by diversity in our nation's past and its importance to our future.
- The urgent need to understand connections between American life and cultures around the globe.
- The responsibility of public media to encourage the exchange of ideas and search for common principles fundamental to a civil society.
- The power of sound and of the spoken word to engage the mind and nurture the human spirit.

(PRI Public Radio International, n.d.: 2)

Like PBS and NPR, PRI receives government funding from the CPB, but most of its operating budget comes from private sources. Corporate underwriting, foundation grants and station fees comprise the bulk of its budget. Major contributors include the Atlanta Philanthropies Inc., the Bill & Melinda Gates Foundation, the John D. and Catherine T. MacArthur

Foundation, Medtronic, Merck and Volkswagon.

PRI (like PBS and NPR) was designed to provide niche programming that the commercial radio stations did not provide because it was not profitable. These have included classical music programmes, cultural programmes, and information and news programmes. PRI has distributed some very popular programmes, including "Classical 24", "Sounds Eclectic", "The Tavis Smiley Show", "The World" and "This American Life".

Pacifica Radio Foundation

The Pacifica Radio Foundation was established in 1946 as the fulfilment of pacifist Lewis Hill's dream: to organize the only independent non-commercial radio system in the United States. The first station in the system, KPFA, went on the air in Berkeley, California in 1949. In 1959, KPFK in Los Angeles, California went on the air. WBAI in New York, New York joined the Pacific Radio network in 1960. The fourth station, KPFT in Houston, Texas went on the air in 1970. The final station, WPFW in Washington, D.C., joined the Pacifica network in 1977.

The Pacifica Radio Foundation saw its mission as promoting "a pacific world" by encouraging creative exchange between people of diverse backgrounds and beliefs and, secondarily, as an advocate of free speech and individual rights (Lasar, 1999: xi). All five of the stations in the Pacific network subscribe to the Pacifica Mission Statement (see box).

The uniqueness of the Pacifica network lies in the fact that it is a strictly non-profit organization. From the beginning, most of the day to day tasks have been accomplished through volunteers. Originally, Hill organized the financial support of KPFA as a subscription service similar to that of magazines. This method did not provide enough funds, so Hill sought outside benefactors. With Hill's death in 1957, KPFA organized its first on-air marathon fund drive (Lasar, 1999: 164). Today, the Pacifica radio stations are financially viable due to a combination of volunteer work, planned giving, pledge drives, donations and special events. The Pacifica network receives minimal funding (in the form of grants) from the CPB. The only corporate funding it accepts are matching gifts from members' employers.

In the 55 years that the five Pacifica radio stations have been broadcasting, the network has produced and promoted thousands of unconventional news, music and call-in programmes that have stimulated, encouraged and outraged listeners and staff members alike. Closely watched during the McCarthy era of anti-communism and investigated by the Federal Bureau

PACIFICA MISSION STATEMENT

- To establish a Foundation organized and operated exclusively for educational purposes, no part of the net earnings of which inures to the benefit of any member of the Foundation.

- To establish and operate for educational purposes, in such manner that the facilities involved shall be as nearly self-sustaining as possible, one or more radio broadcasting stations licensed by the Federal Communications Commission and subject in their operation to the regulatory actions of the Commission under the Communications Act of 1934, as amended.

- In radio broadcasting operations to encourage and provide outlets for the creative skills and energies of the community; to conduct classes and workshops in the writing and producing of drama; to establish awards and scholarships for creative writing; to offer performance facilities to amateur instrumentalists, choral groups, orchestral groups and music students; and to promote and aid other creative activities which will serve the cultural welfare of the community.

- In radio broadcasting operations to engage in any activity that shall contribute to a lasting understanding between nations and between the individuals of all nations, races, creeds and colours; to gather and disseminate information on the causes of conflict between any and all of such groups; and through any and all means compatible with the purposes of this corporation to promote the study of political and economic problems and of the causes of religious, philosophical and racial antagonisms.

- In radio broadcasting operations to promote the full distribution of public information; to obtain access to sources of news not commonly brought together in the same medium; and to employ such varied sources in the public presentation of accurate, objective, comprehensive news on all matters vitally affecting the community.

– (The Pacifica Foundation, n.d.: 1–5) –

of Investigation, the Senate Internal Security Subcommittee and the Federal Communications Commission, the network has been embroiled in many controversies[1]. What remains clear, however, is that the network provides a space for dissenting opinions. In fact, it is this history of providing alternative perspectives that led to the Ku Klux Klan's bombing of KPFT in Houston, Texas twice during its first year of operation.

---

[1] For a good history of these controversies, see Matthew Laser's 1999 book *Pacifica Radio: The Rise of an Alternative Network.*

SAMPLE SPECIAL BROADCASTS ON PACIFICA RADIO IN 2005

- Pacifica had a special broadcast live from this year's GRC [Grassroots Radio Conference].

- Pacifica organized a whole series of labour-related programming around the AFL-CIO (American Federation of Labor-Congress of Industrial Organizations) convention, examining the role and future of labour.

- [When] Telesur-A New International News Network ... [was] Born, Pacific Radio was there to broadcast the sounds of South America's new network launch.

- Coast-to-Coast Coverage of Lesbian, Gay, Bisexual, Transgendered Pride on Pacifica Radio. On, 26 June, Pacifica Radio broadcast a special 10-hour coast-to-coast broadcast of LGBT Pride.

- John Conyer's Hearing on the Downing Street Memo-Pacifica Radio covered this event live, on 16 June.

- The National Conference on Media Reform. Pacifica Radio provided special coverage (including live web streaming) throughout the NCMR weekend, including a four hour special broadcast on Saturday, 15 May.

– (Pacifica Radio, 2005: 2–7) –

KPFT SURVEY

The best practices at KPFT in Houston, Texas were identified by representative listeners, staff and Local Station Board members in an online survey that was completed in 2004. The following provides a summary of the questions asked and the answers that the representatives provided.

1. (Question): In the age of globalization, the broadcasting industry has taken a distinctively commercial face, which has led to the decline of public service broadcasting. What role can Community Radio play in this environment, especially as a counter-weight to global media networks?

(Answers):
- Alternative news, info, dialogue, and music. [Listener, former sponsor and former volunteer]
- By representing the local community, answering local needs with specific programming, going out of the way to find alternative news and news sources to present to the community. [Listener and sponsor]
- Our Pacifica station, KPFT-Houston 90.1 and fm-kpft.org, brings me information I do not hear on any other radio station or on TV. The fact that kpft.org exists means that all people all over the world have access to this information just as I do. KPFT programmes, both locally and nationally produced, give much more detail, background, and on-site reporting of news

events around the globe. The voices I hear on KPFT would never be allowed on mainstream stations. [Listener, foundation member and volunteer]

- Community radio is suited, through practice, to express the interests and concerns of specific localities. This ability assists the localities in two different ways: 1) representation of local viewpoints and 2) dealing with issues in an immediate manner. The historic practice of this by community radio stations has not been superseded by commercial or otherwise conglomerate media. Thus, community radio must continue to serve those purposes and attempt to develop them further so that they can succeed. [Volunteer]

- The better question is "Can commercial radio be compelled to advertise community radio?" [LSB member]

- Given Pacifica's current mindset, it cannot participate to the point where it will make a difference ... More farming of local talent is required and that means hours of work that for which we can not compensate the participants. The free talent, unfortunately, does not always have a positive impact. [Volunteer]

– (Mater, 2004: 1) –

2. (Question): The third paragraph of the Pacifica Mission Statement compels Community Radio to foster creativity for the cultural welfare of the community. How does your station fulfil this mission?

(Answers):

- Introducing varied arts and announcements of cultural events. [Listener, former sponsor and former volunteer]

- By being a focal point for programming about art and artists. [Listener and sponsor]

- KPFT-Houston has many locally produced arts, current events, and news programmes. Most of the programmes on the air originate in Houston. Sometimes the topics are very local, but most of the programmes cover issues which are both local and worldwide in scope. I feel like KPFT is a tool for reshaping our culture into one which as broader horizons than most other broadcast media attempts. [Listener, foundation member and volunteer]

- KPFT generally fulfils the mission of fostering creativity for the cultural welfare of the community, in that the door to the station is always open and that a large number of individuals and organizations have gotten involved due to this openness. On the other hand, in many cases KPFT has failed this mission by deliberately excluding those individuals and groups whose ideas conflict with the people in power at the station or who are seen as potentially getting in the way of the interests of those powerholders. [Volunteer]

- KPFT provides live performance opportunities for local musicians on a handful of shows, but we could sure use more ... [LSB member]

- The local music and programming embodies raging talent! Tune in almost anytime of the day and you will hear something completely different ... creativity is not an issue. [Volunteer]

– (Mater, 2004: 2) –

3. (Question): The fourth paragraph of the Pacifica Mission Statement compels Community Radio to engage in activities that foster intercultural awareness and understanding. How does your station fulfil this mission?

(Answers):

- Encouraging dialogue and understanding between people of different cultural backgrounds. People of Earth, Go Vegan Texas, The CPR Show, Living Art, Arab Voices. [Listener, former sponsor and former volunteer]
- We have programmes like Pan African Journal, the Arabic Hours, Queer Voices, Border Crossings and Latino Voices. [Listener and sponsor]
- Democracy Now! and Flashpoints are two programmes which strongly fulfil this goal. Free Speech Radio News (FSRN) brings daily reports from stringers all over the globe. We have some Spanish language/Latino cultural programmes, including a 30-minute news programme on Fridays at 6:30 p.m. Several programmes are hosted by African-Americans and primarily discuss concerns of the A-A community, while not discouraging non-African-Americans to join in. We also have programmes hosted by South Asians. [Listener, foundation member and volunteer]
- There are many programmes and activities at KPFT that attempt to foster intercultural awareness and understanding, such as co-sponsoring various international, multicultural and ethnic-based public events, and the many programmes on the air that cater to multicultural or culture specific themes. But again, KPFT often focuses much of its attention on some specific groups while ignoring and even excluding others. This based on the will of the powerholders and whatever real or imaginary threats to their own personal survival at KPFT. [Volunteer]
- We have two or three dozen programmes that do this—too numerous to recall. [LSB member]
- We drive stakes of division where this subject is concerned. Talk shows are hosted by biased individuals with biased view points ... A complete overhaul is needed. We fail to meet this criteria. [Volunteer]

– (Mater, 2004: 3) –

4. (Question): The fifth paragraph of the Pacifica Mission Statement compels Community Radio to promote the full distribution of public information and news. How does your station fulfil this mission?

(Answers):

- My local Pacifica Network station does this by broadcasting Democracy Now, KPFT News, FSRNN news, Flashpoints, BBC news and other shows. [Listener, former sponsor and former volunteer]
- By broadcasting alternative news like the KPFT News, Democracy Now, Free Speech Radio News, WINGS, Houston Indy Media, Counterspin, Cultural Baggage, Making Contact, Access This!, Alternative Radio, TUC Radio and Noticerio KPFT. [Listener and sponsor]

- Again, Democracy Now! and Flashpoints do an excellent job of distributing news that isn't available from mainstream news. KPFT-Houston also broadcasts FSRN every weekday, and has our local news programme immediately after FSRN. BBC North American Edition news is broadcast each weekday morning and BBC headlines are heard several times during the day. Many of our other programmes have news segments or are devoted to a particular news segment, such as Cultural Baggage, which is a news programme against the drug war. [Listener, foundation member and volunteer]
- KPFT generally does promote an alternative distribution of public information and news, but certainly not "the full" amount. What is distributed is mostly filtered through various ideological prisms, in the case of politics or through the idiosyncratic interests of particular programmers. In order to properly fulfil this aspect of the mission, KPFT would benefit from bringing in people who are professionally trained as journalists. [Volunteer]
- We have our own full time news department that covers local and regional news. [LSB member]
- Biased news shows with limited scope fail to fulfil—this is a tough nut to crack—I believe we are doing the best we can, however there is lots of room for improvement. [Volunteer]

– (Mater, 2004: 4) –

5. (Questions): Could Community Radio be a better alternative to public service broadcasting in providing the people with a voice in their media, and in turn, assist in better democratic institutions and good governance? How so?

(Answers):
- Programmes that share the dialogue with listeners is one way. The station also encourages volunteers to express their opinions and produce programming. Activities like encouraging voting in elections and discussing political issues and current events. [Listener, former sponsor and former volunteer]
- It does it by its own governance—Pacifica is holding elections to elect members to the Local Station Board using Single Transferable Voting—and by shows on government and democracy. [Listener and sponsor]
- Most of the voices heard on KPFT would not be allowed onto mainstream broadcast media. Examples are Howard Zinn and Noam Chomsky. Both are non-persons to the mainstream, but both have large followings because of public radio. Many topics which do surface on the mainstream media were first broadcast on community radio and were forced onto the mainstream by public demand. [Listener, foundation member and volunteer]
- Community radio is a valuable alternative to public service broadcasting, generally, in that it has its roots and foundation directly in the community at large that it serves, as opposed to the generally institutional nature of many public service broadcasting outlets, such as universities, etc. This direct connection to the community at large provides access to the voices

that support it. The fact that the "common folk" within the community at large possess such access (either real or potential) serves the interests of democracy in that those generally obscure voices and expressions have an outlet, which increases the possibility that those expressions will be acted upon. [Volunteer]
- Your question answers itself, but in order to do this more effectively, we need to pursue advertising so that *if* we do it, more people will listen. [LSB member]
- Not sure—we don't do this at KPFT. [Volunteer]

– (Mater, 2004: 5) –

6. (Question): Please identify your Pacifica station and your role at that station.

(Answers):
- KPFT Houston, listener, sponsor, former pledge drive volunteer. I no longer donate money to KPFT because of a show named Technology Bytes.
- KPFT, I am a listener sponsor.
- KPFT-Houston, 90.1 fm, kpft.org on the worldwide web. I am a listener, Foundation Member, and sometimes committee volunteer. I am primarily a listener, of primarily the news and public affairs programmes.
- KPFT in Houston. Long time volunteer.
- I am on the local station board of KPFT 90.1FM in Houston.
- KPFT [Volunteer].

– (Mater, 2004: 6) –

Challenges and successes for public broadcasting in the United States

The public service approach and the public sphere approach to public broadcasting in the United States face many challenges. These challenges include political criticism, commercial competition and new communication technologies (NCTs). However, there have been some successes and certainly there is the potential for subsequent ones. The most notable success has been the actual democratization of management.

Public service broadcasting has been subjected to right-wing political criticism. Because the CPB is funded by the United States Congress, the CPB Board is appointed by the President and must be confirmed by the Senate. Previously, members have been political appointments and not expert appointments. Increasingly, the CPB has been criticized by the conservative right.

> In the last few months, the ... CPB and the ventures it supports ... have become prominent battlegrounds in the nation's culture wars. Most of the headlines have focused on the criticism from the right, as articulated most forcefully by the CPB's own chairman since 2003, Kenneth Y. Tomlinson, a friend of White House political adviser Karl Rove. Tomlinson has addressed complaints of liberal bias in some of PBS' news programming by encouraging more conservative-leaning programmes to the lineup and hiring two ombudsmen to scrutinize the programmes for balance and objectivity.
>
> (Nather, 2005: 1,503)

Additionally, there have been debates over the size of the CPB's budget because of this "seeming liberal-leaning slant" of the programmes that are on PBS, NPR and PRI. In June 2005, Patricia Harrison, a former Republican National Committee chairwoman, became the chair of the CPB. As a result, criticism by conservatives is expected to continue.

Both public service broadcasting and public sphere broadcasting in the United States face challenges from the commercial competition. The thousands of radio channels and hundreds of network and cable television channels provide consumers with a wide variety of programming. For example, the cable television channels are able to provide the niche broadcasting that PBS has traditionally provided. With corporate dollars at their disposal, radio, network and cable television channels can provide not only more, but theoretically, more high-quality programming.

The problem, of course, is that most of these commercial channels are owned by a handful of corporations. These include Clear Channel Communications, General Electric, News Corporation, Time Warner, Viacom and Walt Disney. According to media expert Robert McChesney (2003: 18), commercial programming is poor because of this.

> The journalism is dreadful and the entertainment is often a hyper-commercialized morass. We may have diversity in the number of stations, but we have a numbing lack of genuine ideological or cultural diversity, not to speak of creativity.

Finally, there is concern about the impact of the new communication technologies (NCTs) on both public service broadcasting and public sphere broadcasting. NCTs like DVDs, hand phones, interactive games, the Internet, iPods and Tivo, all compete with public broadcasting for audiences. Most importantly, they compete to attract younger audiences who are currently forming their media habits. These young audiences are being introduced to the new social and technological world of "continuous computing".

The arrival of continuous computing means that people who live in populated areas … can spend entire days inside a kind of invisible, portable
"information field". This field is created by constant, largely automated
cooperation between:
- the digital devices people carry, such as laptops, media players and
  camera phones;
- the wireline and wireless networks that serve people's locations as
  they travel about; and
- the Internet and its growing collection of Web-based tools for finding information and communicating and collaborating with other
  people.

(Roush, 2005: 4)

There is great potential for public broadcasting to tap into the world
of continuous computing. NPR and PBS have begun to do so with Really
Simple Syndication (RSS) feeds and podcasts of news and shows. The five
Pacifica radio stations are also available for online listening.

One major success for public broadcasting is the fact that the Pacifica
radio network is the only radio (or television) network that is run democratically. In 2003, the five radio stations that constitute the Pacifica network
held elections to constitute Local Station Boards to govern each station.
These Local Station Boards ensure that the needs of the station and the
community are met with regard to programming and budgetary issues.
Moreover, four members of the Local Station Boards are elected to constitute the National Board, which focuses on policies that are relevant to all
stations. The elections are held using the choice voting form of proportional
representation to ensure a diverse board with minority representation.

Conclusion

In my opinion, the greatest hope for public broadcasting is the public sphere
approach. The importance of this general approach lies in the potential for
public communication to serve as a model of society integration, one that
would value citizenship over consumerism (McCauley, Peterson, Artz &
Halleck, 2003: xxiii). This approach is based on Jürgen Habermas' theoretical work on participatory democracies. In his re-conception of public
sphere theory, Habermas (1992/1996: 307–308) lays out two types of public
spheres: 1) general public spheres that develop spontaneously and provide
a medium for unrestricted communication, and 2) procedurally regulated
ones (like parliaments) which try to produce cooperative solutions to
practical questions.

General public spheres not only include organized groups like civic organizations or social movements, but also include less organized groups such as informal gatherings at coffee shops or chat rooms. Moreover, abstract mass mediated public spheres of listeners, readers and viewers exist connected by traditional media (television and radio) and new communication technologies. General public spheres try to raise a "crisis consciousness" about issues like free trade or war. If they are able to get the attention of larger numbers of the public, then "problematization" takes place in which the weight of public opinion requires that the regulated public sphere become involved. Once in the regulated public sphere, the issue becomes the subject of formal methods of deliberation required by that particular institution.

The Pacifica Radio Foundation appears to be the only public broadcasting organization in the United States that is an actual example of Habermas' two-track public sphere. First, the programming that is broadcast at each of the five stations constitutes general public spheres in which on-air hosts and the listening audience exchange ideas and debate each other. Second, with its non-profit status and move to democratization, the listening audience can actually become involved in both the funding and management of station. This could result in a "multiplier" effect:

> Most important, a non-profit media sector is mandatory for providing some, perhaps much, of the journalism and public affairs material befitting a democracy. If such a sector is well funded and well managed, it can have repercussions across the entire media system, across the social culture, and across the entire political culture. As economists would put it, public broadcasting can have a "multiplier" effect (McChesney, 2004: 248–249).

The impact of such an outcome would be more democratic access and participation in the United States, particularly if this model was used to reorganize PBS, NPR and PRI.

References

Habermas, J. (1996). *Between facts and norms: Contributions to a discourse theory of law and democracy* (W. Rehg, Trans.). Oxford, UK: Polity Press. (Original work published in 1992).

Lasar, M. (1999). *Pacifica radio: The rise of an alternative network.* Philadelphia, PA: Temple University Press.

Mater, M. A. (2004). [Pacifica survey]. Unpublished raw data.

McCauley, M. P., Peterson, E. E., Artz, B. L., & Halleck, D. (2003). Introduction. In M.P. McCauley, E. E. Peterson, B. L. Artz & D. Halleck (Eds.), *Public broadcasting and the public interest* (pp. xv–xxix). M. E. Sharpe, Armonk, NY.

McChesney, R. W. (2003). Public broadcasting: Past, present, and future. In M. P. McCauley, E. E. Peterson, B. L. Artz & D. Halleck (Eds.), *Public broadcasting and the public interest* (pp. 10–24). M. E. Sharpe, Armonk, NY.

McChesney, R. W. (2004). *The problem of the media: US communication politics in the 21st century.* New York, NY: Monthly Review Press.

Nather, D. (6 June 2005). Public broadcasting hit from all sides. *Congressional Quarterly*, 63(23), 1,503–1,505.

The Pacifica Foundation. (n.d.). Pacifica mission statement. Retrieved on 29 December 2005 from www.kpft.org/site/ PageServer?pagename=mission_statement

Pacifica radio. (n.d.). Retrieved on 29 December 2005 from www.pacifica.org/

PBS. (1995–2005). The PBS mission. Producing for PBS. Retrieved on 18 September 2005 from www.pbs.org/producers/mission.html

PRI Public Radio International. (n.d.). Mission and principles. Inside PRI. Retrieved on 28 September 2005 from www.pri.org/Public Site/inside/index.html

Roush, W. (August 2005). Social machines. *Technology Review*, 108(8), 44–51.

Siemering, W. H. (1999). National Public Radio purposes. Public broadcasting policy base. Retrieved on 18 September 2005 from www.current.org/pbpb/ documents/ NPRpurposes.html (Original work published 1970).

Websites

CPB: www.cpb.org/
NPR: www.npr.org/
Pacifica Radio: www.pacifica.org/
PBS: www.pbs.org/
PRI: www.pri.org/PublicSite/inside/index.html

Papua New Guinea
Revitalizing Radio with Community Emphasis

Public Service Broadcasting (PSB) plays an active role in presenting and promoting national culture and contributing to strengthening notions of identity and community and establishing interaction between citizens and their immediate wider communities.

This chapter explores how a mission to develop a PSB system on the Pacific Island of Papua New Guinea[1] (PNG) has been challenged by the market for private media, a lack of political will on the part of government, and poor allocation of financial resources.

A PSB radio service that at its peak reached about 80 per cent of a diverse, geographically isolated population, broadcasting in about 60 different languages has been in decline in recent years as the number of privately-owned commercial stations, playing mostly music, based in and around PNG's urban centres, grows.

The chapter discusses this situation in the broader context of the role PSB and community radio plays in aiding development and democracy in emerging nations and how this is threatened by the free market. In particular it shows how the mass media in the free market must rely on delivering relatively wealthy audiences to advertisers and in doing so the traditional role of the mass media as an agency of free ideas and debate, which facilitate democracy, is undermined.

To put the wider discussions in context a case study is made of PNG, an island in the Pacific to the north of Australia. Radio is being

---

[1] Papua New Guinea is a country just north of Australia, occupying the eastern half of the island of New Guinea and numerous offshore islands (the western portion of the island is occupied by the Indonesian provinces of Papua and West Irian Jaya). It is located in the south-western Pacific Ocean, in a region defined since the early 19th century as Melanesia. It is one of the most diverse countries on Earth, with over 700 indigenous languages and at least as many indigenous societies, out of a population of just over five million.

revitalized here by a new initiative that sets out to revive a flagging public service system. At the same time new community radio stations are starting which are giving opportunities to previously voiceless people.

This is important in a society such as PNG which is fragmented with more than 800 distinct cultural groups, each with its own language. About 85 per cent of PNG's population, estimated at five million, live in isolated scattered rural settlements. Poor roads, bridges and air transport are barriers to providing education and health services. About 3.5 million Papua New Guineans depend on subsistence agriculture for their survival and are largely outside the formal economy. Almost one in 12 children still die before the age of five and the maternal mortality rate is one of the highest in the Pacific. Income levels are low with about 37 per cent of the population living below the poverty line, most of these living in rural areas.

PSB in the developing world

The debate about the PNG media will not be viewed in isolation. Today, there is a wide geopolitical consensus that political systems should exist to provide opportunities for all the people to influence government and practice (DFID 2001) and that the media reinforce or foster this kind of democracy (Price and Krug, 2002: 3).

To engage effectively there is an assumption that access to information is the first requirement for an engaged, participative democracy (Roth, 2001: 13). An active citizenry will help prevent governmental excesses and breed trust in the democratic system, thereby enabling the private media to perform their functions (Tetty, 2003: 28) and the media are the major mechanisms by which citizens are informed about the world (Sparks, 1991). There are specific public interest political goals, which the media can be used to serve, including the following:

- Informing the public
- Public enlightenment
- Social criticism and exposing government arbitrariness
- National integration and political education

But the more the media serve the narrow self interest the less able they are to serve the other group of public interests (Ojo, 2003: 829–830).

Public service programming fulfils some of the criteria necessary for democratic participation. Public service programming remits vary from country to country but there is a core of common features that are universally valid. PSB is broadcasting made for the public, financed by the public and controlled by the public. Generally, the "public" is the entire population of the country and ideally means every household in the service area should be in a position to receive the programme service. Programming should be in the fields of information, entertainment and education for people of all ages and social groups. It plays an active role in presenting and promoting national culture and can contribute to strengthening notions of identity and community and establish adequate interaction between citizens and their immediate wider communities (Rumphorst, 2003: 73–74; Yaakob, 2003: 96).

Broadcasting has a role as a partner in development as it can help to mobilize people who are directly affected by a community condition (that is, the victims, the unaffiliated, the unrecognized and the non-participating) into groups and organizations to enable them to take action on the social problems and issues that concern them. For community development to take place, the people must first be conscious of and open to changes for development (Dy, 2004).

People have a right to express their needs and concerns, in development programmes and across society and government. At an operational level, fulfilling people's rights to speak about problems with service delivery will improve service provision. More fundamentally, communication can help create open and responsive government (Burke, 1999). But PSBs should be neutral towards all parties, providing facts, education and entertainment to the people, and not serve as the mouthpiece of those in power (Samuon, 2003: 106).

The free market

Globally, media markets are dominated by the free market and this is especially so in PNG. In a free market, media is said to be agencies of information and debate, which facilitate the functions of democracy. In Jurgan Habermas's account, the free market allows anyone to publish an opinion and ensures all points of view are aired (Habermas, 1989). But, as James Curran summarizes, there are restrictions to this model as information is treated as a commodity. There are high costs of entry into the market; the free market restricts participation in public debate. It generates an information rich media for elites and information poor media for the general public and it undermines rational debate by generating information that is simplified, personified and without context (Curran, 2002: 226).

Developing countries are at a disadvantage in a global market for media commodities as they are essentially importers of cultural commodities.

Today there is a heavy one-way flow of exported media products, from the US to Asia/Pacific, but there is only a slight trickle of Asian/Pacific media products to the US. A very small number of source countries account for a very substantial share of all international media influence around the world.

This applies to electronic equipment used for receiving, recording and replaying images or sound. It also applies to commodities that have been reproduced or published, including books and magazines, records, tapes and films and television programmes. Most developing countries represent secondary markets where additional profits can be made on products, which have already covered their costs in primary markets (Thussu, 1998: 67–69; Reeve, 1993: 11; Boyd-Barrett, 1977: 116–135).

PSB under attack

PSB is under attack all over the world from the market. Satellite and cable technological advancements have enabled an increasing number of new channels to be created by multinational companies, which are focussed on making profits (Shukla, 2003: 21). These channels see people as consumers (of goods and services advertised by broadcasters) rather than citizens. This market undermines PSB's traditional role as an instrument of social and cultural development and instead PSB is being marginalized as an alternative service on the periphery of a vast cultural industry (Shukla, 2003: 22–23).

PSB empowers individuals and social groups to participate more fully and equitably while profit-motivated broadcasting is only interested in creating the largest possible audiences most effectively for the specific objective of the programme concerned.

In practice, although mass media have a role in achieving development goals and contributing to social change, the reality is that privately-owned media groups have little incentive to create development-type material if this threatens profits or works against the interests of capital associated with the media (Reeve, 1993: 27). A basic dependence on advertising means that media groups are invariably promoting a model of consumer-oriented development that in some cases directly contradicts that espoused by governments (Barker, 1997: 162; Herman, 1998: 125–6; Reeve, 1993: 27).

Mass media that operates in a capitalist economy rely on advertising revenue for profit and the way advertisers chose where to spend their money amounts to a political discrimination; this is because advertisers are more interested in reaching people with money to buy things (Herman and

Chomsky, 1994: 16). The predominant influence on spending is income: the rich buy more of most things than the poor (Curran, 1978: 246).

Advertising provides the principal financial backing for commercial mass media (and some public service media) across the world. The overwhelming dominant economic use of media space in capitalist economies is to advertise goods for sale (Van Ginneken, 1998: 55; Reeve, 1993: 149; Herman, 1998: 125).

In order to secure the support of the state and advertisers the media tend to protect and promote the interests of the big companies and sponsoring government units (Ma, 2000: 22). As long as they are organized around capitalist principles the media constitute obstacles to rather than conduits of democracy. The advancement of ruling economic and political interests and the suppression of alternate views lie at the heart of media operations interested in profit-making rather than public information (Waisbard, 2000: 52–53).

Advertising has not only had profound effects on the shaping of audience consumption preferences it has played a role in shaping mass communications. Denis McQuail asserts that advertising has a general influence on the content of media, especially by shaping the structure of markets, the relation between media and their audiences and the balance of types of content offered (McQuail, 1992: 133–134). The logic of media operated for profit under free market conditions is that they work towards maximizing revenue by way of various marketing strategies. One of these will involve the shaping of content and service provided in order to contribute to this goal. Where advertising revenue is being sought, the strategy may be to offer content, which is "friendly" (or even just relevant) to the goods and services likely to be advertised.

Where advertising becomes increasingly important as a source of revenue for media, and entertainment packages of soap operas, music and sports are central to attracting audiences, the nature of news programming is modified. There is less emphasis on development news and lengthy social and political explanation and more stress on relatively brief items whose main concern is to entertain.

Television in PNG

A case study of PNG gives us an opportunity to identify some of the general issues around media and democracy in action. There is little evidence of audience empowerment in PNG, either in broadcasting or the print media. Foreign ownership dominates the media with conglomerates owning the two daily newspapers, the country's only television station Em-TV, and a growing number of commercial radio stations (Rooney, 2003).

Em-TV is a commercial service wholly-owned by an Australian company and it has no formal PSB remit, although it does broadcast schools programmes, produced by the National Department of Education with the support of the Japanese International Cooperation Agency (JICA). Em-TV is prepared to broadcast educational programmes free of charge at non-peak times because it costs Em-TV less to run its transmitters 24 hours a day than to turn them off and it is therefore cheaper to broadcast content than a blank screen (Rooney, 2004).

When TV was introduced into PNG no consideration for issues such as cultural relevance, its effects on people, impact on their culture and the country were taken into account. TV was introduced before any national policy framework was established and thus no guidelines were available for TV broadcasters such as Em-TV (Sinebare, 1997: 34).

Experience elsewhere in developing countries suggested that the effects of television would be detrimental to the indigenous culture of PNG. When it was introduced into PNG there was doubt as to whether television would serve a useful purpose by disseminating information. Information needs of ordinary PNG people vary from village to village. In the traditional context of PNG societies information needs were conveniently met within each village or region (Sinebare, 1997: 35)

The experience of other Pacific Island countries provides good context to the PNG story.

In a report for UNESCO, James Bentley said that it was important for television stations in the Pacific to provide programming content that was created locally because such content expressed the community's locally owned and adapted knowledge and experience that is relevant to the community's situation (Bentley, 2002: 2–3). He said the process of creating and disseminating local content provided opportunities for members of the community to interact with each other, expressing their own ideas, knowledge and culture in their own language.

Bentley studied television across the whole of the Pacific and discovered the lack of local content was evident across all media and information channels. There was an overwhelming presence of content coming from non-local sources, reflecting language, values and lifestyles, which are often vastly different from those of the community "consuming" the content.

Bentley concluded that to create relevant content you need owners or producers with the motivation to create it. To do this in developing countries all levels of the society, including the policy-making, must recognize the need to support those who create, produce and distribute the programmes.

Elsewhere, Michael Ogden's research in Belau and Marshall Islands concluded that TV has intruded into the traditional time of the average Pacific Islanders. This intrusion has not just displaced their time of evening story telling, but it has endangered the continuity of the people's history since they have an oral tradition, which is passed from generation to generation through such story telling sessions (Ogden cited in Anyanwu, 1995: 55).

In the Fijian context, Niik Plange and Bruce Horsfield found the average Fijian family lifestyle has been altered both in speech pattern, family gathering time and meal time because of their need to construct their lives around television schedules so as not to miss favourite programmes (cited in Anyanwu, 1995: 61).

Radio in PNG

PSB radio, in PNG, is controlled by the National Broadcasting Commission (NBC). As the only radio broadcasting authority in the country it is the nation's public service provider. At its peak NBC reached about four million people in about 60 different languages as well as English. NBC is made up of three networks: Karai, Kundu and Kalang services, which broadcast through short-wave frequencies (Nash, 1995: 42–43). NBC has been in decline in recent years as the number of privately-owned commercial stations, playing mostly music, based in and around PNG's urban centres, grows.

The geographical isolation of much of the country makes it difficult for media to penetrate beyond the main urban areas. In rural areas 80 per cent of teenagers and 43 per cent of adults listen to radio every day. No teens and no adults read newspapers every day (meaning that the numbers are so small as to be statistically insignificant); five per cent of rural teens and no rural adults watch TV every day (AusAID, 2004: 16)

In PNG radio is the most widely accessible information and communication technology. Five times as many people own a radio set as a television or purchase a daily newspaper.

NBC has a stated vision of being the leading provider of information and knowledge to the people of PNG; to be a centre for excellence in analytical and investigative reporting of PNG affairs; and to become a PNG voice in today's global village (Ninkama, 2003: 121).

The NBC's mission is to contribute to integral human development via the advancement of knowledge taking into account, without bias, Papua New Guinea's 865 different languages, cultural diversity, religion and politics through the provision of vital information and entertainment, the promotion of Papua New Guinea's national identity, the provision of broadcast programmes of educational nature, independent news bulletins and the facilitation and promotion of debates on issues of national importance (ibid).

The NBC is controlled by a board with a chair appointed by the government and is accountable to Parliament through the minister responsible for communications.

Since its inception NBC has considered its role to be one of a community broadcaster with services provided through a series of provincial radio stations, which provide a forum for local people. These community stations do not generally share content with NBC nationally because the network is defunct, thereby making it impossible for NBC to fulfil one of its main goals which is the promotion on national unity and identity (Rooney et al, 2004).

Poor legislation has exacerbated the challenging situation that NBC has been facing. In 1995 responsibility for meeting provincial radio station operating costs was transferred to provincial government resulting in political interference by some provincial governments that affected the content and forced several stations off-air because of lack of resources or willingness to fund provincial radio (Rooney et al, 2004).

According to Kristoffa Ninkama, former managing director of NBC, the delivery of basic services can be effectively implemented to the majority of the people of PNG through the medium of radio as it is the least expensive and the most accessible tool to inform, educate and entertain. However, NBC is under-resourced, with outdated analogue studio equipment and production facilities, compounded by deteriorating infrastructure. As a result programme quality is compromised and stations are frequently off the air due to technical faults (Ninkama, 2003:121).

In a SWOT (strength, weakness, opportunities and threats) analysis of NBC, Ninkama identified a corporation struggling to fulfil its PSB mission. NBC's strengths, as the biggest radio organization in the Pacific island region, are its nationwide and extensive coverage and its ability to tailor programmes to local audience needs and expectations. NBC's opportunities encompass introducing digital and satellite technology to attract more audiences. On the "down" side NBC's weaknesses include poor infrastructure and equipment, unreliability of service, outdated equipment, and lack of audience research and lack of training for staff. Among the threats to NBC are the increasing number of new commercial radio stations and the need to maintain present audience satisfaction (Ninkama, 2003: 123).

One of NBC's community stations, NBC Radio Southern Highlands Province (NBC-SHP) provides an example of the troubles NBC generally faces. The station offers a service for one of the most remote areas of the country where it is estimated that 80 per cent of radio listeners tune in to NBC-SHP. The station was established as one of the 19 provincial Kundu service by NBC in 1973 when the country was still a protectorate of Australia. Its broadcasting facilities are located in the centre of Mendi town while the transmitter is located at Mt Kape in Longo village, outside Mendi. It broadcasts on short-wave each evening from 4:30 p.m. to 11.00 p.m. (Alphonse, forthcoming).

Like all other NBC stations in the country, NBC-SHP has been forced to meet its own operational costs. This was an outcome of the National Government's decision to decentralize the functions of the Kundu network stations to their provincial governments. A succession of Southern Highlands provincial governments have neglected to fund the operational and maintenance costs of the station, which has been forced to use equipment some of which is more than 30 years old (Alphonse, forthcoming).

The station is ill-equipped, under-resourced and under-funded and it finds it difficult to effectively deliver news and coverage of the province as it did in its heyday. The insufficient funding from the national and provincial governments limits the capabilities to effectively address the issues like law and order, tribal fights and matters of community development in the province.

The station does not have a reliable vehicle to enable its reporters to travel throughout the province to collect news and the staff, mostly, use their own money to travel and buy notebooks and recording tapes.

There is a need for digital equipment as most of the station's equipment is still manual with reel-to-reel tapes, record players and pick-ups. The station broadcasts in Pidgin while the main provincial news is presented in eight local languages, but a further six languages are not represented due to lack of funds to recruit broadcasters who can speak these languages (Alphonse, forthcoming).

Revitalizing radio in PNG

While the public service stations in PNG are failing, the growing privately owned media in PNG have not taken on a role in representing the public; instead, they represent the configuration of power to which they are linked. In PNG power is maintained through a system of patronage that binds together different clans (wantoks) within the structure of a party political coalition in Parliament. A power network extends to include the economic power exercised by shareholders and managers. The media in PNG are themselves part of the economic power structure with conglomerates with international business interests owning nearly all media, except NBC.

Elite groups in PNG predominate in the creation of public opinion, deciding what is talked about and in most cases how it is talked about. Studies of television and daily newspapers found that the government dominates news agendas and there is little opportunity for ordinary people within PNG to communicate through the news media. In the case of Em-TV and the newspapers, the value of the news depends mainly on the importance of the speaker, not on what they have to say. The *National Em-TV News* excludes the vast majority of people in the country from its bulletins and it rarely includes stories about ordinary people and its stories centre on the national capital, Port Moresby (Rooney, 2003; Rooney, 2004a; Rooney et al, 2004).

There is a need to revitalize public service broadcasting to empower communities within PNG and the way to do this is through radio, which is unarguably the best medium of communication in a country with a strong and diverse oral culture.

A revived NBC backed by independent community radio stations could provide the best way forward for PNG. This could improve on the present media landscape by creating a diversity of voices and opinions through its openness to participation from all sectors. It could provide a platform for the interactive discussion about matters and decisions of importance to the community. Community radio stations (whether NBC or other) can overcome the linguistic divide in PNG, which hinders information dissemination from national broadcasters, and strengthen cultural diversity that has been weakened with the spread of English and pidgin through education and migration to urban centres. It can also solve the transmitting problem, as it will be broadcasting locally.

Radio has the greatest chance of providing the presently disadvantaged population with a platform for the public dialogue through which people can define who they are and what they want and how to get it (Fraser & Restrepro, 2002: 70). The advantages of radio are its ability to reach audiences quickly, especially in the country's remote rural areas, and the fact that as an oral medium radio is able to involve communities and individuals in an interactive communication process. Sets are also cheap to own and there are fewer literacy problems (Nash, 1995: 36; Ninkama, 2003: 124).

A major project, the PNG Media for Development Initiative (MDI), headed by Australia's overseas' development agency, AusAID, is underway to transform the NBC and help it to recapture its original mission of service to the community.

In 2005, a five-year media development agreement was signed to support the role of PNG's media and to foster increased access to development information. AusAID concluded that people, especially in rural areas, would welcome better access to better quality and more relevant media content, especially if it is available in vernacular languages.

The project will be funded under the Australia/PNG aid programme with an initial funding of up to US$1.6 million. The initiative will build the media sector, address issues of access and content, and will assist in the training and development of media personnel and strengthen the effectiveness of NBC through a partnership with the Australian Broadcasting Corporation (ABC).

MDI has identified that the media in PNG has the potential to promote development by improving good governance and the delivery of essential services by the following.

- Giving voice to the poor by providing usable information, a platform for discussion and feedback loops between government and citizens.
- Improving the media content by reporting on socio-economic and development issues, and by enhancing information flows surrounding public health, education, agriculture and other development interventions.
- Increasing access between the media and the public through improved services and communications.[2]

The first phase of the initiative will support activities by media related organizations and NGOs that address problems of access, content and voice. The initiative concentrates on improving programme content, making high quality programme content available to media networks and community groups at minimal cost; building a rural network of civil society, media and government agencies that can collaborate to improve the access of rural people to media services; providing practical, accurate and useful means of assessing media operations and performance and contributing to public policy development for PNG; and increasing the knowledge, skills and understanding of media personnel in government, civil society and the media industry.

The second phase is focused on the NBC, strengthening the organization's capacity as the national public broadcaster by building upon an

---

[2] See PNG Media for Development Initiative, 2005.

existing partnership with the Australian Broadcasting Corporation. Four focus areas have been identified: organizational development consultancy; delivering quality programmes; strengthening the Kundu network; and digitizing the archive.

The PNG Media Council is the managing agent for the MDI, given its role as the peak media organization, its extensive networks and its high level of credibility.

Community radio in PNG

The MDI is in its infancy and we do not yet know how successful it will be. It is an initiative that deserves support but the potential resurrection of NBC is not the only way forward for PNG. A healthy, well-funded public service broadcaster can be supported by smaller community radio stations.

The significance of community media is that it provides an alternative to both the profit driven and the public service models. At its best, community media empowers people rather than treating them as a passive audience.

"Community radio" is defined as a "non-profit service that is owned and managed by a particular community" (Fraser & Restrepro-Esrada, 2002: 70). The operations of such radio stations rely on the community and the community's own resources and are comparatively cheap to set up and operate. Its programmes are based on audience access and participation and reflect the special interest and needs of the community as they deal with local issues in local languages and cultural context. There is potential for community media to minimize social unrest by providing a forum for public debates. It can also provide useful feedback to community leaders and government on the concerns of the people thereby affording opportunities to defuse potentially threatening situations.

As NBC is failing in its mission, commercial radio in PNG has not adopted an informational role, and there are no obvious signs that it intends to in the future. It depends on advertising revenue and therefore faces the economic imperative to deliver audiences that are attractive to advertisers, targeting relatively affluent urban listeners (Rooney, 2004).

Community radio is a new concept to PNG despite its wide use in the developing world for several decades. Community radio stations could fill the gap that the mainstream broadcasters and other media forms cannot meet. Having people in the community volunteering or working for a nominal payment, community stations have the potential to strengthen the community by empowering people to take ownership and responsibility of their communication needs.

Papua New Guineans, by their traditional communal culture which is still strong, are people who willingly help each other in times of need. As such, if an educational institution, a church, a women's group or other non-governmental organization was to organize and operate a community radio station that reflected the shared interests of the people, they would probably generate sufficient interest for volunteers and funds to help run it. Projects such as the rural multimedia production centre in the Highlands, part of the media production unit of the Foundation for Rural Development, which produce audiovisual material on rural and development issues can assist by providing content to community radios. At the moment their activities in making more information available to rural communities is hindered by the cost of access to airwaves (Rooney et al, 2004).

However, people need to be aware of this option. Policymakers and opinion leaders need to promote the community radio concept to create interest among the people and also donors.

There have been attempts to introduce community radio into PNG, with some limited amount of success. The PNG government allows for only 10 kilowatts radio transmission capacity so the range that can be covered is not enough for communities that are widespread. There is also electricity problem and most of the villages have no electricity, but experiments have been made using solar energy.

In partnership with the PNG Ministry of Education, the Commonwealth of Learning has established a solar-powered community radio station in Mountain Brown, a remote village high up in the mountains in a largely inaccessible region of Papua New Guinea. The community-run radio station broadcasts national and local news, development information, community education and topical issues to 2,000 citizens living in 10 neighbouring villages. For the very first time, these people are being exposed to mass media production facilities that enable them to communicate among themselves in their own language. Stations such as these that have been running throughout the Commonwealth demonstrate to policymakers within government and international donors how local communities can empower themselves through radio.

The Catholic Church has made a foray into community radio with limited test broadcasts using temporary licences. In 2003, Pangtel, a licensing body of the PNG government approved a community radio licence for CRN PNG and allowed it to start a test broadcast. In the same year the first transmitter was set up at Rabaul and a test broadcast of the National Catholic Youth Pilgrimage to Vunapope and Rakunai was covered live on radio. The youth mass at Rakunai went live on community radio in Rabaul. A small team of five personnel managed to keep the station running for 24 hours a day for a week. Later in the year a second test broadcast in Rabaul was conducted.

The University of PNG, the oldest and largest university in the country, runs a community station in the nation's capital Port Moresby with the main purpose of helping its students to learn the basics of radio production and journalism. In 2003, the UPNG administration embarked on improving the coverage of Campus FM community radio station and boosting training for journalism students, but essentially the station exists as a public relations tool for the university rather than a genuine community station, but it does attempt to promote development and activities within the university to a wider public.

At the other end of the country in Madang, Divine Word University set up an electronic media training facility in 2000 to enable students to be taught programme production skills. Funding was obtained from the European Union to buy minidisk recorders as news gathering equipment and computerized editing suites to enable editing and production skills to be taught. Chevron Niugini has presented the department with the funds to enable a transmitter to be bought so that a campus radio could be set up which would broadcast to Madang and surrounding communities, but to date no progress has been made on this project.

One example of locally-based radio that collapsed under the weight of difficulty was the Kasela Palu Community Radio Station project for rural Enga in the Highlands region. This was set up in 2003 and financed by UNESCO. Equipment was purchased and community members trained in the station's operations. Despite a lot of enthusiasm and journalistic expertise within the community, UNESCO reported implementation of the project has not advanced because of the difficulty of travelling in the mountainous terrain of the Highlands and the socio-political situation in the area which has seen many outbreaks of violence between various Highlands' tribes.

UNESCO concluded that a community radio could make a difference in contributing to and enhancing the sustainable development in the area but a number of obstacles have yet to be overcome (Unesco 2003: 54)

Conclusion

Radio in PNG is at an interesting time in its history. Major inroads are being made into the country by privately-owned, music programming-orientated stations that are gathering growing audiences in urban areas. As this sector of the radio industry has been growing, the traditional public service broadcasting of NBC has been in decline. This decline may be reversed by an Australian-backed initiative that sets out to put local (mostly rural) audiences at the centre of its endeavours. This project is in its infancy and it is too soon to determine its success, but there are hopes that it could improve on the present media landscape by creating a diversity of voices and opinions through its openness to participation from all sectors.

Independently ran, locally based community radio stations are able to supplement this initiative. Community radio is in its infancy in PNG, hindered as it is by geographical difficulties, lack of finance, and government policy restricting the sizes of transmitters. However, if lessons can be learned from experiences in other developing countries this form of radio has the potential to open up new opportunities for empowerment among people who presently are denied opportunities.

References

Alphonse, A. (Forthcoming). Community Media and its Potential Impact on Law and Order Issues in the Southern Highlands Province: a case study of the NBC Radio SHP. In E. Papoutsaki & D. Rooney (Eds.), *Media for Development in Papua New Guinea*. Madang: Divine Word University Press.

Anyanwu, J. (1995). A Clash of Culture and Content. In D. Robie (Ed.), *Nius Bilong Pasifik, Mass Media in the Pacific*. Port Moresby: University of Papua New Guinea Press.

AusAID. (April 2004). *PNG Media for Development Initiative Draft Design Document.*

Barker, C. (1997). *Global Television, an introduction*. Oxford: Blackwell.

Bentley, J. (2002). Pacific Islands Television Survey, Report. UNESCO, Suva.

Boyd-Barrett, O. (1997). Media Imperialism: Towards and International Framework for the Analysis of Media Systems. In J. Curran, M. Gurevitch & J. Woolacott (Eds.), *Mass Communication and Society*. London: Edward Arnold / Open University.

Burke, A. (1999). Communications and Development: a Practical Guide. Department for International Development, London.

Curran, J. (2002). *Media Power*. London: Routledge.

Department for International Development (2001). *Making Government Work for Poor People: Building State Capability. Strategies for achieving the international development targets*. DFID, London.

Dy, M. (2003). Impact of New & Old Media on Development in Asia. 13th AMIC Annual Conference held in Bangkok, Thailand on 1–3 July 2004.

Fraser, C., & Restrepro-Estrada, S. (2002), Community Radio for Change and Development. *Development*, 45(4), 69–73.

Habermas, J. (1989). *The Structural Transformation of the Public Sphere*. Cambridge: Polity.

Herman, E. J. (1998). Privatizing Public Space. In D.K. Thussu (Ed.), *Electronic Empires Global Media and Local Resistance*. London: Arnold.

McQuail, D. (1992). *Media Performance, Mass Communications and the Public Interest*. London: Sage.

Nash, S. (1995). National Radio and Development. In D. Robie (Ed.), *Nius Bilong Pasifik, Mass Media in the Pacific*. Port Moresby: University of Papua New Guinea Press.

Ninkama. K. (2003). PSB n Papua New Guinea. In S. Eashwar (Ed.), *Responses to Globalization and the Digital Divide in the Asia Pacific*. Asia-Pacific Institute for Broadcasting, Kuala Lumpur.

Ojo, E. O. (2003). The Mass media and the challenges of sustainable democratic values in Nigeria: possibilities and limitations. *Media, Culture & Society*, 25(6), 821–840.

PNG Media for Development Initiative (2005). Unpublished Fact Sheet.

Price, M., & Krug, P. (2002). *The Enabling Environment for Free and Independent Media*, USAID, Washington.

Reeve, G. (1993). *Communications and the Third World*. London: Routledge.

Rooney, D. (2004a). "Information for Empowerment and Development, Why Media is Failing the People of Papua New Guinea". Paper presented at World Media Freedom Day Conference, 30 April, Divine Word University, Madang, PNG.

Rooney, D. (2004b). Nambawan To Watch: Em-TV, PNG's Only TV Channel. *DWU Research Journal*. 1(1), 27–36.

Rooney, D., Papoutsaki, E., & Pamba, K. (2004). "A Country Failed by its Media: A Case Study From Papua New Guinea". 13th AMIC Annual Conference, "Impact of New & Old Media on Development in Asia", 1–3 July 2004, Bangkok, Thailand.

Roth, C. (2001). *The Media in Governance: a guide to assistance. Developing Free and effective media to serve the interests of the poor*. Department for International Development, London.

Rumphorst, W. (2003). What is Public Service Broadcasting? In S. Eashwar (Ed.), *Responses to Globalization and the Digital Divide in the Asia Pacific*. Asia-Pacific Institute for Broadcasting, Kuala Lumpur.

Samuon, D. (2003). Public Service Broadcasting Partners for Development. In S. Eashwar (Ed.), *Responses to Globalization and the Digital Divide in the Asia Pacific*. Asia-Pacific Institute for Broadcasting, Kuala Lumpur.

Shukla, T. (2003). The Changing Context of PSB (2003). In S. Eashwar (Ed.), *Responses to Globalization and the Digital Divide in the Asia Pacific*. Asia-Pacific Institute for Broadcasting, Kuala Lumpur.

Sinebare, M. (1997), One Way Information Flow: The Case of Australian Television Channels Received in PNG. *Media Asia*, 24(1), 33–39.

Sparks, C. (1991). Goodbye Hildy Johnson, the vanishing "serious press". In P. Dahlgren & C. Sparks (Eds.), *Communications and Citizenship*. London: Routledge.

Tetty, W. J. (2003). The Media and Democratization in Africa: contributions, constraints and concerns of the private press. *Media, Culture & Society*, 23(1), 5–31.

Thussu, D. K. (1998). Infotainment International, a view from the South. In D.K. Thussu (Ed.), *Electronic Empires Global Media and Local Resistance*. London: Arnold.

UNESCO. (2003), Implementation Report on Recent IPDC Projects, Paris.

Van Ginneken, J. (1998). *Understanding Global News, a critical introduction*. London: Sage.

Waisbard, S. (2000). Media in South America: Between the Rock of the State and the Hard Place of the Market. In J. Curran & P. Myung-Jin (Eds.), *DeWesternizing Media Studies*. London: Routledge.

Yaakob, K. (2003). PSB in the Asia-Pacific. In S. Eashwar (Ed.), *Responses to Globalization and the Digital Divide in the Asia Pacific*. Asia-Pacific Institute for Broadcasting, Kuala Lumpur.

About the Authors

Indrajit Banerjee

Indrajit Banerjee received his PhD with the highest distinction awarded in France from the Sorbonne University in 1994. He has been the Secretary-General of AMIC since January 2004. He continues to be an Associate Professor in the School of Communication and Information at the Nanyang Technological University, Singapore. Dr. Banerjee was the Research Coordinator of the first UNDP Regional Human Development Report on ICTs and Human Development 2005. He has published papers in many prestigious international conferences as well as papers in many top international journals of media and communication studies. He was invited by former Soviet President Mikhail Gorbachev to speak at the World Political Forum in Italy in 2004, along with over 60 international political leaders. Dr. Banerjee is a member of many top international committees in media and communication studies and journals across the world. He was recently appointed to the Steering Committee of the World Congress on Communication and Development and is also the coordinator of the first World Journalism Education Congress to be held in 2007.

Kalinga Seneviratne

Kalinga Seneviratne has an MA in Social Sciences from the University of Technology, Sydney, and a BSc (Hons) in Engineering Science from Reading University, UK. He has taught radio broadcasting, international and cross-cultural communications in Singapore and Australia. He has broadcast on Australian community radio for over 15 years and has received a United Nations Media Peace Award (1987) as well as the Inaugural Singapore Airlines Educational Award of the Community Broadcasting Association of Australia (1992) for his broadcasting. He has been a correspondent for Inter Press Service news agency for over 12 years and currently works as Senior Research Associate at the Asian Media Information and Communication Centre (AMIC) in Singapore.

Andrew Taussig

Andrew Taussig, a member of AMIC's International Academic Advisory Committee, received his PhD in the Kennedy School of Government at Harvard University. He has worked at the BBC in Television News & Current Affairs and in the World Service where he was Director of Foreign

Language Services (1996–2000). He is a Steering Committee Member of the International Institute of Communications (IIC) and associated with Oxford University's Programme in Comparative Media Law and Policy as well as being an Associate Fellow of Chatham House, London's Royal Institute for International Affairs. He is a Trustee and Director of Voice of the Listener & Viewer (VLV), a leading advocate for public service broadcasting in the UK and beyond. He is also an active participant in the Langkawi Smart Partnership International Dialogue.

Karol Jakubowicz

Karol Jakubowicz, PhD, is Director, Strategy and Analysis Department, at the National Broadcasting Council of Poland, the country's broadcasting regulatory authority. He has worked as a journalist and executive in the Polish press, radio and television for many years. He has been Vice-President, Television, Polish Radio and Television; Chairman, Supervisory Board, Polish Television and Head of Strategic Planning and Development at Polish Television. He has been active in the Council of Europe, in part as a former Chairman of the Committee of Experts on Media Concentrations and Pluralism, Chairman of the Standing Committee on Transfrontier Television, and now Chairman of the Steering Committee on the Media and New Communication Services. He has been a member of the Digital Strategy Group of the European Broadcasting Union. His scholarly and other publications have been published widely in Poland as well as internationally. He helped write the report "Public Service Broadcasting in Europe", which was adopted by the Parliamentary Assembly of the Council of Europe in 2004.

Sundeep R. Muppidi

Professor Sundeep R. Muppidi is an Associate Professor of Communication at the University of Hartford, CT, USA. He has a doctorate in International Communication from Bowling Green State University, Ohio. His research interests are in the areas of globalization and new communication technologies; multimedia and video production; and international development communication and media studies. He teaches courses in international communication, research methods, multimedia, television production and new media. He is also an active filmmaker and research scholar in the field.

Venkat Iyer

Dr Venkat Iyer is a Barrister and Senior Lecturer in Law at the University of Ulster, Northern Ireland. He specializes in media law and offers consultancy and training services in this area around the world. He has published extensively on media-related issues and is the Editor of *The Commonwealth Lawyer*, a London publication.

Binod C. Agrawal

Dr Binod C. Agrawal, MS, PhD (University of Wisconsin), is currently Director, TALEEM Research Foundation, Ahmedabad, India. He has been deeply involved in communication research for over three decades and pioneered the use of anthropological methods for communications research. Significant publications include *SITE Social Evaluation* (1981) and *Anthropological Methods for Communication Research* (1985). Dr Agrawal is Founder Director of Mudra Institute of Communications, Ahmedabad (MICA).

Shalini Raghaviah

Shalini Raghaviah is Research Associate, TALEEM Research Foundation, and is currently involved in social science and communication research. Her previous work includes television and documentary film production, environmental communication and feature writing. She has a Master's degree in journalism and has been trained by the BBC World Service Trust at the Asian College of Journalism, Chennai, India.

Elizabeth Jacka

Elizabeth Jacka is Professor of Communications in the Faculty of Humanities and Social Sciences at the University of Technology, Sydney. She has published extensively on various aspects of Australian film and television, including Australian Television and International Mediascapes (with Stuart Cunningham). More recently, she has been researching public broadcasting in Australia, especially the Australian Broadcasting Corporation (ABC). She has published a number of articles and chapters on this subject, most notably "Democracy as defeat: The impotence of arguments for public service broadcasting" (*Television and New Media*, 2003).

Umi Khattab

Dr Umi Khattab is a lecturer in the Media and Communications programme of The University of Melbourne, Australia. She had previously taught and researched in Malaysia where she also freelanced and wrote as a columnist.

Ruth Elizabeth Teer-Tomaselli
Ruth Teer-Tomaselli is a Professor of Culture, Communication and Media Studies at the University of KwaZulu-Natal, Durban, South Africa. She holds a UNESCO-Orbicom Chair in Communication for Southern Africa. Her research interests include the political economy of broadcasting and telecommunications in Southern Africa; programme production on television; radio, particularly community radio; and the role of media in development. She has served as a director on the boards of the national public broadcaster, the South African Broadcasting Corporation, a commercial radio broadcaster, East Coast Radio, and a community radio broadcaster, Durban Youth Radio.

Sigrid Baringhorst
Professor Sigrid Baringhorst has been lecturer at the University of East Anglia (UK) and University of Technology, Sydney, and is currently Professor of Political Science at the University of Siegen, Germany. She works on political communication studies, particularly political campaigning and media politics, as well as political sociology. She is the author of *Politik als Kampagne* (1998) and the editor of *Medien-Demokratie – Mediokratie*.

Joseph Borg
Fr Joseph Borg is the Audio Visual Policy Consultant of the Minister of Culture in Malta. He was the first ever Chairman of the Editorial Board of PBS Ltd between 2004 and the end of 2005. He lectures in communication studies at the University of Malta. Fr Borg has been actively involved in the media scene for the past 20 years.

Ariyaratne Athugala
Ariyarathne Athugala is a senior lecturer attached to the Department of Mass Communication at the University of Kelaniya, Sri Lanka. He is a media researcher and consultant as well as an author of many books in both English and Sinhala. He has directed a number of teledramas on current social subjects. His speciality is in perceptions and communication. A very versatile writer—outspoken and creative—his interests lie in creating a media suitable for Third World countries.

Thomas Jayaprakash Yesudhasan
Thomas Jayaprakash Yesudhasan is a senior lecturer in the Department of Mass Communication at the Curtin University of Technology, Sarawak, Malaysia. He is the joint winner of the Asian Radio Write Award 2000, insti-

tuted by the Radio Corporation of Singapore (RCS) and the Asian Media Information Centre (AMIC), Singapore. He has recently co-convened an international conference in Malaysia entitled "Media and Identity in Asia". He has presented numerous international conference papers in the context of radio and television consumption in Asia.

Kuniko Sakata Watanabe

Kuniko Sakata Watanabe has an MA in social information from the University of Tokyo and an MSc in media and communication from the London School of Economics and Political Science, University of London. She is currently Assistant Professor in the Graduate School of Information Sciences, Tohoku University in Japan, specializing in community media as well as cross-cultural understanding through media.

Marie A. Mater

Marie A. Mater is Associate Professor in the Department of Communications at Houston Baptist University, USA. Her theoretical expertise is the Habermasian concept of the public sphere. She has also taught at the University of Iowa, USA; the ITM/MUCIA Programme, Malaysia; and Nanyang Technological University, Singapore.

Dick Rooney

Dr Dick Rooney worked at Divine Word University, Madang, Papua New Guinea, for two years until November 2003. He has published in academic journals in America, Europe, Australia and the Pacific recently on subjects connected with the press, television, journalism education and academic quality assurance in PNG. He was the founding head of the Department of Journalism at John Moores University, Liverpool, UK, for seven years.

ASIAN MEDIA INFORMATION
AND COMMUNICATION CENTRE

The Asian Media Information and Communication Centre (AMIC) is a non-profit NGO with the mission of spearheading the development of media and communication expertise in Asia within the broad framework of economic, social and cultural progress.

It exists to encourage ethical and social responsibility of the media to support democratic access and participation in media development and production, and to provide opportunities for empowerment of disadvantaged sectors in the communication/media environment.

It performs these roles on many fronts. As a research centre, it examines critical issues in the media and communication sector and their implications for development. As a resource centre, it gathers and disseminates knowledge about communication and its effects in Asia. By conducting training and professional consultations, it is active in capacity building for the media and their users.

AMIC was established in 1971 with core funding support from the Friedrich-Ebert-Stiftung (FES), a private non-profit, public-interest foundation of the Federal Republic of Germany. Core funding was maintained by FES for AMIC's first 30 years. The foundation is a key partner and provides generous project funding to this day. Premises were provided by the Government of Singapore.

AMIC is now housed in the School of Communication and Information (SCI) of Nanyang Technological University (NTU), with whom it has had a close working partnership for many years. SCI provides substantial core funding and is the co-publisher of all AMIC's books and journals. AMIC's and SCI's libraries were recently merged to create the Asian Communication Resource Centre (ACRC), a unified, comprehensive specialist media library.

The Centre is a registered charity in Singapore.

Asian Media Information and Communication Centre (AMIC)
CS-02-28, School of Communication and Information
Nanyang Technological University, Singapore 637718
Tel: (65) 6792 7570
Fax: (65) 6792 7129
http://www.amic.org.sg
E-mail: enquiries@amic.org.sg